Anthropology and Development

In recent decades international development has grown into a world-shaping indus-try. But how do aid agencies work and what do they achieve? How does aid appear to the adults and children who receive it? And why has there been so little improvement in the position of the poor? Viewing aid and development from anthropological per-spectives gives illuminating answers to questions such as these. This essential textbook reveals anthropologists' often surprising findings and details ethnographic case stud-ies on the cultures of development. The authors use a fertile literature to examine the socio-political organisation of aid communities, agencies and networks, as well as the judgements they make about each other. The everyday practice of development work is about negotiating power and culture, but in vastly different ways in different contexts and for different social groups. Exploring the spaces between policy and practice, suc-cess and failure, the future and the past, this book provides a rounded understanding of development work that suggests new moral and political possibilities for an increas-ingly globalised world.

EMMA CREWE is a Visiting Reader in the Department of Anthropology and Sociology at the School of Oriental and African Studies. She has worked as an anthropologist researcher, lecturer, and practitioner in international development in South Asia, East Africa and the UK. In her research she explores inequalities, governance and institutions.

RICHARD AXELBY is a Senior Teaching Fellow in the Anthropology of Development at the School of Oriental and African Studies. Richard has worked with develop-ment and educational NGOs in South Asia and in the UK. He is a fellow of the Royal Anthropological Institute.

Anthropology and Development
Culture, Morality and Politics in a Globalised World

EMMA CREWE
RICHARD AXELBY

CAMBRIDGE
UNIVERSITY PRESS

CAMBRIDGE UNIVERSITY PRESS
Cambridge, New York, Melbourne, Madrid, Cape Town,
Singapore, São Paulo, Delhi, Mexico City

Cambridge University Press
The Edinburgh Building, Cambridge CB2 8RU, UK

Published in the United States of America by Cambridge University Press, New York

www.cambridge.org
Information on this title: www.cambridge.org/9780521184724

First published 2013

Printed in the United Kingdom at MPG Books Group

A catalogue record for this publication is available from the British Library

Library of Congress Cataloguing in Publication data
Crewe, Emma, 1962–
   Anthropology and development : culture, morality and politics in a globalised
   world / Emma Crewe and Richard Axelby.
      pages   cm
   Includes bibliographical references and index.
   ISBN 978-1-107-00592-1 (hardback) – ISBN 978-0-521-18472-4 (paperback)
   1. Applied anthropology.   2. Political anthropology.   3. Anthropological ethics.
   I. Axelby, Richard.   II. Title.
   GN397.5.C75 2013
   301–dc23
   2012018840

ISBN 978-1-107-00592-1 Hardback
ISBN 978-0-521-18472-4 Paperback

Contents

Acronyms

ATO	Alternative trade organisation
BRIC	Brazil, Russia, India and China
CBO	Community-based organisation
CHADET	Organization for Child Development and Transformation
CSO	Civil society organisation
CSR	Corporate social responsibility
DFID	Department for International Development
EZLN	Zapatista Army of National Liberation
FAO	Food and Agriculture Organization
FBO	Faith-based organisation
HTS	Human terrain system
GATT	General Agreement on Tariffs and Trade
GDP	Gross domestic product
IC	Improved cookstove
IMF	International Monetary Fund
INGO	International non-governmental organisation
MDG	Millennium development goals
NGO	Non-governmental organisation
NIC	Newly industrialised country
NSA	Non-state actor
ODA	Overseas Development Administration
OECD	Organization for Economic Cooperation and Development
PRA	Participatory rural appraisal
PRSP	Poverty Reduction Strategy Paper
QUANGO	Quasi-autonomous non-governmental organisation
SAP	Structural Adjustment Programme
SIDA	Swedish International Development Cooperation Agency
SL	Sustainable livelihoods
UDHR	Universal Declaration of Human Rights
UN	United Nations
UNCRC	United Nations Convention on the Rights of the Child
UNDP	United Nations Development Program
UNEP	United Nations Environment Program
UNESCO	United Nations Educational, Scientific and Cultural Organization
USAID	United States Agency for International Development
WB	World Bank
WTO	World Trade Organization

Preface and acknowledgements

Welcome to 'Development World'. The pursuit of development has become a global concern and no one is unaffected. Aspiring to manage change in economic, political, social and cultural arenas, development is a world-shaping project.

The world of development is neither simple nor self-contained. Its cultures, moralities, languages, rituals and symbolic practices relate to what is already there. And, like any political world, it is subject to considerable tensions as differences emerge in the interests and attitudes of its diverse peoples. As geo-political realities shift and understandings of poverty and progress take on new meanings, the old geographical and social divisions – such as developing and developed – can no longer be sustained.

Defining development globally allows us to consider development from a wide range of different perspectives. Moving from the global to the local, from policy-makers to farmers, it is a subject well suited to anthropological investigation. This book offers an anthropological guide to Development World. In it we explore anthropology's varied engagement with and understandings of institutions and social groups. It explains the complex relationships linking donors to government officials and development professionals to project beneficiaries. Anthropological perspectives offer ways of understanding the value judgements, social realities and social practices that make up the world of aid and development.

The idea of a guide emerged out of our own experiences of teaching, researching and practising international development. In the practice of development – working as a 'social development' expert, consultant or manager of an international non-governmental organisation (INGO) – Emma Crewe has increasingly found that practitioners reduce the process of social change to frameworks, tools and formulae. To give an example: consider this story. As part of a due diligence exercise commissioned by the UK's Department for International Development in 2011, an auditing firm visited all charities that were due to receive government funding and conducted a two-day assessment. Armed with a 54-page questionnaire on finance, risk management, strategy, governance, systems, monitoring and evaluation, environmental policy and human resources, the auditor asked the Executive Director (Emma):

> AUDITOR: What are your organisational objectives and Key Performance Indicators [KPIs]?
> DIRECTOR: We have targets in fundraising for income against each stream so the indicators relate to success in achieving these targets. In other

areas – such as getting feedback from the partner organisations we work with – KPIs don't really help.

AUDITOR: But even if they are qualitative, what are they and what is your baseline?

DIRECTOR: I need to explain about our approach to evaluation. But before I do that it would be useful to know that I am an anthropologist – it accounts for where I am coming from to some extent.

AUDITOR: You mean a socialist?

DIRECTOR: No, no! I mean anthropologist, you know, similar to a sociologist.

AUDITOR: Is that the same as anti-capitalist?

Of course anthropology – the comparative study of cultural ideas and social relations – is not a political theory. But anthropologists do take a keen interest in politics and power. Applied to the study of development, anthropological perspectives help to unravel the complex rituals, moralities and politics that shape our changing world.

This book is designed to appeal to two main audiences (in addition to the auditor above). First, we are writing for students of anthropology and of international development. Secondly, we are writing for the development professionals who may find an anthropological approach interesting. Rather than closing problems down anthropology seeks to open them up; it asks questions where others might try to force answers onto ill-fitting and diverse realities. This book seeks to make anthropology simpler and development more complex. Our aim is to allow students to engage critically with development and, at the same time, to suggest alternative perspectives and practices that may discourage development practitioners from taking lazy shortcuts.

We are grateful to Cambridge University Press, and especially Andrew Winnard, for commissioning this book and to Andrew McConnell for his photograph on the cover. We would like to thank Cambridge University Press's anonymous reviewer for comments and pointing out some important gaps.

The foundations of this book sit on an earlier work that Emma Crewe wrote with Elizabeth Harrison (*Whose Development?*, 1989); we would like to extend our thanks to her. We would also like to thank John Campbell and Johan Pottier with whom we taught a Social Anthropology of Development MA course at the School of Oriental and African Studies. They have provided support and encouragement and, in sharing their knowledge of Development World, have helped to shape ours. We have a debt of gratitude to David Mosse, without whom this book would not have been written. Other colleagues at SOAS who have helped us with their perceptive and insightful comments on earlier drafts include David Marsden, Dina Matar, Toni Baum and especially Raymond Apthorpe.

Working at ChildHope (2005–11) was Emma Crewe's most recent fieldwork. She would like to thank all the staff, trustees and partner NGOs in Africa, Asia and South America for the collective demonstration that it is possible to do development with a little more respect, reflection and humility than is customary. Our thanks go particularly to Chris Mowles (Chair) for his comments on the draft and to Richard Livesey-Haworth (former Chair) for alerting us to 'the spaces in between'. Dwan Kaoukji, who works with ChildHope, also made useful suggestions.

Our appreciation goes to all the anthropologists who wrote pieces, gave us permission to use their work or told us stories: Lucy Crisp, Mary Ann Mhina, David Mosse and Dan Taylor in the UK, Anannia Admasu and Girmachew Adugna in Ethiopia, Kelfa Kargbo in Sierra Leone, Harini Amarasuriya in Sri Lanka, Vasundhara Bhojvaid in India and Sabrina Crewe in the USA. Finally we are grateful to our families – Helen, Moya, and Harry Axelby and Nicholas, Cleo and Scarlett Vester – for their good-humoured support.

Over the past four years our students on the Anthropology and Development course at SOAS have been a constant source of inspiration, encouragement and superb questions. This book is dedicated to them.

1   Introduction: hope and despair

The emotional geography of development spans the twin poles of hope and despair. Development is a powerfully affective world that touches us all. Despair at failure, corruption and enduring suffering sit alongside hope invested into how we imagine the future, but they are not the only responses. Guilt, anger, cynicism and piety all charge development encounters with emotion and morality.

Key points covered by this chapter

- This chapter outlines different theoretical bases by which policy-makers, scholars and practitioners have sought to understand development.
- We describe how ways of thinking about development influence practice.
- We look at a number of points of similarity between globalised narratives and describe how these common assumptions may limit understanding of the complex reality of change.
- We outline the basis of recent anthropological approaches to the study and practice of development.
- Finally the main themes and the chapters of the book are introduced.

Viewed from the comfort of social and geographical distance, economically 'poor countries' are conjured up as places of unrelenting misery by the US and European media.[1] They are beset by social breakdown and endemic corruption, where state failure results in endless cycles of civil conflict. Grinding poverty and senseless violence, 'biblical' famines, disasters and killer diseases are depicted. Poor, Third World or developing countries are populated by the starving, the destitute, the displaced and the marginalised. They live in unsanitary conditions, are unable to access clean water and lack adequate standards of healthcare. To make the subject of development 'newsworthy', the mainstream media tend to employ extreme and sensationalist images of suffering and despair. But such portrayals are not restricted to news reports. Fundraising drives and awareness-raising campaigns also rely on the evocation of despair to provoke a reaction. Shocking images are accompanied by passionate pleas for support.

These invented pictures of despair are only one slice of the story. Set against situations of hopelessness, development agencies offer potential supporters an imagined future that will bring miraculous improvements in people's lives. Mission statements ask us to imagine 'a world free of poverty and injustice'.[2] Others inform readers that 'No child is born to die'.[3] Ambitious if not impossible targets were set in 2000 the Millennium Development Goals adopted by the United Nations promise to halve world poverty by 2015. The battle against poverty may be a 'massive challenge' but 'we are winning the battle, right now, in all sorts of ways – big and small'.[4] In rich countries, people are told that our support 'can, and does, make a difference'.[5] The message is clear: 'Dig down the back of the sofa. Empty your pockets. Raid the piggy bank. Why? Because every penny you give will help us realise our vision – an end to poverty'.[6] Proposals and plans chart paths to better futures. Guarantees of a better world are supported with evidence of previous success stories, the tangible outcomes and past achievements that illustrate mastery and competence.

Sensationalistic portrayals of development serve to attract attention, galvanise support and direct practice. But in making these dramatic claims, the realities of life are distorted – not just the 'everyday' experiences of poverty and marginality but other aspects of life are lost: work, play, fun, friends, as well as deals, gossip and quarrels. Nor does the impatient optimism of fundraising literature or planning proposals conform to the sometimes mundane realities of development work, such as the endless committee meetings, training courses and testing of toolkits. Such down-to-earth realities are not 'news'. Meanwhile 'donor fatigue' encourages ever more extravagant claims to be made to save us all from the depths of despair with visionary optimism and hope.

Rather than the polarised pessimistic depictions and exaggerated promises permitted by distance, in this book we will engage with a range of representations and realities through close-up examinations of everyday experience. Important sets of actors in 'Aidland' are the planners, consultants, advisors and policymakers (Apthorpe 2011). Our starting point is aid, but our focus extends beyond at points to consider all who are touched by, involved in or affected by processes of planned (and occasionally unplanned) change, even including celebrities (see Box 1.1). In defining the object of study so broadly, we move constantly between the big picture and the fine details that make it up. This book considers 'the spaces in between', the gaps that exists between the past and the future, between policy and practice, developed and developing or between success and failure. In the space between these binary oppositions lies the real world of aid and development.

So what is development? The meaning of anything interesting is usually unclear and 'development' is no exception. Even concepts with one meaning can be hard to reduce to their essence. When comparing different examples of a phenomenon it can be more instructive to consider the overlapping similarities (like threads in a rope) rather than the one common feature they all share. When you have a concept with many meanings, as you do with development, the task of finding comparative meaning gets even more complex.

Box 1.1. Band aid or brand aid? Celebrities in development

In counterpoint to the anonymous, silent black recipient of charity (see Box 1.2 on page 14), individually named, fabulously wealthy, easily recognisable and (mostly) white celebrities are often chosen as the public face and voice of international fundraising campaigns.

Celebrities have become so integral to development fundraising that agents tend to advise their clients on how to handle the endless requests; some suggest choosing three organisations and giving them twelve days a year. The UN agencies meet quarterly to make sure they are not approaching the same people. From the development agency viewpoint, celebrities often have to be 'tracked' for up to a year before they can be asked to help. For both sides it is about promoting 'the brand' – that of the celebrity and the organisation – but to make it look authentic, some connection has to be found. Anthropologist Dan Brockington writes, 'authenticity is forged in the public domain. It is performed to publics and represented by the media' (2011: 20). Corporates are particularly star struck when it comes to famous people – business people fawn over someone reasonably well known and attractive, according to one informant – so when offering assistance to NGOs they love getting free association with celebrity.

Public figures such as Bono and Bob Geldof are now as well known for fighting poverty and famine as they are for their music. But celebrity involvement in international development tends to polarise opinions. Brockington suggests that activism by famous figures tends to generate more heat than light. He identifies the following two typical types of response to celebrities: (1) celebrities should devote themselves to tackling development problems, speak out against injustice and tackle the root causes of poverty. By using the media spotlight celebrities put their fame to good use to highlight important issues. (2) celebrities just jump on bandwagons, embrace easy causes and shy away from difficult and unpopular issues, all to advance their careers. Celebrities do not understand enough about development issues and cannot claim to speak as experts; they fail because they do not tackle the structural causes of poverty.[7]

The term 'development' was initially used to refer to processes of social and economic change. Starting with the ancient Greeks, Cowen and Shenton trace this sense of development as a *process* that is both natural and inevitable (1996: viii–ix). But the focus of this book is on a slightly different meaning of the word. Here we use 'development' to refer to the purposeful pursuit of economic, social and political goals through planned intervention. Development interventions are conscious acts carried out through projects, policies and programmes by governmental and non-governmental actors. Though primarily applied to efforts to bring about improvements this definition may be extended to encompass attempts to ameliorate the negative effects of change.

Notions of development as *natural process* and development as *planned intention* are not inseparable; nor are the boundaries between aid and development. The contemporary reality in our globalised world is that all planned change involves both indigenous and expatriate stakeholders and therefore it is hard to separate *national* 'development' from *international* 'aid'. If 'development' is used for attempts to produce long-term social, economic or political change then, in contrast, 'humanitarian aid' responds to disruptions and emergencies, such as war, famine and natural disasters, with an emphasis on the short term. But the boundaries are blurred: development usually involves some shorter-term aid – helping the poorest families out when they are destitute – and humanitarian aid often aims for longer-term service provision. In this book most of our examples are drawn from the anthropological literature, much of which focuses on international aid and development cooperation between the global 'North' and 'South', although at points we refer to a fuller range of development encounters. So, while we may relax our definition at times, we follow Cowen and Shenton by asking not 'What is development?' but rather 'What is intended by development?' (1996: xiii). This leads to a further question: 'Who decides what development should be?'

Development has become an industry that has grown up around efforts to engineer social change or eradicate poverty. Again, we find that people working in the development industry use the word in different ways and either understand, or misunderstand, each other in the context of its use. Nandy and Visvanathan recognise development as both an *idea* and a *community*:

> The idea of development has served many purposes in our times. It has served as a reason of state, as a legitimiser of regimes, as part of the vision of a good society, and, above all, as a shorthand expression for the needs of the poor. It has produced a new expertise and created a new development new community of scholars, policy-makers, development journalists, reader of development news, development managers, and activists – who together can be said to constitute the development community.   (1990: 145)

In this chapter we discuss the ideas of development planners and practitioners and how they mobilise and justify action. Planned interventions require desirable destinations to be identified and supposedly linear routes to them to be carefully charted. But questions about desirable ends and the means by which they should be attained are not simple ones to answer. Embedded in the cultures of communities, collectivities and institutions, these questions are shaped by the moral values of those that hold them.[8]

Development as easy

In the search for the foundational text for the idea of development as the fight against poverty, ignorance and disease, a good candidate would be the inaugural address made by President Truman in Washington, DC on 20 January 1949.[9] Truman spoke of the misery that afflicted 'more than half the people of the world'. Handicapped by poverty 'their food is inadequate, they are victims of disease, their economic life is primitive and stagnant'. This could not be allowed to continue: 'For the first time in history, humanity possesses the knowledge and the skill to relieve the suffering of these people ... Greater production is the key to prosperity and peace. And the key to greater production is a wider and more vigorous application of modern scientific and technical knowledge.' After the horrors of the Second World War and with newly independent states emerging from decades of colonial rule, eyes were turned towards the future. Proclaiming the end of the old order Truman spelt out a vision of a better world for all: 'The old imperialism – exploitation for foreign profit – has no place in our plans. What we envisage is a program of development based on the concepts of democratic fair-dealing ... We must embark on a bold new program for making the benefits of our scientific advances and industrial progress available for the improvement and growth of underdeveloped areas.' So began the great progressive project of freedom and prosperity promised for all. The age of empire was at an end; the age of development had begun.

The idea of a global geographical divide between 'haves' and 'have-nots' is one that, until recently, has been central to the idea and the practice of development. In deploying the term 'underdeveloped' Truman identified a new global geography marked by disparities in wealth and technology. Set against the term 'developed', this division highlighted an incompleteness, an absence or backwardness. The peoples and nations of the underdeveloped world needed to improve and to grow. The solution was obvious: development could be effected by the export of money, technology and expertise from the developed to the developing world.

Truman's vision for development is a simple one in the sense of identifying the goal of a world freed from poverty, disease and oppression. Who could disagree? The following decades brought together a powerful coalition of policy-makers, academics and development professions united by a shared belief about the possibilities of development. But, in more than half a century since Truman delivered his address the better, healthier, more prosperous future that he envisaged has materialised only for some. Over the past half-century substantial differences have emerged to account for this failure and suggest what the goals of development should be and how they might be achieved. At the root of these divergent views lie fundamental questions about the meaning of development. These questions entail moral and political judgements about social change as well as technical questions about how to achieve it. However, anthropologists tend to argue that the problems and consequent solutions to development have been simplistically defined, as if development were easy, and even misconceived.

The idea of easy development persists in the face of deepening poverty in sub-Saharan Africa with the Millennium Development Goals (MDG). In 2000 the UN countries agreed to halve poverty by 2015; despite significant decreases in poverty in East Asia, Africa only saw poverty drop from 58 to 51 per cent between 1990 and 2005. Further echoes of this naivety can be found in the participatory development movement (see later in this chapter and Chapter 4). It lives on in fundraising images and the publicity materials of aid agencies of all types and sizes (see Box 1.2). Finally the bureaucratic demands of development require the applicants and supplicants to give an impression that development is easy – with impossible visions, ambitious targets and positive reports (as described in Chapter 9), whereas it is clearly fraught with endless difficulty, difference and conflict, as we aim to show in this book.

Development as modernity

With the dismantling of European colonial rule, the two decades that followed the end of Second World War saw the birth of newly independent sovereign states across much of Africa and Asia. Development thinking during this period was dominated by the notion of a straightforward route leading upwards to the goal of modernity. Alongside the geographical divide identified by President Truman, we find a temporal divide that makes development a question of *time* as well as *space*. Proponents of modernisation theory saw all societies arrayed at various points along a linear progression. Viewing the developed world's past as the undeveloped world's present, it follows that the developed world's present is the undeveloped world's future. To modernisation theorists and proponents, development can be achieved by mimicking the historical experience of the industrial states of Europe and North America.

Modernisation theory has cast its spell across all development institutions at some point in their history and remains in implicit forms. Among the most influential of the modernisation theorists is Walt Whitman Rostow (1916–2003). In his *Stages of Economic Growth* (1960), Rostow outlined a series of evolutionary levels – starting with 'traditional society', and moving through 'preconditions for take-off', 'take-off' and 'the drive to maturity' – through which all societies had to pass before reaching the final age of 'high mass consumption' characterised by high productivity, advanced technology and urbanisation. In this evolutionary schema those countries at the earlier stages of economic growth were bound by 'traditional' modes of social organisation resistant to change. Rostow optimistically promoted the idea that ultimately all societies would progress beyond this initial backward state. Developmental efforts should therefore concentrate on re-orienting conservative norms and values towards those associated with capitalist development: individual initiative, risk taking, innovation and freedom from kinship constraints and customary obligations.

The deficits of underdevelopment could be made good by a simple replication of historical conditions of the already developed. But which conditions should be replicated? Large-scale and capital-intensive infrastructure was the means by which development was to be achieved: centralised states invested heavily in projects of road-building, the provision of irrigation and the promotion of heavy industry. Despite broad consensus on the fundamental desirability of development, agreement on the actual direction that change should take has proved less settled. The early prioritisation of industrialisation and economic growth in the newly decolonised countries of the 'Third World' had, by the 1970s, shifted towards a focus on reducing poverty. Initial ideas of political independence, industrial progress and urban expansion gave way to new notions that suggested development was equivalent to, and achievable through, a greater degree of integration into a capitalist market system. The primacy of the state as the provider of development was replaced by an emphasis on the market as the driver of progress. Structural Adjustment Programmes provided blueprint solutions for taming macro-economic imbalances, dismantling barriers to trade and reorienting production towards export markets. More recently the 'Washington Consensus' of a mix of economic neoliberalism and 'good governance' has attained significant influence among key international policy-makers.

Such explicit modernisation theory has long since fallen out of intellectual fashion in some circles. However, it persists in the mainstream, even if in subtler forms: the hierarchical notions of knowledge and expertise that lay at its heart continue to inform approaches to development. Despite variations in the way development is conceived, the means of delivery through particular institutions and approaches have remained remarkably resilient. These 'travelling rationalities' inform contemporary development policy and influence practice. According to Mosse: 'There is today unprecedented expert consensus on how global poverty is to be eliminated and the poor governed, brought about by new processes of aid "harmonisation" or "alignment"' (2011: 3). Anthropologists have shown that homogenised development policy knowledge is socially produced out of 'locally transient but internationally permanent and close-knit communities of experts' (*ibid*.: 14).

Within aid agencies extraordinary faith continues to be invested in 'global' policy ideas, models or frameworks whose universal applicability is expected to affect predictable economic, social and political transformation around the world. From the capitals of 'Aidland', powerful policy-makers direct the courses of action. Armies of expatriate development advisors and consultants transmit these plans around the world. Later in this book we will examine in detail the international consensus that they promote around issues of poverty (Chapter 4), rights (Chapter 5), technology and knowledge (Chapter 6) and neoliberal economics (Chapter 6).

Assumed to progress in a linear and predictable manner, development projects are planned with predefined objectives, outputs, targets and indicators (see Chapter 8). Development's 'liberal and travelling formalism' constantly works to frame places in terms of lessons distilled from elsewhere. This practice allows 'for the universal to assert itself over the particular, the travelled over the placed, the technical over the political, and the formal over the substantive' (Craig and Porter 2006: 120). The main mode of development can be caricatured as built on external assistance and expertise being delivered to a passive and uncritically accepting local population of grateful beneficiaries. In spite of recent official rhetoric about increased participation, little space is left for debate, contestation and variance from the plan. This is centralised development as conceived from above, and often from the global North, devised and delivered by external experts. Timothy Mitchell's *Rule of Experts* (2002), a study about the constitution of expertise in post-colonial Egypt, illustrates how experts are integral to the process of giving the impression that the logic of modernity is working despite the gaps between intention and reality.

Development as control

In the immediate decades after Truman defined the terms of post-colonial development assistance, successful examples of the predicted take-off into economic growth were thin on the ground. Clearly something was not working. Much of the research of scholars in the development studies departments that have sprung up in universities across Europe and the USA was concerned with explanations of failure. Donor governments and international agencies typically blamed the victim by identifying further deficiencies in the weak and corrupt states of the developing world. While some scholars supported this view, during the 1960s and 1970s counter-arguments emerged. Some neo-Marxists highlighted the way in which developing economies have become enmeshed in systems of international trade and development that were not in their own interests. Responding to the 'rule of experts' offered by the global North, new voices emerged from the South calling for acceptance to be replaced by resistance. Challenging the evolutionary assumptions of modernisation theory, the notion of forced dependency pointed to an alternative understanding of relationships of development and underdevelopment.

As part of a more general challenge to established values, recognition of unequal trade relations between the global North and South grew into a more general critique of the notion of a straightforward linear progression towards development. The modernisation ideal that nations could independently determine their own futures was dismissed as apolitical and ahistorical. Instead neo-Marxist theorists such as Andre Gunder Frank (1966) and Immanuel Wallerstein (1974) adopted a political economy approach to highlight the negative effects on the underdeveloped world of global historical processes, including colonialism and capitalist expansion. Far from progressing along the road to development in the manner suggested by modernisation theory, the countries of the global South were being actively *under*developed through deeper involvement in an unequal and exploitative global economic system. Dependency theory recognised *development* and *underdevelopment* as being different sides of the same coin. Departing from the promise of a brave new post-colonial order, the 'anti-development' critique argues that the formal granting of independence masked a reality of continued dominance by the former colonial powers. With the end of the colonial era, the 'civilising mission' became a modernising one. Again rational external progress would be delivered mainly by foreign experts; central planners would provide progress to the backward and ignorant masses. Aid conditionality meant that the prime 'beneficiaries' were not the poor, hungry or marginalised in Africa or Asia but rather the states donating funds and agencies tasked with delivering aid.

Dependency theory was rooted in the conviction that development as conventionally practised was no more than an exercise in power. Through development, powerful international actors were able to impose their interests, values and beliefs onto the people of the developing world. This was a continuation of colonialism by other means. But, the question was asked, how was the domination of the global North maintained following the dismantling of the structures of formal colonialism? In contrast to the overt political and military force employed during the colonial era, the workings of power in the age of development required new understandings.

Before we move on to the new understandings, it is worth noting that various other strands of development theory have put the spotlight on control. Feminists argued that male-dominated systems at all levels of society ensured that women and girls engage in economic, social and political life on adverse terms. Women are subordinated through poorer access to and control over resources, lack of adequate representation and violence. Until the 1980s mainstream development institutions failed to acknowledge gender inequality in society and the ways that their initiatives were exacerbating it. Since then gender mainstreaming has swept across development bureaucracies as a goal but, many feminists and anthropologists would argue, with only limited impact on women's subordination in many parts of the world (see Chapter 4). Environmentalists have also perceived control as a central mechanism of development. The way we control and lose control over our physical world through development – extracting resources, filling it with pollution, meddling with genes and warming the atmosphere – are major threats facing the globe. As Apffel-Marglin puts it: 'development as greater control by man of his environment … rests on a logocentric mode of thought. In this definition of development is embedded the opposition between man and his culture on the one hand and the environment on the other hand' (1990: 140) (see Chapter 6).

Finally, against the Cold War backdrop, aid and development were used to reinforce political interests; not only the economic but also the *security* concerns of the donor countries have shaped international development. Since the end of the Cold War the threat of interstate war between the communist bloc and western bloc receded but new regionalised forms of conflict emerged (Duffield 2001: 1). Since the mid 1990s the issue of conflict has become central to humanitarian aid and the development agenda and new conflict university departments, NGOs and units in global agencies have sprung up. According to Duffield, new forms of global capitalist expansion means incorporation for some countries but exclusion for others; for example, commercial investment in Africa has collapsed since the 1970s (*ibid.*: 4). The resulting 'Fourth World' – sub-Saharan Africa and poorer areas of Latin America and Asia – is targeted for conflict prevention and the creation of stability rather than capitalist expansion. Reflected not just in policy, but also in the thickening of networks that link UN agencies, military establishments, NGOs and private security companies, development and security concerns have merged (*ibid.*: 15–17, 22–43).

Development as empowerment

Many critics attributed the failures of development to the top-down nature of development processes. The arrogant assumptions underlying modernisation theory, reliance on national statistics and blueprint standardised policy prescriptions doomed development to bringing benefits only to a few. Although he had antecedents (notably the liberation theologist Paulo Freire), Robert Chambers has become the most famous proponent of bottom-up participatory development. When Chambers drew attention to 'bias', and argued passionately in favour of reversals within relationships, he initiated what has become a huge industry promoting participation. The initial method – participatory rural appraisal – is defined by him as 'a family of approaches and methods to enable rural people to share, enhance, and analyze their knowledge of life and conditions, to plan and to act' (Chambers 1994: 953). The point is to try to avoid the dominance of development by outsiders but also by elites within intended beneficiary communities – whether richer, male or older – by using techniques to encourage participation by all. Participation has become so much part of the orthodoxy that all donor agencies require any initiative to have at least an element of PRA or its equivalents.

Paul Francis tells us how the World Bank uses PRA. The repertoire of tools that encourage both verbal and non-verbal communication include mapping, ranking, use of diagrams, all described in manuals and guides (2001: 76). PRA supposedly gives greater value to emic (insider), rather than etic (outsider), viewpoints, which sounds commendably humble but underplays the importance of acknowledging (and dealing with) conflicts and differing views within categories (e.g. between 'marginalised women'). Although wealth ranking does explore differentiation within communities, most of PRA elicits community priorities or plans as if whole communities can share the same priorities despite wealth, gender, caste, and age differences and inequalities. And although its stress on the informal, and non-verbal communication such as drawing pictures on the ground, are well meaning, Francis asks whether the simplification of complex knowledge and views is helpful (*ibid.*: 84). It can be highly manipulative. He relates how the PRA approach is popular within the Bank, and especially its assumption that empowerment involves individual rather than collective transformation. So, it can be interpreted as improving processes through consultation to get better results, rather than forcing the Bank to give attention to class, power or gender inequality.

The critique of participation – for example, by Cooke and Kothari in their book *Participation: the New Tyranny* (2001) – is that it is inherently flawed; in fact, the more participatory a method claims to be, the more it will mask local inequalities (*ibid.*: 12). If it can be saved, they argue, it is only by a far more penetrating understanding of power and its manifestations (*ibid.*: 15). This may only be true of a weak definition of participation. Sarah White points to the different types of involvement and power that are all contained within the one black box of 'participation': nominal, whereby people make it look as if participation is going on by, for example, forming women's groups and persuading women to join; instrumental, meaning that people give their time or labour which may be cost-effective and efficient for the outside agencies but can be expensive for 'people'; representative, where local people form groups through which people express their views and get things done so that the initiative has a greater chance of sustainability; and, transformative, meaning that participation leads to empowerment because people take collective action against injustice. If genuine empowerment is to take place then it can be facilitated but not controlled by outsiders. She writes that 'sharing through participation does not necessarily mean sharing in power' (White 1996: 6). In fact, she goes on to say, 'incorporation, rather than exclusion, is often the best means of control'. Arguably, when you consider the various initiatives carried out by development agencies, the further up the participation ladder you go towards transformative change, the rarer success becomes.

Top-down commitment to others' empowerment is highly contradictory (*ibid.*: 13) because if people are given the space to empower themselves they tend to work outside expected parameters. White tells a story about how an NGO introduced a hand-tubewell programme for irrigation in Bangladesh. The pumps were located in the fields to help with vegetable production but people kept moving them to their homes. The NGO issued immoveable plastic pipes and when they were no longer used, the project turned into a failure in terms of its stated objectives. Too often development agencies are not promoting participation in an open-ended way, but heralding participation within highly constrained limits to ensure that their own goals are met. In part, she writes, it is the multiple meanings and ambiguities in the language of participation that lend it to manipulation by elites (*ibid.* 7–8). Maia Green reinforces the argument: 'despite claims of the empowerment rhetoric, poor people lacking the capacity to bring about social transformation themselves can only participate in development through development agency institutional structures for participation' (2000: 68).

As Williams points out, this is hardly surprising. The idea that participatory events can empower people is absurdly naive: 'most development projects simply do not command enough power to transform radically the structural inequalities that reproduce poverty' (2004: 98). He finds examples where a more radical version of participatory development can inspire the popular imagination. The Kerala Popular Science Movement galvanised mass participation with state support, while the Rajasthan-based MKSS mobilised people against the state by exposing corruption through dissemination of official documents and large-scale protests. In short, empowerment can only genuinely challenge power structures if it is explicitly political.

But even being explicitly political in a rhetorical sense is not enough. Craig and Porter write about how since the 1990s the donors' planning requirements have been laid down in the Poverty Reduction Strategy Process (PRSPs) (2006: 85–7). Donor agencies' neoliberal ideas were dominated by structural adjustment pre the 1990s but by 2000 it has become clearly pro-poor. This means 'making markets work for the poor', improving legal and regulatory arrangements and enhancing their security or 'reducing vulnerability to shocks', all familiar phrases within the reports and plans of national governments and development agencies (*ibid.*). In a shift from conservative to more inclusive neoliberalism, even empowerment has become fashionable. Putting into practice Sen's ideas[10] – following his much quoted book *Development as Freedom* (1999) – and giving a nod to women's inclusion, empowerment through the development of individual capacity has become central (*ibid.*: 86). As Craig and Porter make clear, 'this round table multi-inclusion may feel good at the time, but in practice is not just sociologically, but politically naive. In its full-blown form, it creates a powerful 'inclusion delusion', a perfect ideological smokescreen, legitimating wider Liberal market relations and obscuring the power inequalities they lead to' (*ibid.*: 87). As the rhetoric of empowerment becomes co-opted into development discourse and stripped of its political nature, the potential for transformation melts away.

Development as discourse

Foucault's concept of 'governmentality' describes how rule is accomplished through hegemonic discourse and disciplinary power. A close analysis of the use of language, structures, symbols and rituals reveals the ways in which discourses serve the interests of powerful actors. Discursive power tightly defines the parameters of discussion in ways that order and limit what can be talked about and what cannot. In turn the existence of particular orders is justified and becomes institutionalised in routine processes and events. To put it another way: words work to shape thought and action, and practices determine the way we think about them.

Discourse is a claim to truth, it normalises and makes natural. The analysis – or deconstruction – of discourse reveals the political basis of these claims. By deconstructing a discourse we are able to read between the lines to expose the working of power. Applied to the world of aid and development, the analysis or deconstruction of discourse gave rise to a powerful 'post-development' critique.

Post-development theory emerged out of the criticism of development projects, the institutional arrangements that produced them and the theories that justified them. Theorists such as Escobar (1995), Esteva (1992) and Sachs (1992), worked to uncover the hidden mechanics of power and to reveal how structures of global dominance are reproduced through the silent assumptions and reductive representations of mainstream development practice. Adopting the methodology of discourse analysis these critiques pointed to the ways in which particular practices and ideas were naturalised and, therefore, depoliticised.

The power of discourse lies in its ability to order and define. Words and concepts shape ideas, policy and practice and reshape the objects they set out to describe (Cornwall 2010). Gustavo Esteva turned on President Truman's inaugural address to challenge the very meaning of the term 'development'. To Esteva 20 January 1949 marked the day that 'two billion people became underdeveloped' (1992: 7). Ignoring their varied cultures and histories, Truman depicted the inhabitants of the developing world (poor, primitive and stagnant) as the simple antithesis of the developed world (rich, advanced, progressive). Having objectified the undeveloped world in ways amenable to external intervention it was decided that 'they' need to become more like 'us'. For Esteva the speech marked the launch of 'a political campaign on a global scale'. Through the construction of this hierarchical framework for action 'development' becomes equated with 'westernisation'. Denying difference in the countries of the underdeveloped world, Truman's address established a still widespread view of globalisation as a process of homogenisation.

Having established the geographical contours of development, hegemonic development discourse worked to reshape the realities of First and Third Worlds in particular ways. Arturo Escobar describes the discourses of development as a mechanism used first to produce and to manage the Third World. He argues that in the same way that colonised people were construed as degenerate on the basis of race, so too are poor people represented as impoverished and lacking (see Box 1.2). These representations are made real through the practices of development: 'the body of the malnourished – the starving "African" portrayed on so many covers of western magazines, or the lethargic South American child to be "adopted" for $16 a month portrayed in the advertisements of the same magazines – is the most striking symbol of the power of the First World over the Third. A whole economy of discourse and unequal power relations is encoded in that body' (1995: 103).

Treating national and international development policy as in part an ethnographic object allows us to ask how orders of policy are produced and how, in turn, they produce their objects (people, nations, regions). In his book *The Anti-Politics Machine* (1990), the anthropologist James Ferguson writes about World Bank engagement with Lesotho in the period between 1975 and 1984. Contrary to a long-standing reality of market integration, proletarianisation and labour migration to South Africa, the World Bank consistently chose to characterise Lesotho as a traditional, isolated, subsistence economy. Through this particular framing of Lesotho's 'problems' it fell to the state to introduce the necessary roads, markets and credit deemed necessary to stimulate development. Built on shaky foundations it is unsurprising that this approach did little to solve the very real problems (low wages and negligible employment rights) that afflicted many people in Lesotho. With the World Bank mission to Lesotho unable to mount a political challenge to inequitable and exploitative South African labour laws,

---

Box 1.2. A black-and-white issue?

International fundraisers' frequent reliance on images of the pain and suffering of anonymous Ethiopians during the famine of 1984–5 was later described as the 'pornography of poverty' (Plewes and Stuart 2007). But when in July 2011 famine in Somalia, Kenya and Ethiopia left millions of people without food, the fundraising departments of many major INGOs opted to fall back once more on the familiar pictures of starving African children. These images have a powerful hold over the public imagination and can prove highly effective in generating financial donations. But at what cost?

Homogenising the many different issues that countries in Africa face encourages the belief that famine, for example, is a fundamental part of the 'single story' of Africa. Whilst images of starving children reflect part of the reality that some regions in East Africa are subject to, they also risk reinforcing the view that black victims require the assistance and knowledge of organisations run by white people to help them survive. Rarely depicting the local organisations that are already working to cope with a crisis, and preferring a foreign celebrity over a local expert (see Box 1.1), these representations create an image of the 'other' which reinforces white peoples' place at the top of the hierarchy of development.

The dilemma faced by INGOs when choosing fundraising images is that the demand for short-term financial gain often outweighs the desire for long-term advocacy and development education. Though possibly effective as a fundraising tool, sensationalist images of abject suffering do little to educate people about the complex realities of development. Fundraising materials do have the potential to change peoples' perceptions of development but many INGOs persist in reproducing images which depict a hegemonic 'single story' of development.

(Lucy Crisp 2011)

---

they instead opt to reorder reality in ways that recognise possibilities for technical assistance. The situation on the ground is made to fit with the institutional needs of development agencies and their blueprint package of external intervention.

'"[D]evelopment" institutions generate their own form of discourse, and this discourse simultaneously constructs Lesotho as a particular kind of object of knowledge, and creates a structure of knowledge around that object. Interventions are then organised on the basis of this knowledge, which while "failing" on their own terms, nonetheless have regular effects' (Ferguson 1990: xiv). The regular effects that Ferguson mentions are the expansion and entrenchment of the bureaucratic power of development agencies including the state. His point is that failed projects get replicated again and again because although they may fail for the 'people', they succeed for the state. In this way development policy is de-politicised; that is, made to appear natural, neutral and amenable to technical intervention. This is the Anti-Politics Machine in action.

Ferguson's empirical case study characterises development not as an effort to confront inequalities or reduce poverty but as the conscious imposition of western hegemony over the world. Wolfgang Sachs writes: 'it is not the failure of development which has to be feared, but its success' (1992: 3).

To post-development discourse theorists such as Escobar the need for change cannot be denied. However, change should be conceived in terms that emphasise equality, democracy and genuine (rather than merely cosmetic) respect for other traditions, technologies and forms of knowledge. To Majid Rahnema (1997: 391) the answer is not development but the 'end of development'. But what does this mean? If not development, then what?

Alternatives to conventional development are seldom clearly spelled out. For some the answer lies in people driving development themselves, while others emphasise the need for localised strategies determined by group participation or appropriate technologies or redistributive justice. Escobar, for one, sees social movements as offering a solution to the stifling bureaucratic norms imposed by self-serving NGOs and states. Collective self-mobilisation allows the poor and marginalised to exercise power and seize control over the direction of change. As examples we might point to the Chipko movement where villager women in the western Indian Himalayas hugged trees to protect them from felling (Shiva 1988). Protesting against globalisation, neoliberalism and unfair trade, Mexico's Zapista Army of National Liberation is also held up as exemplifying anti-development resistance. Hailing from the southern state of Chiapas, the Zapatistas are a revolutionary group whose figurehead styles himself as Subcomandante Marcos to reflect the non-hierarchical nature of the movement and a commitment to promoting participatory democracy (see Box 7.4 on page 171). From the despair of environmental destruction and capitalist exploitation, these movements imagine the hope of a better, greener, fairer future.

So are discourse theorists right about the power of the developers and the possibilities for resistance? The reality is not so polarised. In this book we refer to the many anthropologists offering more nuanced interpretations. While recognising the insights offered by the analysis of development discourse, we do not have to accept all the conclusions of the post-development critique.

Moving beyond discourse

So far in this chapter we have outlined contrasting ways of viewing the world that advocate distinctive visions of progress and the methods by which they may be achieved. The most recent critique of development – the post-development discourse theories – provides an important questioning of the ethnocentric assumptions of mainstream development (neoliberal economics, modernisation and de-politicisation). But, despite the differences, some discourse theorists share a number of key assumptions with their ideological opponents. These common beliefs can be summarised as follows:

•   both mainstream and the discourse theories maintain a sharp dichotomy between the global North and South as agent and object of development respectively;

- both see development as a monolithic enterprise that is easily defined and internally unified: development is an industry or machine able to deliver predictable and uniform programmes;
- local agency is limited; the objects of development are either grateful beneficiaries or passive victims of externally determined change; 'development' is something to be resisted (whether rationally or irrationally) but possibilities for collaboration, adaptation, contestation and compromise are less considered.

These two contemporary extremes of development thinking identify similar sets of protagonists and share an understanding of their respective roles and positions. Extreme versions of pro- and anti-development positions divide the world into two distinct camps in ways that simplify the relationships that exist between them. In a bipolar world development is seen to be gifted, or imposed, by the developed North on to un(der)developed countries of the global South; from helpers to the helpless; from perpetrators to victims. In some ways the spatial and temporal geography of development found in Truman's address continue to define the possibilities for action. In order to mobilise support and galvanise action, both modernisation theory and its post-development critics rely on visions that counterpoise a grim present reality against the prospect of a bright future.

Post-development discourse theory is unconvincing in part because it attributes the idea of development with a narrow, singular meaning and consistency that are not matched either in theory or in policy (Pieterse 2000: 188). Some post-development theory itself produces a caricature of development that homogenises the motives and beliefs of those involved and ignores the differences between them. The notion of simple 'westernisation' suggests that such a thing as an undifferentiated 'West' exists – that development as promoted by North American agencies is the same as European or Scandinavian models. But what is 'the West'? Modernity in the USA – with its frontier mentality and technological and economic prowess – is different from European modernity. This simplistic notion also denies the alternative models of change that have emerged and are emerging out of Japan, or, more recently, China, India, Brazil and the Middle East. All are better understood as complex hybrids that draw on their own cultures and histories as much as anywhere else.

The development industry is neither a simple 'aid chain' nor a machine of domination (a theme we return to in Chapters 3, 8 and 9). Development institutions are not necessary as omnipotent or as coordinated as their supporters or detractors might claim. Development organisations are very different from one another, they follow different agendas and utilise different means to do so. Furthermore within single organisations there exists considerable internal differentiation; the intentions or effects of their activities are varied or even contradictory. Taking the example of the World Bank, the impact of the institution is huge and there is much to criticise. But a simple critique is not convincing: we see substantial changes in the institution's policy recommendations over time (from prioritising growth to basic needs to structural adjustment to good governance) and the Bank may be subject to considerable internal differentiation, with different departments and individuals holding diverse aims, motives and working practices. In classifying the world into distinct and fixed categories, contextuality is underplayed as is the fluidity of identity and social relationships. The idea that developers dominate through policy is also over-simplified (see Chapter 8); in reality developers are rarely able to shape practice in the way they (and their detractors) like to claim. Jean-Pierre Olivier de Sardan points to the important difference between the public discourses of development officials in Northern countries and the private conversation of experts in the field, who are often aware of the complexity of real-life situations (2005: 4).

And what of *intentions* and the ways they are shaped by institutional cultures? Can we really say, as the likes of Escobar and Ferguson seem to, that all international development efforts ultimately fail those they aspire to assist? Is it fair to say that the intention of development agents is only to help themselves rather than the beneficiaries identified in project plans? While the record of international development certainly includes endless instances of failure, its successes should also be acknowledged (as they are in this book). At the same time, no initiative can be described as pure success or failure. As we explain in Chapters 8 and 9, most initiatives have both winners and losers at all levels that often change at different times. If you take the empirical data seriously, then the idea of development as success or failure and operating as one system or machine must be treated with suspicion. Recent ethnographic studies referred to in this book maintain that almost all development theories and approaches fail to recognise that the complex relationships and identities of different actors are best understood when set within their particular historical and social contexts.

Over the last decade anthropologists have adopted different, critical perspectives that recognise the varied possibilities of development, while acknowledging the limiting effects of uneven power relations. Development outcomes are negotiated in ways that deny either the bland optimism of the modernisation model or the pessimism of post-development theory. Anthropology's eminently empirical and analytical approach is able to reveal the fluid details of how actors exercise agency and the manner in which they respond and relate to one another, not just as individuals but also as collectives.

Moving beyond the absolute separation of actors, institutions and knowledge systems, recent ethnographic studies of development have recognised development encounters as dynamic interfaces involving multiple acts of brokerage and translation (Lewis and Mosse 2006). No longer separating the different sets of actors away from one another, these approaches depend on examining development projects and processes as a whole – from policy design, through implementation and extending to a consideration of the experiences of local people. To understand how so-called beneficiaries experience development you have to consider their perspectives as central to their respective worldview rather than 'peripheral' to those of the developers. The idea of development as machine only tells us so much about the complex cultural interface between development projects and those that they target.

Rather than maintaining that development discourse is owned and controlled by the global North, anthropologists have revealed how actors in the global South shape new understandings as well. For example, Pigg describes how an ideology of modernisation is assimilated into local culture in Nepal not as a process of domination but as a social positioning of different people within Nepal (1992). How Nepali villagers conceive of development – or *bikas* – is influenced by the West but not identical, it takes a local form. To explain why Nepalis see development as a mixture of foreign and local, Pigg goes into their history. Nepal was governed by the elite Rana oligarchy until 1950–1. When they were overthrown the new government invited international aid in – constructing schools and hospitals for example – whereas the Ranas had maintained isolation. Thus, unlike some of their neighbours, development is not the residue of colonialism (as Escobar describes it for the Third World); it is a new and overt link between it and the West. Even now, '*Bikas* comes to local areas from elsewhere; it is not produced locally' (1992: 499) – so villages tend to have little *bikas* – and it is mostly found in material things like videos, roads and medicines. Pigg talks about *bikas* as a way of categorising people as well as places so that city-dwelling elites are more modern than poor rural villagers. There is also differentiation within villages. In contrast to development agency staff who make generalisations about 'the village' so that their models can be applied nationally, villagers differentiate their own local world from others. They apply the same *bikas* logic that polarises *bikas* versus village, within the village between themselves and 'other' ignorant poorer people in a context of hierarchies based on gender, age, caste or ethnic group. They aspire to be agents rather than targets of *bikas*. She concludes that 'the ideology of modernisation in Nepal is not simply a matter of western influence, but a matter of simultaneous nepalisation and globalisation' (*ibid.*: 512).

When discourse theorists identify the challenge to development orthodoxy as coming from local, democratic, community-centred social movements, they can overlook the diversity of approaches such movements may choose to adopt. Rather than opposing development in absolute terms, the object of people-centred campaigns may be to make claims to the benefits of development. In contrast to Vandana Shiva's characterisation of Chipko activism as a feminine reassertion of traditional ecological values (1988), others have posited that the protests stemmed from contemporary concerns for social justice and political democracy (Sinha *et al.* 1997: 84). Ethnographic research by Antje Linkenback in the Garhwal Himalayas suggests that as the Chipko protests gained international prominence local experiences were subsumed into global discourses of environmental activism. As part of this process, the varied messages and meanings of villager's struggles were homogenised, changed and rewritten in ways that removed Chipko from the local context (Linkenback 2007). Far from being uniformly anti-development, social movements may seek *better* development through participation, decentralisation and inclusion.

In order to understand the working and impacts of international development, it is necessary to go beyond a view of the world as being made up of donors and beneficiaries, perpetrators and victims. Olivier de Sardan, in his book *Anthropology and Development*, argues convincingly for adopting an *empirical* approach – where our understanding grows out of the social realities of people rather than the assumption of a particular grand theory such as deconstruction – and be aware of the value judgements we ourselves are making (2005).

Aims of this book: complicating development and simplifying anthropology

This chapter has reviewed some of the meanings that attach to development. The least critical approaches remain hugely influential in terms of development practice but offer only a very limited understanding of development as a process. The more critical approaches are more complex and theoretically interesting, especially in their understandings of the working of power, but their influence has not been translated into practice. But that is not a good reason for glossing over complexity.

In contrast to the narrow regularities of the pro- and anti-development positions, in this book we argue for proper recognition to be paid to the possibilities for complexity, contestation and creativity in development. Rather than viewing behaviour as determined simply by the reproduction of power relations through discourse, we need to consider how cultural politics work at different levels and times. To approach the idea of development from just one direction is limiting; it can be, in part, a discourse of control but it can be a 'discourse of entitlement' at the same time. The reality is of a multiplicity of voices, some louder than others, but all worthy of attention.

Focusing narrowly on their own plans and projects development workers may fail to look up to see a bigger picture. For policy-makers and planners the fine grain of multiple local realities is concealed in flows of data that suggest 'average' situations and generalised truths. Pursuing their own narrow agendas, critics of development may similarly be guilty of simplifying intentions and outcomes. Attempts to define the character of major development bureaucracies that rely only on a reading of textual output ignore the complex interplay of individual motivations, the cultural making of meaning and institutional structures involved in the production of both. Universal policy models are not enacted unaltered but undergo significant changes through being translated into local social and political arrangements in diverse and unpredictable ways.

In the search for universal explanations complex realities are manipulated and simplified until they conform to a convenient narrative. Limited fields of vision reinforce themselves by avoiding and excluding ideas, people and experiences that do not conform to expectations. Institutional and ideological structures try to bend reality to their perspectives rather than extending their visions to encompass the full diversity of reality. Unable to look beyond the obvious, values are left unquestioned and unchallenged by alternative perspectives, so that complexity, externality and contradiction are dismissed. In an increasingly complex and multi-polar world, processes of displacement and exclusion mean that the rhetoric intentions of development – empowerment, poverty reduction and protection for all – still elude us. There are no easy short cuts in development; it is always difficult and pretending otherwise can do harm.

This book advocates the need to re-engage, to make connections, to accept contradictions and to acknowledge complexity. Those engaging in development, including anthropologists, function well when self-reflexive and respectful towards those with whom they engage. In order to break out of restricted worldviews it is necessary to take on different perspectives, to view the world of development from above and below, close up and from a distance. Theory and practice are advanced when we ask questions of ourselves as well as others.

This approach is firmly rooted in the discipline of social anthropology. Social anthropology is the study of people's values, relations, meanings and practices as created, reproduced or transformed in social collectivities. A collectivity might be a community (or communities and relationships between them), an institution or a group of people interacting regularly across different sites (e.g. global environmental activists, migrants, or an international coalition such as the North Atlantic Treaty Organisation). As the most interesting aspects of social behaviour are complex and only understood over time, anthropology requires a commitment to in-depth investigation and observation. Lengthy periods of fieldwork involve complete immersion in other cultures or settings.

Anthropology is different from other social sciences in its empirical research methods *and* interpretation. It departs from a deductive scientific method that involves proving or disproving hypotheses by starting with a theory and then looking for evidence to substantiate it (Geertz 1973). Combining participation and conversations with observation, anthropological research produces descriptive accounts rich in detail, context, history and theoretical explanation. Unlike other disciplines, anthropology does not seek to divide up aspects of a culture into separate parts. Ethnographic accounts are not restricted to the narrow study of either politics *or* economics *or* religious beliefs but instead are likely to consider how different aspects of a culture relate to one another holistically.

As Gledhill explains, while it is often said that what is unique about anthropology is its methodology, it is also the way anthropologists *explain* social life that makes the discipline interesting. Examining 'social realities in a cross-cultural frame of reference anthropology makes a significant theoretical contribution as a social science. In striving to transcend a view of the world based solely on the premises of European culture and history, anthropologists are encouraged to look beneath the world of appearances and taken-for-granted assumptions about social life in general' (Gledhill 1994: 7). So to understand a society you have to consider the different levels on which it operates, that is, people's worldviews, their rhetoric and rules, and their practices. Anthropology raises questions, delves deeper and refuses to accept surface appearances. Probing into what lies behind surface representations and everyday rituals, anthropologists often focus on the eccentricities and controversies of a situation. In doing so they expose what is taken for granted, including the moral and political assumptions that support power relations at all levels.

Like all researchers, anthropologists face the problem of representing other people's realities through the lens of their own views. It is a challange for writers and artists as well and different schools respond to it differently. While Realist painters once gave the impression that there is only one way to see and represent a scene, Cubists aim to reflect how we all 'see' from different angles or perspectives. Anthropologists have similarly shifted from aiming to represent reality objectively, as if the researcher does not influence their perception of the object, to acknowledging their own subjectivity (Clifford and Marcus 1986). In part in response to feminist anthropologists – who pointed to how male anthropologists once tended to treat women as if they were peripheral or invisible – anthropologists have become keenly aware that how they see, interpret and depict will be influenced by their own identity, relationship with informants and their own worldviews.

For example, consider this story. When Emma went to Colombo for the first time in the late 1980s, as a young female British white NGO worker and doctoral student, she found herself having dinner with an older male white British engineer. They did not discuss work at all; they talked about books, marriage and politics. This may sound irrelevant to the politics of aid, the subject of Emma's PhD thesis, but much later she reflected on this encounter. She compared this encounter with hundreds of others and noticed that when British development workers socialised with each other they established trust and ease very quickly – gossiping, flirting, sharing ideas or useful pieces of information – whereas when they had lunch or dinner with nationals (in East Africa or South Asia where she visited regularly), then they were at work and less relaxed. The more socially embedded the expatriates were in that society, which often included anthropologists or those who had married into that place, the smaller the social distance.

The point for anthropology is that reflecting on one's own role in the research has become highly relevant to the researcher's understanding. Some anthropologists have gone as far as saying that ethnography is so much the product of a particular's anthropologist's view and experience, that it is a form of autobiography. But most would explore the relationship between researcher and object, rather than giving the anthropologist such a central role. At the least anthropologists try to reflect on how they see and interpret and what role has been played by their own gender, race, age, class, politics, assumptions and so on. When conveying their findings, they write themselves into the account where relevant, showing for example how their own assumptions or social position have shaped what they found.

It is becoming clear that anthropologists take a multitude of standpoints. They are interested in more than describing different collectivities; they aim for cross-cultural comparison – looking for convergence or divergence between the ways the state operates or religion is organised in different societies or cultures – and they theorise this in extremely different ways. Anthropology theories historically shifted from early functionalism, through structuralism, Marxism, feminism and postmodernism, or mixtures of these, in different ways in the UK, continental Europe (especially France), the USA and elsewhere, as explained by Barnard in his *History and Theory in Anthropology* (2000). Furthermore, at any one time anthropologists disagree about how to make sense of economics, kinship, politics, religion, art or indeed development.

Anthropology's position at the intersection of the social sciences and the humanities has given anthropology an image as 'the difficult science'. But this is not to suggest that fierce arguments of this apparently hostile and well-armed tribe are without value. Asking awkward questions should not disqualify anthropology from engaging with an issue on a practical level; the anthropologist's war cry 'it's not that simple' is a worthy response to attempts to streamline, abstract and generalise. With regard to development, anthropologists have undoubtedly been critical, but this is not to imply that criticism cannot be constructive.

Olivier de Sardan outlines three broad approaches (each further subdivided) that anthropologists have adopted in the study and practice of development (2005). His first group contains the discourse theorists discussed earlier in this chapter. Although the members of the group share an interest in deconstructing the development discourses of developers, and describing how developers dominate or rule aid recipients, they vary in subtlety: some are mainly ideological, while others build their critique on strong empirical foundations. The second group consists of the populists. Here he makes a useful distinction between the following: (a) methodological populism – the valuable method of taking as your starting point the study of grassroots social actors' knowledge and strategies; and (b) ideological populism – the sometimes nostalgic exaltation of 'the poor' as heroic, long-suffering and ingenious (*ibid.*: 117–18). Idealising and romanticising 'the poor' has no empirical clout but also holds within it the seeds of the opposite, that is negative stereotypes of the poor as environmental destructive or ignorant. His final group take an 'entangled social logic' approach – further divided into two sub-groups: (1) 'actor-oriented approaches', whereby different perspectives meet and are negotiated or clash, as promoted, for example, by Norman Long; and (2) a more diverse set of anti-ideology perspectives that explore the embeddedness of various social logics, placing development within broader fields (of the state, contemporary Africa, or African modernity) (*ibid.*: 11–15). We draw upon and compare these different approaches throughout this book and contrast them to the view from other disciplines (see Box 1.3 for some key texts).

The themes and structure of this book

Of the books written on the subject of anthropology of development some are designed to improve development practice (e.g. Gardner and Lewis

Box 1.3. Anthropology and the study of development: some general texts

These recent key texts have had an influence on the anthropology of development and demonstrate the range of possible approaches that anthropologists may take to aid and development:

- Wolfgang Sachs's *The Development Dictionary* is an edited A–Z of post-development thinking (1992; second edition 2010). In this 'Guide to Knowledge as Power' key concepts of development discourse are deconstructed by Gustavo Esteva, Majid Rehnema, Arturo Escobar, Vandana Shiva and many others.
- Katy Gardner and David Lewis's *Anthropology, Development and the Post-modern Challenge* (1996) delves into the deconstructionist critique to make a positive argument for the continued application of anthropological knowledge to development.
- Edited by Ralph Grillo and Roderick Stirrat, *Discourses of Development* (1997) applies anthropological perspectives to development. Health projects, cookstove dissemination and official panics over lost forest cover are all subjected to anthropological analysis.
- Emma Crewe and Elizabeth Harrison's (1998) *Whose Development?: An Ethnography of Aid* combines their ethnographical research on relationships between aid workers and 'beneficiaries' in Sri Lanka, India, Kenya, Zambia, Germany and the UK. They also provide an overview of the intellectual heritage of aid and the disjunction between policy and practice, and argue for a nuanced and relational approach that takes account of people's lived experience.
- Alberto Arce and Norman Long published *Anthropology, Development and Modernities* (2000) as an edited volume offering a critical review of interpretations of development and modernity and case studies from Guatemala, Sri Lanka, West Africa and Europe. They frame the work through a lens of their actor-oriented and interface approach.
- Marc Edelman and Angelique Haugerud's *Anthropology of Development and Globalisation* (2005) is a comprehensive reader that collects together key texts from classical political economy to contemporary neoliberalism, from the foundations of thought underlying development through to contemporary debates on globalisation and the future of capitalism.
- Jean-Pierre Olivier de Sardan's *Anthropology and Development: Understanding Contemporary Social Change* (2005) is a theoretical monograph about anthropological perspectives on development. Olivier de Sardan critiques populist approaches and discourse theories for their simplicity and failure to take account of the complexity of people's real lives and offers an empirical and interpretative approach.
- Edited by David Mosse and David Lewis, *The Aid Effect* (2005) brings together eight ethnographies of international development and governance that reveal the new global architecture of aid.
- *Deconstructing Development Discourse* edited by Andrea Cornwall and Deborah Eade (2010) examines the language of development.

> Contributors show how meanings of key terms are transformed as they enter mainstream development practice as *buzzwords* and *fuzzwords*.
> • David Mosse's edited volume *Adventures in Aidland* (2011) looks at the social life of development professionals, the relationships they form and the networks to which they belong.

1996), while others offer more theoretical reflections on the institutional workings of development (e.g. Mosse 2005; Olivier de Sardan 2005). We aim to combine these approaches and illustrate them with examples drawn from across the world. During the 2000s there has been a rush of journal articles offering ethnographies of aid and development and increasing numbers of anthropologists going into development professionally. Our book offers a comprehensive examination of the key topics in the anthropology of development as it enters the second decade of the twenty-first century.

This book is primarily written for students of anthropology or sociology and of international development or international relations. Reflecting on development from anthropological perspectives we offer signposts through an interesting and penetrating literature – both primary and secondary sources – and make suggestions about how to navigate through it. The book may also be of interest to planners, policy-makers and practitioners. It will not make doing development any easier – in fact it may mean that their frameworks, tools and formulae become highly unstable. But if they take the insights of anthropological colleagues into their practice, then they are more likely to question their everyday working practices and to recognise the needs and abilities of those they work with and for. In short it provides an alternative way to understand the perils and possibilities of processes of planned change.

This book reviews, from anthropological standpoints, the competing ways of thinking about and practising development. Each chapter subsumes a number of linked beliefs to present arguments concerning processes and agents of development and the likely effects of change. Running through the chapters of the book these recurring themes will be subjected to anthropological analysis to reveal the assumptions and ethnocentric representations upon which they depend.

1. There are multiple *cultures* of development, the categories and concepts that constitute the way people think about and make sense of the development industry, whether structure and agency for anthropologists or tradition and modernity for development actors. In this book we introduce these categories and concepts: structure and agency; tradition and modernity; state and society; policy and practice; local and global; and ritual and representation.

2. The *politics* of development in the sense of how people and resources are organised – hierarchically in explicit and implicit ways – and

what values attach to these. The governance of the industry has been transformed and the recent history of the relations between state, civil society, private sector, social movements, families and individuals will be described.

3.   *Moral* judgements by and about development actors and anthropologists are the final key theme. Anthropologists tend to probe hard into the worldviews of subordinated people but also try to avoid romanticising them. A further central consideration is a concern with the ethics of applied anthropology and the dilemmas of engagement.

In this chapter we have outlined significant differences between conventional modernisation approaches to development and an alternative 'post-' or 'anti-'development critique. We then identified and questioned a number of simplistic (and simplifying) assumptions common to both. These shared limitations restrict understanding of the complex realities of development. Arguing that development is rarely simple the rest of the book draws on anthropological approaches to illustrate the complexity of contemporary thought and practice.

The structure of this book divides into three distinct but interrelated parts. The first three chapters provide an introduction to major ideas and actors. The two chapters that follow this one introduce the main protagonists in the world of development: Chapter 2 provides a historical overview of anthropological engagement in development and considers some of the ethical issues that arise out of applied work. Chapter 3 presents anthropological perspectives on aid agencies and actors and charts the shifting relationships between them.

The subsequent four chapters take topics around which development interventions have been shaped and subject them to anthropological scrutiny. We examine ingrained assumptions about poverty, rights, technology and knowledge, and production and exchange. Looking at how development actions have been influenced by these beliefs we question some of their ethnocentric foundations.

Bookending these detailed overviews is a chapter that looks under the surface of Development World to examine the rhetorical forms, bureaucratic structures and representation tropes through which the idea of development is produced. The final chapter offers a look into the possibilities for the future by explaining how actors and agencies imagine alternative futures and by offering a range of questions that both development and anthropology must deal with if they are to catch up with recent events and paradigm shifts.

This guide to Development World is not intended to be comprehensive. Our space is limited and the world of development is ridiculously large: much that is important receives only passing attention; much is left out. But we hope to convey how anthropological approaches can be applied to some of the patterns, relations and cultures of Development World on the assumption that they may be equally relevant to others.

The book is not an instruction manual. It does not attempt to dictate how development should be done or what the reader should believe. Instead what we offer is a guide; it is intended to serve as an introduction to the complexities of location, language and culture, to be found in the world of development. It seeks to assist the reader in finding their way, recognising the complexity and controversies that underpin notions of development.

Challenging questions arising from this chapter

What does development mean?

How is development similar and different in different countries and regions?

Why is development portrayed as if it were easy?

Is it possible to construct a convincing uncritical perspective of development?

What impact do critiques of development have on policy and practice?

What are empowerment approaches and what impact have they had?

How convincing do you find discourse theories of development?

2   Anthropologists engaged

The origins of anthropology pre-date those of development as we know it. Charting the history of engagement, this chapter outlines the opportunities and dilemmas that face anthropologists as they seek to apply their distinctive approach and specialist knowledge to the world of development.

Key points covered by this chapter

- This chapter charts anthropology's evolving relationship with applied work from the nineteenth century to the present.
- A historical review of the changing relationship between anthropology and development allows us to understand concerns over engagement and point to some of the ethical challenges manifest in applied work.
- Opportunities for the application of anthropological expertise to development work are outlined: anthropologists have provided important contextual knowledge, assessed social impacts of development schemes and advocated for indigenous rights. The limitations of these approaches are also described.
- Central to this review is a consideration of the ethical, political and moral considerations that arise when anthropology is applied to development.
- In recognising the disciplinary and political compromises that arise from engagement, we consider how such pitfalls might be navigated.

From the discipline's establishment in the late nineteenth century, anthropology was disinclined to deal with the idea of 'development'. In part this reluctance stems from the implication that societies can be ordered hierarchically along a line of evolutionary progress. But no man (or culture) is an island and anthropologists have been forced to contemplate the complex processes by which communities are incorporated into wider political and economic systems. The notion that anthropologists should engage in applied work has an equally troubled history. For some, engagement involves an implicit acceptance of particular regimes of change. Other anthropologists have promoted the notion that their understandings could be turned to practical purposes. Over the second half of the twentieth century opportunities for applied work expanded as development grew into a global project. Engaging in development, anthropologists have established a role for themselves as social development advisors capable of injecting a degree of cultural appropriateness into external interventions. Having accepted these positions, anthropologists were left well placed to turn their attention to the institutions, projects and programmes of the development industry itself. Whether writing from inside or outside the development industry, anthropologists have been highly vocal in their critiques of the bureaucratic practices and cultural assumptions through which the world is reshaped.

Despite the entry of anthropologists into Development World, anthropological insights have often been ignored or overlooked by policy-makers and planners. Anthropologists frequently find themselves treated with suspicion within groups of development professionals. In their efforts to empathise with and understand 'the other', they are viewed as becoming too close to 'beneficiaries'. The questions they ask and the methodologies they adopt frequently fail to fit in with the short-termism and simple narratives required by development agencies. The descriptive accounts produced by anthropologists are not readily reducible to sound bites or easily translated into solutions. As a result anthropological insights have often gone unrecognised by key decision-makers.

Following a brief note on history, the chapter is structured by areas of objection to anthropological engagement – first methodological, then political, then postmodern. Each of these critiques has produced responses leading ultimately to the production of nuanced ethnographies of aid. In examining the sometimes troubled history of applied anthropology, this chapter asks fundamental questions as to the purpose of the discipline, the extent of its influence and how best to navigate the ethical dilemmas that are raised by engagement.

Early beginnings: anthropology and colonialism

To understand contemporary anthropology and the practice of development we need to return to the origins of the discipline and its wider political context. Asad points out that social anthropology emerged as a field of study at the beginning of the colonial era, and had established itself as a flourishing academic profession by its close (1973: 14–15). This historical association of anthropology and colonialism has left a legacy that cannot be ignored.

Over the course of the nineteenth century a disciplinary divide separated the sociological study of industrial society from social anthropology's concern with 'exotic', small-scale, non-western cultures. In its formative beginnings, anthropology was thus defined as the study of the 'less developed', its focus was a primitive 'them' as differentiated from civilised 'us'. Requiring accurate information about little-known populations and territories, colonial rule extended opportunities to anthropologists to conduct research. Early thumbnail sketches of the 'customs and manners' of native people progressed into increasingly sophisticated and sympathetic efforts to delineate and describe social relations and cultural practices based on long periods of fieldwork. The early twentieth century saw the emergence of a recognisably modern form of anthropology as a discrete field of understanding. As described in the previous chapter, the purpose of anthropology was the comparative study of society. Using immersive, long-term empirical research (or 'fieldwork') anthropologists were able to generate rich qualitative data. But, almost from the start, differences in opinion emerged about the value and application of anthropological knowledge.

Initially at least, the 'founding fathers' of this new discipline were keen to emphasise the significance of their work to colonial administrators. In the early 1920s Alfred Radcliffe-Brown offered courses in 'applied anthropology' at the University of Cape Town. A strong advocate of engagement, he wrote:

> The white races, and particularly the members of the British Empire, have adopted the view that they have the right to take over immense areas of territory of Asia, Africa, and Oceania, containing in all many millions of inhabitants, and to impose upon the peoples of those countries many important changes in nature ... Here, therefore, in the deliberate attempt made to control and alter the civilisation of other peoples in administration and education there is a field for applied anthropology.   ([1930] 1980: 124)

The application of social anthropology lies 'in the control of the process by which culture or civilisation changes' (*ibid.*). This bluntly defined the terms of engagement: empire was a political fact, and anthropological understandings could contribute to its efficient implementation. Though his attitude to empire was perhaps more ambiguous, Bronislaw Malinowski was also keen to promote anthropology's potential contribution. In his article on 'practical anthropology' (1929: 23) he suggested that a period of anthropological training offered to colonial officials would produce more effective rulers.

British and French anthropologists benefitted from colonial rule in the form of access to restricted sites and other forms of practical support. In the USA similar help was provided to anthropologists by the Bureau of Indian Affairs, which sponsored research into the customs, political institutions and landholding patterns of Native Americans. Talal Asad later concluded that 'the basic reality which made pre-war social anthropology a feasible and effective enterprise was the power relationship between dominating (European) and dominated (non-European) culture' (1973: 17). Colonial rule made the objects of study accessible and safe for anthropologists; it also guaranteed the 'one-sided and provisional' intimacy required for fieldwork (*ibid.*: 13).

What of the more contentious argument that anthropology served colonialism? Certainly the direction of anthropological study reflected and reinforced the racial hierarchies that underpinned colonialism. At the extreme end, anthropologists were accused of serving as spies, providing colonial governments with details of the natives' lives that would normally remain hidden from view. Such views challenge the image of the 'scientific' anthropologist as a detached and neutral observer separated from political influence. The colonial contexts are represented as fostering 'an essentially conservative subject, shaped within the same political ideology as colonial domination itself and bolstering its interest' (James 1973: 41).

The Second World War furthered the deployment of anthropological knowledge in the service of the state (Price 2002). Anthropologists, including Ruth Benedict (1989 [1946]) and Gregory Bateson (see Price 1998), were employed to analyse the behaviour and psychology of 'the enemy' and to provide propaganda material for domestic consumption. Others went further: Tom Harrison returned to the site of his fieldwork to recruit the native people of Borneo into the war against the Japanese (1959). The war years marked the furthest extent of anthropology's initial foray into applied work. But the dubious methods adopted and the ends to which their work was put led many anthropologists to question their contribution.

Clear lines of continuity exist between colonial era engagement and contemporary applied work. Perhaps the most extreme example concerns the application of anthropological knowledge in conflict situations. 'Fighting with both books and guns', anthropologists have applied their special skills and understandings in times of war (Price 2002: 14). So it should not come as a surprise that the US-led invasions of Afghanistan and Iraq have seen a resurgence in the employment of anthropologists in the military sphere. In 2008 the US Department of Defence announced plans for the annual disbursement of up to $18 million under the Minerva Research Initiative. The money was made available by the Pentagon to fund social science research on issues of 'national security'. As outlined by the Pentagon, security issues requiring investigation included 'Chinese military and technology research', 'studies of terrorist organisation and ideology', and 'future ideological trends within Islam' with an eye to 'solving terrorism challenges' (Lutz 2008: 1). The Minerva Initiative's supporters see anthropologists as capable of providing contextual and cultural data, leading to more appropriate and less destructive policies. Anthropology, it is hoped, might function as a corrective 'to the ideologically driven and ill-informed policies, large and small, that have sent US soldiers and Marines into the deserts and mountains of the Middle East and Southwest Asia' (*ibid.*: 1).

Alongside the provision of funding for academic research, the Pentagon has adopted a distinctly more direct approach. The 'Human Terrain System' (HTS)[1] counter-insurgency programme has, since 2005, directly employed anthropologists and other social scientists to serve as adjuncts to the US Army in Iraq and Afghanistan (Gonzalez 2008). Here 'human terrain' is used in counterpoint to 'geographical terrain': in the asymmetrical wars of the twenty-first century the control of *people* is as important as the control of *territory*. HTS operatives are assigned to brigade combat team headquarters and spend time accompanying military units on patrol. Their role (as detailed on the BAE careers webpage) is as follows:

> The Human Terrain System (HTS) is an Army program designed to embed socio-cultural experts with tactical commanders to integrate socio-cultural understanding into the military decision-making process. Human Terrain

Teams help military commanders reduce the amount of lethal force used, with a corresponding reduction in military and civilian casualties. Allowing the commander to make decisions that will increase the security of the area, allow other organisations (local and international) to more effectively provide aid and restore the infrastructure, ensure that US efforts are culturally sensitive, promote economic development, and help the local population more effectively communicate their needs to US and Coalition forces.[2]

Serving alongside military personnel, civilian HTS team members are issued weapons at their discretion and that of the supported unit.

Should we recognise the HTS programme and Pentagon-funded research exercises as valuable attempts to temper the 'kinetic' power of military force with gentler, more culturally appropriate social scientific understandings? Or are they crude attempts to co-opt academic expertise to further the prosecution of war? With the Pentagon responsible for determining the topics to be researched, concerns exist that the acceptance of military sources of funding might lead to the distortion and militarisation of academic investigations (Lutz 2008: 2). Engagement on these terms contradicts ideal standards of professional conduct (see Box 2.1).

What might be the long-term results of embedding anthropologists alongside military personnel? For some of these anthropologists a strong temptation may exist to document the cultures, practices and social structures not of the civilians they encounter, but of the American soldiers they accompany. That unintended outcome of the HTS programme might have more significance for the way future wars are fought than the collection of data on 'human terrain' has on current ones.

From academic purity to dirty engagement

The end of the Second World War and the unwinding of colonial rule marked a new international commitment to the promotion of development. Modernisation theory suggested that the newly independent nations of the Third World should follow the route taken by the industrialised countries of the developed world. But what could anthropology contribute to this new project of development? Initially at least, the answer seemed to be very little.

In the immediate postwar period, anthropologists seemed disinclined to apply their knowledge to the practical goals of development. In part their isolation was rooted in the widespread view that applied work would compromise independent scholarship. Concerns were raised over the influence funding agencies might exercise in setting the limits of research and the uses to which they might apply the information gathered. Writing in 1946 Evans-Pritchard determined that any practical service rendered by anthropologists should be subordinate to academic detachment and scientific goals (see Pels 1999: 108). A divide opened up between the 'autonomous' academic ensconced in academia and the 'compromised' practitioner beholden to other interests.

Box 2.1. The use of ethical codes in anthropology

All of the major anthropological associations offer guidance to their members by out-lining ideal standards of ethical conduct. The American Anthropological Association's *Code of Ethics* (2009)[3] outlines four main areas of responsibility that its members are encouraged to consider:

* responsibilities to the people with whom anthropological researchers work and whose lives and culture they study;
* responsibility to scholarship and science;
* responsibility to the public; and
* responsibility to students and trainees.

The UK Association of Social Anthropologists similarly makes recommendations with responsibilities towards research participants central to its *Ethical Guidelines for Good Research Practice.*[4] This professional code outlines the anthropologist's duty to protecting research participants and honouring trust; anticipating harms; avoiding undue intrusion; negotiating informed consent. Rights to confidentiality and anonym-ity should be respected; fair returns made for assistance and services. Also considered are the researcher's responsibilities to sponsors, funders and employers; to colleagues and to the discipline; to the anthropologist's own and host government; and to the wider society.

Claims to be able to provide a set of 'universal' norms of practice that are time and context free do not sit easily in a discipline that places such emphasis on cultural difference. Areas of possible contradiction between the different requirements are readily apparent in both of the above outlined codes of conduct. We should perhaps regard these professional codes as only starting points illustrating possible choices as a means of promoting discussion. It is worth quoting at length from the epilogue to the ASA's code:

> These guidelines are aimed at helping anthropologists to reach an equitable and satisfactory resolution of their dilemmas. This statement of ideals does not impose a rigid set of rules backed by institutional sanctions, given the variations in both individuals' moral precepts and the conditions under which they work. Guidelines cannot resolve difficulties in a vacuum nor allocate greater priority to one of the principles than another. Instead, they are aimed at educating anthropologists, sensitising them to the potential sources of ethical conflict and dilemmas that may arise in research, scholarship and professional practice, at being inform-ative and descriptive rather than authoritarian or prescriptive.[5]

When considering the ethics of engagement it would be a mistake to assume that all forms of applied work necessarily promote the interest of dominant discourses or that all forms of participation in development work implies collaboration. Instead, it would be better to understand opportunities for engagement on a case-by-case basis. We should direct attention to the form and objectives of projects and programmes and look at the working practices of particular institutions. Hard questions must be asked about whose interests would be served by professing to have adopted an anthropo-logical input. Will the anthropologist's input occur sufficient early and be given a level of priority necessary to make a genuine contribution? Will a hard-hitting political

analysis and recommendations for challenging the status quo of the kind that anthropologists tend to offer make any headway? It means asking about the opportunities
that exist for input, seeking assurances that research will be sufficiently independent
and findings properly considered and respected and that the relevant people have room
for manoeuvre.

Anthropology's retreat into the expanding postwar university sector might
also be attributed to a lack of opportunities for employment in the grand modernisation projects of development. The 'hard', 'scientific' data produced by
economists was privileged; the 'soft' qualitative knowledge of anthropology
considered to be of little relevance or value. The emphasis on western expertise and imported technology saw no value in anthropology's holistic approach
and perceived focus on 'tribal' culture or 'traditional' societies. In practical
terms, the fieldwork methodology central to anthropological investigation was
viewed as being too slow in yielding information and having uncertain results.
Firmly oriented towards understanding other cultures rather than seeking to
change them, anthropologists had little part to play in the early decades of
development.

Narrowly defined as the promotion of economic growth, industrialisation and
infrastructural modernisation, the field of development was initially monopolised
by economists, planners and engineers. Anthropological expertise was firmly
sidelined. And it was from this position that anthropology articulated significant
critiques of the idea of modernisation both as theory and as a set of practices
for achieving development. Ethnocentric assumptions that future economic and
social development would conform to the past experience of western developed
countries were challenged by empirical evidence that revealed the diversity and
complexity of change. Development is better recognised as a set of culturally
constructed ideas encompassing a range of promises, hopes and disappoint-
ments. The forms it takes are rooted in particular historical, cultural and political
contexts. Though some of the tenets of modernisation continued to retain considerable hold over development planners and bureaucrats, from the late 1960s it
began to attract criticism as a means of understanding the process and direction
of planned change.

Anthropological analysis of development gained prominence as the poor performance of the state-promoted, expert-led, 'top-down' modernisation model
was becoming apparent. Rates of economic growth, the criteria on which modernisation was to be judged, were often disappointing given the heavy investment
in capital-intensive development efforts. Ill suited to diverse local cultural and
environmental contexts, big infrastructure projects beloved by central planners
often met with local indifference or even resistance (see Chapter 8). Even apparently successful programmes might, upon closer examination, be shown to have
substantial negative impacts on the poor and marginalised. The global recession
of the 1970s and the resulting crisis of Third World debt further undermined the

modernisation model. New ways of understanding and doing development were required.

Though limited in numbers and influence, from the start of the 1970s opportunities began to open up for anthropologists seeking employment outside the academy. In part this stemmed from the failure of conventional approaches to appreciate social and cultural factors in project planning. A dual role offered opportunities for anthropology both as a body of specialist knowledge (a kind of ethnographic database) but also as a methodological approach capable of generating understandings that others might overlook. Anthropologists established themselves as mediators between stakeholders, doing social impact analysis with a sensitivity to prejudice and ethnocentrism.

This period saw an important symbolic shift away from the previous narrow concentration on economic growth. Under Robert McNamara's governorship the World Bank began to consider the needs of the poorest. 'Poverty-oriented' programmes directed attention towards those that were previously excluded. At the same time other development institutions, notably donor governments in the USA, the UK and Sweden, integrated analysis of local knowledge, attitudes and practices in their programmes for the first time. Whether as short-term consultants or full-time employees, scholars such as Raymond Apthorpe (1970) spearheaded anthropology's re-entry into the field of development work. This pioneering trickle of applied social scientists was tasked with interpreting cultures to outsiders and acting as a translator of local needs, interests and cultural practices and proposing how to overcome cultural obstacles and conservative attitudes. 'They brought with them a method of long-term immersion in fieldwork, an ideology of joining the people where they live, concepts drawn from ethnographies around the world and a general indifference or hostility to numeracy, literate records and all the techniques of bureaucracy' (Hann and Hart 2011: 107–8). Consulted over aspects of project implementation, appraisal and evaluation, the hope was that employing anthropologists as 'social development advisors' would inject a degree of much needed local appropriateness into externally devised projects (see Box 2.2).

Problems of engagement: compromise and complicity

The hierarchical segregate of 'pure' and 'applied' anthropology, so apparent in the decades immediately after the Second World War, is something of a historical anomaly. Both before this period, and after it, anthropology has advertised itself as a distinctly practical discipline. But engagement was not without problems. Just as anthropologists were being welcomed into the world of development practice, new concerns were raised about the issue of engagement.

The perceived failure of planned 'modernisation' fed into a critique of the institutions and methods by which it was supposed to be produced. And this attack on orthodox development practice predictably extended to a growing

Box 2.2. Working in and writing about development: an interview with anthropologist David Mosse

David Mosse studied human sciences at Oxford and found that anthropology had the most interesting perspective. He had spent over two years in two villages in South India – volunteer teaching and doing fieldwork for a PhD – and then, in a climate of few academic jobs, became an Associate Professional Officer with the British government's Overseas Development Administration (ODA, later DFID) in 1987. ODA had two social development advisors to start with – Sean Conlin and David Butcher – and David was another early recruit. They specialised in poverty, participation and gender in the days when all of these were marginalised; social development was a section of the Economic Service. He was the first who did not have to retrain as an economist (at Wye College) but had to wade through logistics, quantity surveying and 'critical path analysis' within a course called 'Project Planning and Management' at Manchester. He had to learn a new language and reframe himself to get socialised into the aid world.

His first task was a review of how the plans for a dam in Sri Lanka had been handled during the 1970s. The displacement of people by dams was beginning to be seen as problematic – resettlement was badly planned and people were often given no or insufficient provision. The inadequate social planning of dam projects was an important entry-point for social development advisors to point out the significance of the social dimensions of aid. These dimensions were no longer just the residue. It was the Hilyard report on dams that opened up debate; it led to a recognition that resettlement was important. It was a tangible social problem that economists and technical experts could grasp; they were forced to think more holistically as a consequence.

His second mission was in Bangladesh in 1987. Together with a fisheries specialist and fisheries economist, they had three weeks to define the critical factors in fisheries development and plan a project. David's role was to establish the likely impact on the poor, involve NGOs, consider gender and find out how existing systems worked. He raised questions about whether ODA's planned project would demolish existing systems. Two days before his departure, he was asked by the head of aid in Bangladesh to stay behind for a few days to look at tractors. It was the practice of aid in those days to find a place for British goods and services under 'Commodity Aid' – including Massey Ferguson tractors in this case – by identifying a need. He found that tractors were not that much used for agriculture in Bangladesh but for the transport of people and goods (e.g. bricks). In those days aid decision-making was fast, informal and sloppy.

Later in 1987, David carried out a mission in Tanzania. In only a few weeks, with an old land rover and an interpreter, he found out a surprising amount about fisherfolk and trading. He was asked to look at why fisherfolk were using dynamite to fish and thereby damaging the coral. Was it a shortage of nets or the fishing gear they used, ODA wanted to know? He discovered that the situation in the south was quite different from the north and neither fitted with ODA's assumptions. In the south of the Tanzanian coast he found collective ownership of equipment and sharing of the profits whereas the north was more individual-based with bigger vessels and more capitalised, passive forms of fishing. In neither case was it the fishermen who were responsible for blowing up coral. There was an allegation that the Fisheries Department was implicated in informal profiteering from aid. This mission brought his attention to the amazing amount you can find out in a short period of time if you have had experience of conducting in-depth anthropological research. After a year of research in one village you have a sense of what can be found out, how things are connected to each other and how to make sense of the incomprehensible. You can produce results relatively quickly (even if turning such results into a publishable form takes far longer), but he couldn't have done it without the experience of doing ethnographic research.

'What are anthropologists doing? Having the arrogance to make sense of seemingly unconnected things. Making links between things, going with a hypothesis and continually testing out of ideas, which others can then keep testing,' David explains. Anthropologists raise questions that aid workers tend to ignore and focus on the actual instance of events. That is, they respect the descriptions by those directly involved rather than, for example, trusting second hand accounts. Anthropologists avoid vague generalisations and are more interested in practice, the actuality of what happens. It is a different view of the world.

Explaining anthropology to non-anthropologists can be challenging, as he found in ODA but also later in Oxfam. David elucidates, 'A paradox arises: the more your ideas are taken on as an anthropologist within an aid bureaucracy, the more anthropology is institutionalised as "social development" which becomes very unanthropological. The World Bank has hundreds of social development specialists, DFID has gone from seventy to eighty but they have very little to do with anthropology in the sense of ethnographic research. Anthropological insight is buried at a high level by being absorbed into the institutional frameworks. We have been victims of our own success.'

Anthropologists have an open view of what is relevant to a situation. One of the main criticisms of David Mosse's book *Cultivating Development* (2005) by other team members was that there was too much within it that was irrelevant to the project he was writing about and, therefore, not 'professional'. For example, the observations about the creation of relationships of dependency and the giving of gifts to make bureaucracies function was considered highly disparaging and irrelevant. Aid workers, like missionaries, are trying to keep ideas about themselves, their identity and the power of planning intact. By saying that it was not the design of the project that lead to a mix of success and failure, David was committing a blasphemy.

(Interviewed by Emma Crewe, 21 February 2011)

questioning of the role that anthropologists were playing within this system. The equation of postwar development with earlier imperialism once again cut to the heart of the question of anthropological engagement.

Already the reputation of applied anthropology in the USA had been tarnished by complicity in US anti-insurgent operations in Latin America and South-East Asia (e.g. in Projects Camelot and Agile). Out of this earlier unease, a new politically inspired critique accused applied anthropology of helping to maintain an international infrastructure of global inequality. These attacks were also levelled at the growing number of anthropologists directly employed or working as consultants with development organisations. The disengaged and value-neutral promise of enlightenment science was dismissed as a fig leaf covering anthropologists' collaboration with ethnocentric and dominating models of development.

Clearly, anthropologists' deep understanding of local context provided a useful corrective to the simplistic assumptions of central planning regimes. But what use is anthropology's local knowledge in situations where a global imbalance of economic and political power was identified as the prime cause of continued underdevelopment? With the provision of 'specialist knowledge' to development planners viewed as politically suspect, accusations of collaboration were cast on anthropologists adopting the role of 'translator' or 'mediator'.

Questions continue to be raised about the extent to which the mind-set and actions of development anthropologists are shaped or constrained by employment within mainstream development institutions. The demand for simple off-the-shelf tools to solve complex problems and the protection of dominant paradigms blunts the influence of anthropologists. Under pressure to simplify and standardise, the anthropological appreciation of nuanced local context is ignored by development agencies with global reach. At best it is suggested that by collaborating, anthropologists take 'development doctrine' for granted and thus contribute to its naturalisation. At worst anthropology is charged with working to extract knowledge and facilitate external management and control. Those anthropologists who have benefitted from the discipline's re-engagement with the world of practice are accused of betraying the subjects of their research. For example, Ovesen explains how he has been criticised by environmentalists for his favourable assessment of a proposed dam (2009 and see Chapter 8).

To some the obvious solution to the idea of the harmful collaboration of applied work was a complete withdrawal from a system that treated local beneficiaries as passive objects to be acted upon and controlled. Theoretical interest might be maintained by turning on the apparatus of development itself as an object for ethnographic study (e.g. Ferguson 1990). For others, the only acceptable form of engagement was to align with indigenous actors fighting to regain control over their lives (Escobar 1992 and see Chapter 7). The anthropologist as activist adopts an explicitly political stance in alliance with indigenous communities. Activist research as defined by Charles Hale is 'a method through which we affirm a political alignment with an organized group of people in struggle and allow dialogue with them to shape each phase of the process' (2006: 97).

These ideas depend on the existence of an unbridgeable divide between the (dominant) developed and the (subordinated) underdeveloped world. Ferguson describes the curious duality that binds anthropology to development:

> the field that fetishises the local, the autonomous, the traditional, locked in a strange dance with its own negation, its own evil twin that would destroy locality, autonomy, and tradition in the name of progress. Anthropology resents its twin fiercely ... even as it must recognise a certain intimacy with it, and a disturbing inverted resemblance. Like an unwanted ghost, or an uninvited relative, 'development' haunts the house of anthropology.   (1996: 160)

But divides may be bridged and ghosts only exist in stories. Exorcising the phantom permits new possibilities for engagement.

The crisis of modernity and the postmodern turn

Some critiques of applied anthropology charge the discipline with the corruption of what is seen as academic detachment and objectivity. Anthropological engagement has also been accused of lending practical and ideological support to dominant hierarchies of power. Questioning the basis of knowledge and the working of power, the extension of postmodernist thought into the social sciences has challenged the very basis of anthropological understandings and the ways they could be applied.

The crisis of 'modernisation' as a way of doing development can be seen as part of a more general crisis of modernity itself. Rejecting grand narratives of unified theory, postmodernism questions the claims of positivist science to offer objective truths. Anthropology is not immune to this line of questioning. Recognising the social embeddedness of scientific ideas refocused attention back onto the workings of anthropology itself: 'no longer were distant peoples studied, but the European scholars that had studied them' (Vermeulen 1999: 16). Ever alert to ethnocentric bias, anthropologists have been forced to reflect on their own disciplinary shortcomings.

The anthropological principle of cultural relativism – that beliefs should only be understood according to the viewpoint of those that hold them – pre-dates postmodernism's celebration of multiple and equally relevant perspectives. However, following the 'cultural turn' of the mid 1980s (Clifford and Marcus 1986), new forms of scrutiny were applied to the presentation of anthropological knowledge. It was argued that 'difference' – the core of anthropological study – could only be understood in relation to the position of the observer; and observers' positions are varied and never truly neutral. The object of anthropology, the 'other', was thereby revealed as a cultural construct. The importance of context became central to notions of identity: interests shift, overlap and diverge. All this makes apparent the artifice in anthropology's tendency to group heterogeneous individuals together as bounded, easily distinguishable entities – the 'tribe', the 'village' or the 'community'. Thus we must consider the legitimacy of anthropologists affecting to speak on behalf of a group of people or to present information about them.

The recognition of 'community' as a construct raises questions about advocacy and activism more generally. Calling for a primacy of the ethical, Nancy Scheper-Hughes (1995) argues that a slavish devotion to cultural relativism allows anthropologists to suspend moral responsibilities. Drawing on her fieldwork in the shanty town of Alto do Cruzeiro in north-east Brazil and the South African squatter camps of the western Cape, she writes of the impossibility of remaining neutral, detached and objective in the face of extreme poverty and violence. To Scheper-Hughes, anthropologists have a duty to be both politically committed and morally engaged. She envisions a new cadre of 'barefoot anthropologists' capable of producing politically complicated and morally demanding texts 'capable of sinking through the layers of acceptance, complicity and the bad faith that allow the suffering and the death to continue' (1995: 417). When confronting situations of suffering in their field sites, they have a duty to act even when the other participants object.

The crisis of representation also opened up other possibilities for the anthropological analysis of development. With its status as a producer of objective facts queried, anthropology turned to 'discourse' analysis – the use and manipulation of signs, images and texts to represent particular viewpoints – as a means of revealing the hidden workings of power. Doing so revealed the ways in which unequal power relations shaped the collection, dissemination and reproduction of knowledge. This was a subject eminently suitable to anthropological study. Post-development anthropologists such as James Ferguson and Arturo Escobar adopted discourse analysis to interrogate the institutional structures, policies and programmes of development.

The final decade of the twentieth century saw the very idea of 'development' increasingly questioned. Gardner and Lewis have argued that within some intellectual circles 'development' had 'become a non-word', its use only possible when accompanied within 'the inverted commas of the deconstructed 1990s' (1996: 1). But while useful in helping us understand how development *works*, they suggested, the political and postmodern approaches of the 1970s and 1980s were of little practical assistance to those involved in development *work*: 'Reading through some of the texts produced by post-structuralists it might appear that the problems of Southern countries are simply a construct, a figment of the post-colonial imagination, and a justification for the continuing domination of the South by the North' (Gardner and Lewis 1996: 156).

But can malnutrition, disease or poverty really be dismissed as merely being cultural constructs? Clearly they cannot. Anthropologists have an excellent understanding of the empirical realities of health and deprivation. Furthermore this kind of cultural relativism relies upon the long abandoned notion of bounded and separate cultures all in possession of their own internal logic (*ibid.*: 156). Yet those who fail to take on the postmodern critiques also face dangers. Gardner and Lewis warn us that some anthropologists working in and for development organisations have found that their insights have been co-opted and their critical faculties numbed (*ibid.*: 24–5). They have been used to support the dominant discourses and have failed to challenge harmful patterns. Between the self-absorbed nihilism of deconstruction and the 'compromise' and 'infidelity' of practice there existed little possibility for mutually beneficial dialogue. The renewed separation of theory and action risked creating a stifling impasse between anthropology and development. However, as Gardner and Lewis have shown through a range of case studies – along with other anthropologists looking for a way through the impasse since the 1990s – engagement within development can be both critical and constructive.

Beyond the impasse: anthropology *in* and *of* development

Postmodern and post-development perspectives have contributed much to our understanding of the workings of development. However, we should be careful to recognise some of the limits of this view particularly with regard to anthropological engagement in development practice. Is the collection of ethnographic knowledge nothing more than an adjunct to systems of bureaucratic control? Should anthropological study be limited to the analysis of discourse and the critique of all forms of development intervention? Must anthropologists deny themselves the right to speak on behalf of communities or articulate particular desirable outcomes? We would suggest that to argue *for* or *against* engagement represents something of a false choice. No longer able to maintain a position of pure detached objectivity, all anthropology, in some way, concerns itself with questions of change and development.

The dual crisis that afflicted both anthropology and development in the wake of the postmodern critique might easily have led to a process of withdrawal and mutual separation. This has not happened. Breaking out of the impasse of the 1990s the last decade has seen a burst of creativity by anthropologists whose work has opened up new areas for engagement in ways that combine or blur rather than divide the pure from the applied.

New opportunities have arisen for anthropologists to apply their theories and methods to the problems of applied work. Since the mid 1990s social scientists have been recruited in significant numbers to the World Bank, the International Monetary Fund and bilateral institutions including the UK government's Department for International Development. Anthropology is now recognised in the dark corners of many official aid agencies as valuable both for the analysis and the practise of development. The two areas of advance are not unconnected. Reflecting on their own activities, practitioners may theorise on their work (see Box 2.3), while academics benefit from taking on employment as consultants in the short or long term. In doing so the divisions that separate theory from action, subject from object, pure from applied work are broken down.

So far in this chapter we have seen how evolutions in development thinking have opened up new spaces for anthropological engagement. And the creation of new opportunities for applied work has simultaneously fed back into advances in thinking about development. The employment of anthropologists within the development industry provided first-hand opportunities to advance the analysis of organisations (rather than people) as a major strand of anthropological investigation. 'Organisational ethnography' – an approach to understanding how institutional structures operate – saw a shift away from locally bounded subjects of development programmes and onto the powerful shapers of these plans. Emma Crewe and Elizabeth Harrison mined their experiences working respectively for Practical Action and the Food and Agricultural Organisation (FAO) to produce 'an ethnography of aid' (1998). Similarly David Mosse's *Cultivating Development*

Box 2.3. Socialising stoves: how anthropology helped explain technology adoption, by Vasundhara Bhojvaid, The Energy and Resources Institute, New Delhi

Fresh out of my anthropology course I found myself in the development world of cook stove programmes, which placed me outside my comfortable academic bubble. A process of learning and de-learning ensued wherein I realised to provide nuance was not enough; the aim was to arrive at quantifiable and measurable solutions. That being said, the training that anthropology had given me allowed me to see things beyond the 'interpretive grid' (Ferguson 1990) of development not the least of which was the workings of what Escobar terms as 'development planning' (Escobar 1987).

One of my first assignments was to visit the field wherein an improved cookstove (IC) programme had been implemented to evaluate hindrances to technology adoption. I wondered what it was that I could add, as most field personnel were already conscious of the deficiencies in the technology of the stove with regard to the specific cultural cooking patterns of the region.

While in the field I was addressed as a 'stove-walli' (stove person) due to my affiliation with the implementing organisation. My purpose was predefined by the locals – to watch, document them cooking and leave. The fact that I was spending extended periods in the village beyond the cooking period allowed me to intermingle more freely. The play of everyday talk served to help promote IC adoption. For instance at the time of IC dissemination (which were given free of cost) about 20 per cent of the male population had migrated to urban centres. On telephoning the migrant male members, the women-folk were asked to do as the other families in the village unit. Similarly, throughout the life of the project the 'community' pitted itself against the intervening organisation in almost all the decisions that were made. The people of the village were conscious of the fact that, while the implementers would leave once the project had come to an end, they would remain beyond the intervention. Consensus within the community was established through the everyday conversations the villagers had with one another. It emerged that accepting the IC, the manner in which the implementing organisation had gone about defining its interactions and personal experiences of cooking on the IC, were discussed and shared emphatically in evening chat sessions. Group approval of the stoves created a general willingness to engage with the device and even to overlook small flaws in the design.

Another lacuna is that reactions to cooking experiences on the IC are imbued with what the IC as social agent connotes in the larger social network – a device that is alien, new, from the outside urban world which was being given for free to the villagers – the lack of a price tag baffled many locals. (The decision to disseminate ICs free of cost was to guarantee maximum IC uptake in order to scientifically quantify variations in ambient air-quality before and after IC usage.) The low adoption rate for free stoves cannot be fully accounted for by the observation that people do not highly value things that are given to them. The important point becomes – how is the value of things constructed during dissemination processes? The construction of this value varied across the village unit owing to different subjective positions and how they intermingle with intervention acts. These issues seldom have anything to do with the type of IC being distributed but are a result of external factors tied to the project implementation plan and the specific micro-political position of the beneficiary. For instance, in the most economically underprivileged and spatially segregated part of the community, those in the lower caste 'Harijan settlement', the IC registered minimal adoption. In this segment the power dynamics of the intervening group were doubly compounded by the selection of volunteers (daughters of the village landlord), who were from the upper caste and class of the community. The starkly differing relative positions between the disseminators (intervening organisation and especially the upper-class volunteers) and the local community (*Harijan* segment) became the driving detrimental force to IC adoption. The place of such insights, however, in the development sector remains uncertain owing to its dominant discourse of a time-bound deliverable model with quantifiable results.

(2005) reflected on the decade in which he was employed as an anthropologist-consultant on an aid project in rural India funded by the British Department for International Development (DFID). Other anthropologists gained access through different roles: whether as critics (Michael Goldman on the World Bank (2005)); supporters (Stephen Hopgood in Amnesty International's International Secretariat in London (2006)) or affiliates (Dorothea Hilhorst in a 'progressive' NGO in the Philippines (2003)). By 'studying up' these and other ethnographers of organisations have undermined simplistic notions about the workings of institutions to reveal internal tension, divergent interests and conflicts over future directions.

From the provincial peripheries of Development World, anthropologists have now made the long journey to its metropolitan capitals. Working from fresh perspectives and engaging with actors at different levels, new and subtle understandings of the workings of the development have moved us beyond the pessimism that characterised the late 1990s. 'Studying through' – examining policies in the round from creation through dissemination to impact – anthropologists such as Anna Tsing (2004) or Tania Murray Li (2007) have moved beyond the constraints of geographically and institutionally bounded studies. Encompassing multiple locales (indeed continents) such approaches allow a holistic overview of the interconnected experience of those working in and affected by development. Applied in the interstices of more formal structures, this new wave of analysis reveals the internal workings of development bureaucracies. As such it allows us to appreciate the hidden processes of interaction, contestation and negotiation by which discursive regimes are produced and reproduced.

In 'studying-up' and 'studying though' anthropology has not abandoned its commitment to locally sited micro-studies. Rather these are new approaches to understanding how the local and the global intertwine by looking at the relationships and points of connection on wider scales.

Accusations of neo-colonial knowledge extraction are blunted when attention is turned to the assumptions and practices of development workers and institutions.

In focussing on the powerful shapers of development, anthropologists have been able to sidestep some of the moral conundrums that have been levelled at engagement. But the publication of 'insider ethnographies' has, on occasion resulted in considerable acrimony. David Mosse's *Cultivating Development* (2005) demonstrates anthropology's potential to go beyond the simple normative policy statements of organisations to look at wider context and understand how policy is made, instituted and implemented. But when Mosse offered the initial manuscript to key informants for comment the reaction was overwhelmingly negative. Mosse later described their response:

> Objections were made by my co-workers and informants to the publisher, to my university research ethics committee, my Department convenors, the Dean and the academic head of my university, as well as to my professional associations the ASA (Association of Social Anthropologists of the UK and the Commonwealth) on the grounds that the book was unfair, biased, contained statements that were defamatory and would seriously damage the professional reputation of individuals and institutions and would harm work among poor tribals in India. Those of my project colleagues who raised these objections sought to interrupt the publication process and to ensure that many parts of the book were rewritten. (2006: 935)

His employment as a project consultant has allowed Mosse to establish 'personal relationships of understanding, trust and respect' (2005: viii) with field staff, officials and consultants within India and the UK. Upon seeing their shared experiences transformed into data disseminated in public forms, Mosse's former colleagues felt a sense of betrayal. Having in effect joined the communities they wish to study, researchers such as Mosse were to find they had, 'substituted a set of boundaries that kept us *out* (the problem of access) with another set that kept us *in*' (2006: 936).

Old ethical problems and new dilemmas

The recognition that the development industry is a complex, heterogeneous and frequently contradictory collection of institutions and practices, has at least partially negated accusations of anthropology's complicity with development. But the question still arises of whether the alternative perspectives offered by anthropologists are necessarily diluted and compromised through involvement in the mainstream of development. Within institutional structures, linear ways of thinking and essentialised messages retain their descriptive power. The anthropologist wanting to 'open things up' is still confronted by established interests and ways of working that seek to 'close things down' (Marsden 2010: 1). 'For those with a job to do', Marsden writes of how 'the deployment of social development specialists was, to put it politely, a challenge. Here were specialists wanting to explore the ambiguities of engagement, rather than ... giving managers concrete solutions' (2010: 2). So the job of anthropology becomes about the nature of our own engagement and not just the processes and impact of aid.

This chapter has reviewed anthropology's engagement with development and the objections that have arisen from them. When considering questions of compromise and complicity, it is worthwhile returning to the origins of anthropology during the late colonial period and to chart areas of similarity and difference with the present. Breman and Shimizu argue that it is a mistake to dismiss anthropology 'as primarily an aid to colonial administration, or as a simple reflection of colonial ideology' (1999: 5). Anthropology, they point out, 'is a complex thing … It thrived in the colonial period but is not inherently of it' (*ibid.*: 2). If western imperialism provided suitable conditions in which the discipline might be born, it would perhaps be better to recognise anthropology as 'the *problem child* of the colonial encounter' (James 1973: 43).

The anthropologist's concern that culture should only be understood from the viewpoint of its own participants was diametrically opposed to the colonialists' intent to impose his own culture onto the colonised subjects. By celebrating the sophistication and rationality of indigenous systems of thought anthropologists challenged the ideologies of racial superiority that justified European Imperialism. While Malinowski was keen to offer anthropological knowledge in the service of colonial administration this position should not be seen as simple supplication. With regard to his later writing James suggests that Malinowski displayed signs of 'increasing disaffection with the apolitical, amoral natural science approach … and of a deepening personal radical commitment' (James 1973: 67). Denying the divide between applied and pure work, Malinowski wrote: 'research in order to be of use must be inspired by courage and purpose … It must be briefed by that constructive statesmanship and use foresight which establish the relevant issues and have the courage to apply the necessary remedies. Shall we therefore, mix politics with science? In one way, decidedly "yes"' (1945: 4). This was 'anthropology as a vehicle for criticism of that authority' with the discipline reaching 'beyond the bounds of received western civilisation in search of alternative modes of understanding and living' (James 1973: 69, 42). Writing in 1981 Raymond Firth recalled Malinowski's belief that an anthropologist's primary duty is 'to present facts, develop concepts, [and] destroy fictions and empty phrases, and so reveal relevant, active forces' (Firth 1981: 195). And if this can be true of anthropology's involvement with the colonial enterprise, why cannot similar advice be applied to its engagement in development today?

What relevance does this history have for the rest of the book? In it we have charted the general ways in which anthropologists have applied their practical skills and theoretical perspectives to the field of development. The underlying theme is that these points of contact inevitably generate frictions and lead to questions about the ethics of engagement.

Substantial (and sometime vicious) disagreements exist within and between academic disciplines and anthropology is no exception. Anthropologists engaged in development work intervene, act, speak and think, in different ways. At its best, the application of anthropological perspectives can shed light on and help to overcome discursive gaps in ways that bring people together. Anthropologists in development can be a bridge between diverse actors and interests. Practical work, especially when underpinned by theoretical rigour, requires constant processes of engagement and disengagement as the researcher establishes relationships with the constituent groups of interventions as well as with development workers, government officials, planners and policy-makers and, of course, with other academics. The process of moving in and out of these diverse worlds, collecting and communicating information inevitably raises questions and ethical issues. Each point of collaboration creates new possibilities for compromise. But judging when this becomes a harmful betrayal of a diversity of views and contexts is part of the work of any engaged anthropologist. At the same time by paying proper attention to the politics, culture and morality of the institutional structures within which they are employed, anthropologists can hope to be better at both understanding and, possibly, doing development. The two outcomes can be mutually beneficial, as we aim to demonstrate in the rest of this book, but cannot be assumed. Improvements in development policy and practice require transformations of power hierarchies and the mechanisms that sustain them. Anthropology is not enough. But anthropological insight can assist in determining what needs to be done and give support to those pursuing strategies that are well thought through and respectful. The problem is not lack of opportunity but that there is too much to be done. As Keenan puts it, 'The question, both as anthropologists and citizens of the world, is not just whether we did the right thing, but whether we could have done more' (2009: 18).

Challenging questions arising from this chapter

What is social anthropology?

What are the different anthropological approaches to development?

Did anthropologists serve colonialism and do they help or hinder development?

What is the difference between anthropology in development and anthropology of development?

Why do anthropologists have limited influence in development institutions?

How have development professionals and other informants reacted to anthropological contributions?

What are the ethical challenges facing anthropologists who engage (or choose not to engage) in development?

3   The social and political organisation of aid and development

---

Key points covered by this chapter

- This chapter outlines the shape of Development World through the labelling of the people and places within it. We explain what anthropologists find problematic in geographical classification of development.
- We introduce the key state and government categories – governments giving aid, states receiving aid and global intergovernmental agencies.
- We describe the non-state actors within the categories of the private sector, civil society and constituent groups (beneficiaries, activists and development professionals).
- The changing governance and architecture of aid is discussed. States are being displaced by both NGOs and global intergovernmental agencies and aid is being globalised.
- Finally institutional global partnerships are explored, particularly between international and national NGOs, through the lens of race and nationality.

How big is the world of aid? A crude measurement of the scale might consider how much money is involved. But such measures raise further questions about what exactly should be classified as aid money, what should be included and what should not. According to the World Bank all aid amounted to $457 billion in 2007, $294 billion in 2008 and $390 billion in 2009. But these figures include debt relief. They also seem rather small when compared to the cost of the Iraq war at $500 billion.[1] Remittances are almost as big as aid; in 2009 $319 billion of remittances were sent to the 'developing' world.[2] Although OECD member countries pledged to spend 0.7% on aid, only Sweden, Norway, Luxembourg, Denmark and the Netherlands had achieved this by 2009. The amount of aid received per head ranges from $1 in Brazil to $12,923 in Niue (a small island country in the South Pacific), while the percentage of Gross National Income that is aid spans 50% for Burundi to less than 1% for South Africa. In 2009 the Bill and Melina Gates Foundation gave $2.5 billion to global causes while the Ford Foundation disbursed $490 million. Most foundations, trusts, companies or individuals give far smaller amounts but the vast number of donors means that large sums are raised. The American Red Cross spends over $3,422 million, while Food for the Poor £1,516 million and World Vision $1,206 million. Save the Children's income was $1,276 million in 2008, 31% of which came from individuals. ActionAid alone has 320,000 supporters in Europe.

But development is not just about financial gifts or other transactions. Development agencies deliver services, keep peace and educate policy-makers or the public. The UN's permanent staff amounted to 36,239 people in 2010, receiving salaries of between $36,651 and $201,361, while USAID had only 2,417 in 2007.[3] According to their 2009–10 Annual Reports, staff costs amounted to £113 million in DFID as opposed to £595 million for programmes, whereas in USAID staff cost $114 million, while the programmes required $1,087 million. NGOs can employ even larger numbers – Oxfam employs 4,000 staff and has 22,000 volunteers while the Save the Children Alliance has a global staff of over 14,000 working in 120 countries. What these public sector and NGO workers do when providing technical assistance, training, advice or advocacy support is one of the themes to which this book will continually return.

The size of the aid industry is a rather superficial starting point; its social and political organisation is of greater interest to anthropologists. This chapter seeks first to define and then to complicate our social map of the people engaging in aid and development and their organisations and relationships.

Labelling places and people

The world has been geographically divided by aid agencies into two camps according to levels of material and economic progress (see Box 3.1). In one camp we find the 'developed' world, rich, urbanised and (post-)industrial, with effective state machinery and material comfort. The other camp holds the 'Third World', which is characterised by high levels of poverty, ineffective government and disasters of various kinds. This act of classification implies that the diverse countries of Latin America, Asia and Africa share certain common social, political and economic features. Similar homogeneity is expected in North America, Europe, Japan plus Australia and New Zealand.

The simplistic division of the world into two opposed categories has become strained to breaking point. The diversity and dynamic of the real world is reflected in the emergence of the following new groupings over recent decades.

*   The four 'Asian Tigers' of Singapore, Hong Kong, South Korea and Taiwan rose to prominence in the 1970s; their growth was based on export-led models of development assisted by interventionist states.
*   The term 'newly industrialised countries' (NICs) was later applied to nations including Mexico, Turkey, South Africa, Malaysia, Thailand and the Philippines. Rapid economic growth differentiates these nations from the classic model of the poor 'Third World' country yet all followed trajectories quite different from those of the 'developed nations'.

Box 3.1. Regional labels

Out of the colonies, dominions and protectorates of Empire, the decades after the Second World War saw a reconfiguration of global geographical divisions and political relationships. Against the backdrop of the Cold War, the term 'Third World' was coined to describe non-aligned former colonies that positioned themselves in distinction to the capitalist 'First World' and the 'Second World' of the communist bloc. This initial political meaning proved short-lived with the term soon taking on negative connotations to describe those parts of the world blighted by instability, poverty and hunger.

The distinction between Third and First World finds parallel in the division between *developed and developing* countries (with developed/less developed also used). Corresponding to the evolutionary stages of progress put forward by modernisation theory, these labels imply the former have already achieved the ultimate end-state of development while others are on their way there. Dependency theory challenged such assumptions by considering the way that the capitalist 'core' worked to actively undermine the position of the *underdeveloped* countries of the periphery. Other distinctions use purely geographical terms to separate the *global North* from the *global South* in an attempt to avoid implications of hierarchy (which puts Australia and New Zealand into the 'wrong' camp).

- The end of the Cold War marked the beginning of a 'new world order' and the creation of 'transition economies' in Eastern Europe and the Former Soviet Union.
- More recently, the term 'BRIC' nations (Brazil, Russia, India and China) is used to refer to the four largest emerging economies able to exert growing influence on the world stage. The 'next eleven' are those countries – including Bangladesh, Vietnam, Pakistan, Nigeria, Iran and Egypt – that have been identified as having the potential to become among the largest economies of the twenty-first century.
- Meanwhile in the northern hemisphere the last decade has seen America's claim to sole superpower status increasingly questioned; while Europe has been subdivided into old ('west') and new ('east') and north (Germanic/Protestant) and south (Latin/Catholic).

These processes defy the simplistic labels 'developed' and 'developing': poverty and social marginalisation are to be found alongside material wealth across the world. Defined according to shared economic trajectories or by geographical proximity the new terms reflect tectonic shifts away from the old binary distinction between the rich, industrialised, urban developed global North and the poor, predominantly rural, undeveloped South.

But development is not just ordered geographically. Further acts of categorisation are used to denote the key actors and institutions engaged in carrying out development. The idealised categories could include the following:

- global intergovernmental agencies (multilaterals)
- bilateral donor governments (states)
- aid-receiving governments
- private-sector organisations
- civil society and social movements
- policy-makers, development professionals and volunteers
- activists and academics
- intended beneficiaries.

These agencies and groups, and the relationships between them, are in part shaped by the ways in which they are categorised. But the boundaries are blurred, goals are complex and the relationships between them exhibit considerable dynamism. This chapter reviews recent anthropological research that provides new insights into the worlds of these agencies and actors and the relationships they create and recreate.

Governments, states and global institutions

Of the agencies that populate the world of development, it is assumed that governmental and international intergovernmental institutions are the donors with the greatest power. The hierarchical vision of development entails funds and expertise passing down from policy-makers, planners and bureaucrats in these donor agencies. Certainly, as major sources of finance and policy, national governments and the intergovernmental agencies are both influential and powerful. But, as we shall see in this book, behind the illusion of coherence, the framework of governance at times exhibits a surprising degree of contradiction, contestation and complexity. We will introduce the global intergovernmental agencies, government donors and then the aid-receiving states.

Global intergovernmental agencies

The following multilateral agencies were formed by international agreements and depend on funding from many governments:

- Bretton Woods institutions, including the World Bank and the International Monetary Fund, created by the agreements established in 1944 at Bretton Woods and ratified in 1945;
- United Nations, created in 1945 to replace the League of Nations;
- European Investment Bank, formed in 1958 under the Treaty of Rome;
- Organization for Economic Co-operation and Development, established in 1961 to stimulate economic progress;
- Inter-American Bank, African Development Bank, Asian Development Bank, European Bank for Reconstruction and Development, founded

in 1959, 1964, 1966 and 1991 respectively to promote economic and social development in their regions;
*   International Organization for Migration, created in 1951 to promote the humane management of migration.

The notion of developing certain regions of the world began to take institutional form during the immediate postwar period. Out of the Bretton Woods Conference of 1944 a new architecture of development was established. The International Monetary Fund (IMF) was tasked with regulating the rules for commercial and financial relations between states while the International Bank for Reconstruction and Development (later to become the World Bank (WB)) was responsible for financing economic development. The United Nations was created in 1945 to promote cooperation and prevent international wars. Although the European Investment Bank was formed to lend to European countries, and is far less well known than the World Bank in Aidland, it has expanded its remit to the world. It gave loans amounting to $3 billion in Africa during the 2000s and has been accused of a lack of transparency and accountability for its work outside Europe by the NGO Bankwatch Network.[4]

All major intergovernmental agencies exclusively derive their funding from and are governed by national governments. The USA is the largest single share-holder in the World Bank and the IMF with the governments of France, Germany, Japan and the UK also making significant contributions. These funding agree-ments have guaranteed a monopoly over leadership roles; since their inception the presidency of the World Bank has been reserved for an American and the dir-ectorship of the IMF allocated to a European. At the UN the Permanent Security Council continues to be made up of the 'victors' of the Second World War – the USA, the UK, France, Russian Federation and China. These arrangements reflect the global power configuration that existed nearly seventy years ago. Continued influence is built on funding arrangements with the USA contributing a large proportion of funding to WB, IMF and UN total income and getting the highest proportion of votes.[5] By withholding its commitments, or threatening to do so, it is able to exert considerable influence. In 2010 the voting power on the gov-erning boards of the IMF and the World Bank of some 'developing countries' was increased, including China, but most lost votes. While the World Bank and European Investment Bank borrow and lend funds, the UN and IMF depend on donations from their members (see Table 3.1).

These institutions have been criticised by anthropologists (and a wide range of NGOs) for their bias against the poorest countries. For example, Michael Goldman managed to penetrate 'the belly of the so-called beast' (2005: xiii) to describe how institutional cultures and politics at the World Bank prioritise the interests of funders over and above those of developing nations and the poor. The most significant impact of the Bank is that more capital flows *out* of the countries borrowing the loans than *in*; thus, the Bank's beneficiaries of aid are primarily in the North not the South (*ibid.*: xi). As an economist in the South, the offer of

Table 3.1 *Funding by top ten member state donors to the*
UN (as a percentage) in 2011

Member state	United Nations	IMF
USA	22.00	16.76
Japan	12.530	6.24
Germany	8.018	5.81
United Kingdom	6.604	4.29
France	6.123	4.29
Italy	4.999	3.16
Canada	3.207	2.56
China	3.189	3.81
Spain	3.177	1.63
Mexico	2.356	1.47

Sources: United Nations – http://data.un.org and the International Monetary
Fund –www.imf.org/external/np/sec/memdir/members.aspx. Accessed 30 September 2011.

a consultancy with the Bank that pays thirty times your usual salary makes it
extremely difficult to say 'no' (*ibid.*: 4). Paying particular attention to the hierarchical structure and the discourse it deploys, Goldman applies an anthropological lens to the World Bank as an institution. The result offers us a glimpse
into the workings of the global political economy and the hegemonic powers that
maintain it. He writes:

> one can hardly imagine the world today except through the lens of World
> Bank-style development. As the chief arbiter of development, the World
> Bank has become so much a part of our everyday lives, with its practices
> and effects so highly dispersed across the world, that it is difficult to know
> precisely where the World Bank starts and where it ends.   (Goldman
> 2005: viii)

The hegemonic power of the World Bank universalises knowledge in ways that
abstract people and places away from the particular context, politics and history
that form them (Goldman 2005: 6). In this view, the prescriptions of World Bank
officials are oriented towards reproducing their power even if they are resisted and
contested (*ibid.*: 272–91). This view may rather overstate the idea of the World
Bank as a fortress, characterised internally by consistency and unity of purpose
and protected externally by impenetrable walls. It assumes that policy impact is a
linear and logical process by which commands are passed down through various
levels of international and national administration to be delivered unchanged at
the local level. Bebbington *et al.* (2004) recognise the World Bank to be a 'battle-
field of knowledge', in which different perspectives on development coexist and
compete. Moving away from the idea of a predictable development 'machine'
more nuanced insights are revealed. Peter Griffiths's account of a consultancy funded by the World Bank in Sierra Leone depicts 'expert knowledge' as

'semi-clandestine detective work, negotiating gossip, absent data and misinfor-
mation, wishful thinking or deliberate lying, not to mention dangerous driving,
loneliness, alcohol and sex' (as cited by Mosse 2011: 10). Quick impressions
and hunches are stabilised as statistics, procedures and directives that provide the
appearance of certainty. Bureaucracy works to transform unstable knowledge and
shifting relationships into official narratives and formal documents that represent
the outwardly turned face of institutional consistency.

    An example from Mexico unpacks some of the assumptions about the rela-
tionship between powerful actors and the political motives that drive them.
Schwegler describes how most scholars perceive the World Bank as having
played a pivotal role in promoting the neoliberal policy reforms that swept across
Africa, Asia and Latin America from the 1980s (2011: 130). However, her field
research in Mexico discovered contestation between World Bank officials and
Mexican policy-makers, with both claiming responsibility for pension reforms.
Rather than assuming that she has to find out who is telling the truth versus lies,
Schwegler looks into the political significance of how views diverged and why
these two competing claims could happily co-exist.

    In order to explain her findings, Schwegler – like all good anthropologists – pro-
vides some context and investigates relationships between World Bank officials
and Mexican technocrats. The two groups share similar educational backgrounds,
often PhDs in economics from top US or European universities, but have to please
different constituencies and interests. The World Bank has different levels of influence on different governments; India, Russia and Mexico have negotiated more
room for manoeuvre than most (*ibid.*: 135). For political reasons Mexican technocrats need to assert their autonomy from the World Bank and apply their sensitivity
to unique local conditions, while the Bank officials have to look as if their advice
has a strong influence on policy but that they are not issuing orders. These political needs obscure the intense negotiation that went on behind the scenes. Some
of the discussion between personal contacts in the Bank and Mexican institutions
left no bureaucratic footprints, such as minutes of meetings. That meant that either
side could deny that the meetings took place (*ibid.*: 141). A Bank official explains,
'The Bank does not want to show that it was involved. The ultimate goal is that
the government undertakes the reform and the credit goes to the government'
(*ibid.*: 142). Curiously, the two groups are not competing over who should claim
credit for reforming the pension system through privatisation but who identified
problems in the old system first. The Bank claims superior wisdom about *regional*
trends while the Mexican technocrats need to assert their independence and demonstrate their specific, local expertise. But it becomes more complex; the Mexican
group contains sub-groups. The Mexican Institute of Social Security portrayed the
Ministry of Finance and the World Bank as collaborators in their determination
to copy pension reform in Chile. But the Ministry of Finance put it differently –
they say that they merely took advantage of the similarities between their already
formulated plans for reform and the World Bank's reform model in order to obtain
a loan. Thus, the World Bank's 'political function shifts as the political process

evolves,' depending upon whom you speak to and at which point (*ibid.*: 144). It is clear that their role is not the pursuit of simple domination.

Anthropologists are skilled at getting beneath the surface to distinguish what we say we do from what we actually do, whether we are in African villages or the World Bank. Focusing on the internal interaction of a range of specific actors (rather than looking only externally at the whole) allows for an understanding of institutions as networks within which decision-making is a messy and political process that often involves considerable internal debate. Viewed as social organisation it becomes clear that policy-making in the World Bank or IMF depends on the creation of 'epistemic communities' which establish agendas, set the terms of debate and determine the extent to which actors may have input into decision-making processes. Institutional cultures certainly exert a powerful pull, and bureaucratic structure will privilege some interests and information over others. But the outcomes cannot be read from policy proposals and statements espoused by the upper echelons of international institutions. The generation of policy is subject to considerable contestations between and within organisations; outcomes and external representations (made visible as policies, programmes and documents) should not be privileged in our scrutiny over the processes involved in creating them. Once policy is settled and communicated it is altered again as it moves out into the real world of development and into the untidy field of practice. Intergovernmental agencies face two ways. To some extent they must bend to the influence of powerful funders; yet at the same time policies must be passed on to aid-receiving countries who then implement plans and projects (or give the appearance of doing so) in different ways.

A rough tour around the rhetoric of donors and lenders gives the impression of universal standards but the reality is far more confusing. Most of the conventional aid-giving donors – governments and global institutions – have organised themselves around the Millennium Development Goals to be reached by 2015.[6] These are to end poverty and hunger, ensure universal primary education, promote gender equality, reduce child mortality, improve maternal health, combat HIV/AIDS, malaria and other diseases, ensure environmental sustainability and develop a global partnership for development. But the forms these take, and rates of progress, are extremely variable. In this book we describe instances of global policies and multilateral funded projects as studied by anthropologists in different places to illustrate this mix of hegemonic global discourse and diversity of national or local practice.

States sending aid

We *nearly* know how many national states there are. The formal succession of the Republic of South Sudan from Sudan in 2011 brought to 193 the number of UN member states (two non-member states – the Holy See and Palestine – hold observer status although Palestine applied to the UN for state status in September 2011). This number does not include sovereign states like

Taiwan nor other territories that make claim to independent sovereignty (western Sahara and Kosovo are the most widely recognised ones). Each of these states has a system of administrative apparatus that can be recognised as government (except Somalia).

In terms of aid and development governments were once neatly classified into aid donors and recipients.

- Aid-sending governments: the ten most generous aid donor govern- ments in 2007 were the USA, Germany, France, the UK, Japan, the Netherlands, Spain, Sweden, Canada, Italy, Norway and Australia.
- Aid-receiving governments: the twelve countries receiving the most aid in 2007 were Iraq, Afghanistan, Ethiopia, Pakistan, Sudan, Nigeria, Cameroon, Mozambique, Uganda, Bangladesh, China and India.[7]

But some governments both send and receive aid (e.g. India, Brazil, China, Israel). We will consider the act of *aid-sending* first before looking at *aid-receiving* in the next section.

Aid sending by governments is typically organised through departments responsible for promoting international development (examples include DFID, USAID, Swedish International Development Cooperation Agency (SIDA)). Even if development is a common project for all aid-giving governments, the intentions of states tend to be not only different but even contradictory and con- tinually changing within organisations. And the evolution of development assist- ance reflects the changing circumstances and politics of the giver rather than the receiver. For instance the end of the Cold War forced western policy-makers to rethink a model of foreign aid that had, in part, been (mis)used to bolster inter- national support. Until the 1990s former colonial powers such as Britain and France had maintained close ties with the 'elites' of particular client states. The collapse of the Soviet Union changed donor priorities: the earlier economic con- ditionality was now combined with calls for political reform under the banner of 'good governance'. It was clear that the old ways of giving were no longer appropriate – globalisation needed global development.

Acknowledging that for aid to be effective a degree of harmonisation between donors was required, 100 countries signed the Paris Declaration in 2005 and the Accra Agenda for Action in 2008. The aim continues to be to coordinate more effectively so that better results can be achieved.[8] The drive towards harmonisa- tion and alignment presents us with an image of stable consensus. However, in practice huge variation between donors continues in the ways goals are articu- lated. USAID spend huge amounts on health and water while SIDA covers a broad range of priorities including democracy, peace, environment, economic opportunities and so on. Goals within aid donors change as governments come and go. DFID's Secretary of State from 2010, Andrew Mitchell, a Conservative, has different politics from his Labour predecessor. His interest in tangible results entailed a seismic shift within DFID away from an emphasis on governance, economic growth, climate change and reform of global institutions and towards a concentration on health (especially child and maternal health). We will see in later chapters that even at any one time within a particular institution, contradictions in policy, and even more clearly between policy and practice, are commonplace (see Chapters 8 and 9).

Accountable to citizen taxpayers, western democracies increasingly justify aid budgets not just on moral terms but also as a means to support national interests. USAID is open in admitting that US foreign assistance serves the twofold purpose of improving the lives of the citizens of the developing world while at the same time also furthering America's foreign policy interests in expanding democracy and free markets.[9] USAID's two largest assistance programmes are to Afghanistan and Pakistan. They claim that assistance in 'agriculture, democracy and governance, economic growth, education, energy, health and infrastructure provide Afghans and Pakistanis with the tools, technical support, capacity building and institutions for stability, sustainable development and self-sufficiency'.[10] These programmes reflect the US government's 'commitment to the region's long term stability and human progress' but also their national security strategy 'to disrupt, dismantle and defeat al Qaeda and to prevent its capacity to threaten the United States'. In the UK, security and moral concerns have coalesced in a similar manner. Mitchell has advanced a moral justification for the ring-fencing of DFID's budget by arguing that people will look back at and be shocked at poverty in the same way as we now perceive slavery.[11] But with polling data revealing a decline in public support for aid, Mitchell has sought to claim particularly forcefully that development is also in the UK's national interest.

Aid is given with strings attached and the strings are partly shaped by domestic considerations. Patty Gray looks '"the gift" in the mouth' to show how Russian aid is a cultural phenomenon (2011). In its time the Soviet Union had been a major player in international development. The funds and expertise it dispensed can be viewed as part of the Cold War competition between capitalist and socialist models of progress. But the tables were turned with the dismantling of the Soviet Union. Since the 1990s a generation of Russians have been demoted to the position of 'recipient' in the global geography of development. Russia was recast as a 'transitioning economy' reliant on the financial assistance and expertise of western donors in ways that mirrored, in all but name, 'the Third World,' with consequences for their status: 'It could be argued that charity – or development aid – becomes wounding precisely in those circumstances when it is framed as a *free* gift with no return expected (possibly implying the recipient is incapable of return), rather than as a Maussian gift that would imply ongoing mutual obligations' (Gray 2011: 6).

It might be argued that aid is sometimes given with no obligations (e.g. by charity), sometimes with conditions (e.g. by a government expecting assistance in the war on terror) and sometimes not given at all (e.g. loaned with interest). However, it has the public image of generosity. So the demotion from 'giver' to 'receiver' was a blow to Russian prestige and one that was to be reversed. In

2007, Russia officially signalled its (re-)emergence as an aid donor. The message was clear: by refusing to play the role of non-reciprocating aid recipient, and insisting on being taken as a legitimate player in the aid game, Russia was resisting its lowly placement in the global political economy (Gray 2011: 6).

Equally revealing is the international response to Russia's shift from recipient to donor. For many observers, Russia's emergence was viewed not as a cultural or even economic phenomenon, but rather 'as a political phenomenon, and a negative one at that' (ibid.: 7). Gray suggests that certain countries are placed in a separate category – as 'new' donors rather than 'traditional' ones – simply because they may not share the same concerns of the (imagined) existing transnational development community. The spread of aid from these 'emerging donors' challenges western ideas of 'the right sort of giving' (ibid.: 7). China's recent engagement as a major investor in Africa exemplifies these fears in ways that raise fundamental questions about the purpose of international development assistance and the ability to impose conditions on aid recipients when China places so few. Themed under the banner of 'friendship, peace, cooperation and development', the two-day Beijing Summit of the Forum on China–Africa Cooperation was held in early November 2006. In an opening speech to heads of state or senior government officials from forty-one African countries, Chinese President Hu Jintao announced a package of aid and assistance measures to Africa including $3 billion of preferential loans and significant exemptions from the repayment of debt. Added to previous pledges made to a number of African countries, these would lead to China overtaking the World Bank as the continent's main financial provider. The Declaration of the Beijing Summit established a new type of strategic partnership between China and Africa, one that would be built around 'political equality and mutual trust, economic win-win co-operation and cultural exchanges'.[12]

Not everyone has welcomed China's new commitment to international development. Speaking in 2008, Hilary Benn, the UK Secretary for State for International Development, expressed concerns that Chinese aid to Africa might do more harm than good.[13] The suggestion was that China's growing involvement would undermine the work that had been done on debt relief and on promoting good governance. Criticism is levelled at China for doing business with abusive regimes such as Zimbabwe or The Sudan, plundering natural resources and exporting its own low standards of human rights and environmental protection.

In her book *The Dragon's Gift* (2009), Deborah Brautigam draws on perspectives from anthropology, economics and political science to assess how Chinese aid differs from that of other donors and calculate the impact it has had on African development. While recognising that the Beijing Consensus contains significant differences from the Washington one, Brautigam suggests that the simple assumption that it is necessarily 'worse' reveals more about China's critics than it does about China's commitment to promoting development. In particular these critics ignore the West's history of exploitation and support for unsavoury regimes. Perhaps the negative reaction to China's engagement in Africa stems from the way it 'de-naturalises' western models by pointing out alternative possibilities for development. With Russia, China, Brazil, India and South Africa now established as 'aid donors' the old binaries of global North and South have become terminally confused. It is even possible that the new donors will, could or should change aid forever. Sceptical of the Paris Declaration, with its unequal opposition between those who send and those who receive aid, some argue that South-to-South cooperation and mutual benefit should replace the apparent altruism of the 'West' and its inevitable colonial-like forms.[14]

States receiving aid

A fundamental distinction is often made between the way that state power works in 'developing' as compared to 'developed' countries. Politics scholars tend 'to reproduce the Weberian argument that formal legal rationality eclipses substantial cultural factors, so that all modern states are fundamentally the same' (Fuller and Harriss 2001: 2). The standard view of the *modern* state presupposes a centralised system of administrative and legal order characterised by unified intentionality and internal consistency. This is the kind of state assumed to exist in so-called 'developed' nations. And, in opposition to this picture of unified state rationality, the state in developing countries is assumed to be 'weak' or 'soft', and the apparatus of power limited in reach, unreliable and corrupt. Power in such situations is exercised though networks of patron–client relations that bypass the rule of law. Culture, not rationality, apparently informs the working of the 'pre-modern' states of the developing world.

This crude opposition can be challenged from two directions. First, if aid-sending states operate according to different logics and rationalities from aid-receiving states, then it is for political reasons partly connected to aid rather than natural causes. But it is a big 'if'. From the anthropological perspective, it is more convincing that cultures, patron–client relations, rituals and class–gender relations are critical to the everyday working of all states. Secondly, opposing developing versus developed states conceals a wide variety of empirical possibilities within each category. Aid comes with different conditions attached by different donors and different expectations on the receiver. Cultural and political factors determine who, when, how and how much assistance is given. But also there are clear differences in the relationship between state and society within different aid-receiving countries and in multi-party democracies such as Brazil, India and South Africa compared to those of single party states such as China and Zimbabwe. In some cases the reach and capability of the state is limited – revenue from taxation in the Democratic Republic of Congo is a fraction of what it is in the USA. But in other cases – for example North Korea or Cuba – the governments of so-called developing nations have constructed elaborate state machineries that allow them to intervene intensively in the lives of their citizens. Aid agencies rank the capacity of the state, often in simplistic ways and by attaching demeaning categories. The label of 'failed state' is applied to situations

---

Box 3.2. 'Guardians of childhood'. Amarasuriya's study of state bureaucrats in Sri Lanka, 2010

Amarasuriya's ethnography of a unit within a state bureaucracy in Sri Lanka is about how civil servants respond to child protection cases. Their decisions and practices are embedded in their wider social world: nationalism, class and culture. State-sector employment is a significant source of social mobility and respectability – it can be seen as producing or reproducing middle-class identity. Their responses to cases embody moral judgements in part shaped by middle-class Sinhala ideas about how good Sinhala women, men and children should behave and how foolish the 'lower classes' can be (2010: 33). For example, in the cases of teenagers having love affairs and running away from parental wrath, it was sometimes assumed that the girl, in particular, could not come from a 'good' family (*ibid.*: 220–1). On one occasion a priest abused a girl and the official implied that the girl was at fault (*ibid.*: 225). The primary responsibility for the protection of children and family harmony lies with women – 'When you are a woman, you have to make sacrifices for your children' – and even the violence of a man can be blamed on his wife (*ibid.*: 230–1). When a man is unfaithful he is foolish but when a woman commits adultery she is immoral and moral decay is associated with either poverty or western decadence. Thus, it is clear that bureaucrats' assumptions and practices reproduce hierarchies in multiple ways. By showing how deeply embedded development encounters are in enduring, everyday social relations, she offers an explanation of why development continues without achieving the transformations that it intends.

where governments are considered to have been unable to fulfil some of their basic functions and responsibilities: control of territories, provision of services, and inability to act as a 'responsible' member of the international community. Social, economic and political dimensions of failure have long histories and are as wide as possible causes but are rarely differentiated or explored by aid agencies in any depth. Somalia, the Sudan, Afghanistan and Ivory Coast all feature in the top ten Failed States index with Pakistan not far behind.[15] However, these nations display substantial differences both internally and in comparison with one another. There is no such thing as the typical state, whether it be 'failed', 'fragile', 'modern' or somewhere in between.

Scholarship and policies on states, and programmes to build their capacity, treat them as if they are monolithic. The increasing number of ethnographies on the state show that the boundaries between states and societies are porous, policies and practices are endless in contradiction, and inconsistencies in following rules abound (see Chapter 9). Both state institutions and the actors within them are embedded within their social worlds as much as any other social group and these have to be understood before we can consider the possibility of reform. Amarasuriya's recent research with state bureaucrats illustrates how development is embedded in class, culture and morality (see Box 3.2). Development workers are shaped by the social worlds, bureaucratic cultures and institutional

networks of which they are part. But at the same time they also belong to informal networks that transcend narrow institutional affiliations.

By studying the culture of the state's administrative machinery, anthropologists have questioned the normative statements made by institutions regarding
their role, function and manner of operation that give the impression of a straightforward, predictable bureaucracy. The gaps between the 'ideal' administrative
framework and the reality on the ground are explained not by a lack of manpower
or insufficient budgets but by people doing and remaking culture. By taking this
more rounded view, agents of the state are no longer simply 'faceless automatons
in the Weberian mould' (Corbridge *et al.* 2003: 2378), but become members of
civil and political society as well as of particular faiths and communities.

As part of the anthropology of the everyday state, studies by Sudha Vasan and
Paul Robins have explored the activities of forest guards in India. In contrast to
the orthodox view of development officials as 'an instrument of state power with
little agency or efficacy', Paul Robbins argues that forestry officials in Rajasthan
act as crucial interpreters and brokers in the encounter between global and local.
He writes, 'the fictive partition between the global and the local is undermined
by the actual practice of those who are supposed to enact it'; forest officials
are 'enmeshed in local networks and relationships' (2003: 379, 390). Parallel
research by Sudha Vasan in Himachal Pradesh reached similar conclusions. Her
ethnography of forest guards examines the multiple pressures, actual interactions, conflicts and negotiations that influence the actions and discourse chosen
by the lower levels of officialdom. Vasan recognises that although forest guards
are part of the states' administrative machinery their positions are significantly
different from other representatives of the state. Unlike their superiors, many forest guards are recruited locally and are therefore culturally integrated into rural
society: 'in terms of language, urban exposure, lifestyle and belief-systems, the
forest guard is closer to the villagers than to higher officials in the forest department' (2002: 4130). The embeddedness of these officials in local society means
that public policies are more often negotiated in the field rather than in the office.
Denying the top-down 'blueprint plan' notion of policy implementation, Vasan
describes a complex social process involving far more than a mechanical translation of state goals into activities:

> It is a process influenced and mediated by the perceptions, attitudes, and
> compulsions of multiple stakeholders, including implementers and bene-
> ficiaries. Most public policies are reinterpreted and translated in ways by
> individuals charged with the responsibility of implementing them. These
> translations of policy are influenced by the nature of the policy as well as the
> context in which they are implemented ... The forest guard ... is the primary
> bridge across the public-private divide.   (*Ibid.*: 4125)

Subordinate state officials working in rural societies exist in a 'twilight
zone', torn, as they are, between satisfying the pressures of the state for which
they work, and responding to the demands of those with whom they live and

socialise. 'It is they who face the immediate wrath of local people for policies perceived by them as against their interests, and they who reap the immediate advantages of policies that provide them with discretionary power. The most intense state–society interactions occur at the field-level, and the conflicts and contradictions of policy implementation are confronted by the field-staff' (*ibid.*: 4126).

With the dichotomy between professional and personal life often indistinct, and with policies ultimately implemented low down in the bureaucracy, we find that policies are frequently reinterpreted beyond recognition. The capacity of the centre to implement its plans is undermined by the action of what could be termed the 'unofficial state' operating at the lower level of the bureaucratic machinery. Indeed, as Axelby's (2007) study of nomadic pastoralists in the Indian Himalayas suggests, the divide between state and society becomes increasingly fluid the further away from the urban centres and down the administrative hierarchy you go. He describes how the guards employed to protect wooded tracts are also the brothers, sons, uncles and friends of the shepherds whose flocks trespass into restricted pastures. Together they creatively reinterpret official policies to co-produce intricate arrangements for grazing access that unite varying degrees of the official and the informal, the personal and the bureaucratic.

Given this evidence we need to rethink the idea of the state as a homogeneous, monolithic and unified entity 'acting' impersonally above and outside of local society. Alongside the horizontal departmental fissures identified by Saberwal (1999), you find a series of silos within which different interests are entrenched. Jeffery and Lerche describe the core dichotomy in India today as existing between the modern discourse of the elite and its state, and a public 'community' or 'lower' discourse (2001). Not only are there conflicts within and between different agencies of the state but these agencies are themselves penetrated and challenged by different groups within political and civil society. Religion, caste and other forms of identity play a role in determining the ways in which policy is implemented and resource access assigned. Social linkages may result in officials turning a blind eye to infringements or ensuring policy is implemented in favourable ways to certain segments of local society. The 'unofficial' parallel state can also be recognised in the payment of bribes or other inducements. The assumption of the existence in India of a mechanical and impersonal model bureaucracy unravels; far from being rigidly defined, the boundaries of the state are difficult to delineate.

Moving up and down bureaucratic hierarchies, the supposedly inflexible regulation of written law is considerably de-rigidified. Higher-level policy is not imposed unchanged onto diverse localities – whichever state we are concerned with – it is substantially reinterpreted into local vernaculars by lower-level officials subject to the politics and pressures of local society. Limits to the authority and capacity of states, combined with the grounded reality of state agents, ensure a degree of flexibility, subtlety and local appropriateness.

Non-state agencies and actors

It is hard enough to delineate boundaries around states; state and society intermesh. But mapping *non*-state agencies and actors is even more difficult. In this section we have divided these roughly into private sector, civil society organisations and constituency groups but offer them as porous and fluid categories. Agencies can fall into more than one category and individuals can move from one sector to another and back again.

Private-sector organisations

It is often assumed that the 'private sector' aims for profit. But some private enterprises are cooperatives seeking no profit while some civil society organisations can be hugely profitable. Rough categories (for our purposes of explanation) might include the following:

- Multinational, national or local companies selling or trading products or providing services;
- Companies funding development (either directly or through foundations);
- Consulting companies;
- Private-sector support organisations (including Fair Trade);
- Small enterprises, producers or traders benefitting from development.

The number of private-sector organisations is huge. And, unsurprisingly given neoliberal globalisation, the involvement of the private sector in development is growing. Broadly defined, the private sector is probably the largest sector in development but also the most diverse and difficult to study. When you bear in mind its impact, the private sector deserves far more attention from anthropologists. We will merely hint at some of the patterns of private sector involvement in development in this section but return to some aspects of this in Chapter 7.

In some countries the private sector employs more people than the state. Figures for the UK for 2010 show the private sector as employing 23 million people (although that included not-for-profit organisations), while the public sector employed only 6 million.[16] But in China the state employs more than the private sector. This is changing, as China joins the globalised world with its neoliberal assumptions, a World Bank report claims:

> While China has made great achievements in the transition to a socialist market economy, a reconsideration of the role of the state in the service sector is warranted. Many of the activities performed by the state could be considered commercial production of private goods or services, which can best be left to the market. The concept of 'public benefit relevance (*gongyi xing*),' which is often considered the defining criterion for government involvement,

> is only a necessary, but not a sufficient condition for government interven-
> tion. Only in the case of market failure should government intervention be
> considered.   (World Bank 2005: ix)[17]

Three decades of privatisation, deregulation, outsourcing and subcontracting
have led to a blurring of the boundaries between state and private actors, between
national and international spheres of operation. Many non-state actors now fulfil the sorts of activities that were previously allocated to governments. For
example, in the UK DFID's own staff used to assess the eligibility and quality
of applications submitted to the Civil Society Challenge Fund for UK NGOs. In
the late 1980s they subcontracted this to universities but finally shifted this con-
tract to private companies (currently Triple Line Consulting, a firm that works
with governments, aid agencies, IFIs and others on development issues). Studies,
consultations and evaluations are frequently carried out by private consultancy firms and some specialise in working for particular donors (such as Social
Development Direct in the UK for DFID) or topics (like Agrifood International
Consulting in the USA and Vietnam on food and agriculture).

Some actors actively exploit the boundaries between categories by crossing
and re-crossing borders as it suits them. While studying foreign economic aid to
Russia in the 1990s Janine Wedel coined the term 'flex organisation' to describe
the emerging phenomena of organisations that interpenetrate the state and private spheres: 'These organisations violate the rules and regulations of both the
state and the private sphere – the state regulations governing accountability and
the private rules governing competition. Yet they drive and implement policy in
crucial areas and wield more influence in governance than the otherwise relevant
state organisations, rendering state agencies ineffectual' (Wedel 2004: 218).

Straddling the borders between state and non-state, flex organisations are able
to exploit the possibilities and avoid the constraints that apply to the 'pure' form
of either activity. Flex organisations also undermine the idea of formal structures
through the informal overlap of individuals and social networks:

> non-state actors now fulfil functions once reserved for government ... The
> blurring of the traditional boundaries of state and private encompasses
> long-practices [*sic*] of governance 'reorganisation' such as the outsourcing
> and subcontracting of government work ... the acceleration of this famil-
> iar practice fails to convey the processes under way in governments, which
> are increasingly labyrinths of interconnected state and private structures.
> Indeed, in some settings, governance is reordering itself in ways that stand-
> ard vocabularies are ill-equipped to characterise.   (*Ibid.*: 217)

Some private-sector organisations get involved as part of their core business – explicitly to make money for their own company in an immediate sense;
others offer support from a distance. Corporate social responsibility (CSR) is
increasingly promoted as a path that avoids the uncompromising harshness of
self-interested capitalism and the soft inefficiency of the state. Private-sector
organisations and especially Transnational Companies (TNCs) are encouraged

to contribute the money, time and expertise of their staff as part of their CSR programmes. The hope is that the reach, expertise and resources of these companies may be harnessed in the service of local development and social improvement. CSR entails developing social auditing, codes of conduct, ethical principles and standards. For example the UN Global Compact is 'a strategic policy initiative for businesses that are committed to aligning their operations and strategies with ten universally accepted principles in the areas of human rights, labour, environment and anti-corruption.'[18] In 130 countries, 8,700 corporates are participating in this initiative, implementing and reporting on the ten principles and contributing to the MDGs. The Indian government is even trying to make it mandatory for companies to earmark a proportion of their profits for CSR initiatives. But much of it is voluntary. Deloitte, for example, was expecting its number of pro-bono days to increase from 500 to 1,000 between 2008/09 and 2009/10.

The business case for CSR is that by developing an appearance as moral and generous, they should impress customers and increase sales. But that is not the only business reason. The Deloitte partner leading on CSR explains why it is becoming popular with companies: 'Being able to offer our people the chance to take on a pivotal role and really make a difference in an international relief charity, for example, is a very powerful tool to attract the best people then keep them interested and motivated. It enables them to work for a cause that isn't purely financial and also make use of disciplines and skills developed in the private sector to great effect in the charity sector.'[19] Companies make sure that their members of staff are not only aware of their generosity to charity but encourage them to volunteer and voice opinions about where they donations should go. However, there can be tensions between the corporate social responsibility departments – who become more knowledgeable about grant-making – and individual staff members who want to give to rescue-type missions and to volunteer for local causes that might need them least.

Other motives are less benign. An important driver for corporate social responsibility is the mitigation of harm caused by companies keen to improve their external public relations. Dinah Rajak conducted ethnographic research on the CSR programme of the world's third largest mining company: Anglo American. She concludes that nothing is straightforward about this apparent marriage of moral imperative and market discipline: 'The rise of CSR has established TNCs as more the solution to the challenges of global poverty and underdevelopment, than the cause. Companies themselves have become purveyors of best practice and ethical standard-bearers. The moral high ground once occupied by NGOs has been usurped, so to speak, by the former targets of their campaigns' (2011: 8).

In a collection looking at corporate social responsibility – *Hidden Hands in the Market* (de Neve 2008) – anthropologists argue that it is designed to give an image of morality, but in reality maintains unequal power relations in trade by handing power to global corporations over producers in poorer countries (Freeman 2011).[20] Welker explains one of the reasons why CSR emerged:

The industry's rapid consolidation was galvanized in part by transnational social movements that targeted industries and corporations with creative campaigns (e.g., consumer boycotts, shareholder resolutions, and lawsuits see Keck and Sikkink 1998) and called into question undemocratic international institutions, such as the World Trade Organization, that make and enforce the neoliberal conditions under which companies operate (Graeber 2007). Threatened with external interventions, corporate actors turned to CSR as a means, to paraphrase Hewlett Packard's erstwhile CEO, Carly Fiorina, for seizing control of the movement before it seized control over them.   (2009: 145)

She tells a shocking story about a mine in Indonesia that illustrates the limitations of CSR. The Batu Hijau copper and gold mine has been operated by a Denver-based mining company, Newmont, since 1999. When an Indonesia NGO (LOH) produced a critical report of the company in 2002, Newmont commissioned international consultants to work out how to discredit them (*ibid.*: 158–9). They amassed information about the vices of the NGO's stakeholders (e.g. womanising, drug habits), offered to run an extensive PR and lobbying campaign for $1 million and suggested getting other NGOs to introduce standards of accountability so that the consultants could try to ensure that LOH were included in a list of irresponsible NGOs. They were not hired – they were too expensive – but they provide clues about the tactics employed as part of 'corporate social responsibility'. When a critical newspaper article appeared in the same year, the company distributed it among the neighbouring village elites that were sympathetic to the mine, pointing out the inaccuracies that the article contained (*ibid.*: 161). These elites were gaining considerable benefits from the company (services, transport infrastructure, micro-credit and so on), even setting up NGOs to receive goods, contracts and employment. So when the NGO critics mentioned in the article held a meeting in a village near the mine, Newmont workers intimidated them as they went in and members of the village elites attacked them viciously as they came out.

Welker considers what underlies Newmont's intentions. The motives of the company's senior executives cannot be reduced to moral platitudes – villains in the eyes of some, heroes for others – rather they should be seen as having 'their roots in shared knowledge practices, rituals and narratives' (*ibid.*: 148). They engage in various environmental rituals, such as stocking a small turtle hatchery, not just to look as if they are protecting precious creatures, but to remind themselves that they are enlightened, scientific and responsible environmental custodians. They reassure themselves that the real cause of environmental destruction is not their mine but the actions of poor and ignorant villagers, while they see the activists in an even worse light: they are greedy, corrupt, violent and insincere (*ibid.*: 153–4). So while the violence of village elites, with the tacit approval of the mining company, can be seen as a defence of capital, Welker points out that there is more to it. As she puts it, 'we need modes of analysis that carefully show how the moral commitments of capitalism's defenders emerge and cohere in an era when grassroots approaches to corporate security are nourished by the CSR industry, development projects, and corporate mimicry of environmental values and discourse' (*ibid.*: 166). The villagers who were critical of Newmont were seen as backward, but those who defended it were an indication of their success at integrating into the community. From the viewpoint of the village elites, whether attacking or protecting the mine they were successfully enhancing their control over their own destinies. These are the kind of hybrid moral and political allegiances that are emerging as capitalism becomes globalised and that anthropologists have to understand if they wish to make sense of the private sector.

Civil society and social movements

Civil society is no easier to define than the state or private sectors. It has been described as incorporating everything that exists between the family and the state (a definition that stretches to incorporate the private sector). In practice all boundaries between the state, private and civil society sectors are porous and tidy definitions are impossible. Civil society might span the independent sector, volunteer sector, grassroots organisations, transnational social movement organisations, private voluntary organisations, self-help organisations and non-state actors (NSAs). It may be as amorphous as informal networks, social contacts or norms of social conducts, or it may be more tangible, such as organisations with institutional structures that exist in particular physical spaces. In the latter sense 'third sector' organisations are defined by what they are *not – not* for profit (usually) and *non*-governmental – but some transgress into profit and the state arena. They may be local (grassroots), regional, national or global. In short civil society is a massive catch-all category and varies according to culture, history and context. It might include some or all of the following according to different perspectives:

- private grant-makers, foundations and trusts;
- social, women's and youth movements or activists;
- registered charities (or equivalent), working in one country or more than one;
- informal non-governmental organisations;
- community-based organisations or groups;
- charitable research institutes;
- trade and student unions;
- media (press, radio, TV, Web);
- crime associations, secret societies and militant/terrorist groups;
- religious institutions;
- information providers (newsletters, journals);
- think tanks;
- faith organisations;
- diaspora groups; and
- environmental and anti-globalisation movements.

The scale of civil society is completely unknown and unknowable. Collectively CSOs have hundreds of millions of supporters, followers, activists and staff worldwide. The most bureaucratised CSOs tend to be registered as NGOs, voluntary organisations or charities (depending on the specific terminology in a particular country). Even so the number of NGOs is hotly disputed. Some sources claim that there are 50,000 local NGOs operating in the 'global South', another says that there are 3.3 million in India alone, while the range in China is between 700,000 and 8 million. Much depends on the definition used and how NGOs are divided from the less formal CSOs.

The term 'NGO' is a claim-bearing label. The claim such organisations make is that they are 'doing good for the development of others' (Hilhorst 2003: 6) A rich etymology has built up to describe these organisations: a QUANGO is a quasi-autonomous non-governmental organisation, set up by governments but operationally independent of the state; a GRINGO is a government-run NGO; an INGO, or international NGO, operates in more than one country; a BINGO is a big INGO; a BONGO is business-oriented; a DONGO is donor organised; a TANGO is a technical assistance NGO; and a MANGO is a market advocacy NGO. To this list Hilhorst adds the COME 'N' GO to denote the 'fly-by-night NGO entrepreneurs who never, or only briefly, operate' (*ibid.*).

In this book the wide range of work by civil society agencies and actors will emerge. They respond to the full range of human need and interest: humanitarian assistance in response to war or famine; provision of services in the long term or to pilot new ideas; campaigning, advocacy or lobbying to scrutinise, criticise or change law, policy and practice; education, missionary work or awareness-raising; protesting about or challenging the status quo; or carrying out research and evaluation. The rise of civil society to prominence in the 1980s may partly be explained by the vagueness of the concept (although aid agencies' and international finance institutions' dissatisfaction with governments had a bigger role to play). Practitioners are able to attribute civil society with all kinds of virtues: to some it appeals as a dynamic alternative to oversized and bureaucratic state machinery; to others civil society represents the voice of the people and an expression of grassroots democratic will. Others are more cautious. Mohan and Stokke argue that much of the literature about social movements tends towards homogenising and romanticising. They point out that some assume that social movements are always anti-state but actually they are often co-opted by the state or by political parties and there is a tendency to downplay the power and effects of both the state and market forces (2000: 261).

John Clark, who previously ran the World Bank's civil society unit (and worked for Oxfam before that), attributes CSOs with a strong moral authority (2003: 129). Their goals are closer to the 'people'. Clark describes the rhetoric of civil society's purpose as redressing deficiencies in democracy and in the market – it builds bridges between decision makers and the people. Civil society has a role for championing the interests of those that lose out as a result of this failure of markets and how they are regulated. In international relations an important deficiency of the market is caused by unfair trade rules. Underlying the trade rules is a hypocrisy, he argues; the powerful nations promote neoliberal ideas, including free trade, but they indulge in a protectionism that guards the interests of their own nations, at the cost of countries in the global South, in three ways: (1) restrictions on imports to protect national industries in the global North; (2) protecting their jobs, workers in the global North go along with these restrictions despite the mechanisation of production that leads to job losses; (3) investors then invest in protected economies. Poorer countries depend on exporting commodities but the prices of non-oil commodities have halved in the last twenty years. Clark explains how these, and many other comparative disadvantages created by international rules, combine to mean that globalisation is bad for poorer countries (2003: 9, 12–13).

NGOs are also vital for democracy, or so Clark argues:

1. democracy does not ensure that elected representatives listen to the views of the voters on the issues that they care about and throughout their term;
2. the tyranny of the majority means that persecution or neglect of minorities is always a possibility;
3. numerically substantial groups are under-represented – especially women – or unrepresented in the case of children;
4. civil society can cross national boundaries and form global movements for global problems such as climate change (*ibid.*: 65–87).

According to Clark, civil society can redress the cynicism towards politicians and the gaps left by representative democracy. NGOs rely on elected representatives (e.g. as trade unions) or act as conduits (e.g. registered charities) that articulate the views of interest groups so they complement what governments do.

Clark reflects a widely held view among policy-makers and practitioners that NGOs make up for the shortcomings of states and markets: 'civil society offers a partial solution to the democracy deficit and to politically induced market injustices' (*ibid.*: 13). Is this just rhetoric or does this work in practice? Even Clark's answer is that NGOs do not fare terribly well; they do not send enough funds to Southern NGOs, tend to be timid and conservative, and focus on more prosperous areas. For others the record is mixed. Fisher finds examples of NGOs contributing to the political empowerment of marginalised groups but also of where they failed the people they intended to help (1997: 455–6). But the value of NGOs cannot really be assessed unless you look at the relationship between NGOs and the state (see the section on governance below) and the private sector (see Chapter 7).

The record of faith-based organisations (FBOs) has provoked particularly strong reactions: some view them as being particularly effective, while others criticise their evangelising and discriminatory practices. Anthropologists have only begun to study FBOs fairly recently. These anthropologists point to the differences between FBOs that conceptualise their work as charity as opposed to those who prize social justice in the tradition of Paulo Freire, those that evangelise or avoid it, and respond to different historical and cultural contexts. From a position of contempt towards missionary work, anthropologists are beginning to understand FBOs' different philosophies and practices (Hefferan and Fogarty 2010: 8). At the positive end, Greenfield finds a highly successful mental health programme in the slums of Brazil directed by a Catholic priest, with elements of group therapy, liberation theology and anthropology (2010). On a more negative note, World Vision – the largest non-state organisation in development and relief – has been criticised by several anthropologists especially for its child sponsorship programmes. Its mission is to be 'an international partnership of Christians whose mission is to follow our Lord and Saviour Jesus Christ in working with the poor and oppressed to promote human transformation, seek justice and bear witness to the good news of the Kingdom of God' (Yuen 2008). Their child sponsorship programmes once involved collecting money from mainly white, middle-class, Christian westerners and donating it to poor individual children (*ibid.*: 43). After they acknowledged the discrimination of singling out individual children for assistance, they broadened the support to communities but still extracted 'thank-you' notes from individual children to ensure that the donors felt connected (*ibid.*: 43–4). Although World Vision has banned proselytising they promote education on Christian values and non-Christians are referred to Christian events if they show an interest. World Vision have come under attack for this Christian infused sponsorship: they are commodifying friendship, portraying children in demeaning ways in fundraising, sidelining families and ignoring children's cultural contexts that sometimes mean sponsorship is received with some resentment (*ibid.*: 47–50).

In the labelling of NGOs, a division is assumed between the big international NGOs and those that are national or local in scale. The assumption is that INGOs are based in Europe or the USA and operate in several countries of the global South. But the number of NGOs in Africa, Asia and Latin America that operate in other counties is booming. ActionAid now has its headquarters in South Africa. Both BRAC and the Grameen Bank, originally Bangladeshi NGOs, are working internationally. Instituto Promundo calls itself a Brazilian NGO but runs projects in Asia, several Latin American countries, sub-Saharan Africa, the USA and Canada. Many organisations that started in aid-receiving countries are opening up branches in Europe and the USA to raise funds, offer training or do advocacy.

At the same time the idea of South-to-South learning, or even capacity development, was once fashionable but the recent drive for measurement of impact seems to have pushed this ideal to one side. Little has been written about the experience of people from aid-receiving countries giving technical assistance or advice to agencies in Europe or the USA, mainly because opportunities for this to happen are rare. But when opportunities are created, the results can be interesting. The Tutu Foundation UK aims to bring the spirit of Ubuntu from South Africa – a philosophy that emphasises our common humanity – into fractured communities in urban areas of the UK.[21] In 2007 DFID held a workshop for government and NGO staff from fifteen countries to share their experiences in participation and local democracy.[22] Shazia Hussein, from Tower Hamlets London, was so impressed by the case study of participatory budgeting in Porte Alegre, Brazil, that she returned home and persuaded the local council to allocate £2.4 million to similar participatory processes. But in-depth research into how these South-to-South and South-to-North encounters are embedded in social relations has yet to be done.

Another important component of civil society are the activist organisations that seek to advance a diverse range of political, social and environmental causes. As David Gellner has shown (2010), a common thread linking the variety of activist methods and causes is found in the connections they make between the political and the legal, the economic and the political, and the local and the international. The accounts of South Asian activist experiences brought together in Gellner's edited collection demonstrate the difficulties of disentangling their activities from identity politics, social movements and civil society more generally. To posit such movements in simple opposition to an overarching grand neo-colonial project of development is to ignore the complex and conflicting aims and motives contained within them. By romanticising resistance, we ignore other possibilities that range from exchange to compromise, negotiation or subtle manipulation.

Constituency groups: professionals, activists and beneficiaries

Potentially encompassing *everyone*, *everywhere*, this final category is the hardest of all to describe. The most significant constituency – or stakeholder group as they are often called – are the 'beneficiaries'. In the rhetoric the main gains are supposed to be directed towards the poor, marginalised or disadvantaged. This might involve a whole population (in a poor country like Sierra Leone) or the poorer sections of a nation. More often, the intention is to help a particular group, and their identity is essentialised: groups are defined by their problem, such as (living with AIDS, street children) their residence (poor people in a particular region), their occupation (farmer), their need (women who need credit), or their age (pre-school children). These groups are socially constructed, but the categories are treated as if they natural and the ones of greatest significance to the people concerned.

Intended individual beneficiaries have multiple identities because they belong to many different groups either simultaneously or in different contexts. Within their highly complex social worlds they are part of families, communities, economic classes and occupational or educational groups. The contrast between the detailed ethnographies of kinship, social organisation, class and work by anthropologists, and the crude labels that are attached to groups beneficiaries, are a reminder of very different priorities. Anthropologists delve into the perspectives of groups within micro (and increasingly macro) societies and produce multiple narratives, while development policy-makers and planners have to use simple categories and classifications of needs, problems and solutions (see Chapters 4–7). Families and communities can be sites of difference and inequality and are subject to continual dynamism. But development planners and practitioners conceptualise them as if they are fixed, harmonious and reasonably static.

Three other key constituent groups in development appear to be strictly separable from the intended beneficiaries but actually merge in interesting ways: activists, development professionals and academics. Beneficiaries move into the category of development worker – certainly as activists and volunteers but even as paid staff – with surprising regularity (see Box 3.3) but also may not benefit as much as other constituent groups, certainly in financial terms. Development professionals are paid salaries on the back of beneficiaries' poverty while academics in development studies and anthropology departments are awarded lucrative consultancies and research grants. Understanding development means understanding development professionals, as much as beneficiaries, but also the many hybrid people who do not fit into categories in a tidy way, as Conjit's story illustrates (see Box 3.3).

Ethnographies of expatriate or travelling aid, development and human rights workers make it plain that they are as deeply embedded in culture, morality and politics as any other group of people. Crewe wrote about how development workers, especially the expatriates, in the British charity Practical Action operated with their silent traditions (technology is the driver of development and poverty reduction, participation is the magical process and projects either succeed or fail), a disjunction between policy and practice, and an endless fission and fusion of factional groups in the head office (Crewe and Harrison 1998). Staff in NGOs in aid-receiving countries have been the subject of study, including by anthropologists; for example, Hilhorst describes the everyday experiences of working in NGOs in the Philippines, showing how you can understand them only if you see how they operate within their specific histories, politics and social worlds (2003).

Stirrat draws to our attention stereotypes about expatriate development workers that have currency in development literature. One group are the mercenaries, mostly working for global agencies, governments or the corporate sector and depicted as overpaid, out of touch and lacking in morality. A combination of their incompetence and vested interest in the perpetuation of poverty means that projects have little chance of success (Stirrat 2008: 408). The argument that official aid workers have vested interests in the development industry as individuals, which means that they have little incentive to make it succeed, is most forcefully made in Hancock's 'Lords of Poverty' (1989). He finds corruption, inefficiency and, above all, failure. Another of Stirrat's groups is the missionaries who mainly work for NGOs. They are apparently committed, sacrificing self in service to a greater goal and in touch with 'real' people (*ibid.*: 412). Seen by the mercenaries as misguided and romantic, naive to the macro processes that need to be understood to achieve impact, the missionaries are ineffective. However, these stereotypes tell us more about how aid

Box 3.3. An Ethiopian child sex worker becomes a peer educator: Conjit's story

"I was born in Addis Ababa. I don't know my father. My mother soon left me and went to the countryside. I was adopted by a lady who earned her income by renting beds in the Merkato district of Addis. She had three beds in one room together with other bed owners – there were altogether four bed owners in one collective property.

I was one year old when my mother left. She had worked for this lady before I was born. My father was not her husband – he was a guest in the house. Unofficially my mother was a sex worker. I pressed my adopted mother hard to tell me the story of my mother. When she left me, my mother had told her only that she was going to visit her family in Wollo, but she never came back.

My adoptive mother was childless and so she wanted a child. She was also old (about 70) and her husband had died. My adopted mother gave me love, and I completely accepted her as my mother, at least until I reached a conscious age, at 7. She never allowed me to be abused by the guests – in fact she would weep if I was mistreated by anyone. She would even carry me on her back to school.

My adopted mother always worried about my future and what would happen to me if she died. I was 11 years old when she died. I stayed in the house and in school for one year – my education was important to my adopted mother and I was determined to keep going as long as I could. But the owners threw me out of the house. For one or two weeks, I stayed with a kind neighbour. Then I started street life in Merkato. I was very upset and almost reached the point of killing myself.

By this time I was about 13 years old and I was slowly dragged into sex work. I was not at all ready for this kind of work, but I was not strong enough to resist. The men prefer very young girls. I was a sex worker for four years, from the age of 13 to 16 or 17. I had friends also working on the street, and sometimes we would stay together, four in one bed. I was scared because I frequently saw people dying from TB and AIDS, and this haunted me.

The men would pay 20 birr (US$1.17) for the whole night, less for short services. The men did not use condoms, but I used protective pills. Some men would promise 20 birr and then not pay it, or they would even give it to me and then grab it back in the morning. I received beatings many times. When men demanded abnormal sex, I would refuse and they would get violent.

Sometimes I encountered another terrible thing. One man would take me to a house, and I would go, thinking he was my only client. But after he was finished, he would leave me with his friends also to have sex with me. They would go on all night in turns. In the morning they would send me away with a few coins.

When I was 14 I had a client who was very frequent and very kind. He took me on many dates and I thought he loved me very much. I did not know he was married. I forgot to take my pill, and I became pregnant by this man. I told him I was pregnant and asked him to help me with money for an abortion. He said he could not trust me and that the baby may not be his. He did not help me and he stopped coming to see me. People advised me to go to the courts, but I did not want to disturb his family.

I gave birth to my son Yohannes. Now he is 6 years old and he is very wonderful. I love him very much and have always kept him with me. The best lesson I have learned from my childhood is to care for my child. When he was little and I was working, people would help me to care for him – everybody is very fond of him.

When I was 17, I was informed about CHADET.* I came to talk to Elias at the drop-in centre, and he could see my bruises. I told him my story and that I wanted to go to day school. CHADET agreed to help me go to school, and I joined Grade 7. I stopped sex work immediately. I was looking for a way out of that business, and when the opportunity came, I grabbed it. During the day, I went to school. Until late evening I would study, and then I would go to work hiring out beds. The guesthouse I worked for gave me a space to sleep on the floor.

I stayed in school for four years. During this time, I also trained to be a peer educator for CHADET. They taught me how to persuade young girls, to communicate to them the dangers of their lives, to show that there are other choices, and to explain about the facilities offered by CHADET.

Mostly I work with girls aged 14–18. I know the sleeping areas where the girls work, and I go to these places in the evening. I can easily recognise the young sex workers. First I make friends with them, and then when they are comfortable with me, I start to talk about my work. Often they will get angry and reject what I tell them. I try to persuade the younger ones to come to CHADET. With the older ones, I simply give them condoms.

I feel I am successful at this work – I can tell the girls about Addis because I was born here and many of them come from rural areas. 'A dog is a lion in his own community' – this saying applies to me. There are many younger ones, especially from Tigray. I use their words and language, and then they laugh and come to me. I take it as my responsibility to save lives. It is deep inside me.

My situation today is very different. In the evening I still work as a peer educator, but I have finished school and I am now employed full-time as the librarian at the CHADET drop-in centre where I first came. Many girls come to the library to study, especially those who are in evening classes. Once a week, I hold a group meeting for the girls who come to the library. I discuss many topics with them, such as AIDS or life skills.

I have my own room in Merkato, where I live with my son. He is in kindergarten now. My future dream is to train to be a nurse. If I am a good student, maybe CHADET will help me with my training. If there was no CHADET, I would have been useless."

* CHADET – or the Organisation for Child Development and Transformation – is an Ethiopian NGO working in Addis, Oromiya and Amhara with children facing abuse or affected by HIV and/or AIDS. (This interview was conducted by Sabrina Crewe in January 2008 for their UK-based partner, ChildHope.)

workers' perceptions of each other than their characters or behaviour in practice. Despite these ideal types, all aid workers tend to share some features in common: they all benefit financially, they infuse their conversations about their work with moral and political assumptions and they articulate their intentions as seeking good for others. At the same time, a continuity with the colonial past can be found in their belief in the need for conversion (whether to neoliberal orthodoxy or bottom-up participation by the grassroots), as we will see in the coming chapters. The differences between those who work for development organisations may be less significant than their similarities. As Stirrat puts it, they are all part of a common project 'to produce the modern person in their own image' (*ibid.*: 416).

Lewis and Mosse ask observers not to attach easy moral labels to development professionals any more than we do to farmers:

> In their ethnography, Bierschenk and colleagues (2002) go beyond the heavily normative presentations of such people that is common in development discourses, where they are depicted either as 'parasites' preying on mismanaged aid' or more positively 'as emanations of "civil society" confronting adversity,' to reconstruct the 'social and historical reality' of the phenomenon itself. They locate brokerage with the fragmented politics of the postcolonial state, where power is exercised both through formal bureaucratic logics and through a diverse range of 'supra-local' associations and networks, in which there is a flourishing of intermediate actors and organisations.   (2006: 12)

They refer to the work of Bruno Latour to remind us that all social actors, including development professionals, produce narratives and powerful actors have their scripts adopted by others not because they plot or strategise but as a result of the logic of the way that development is organised: 'development projects – always unforeseeable – become real through the work of generating and translating interests, creating context by tying in supporters and so sustaining interpretations … The concept of "translation" here refers to mutual enrolment and the interlocking of interests that produces project realities' (Lewis and Mosse 2006: 13).

Thus, the idea of development operating as one 'system', 'machine' or 'chain' – with development professionals dominating beneficiaries – is hard to sustain. Olivier de Sardan suggests we avoid replacing economic determinism (actors are motivated by material self-interest) with discursive determinism (people's actions are determined by discourses that reproduce power relations) (2005). Instead, we need an understanding of how institutional pressures and cultural politics work at different levels and times and within different constellations as well as the continuities of social relations and the new forms created by development. Power hierarchies may be a feature of all aid constellations but they are not patterned in a predictable or simple way. Development can be taken up by even those participating on adverse terms and then contested and reworked through grounded everyday struggles (Moore 2000: 673). Social relations in development are not just about power hierarchies – there are other aspects to development that are worthy of our attention. As we shall outline in Chapters 8 and 9, development encounters are embedded in social relations that matter to people, through kinship, friendships, sexual liaisons, or patronage, and in emotional and moral reactions.

The governance of aid in transition

Having outlined the different institutions and actors that populate Development World, we now go on to describe shifts in the relationships between them and the ways this impacts upon the governance of aid.

The World Bank's 1996 World Development Report sought to promote better partnership between governments and NGOs. This confirmed and encouraged an existing and widespread tendency by donors to invest in NGOs and divert funding from governments to civil society. The New Policy Agenda or New Aid Framework with its stress on neoliberalism, privatisation, the retreat of the state and the reliance on NGOs – 'the darling of foreign donors' (White 1999: 313) – is having clear, and for some worrying, consequences. When co-opted by the state, NGOs arguably lose their distinctive character. As Farrington and Bebbington put it 'they operate in a manner that is more akin to the state than to any organisation of the poor' (as quoted by Hulme and Edwards 1997: 276). NGOs handle ever-larger amounts of funding, employ more staff and, if tempted by the huge funding on offer, become increasingly bureaucratised. Some become huge bureaucracies – like World Vision, BRAC or the Save the Children Alliance – and they share as much in common with government departments, or even corporate entities, as they do with other NGOs. Meanwhile other 'suitcase' or 'briefcase' NGOs have the character of tiny enterprises, formed merely to access funding but with hardly any people, organisation or clarity about their social and political purpose.

In this new role NGOs are no longer supposed to be critics of the state – they are now 'partners'. As well as losing some of their ability to criticise, this can lead to a bypassing and weakening of states. NGOs claim to speak for the poor, direct funding away from the state, and they take the pressure off governments to deliver services to the people. However, unlike most states, they rarely have clear democratic accountability, often fail to coordinate with each other and other agencies and their services or actions exclude many, partly because they do not have national reach. The role of NGOs and the state has been changing but with different consequences in different countries or even within them (see Lewis 2001).

White writes about different agencies in Bangladesh; some of her observations are relevant to all aid-receiving countries but some are unique to this particular context. In Bangladesh donors often point to the weakness of government and success of NGOs, with the latter often seen as more in touch with the grassroots and the poor (1999). She quotes the World Bank as saying in relation to Bangladesh, 'Pluralism is also important for social cohesion and can be encouraged by creating an environment where these civil society groupings (i.e. all those organisations that are neither part of government, nor part of business) can be involved in pursuing the goals of national development' (*ibid.*: 309). She points out that NGOs are often happy to work closely with government to gain influence and reach more beneficiaries while the government assumes that it will retrieve donor funds and possibly dilute political opposition. But then, what do those living in poverty get out of the partnership? In Bangladesh NGOs work in 78 percent of its villages and attract a larger slice of foreign funding each year; some governmental officials have become so envious that they have set up their own NGOs (*ibid.*: 313). Bearing in mind that Bangladesh has a weak state in some senses – e.g. unable to raise enough taxes to provide services for all its people – and a strong society of social organisations, pouring more funding into NGOs could, arguably, just add to their problems (*ibid.*: 319). White asks: if NGOs' services bypass the state – effectively displacing them as service providers – then who should people go to when service provision falls short? So the specific point for this context is that donors have colluded in a further weakening of the state in Bangladesh by funding a vibrant civil society while similar behaviour in a country with a strong state may not have such damaging consequences. But the general point is that donors should be better informed about the impact they are likely to have on the state and civil society when they allocate resources between them.

Arguably, those opposing the neoliberal framework, many of whom can be found in civil society, do not have a clear stand on governance, including appropriate roles for civil society and the state. Development agents who believe in social change and equality are caught, as Whaites says (2000: 131), 'in the paradox of seeing the state as part saviour, a vehicle for social change and equality, and part villain, an intrusive monolith with a propensity to lose sight of the common good in pursuit of its own bureaucratic agenda' (a point we will return to in Chapter 9). While NGOs might be confused about who the villains are, at the same time donors are increasingly ambivalent about NGOs. They continue to receive more funding each year – David Lewis offers figures that show an increase from nearly $60 billion in 1996 to $80 billion in 2004 for NGOs. But they are no longer 'flavour of the month' (Lewis 2007: 11). Donors do not assume that they are the magic bullet that will solve development problems any more. They criticise their lack of accountability and their failure to coordinate and complain that NGOs are not achieving large-scale growth and development. In short, even though NGOs have been getting higher levels of funding each year, at the same time, they are being criticised by people from different directions, both for (a) being co-opted into donors' and governments' agendas and losing their distinctive role, and (b) for failing to help governments reach their goals more effectively on a big enough scale.

It is not just NGOs that are displacing the state. There are even examples of multilateral agencies charging into the fray of direct community development themselves. One of these programmes was run by an anthropologist working at the World Bank – Scott Guggenheim – who describes a programme in Indonesia that aimed to reduce poverty and corruption but was critiqued by another anthropologist, Tania Murray Li (2005). Guggenheim sets the scene by explaining that despite claims that Indonesia was reducing poverty, the reality was quite different. Corruption, the erosion of local leadership and poverty left the country in a terrible state by the late 1990s. Guggenheim wanted to find out what was really going on in villages but also to test out some ideas about 'social capital'. For this he drew on Robert Puttnam's definition of social capital as 'the features of social organisation, such as trust, norms and networks, that can improve the efficiency of society by facilitating coordinated actions' (Li 2005: 12).

Guggenheim's team carried out research in forty-eight villages and found that so-called 'community-owned projects' performed better than government or NGO projects funded by the World Bank (Guggenheim 2006:17). Guggenheim does not reveal what he means by 'performed better' but goes on to talk about problems with 'projects' rather than community-based processes: elites were capturing development project organisations, the participation of the poor was low and such organisations weakened the community-based organisations that the poor did participate in. They recommended a departure from 'projects as tools for resource delivery' towards support for processes where villagers solve self-identified problems. On the basis of this research a bottom-up programme was born called Kecamatan Development Project (KDP) funded by a World Bank loan of $1bn. There were problems – they did not reach the poorest and it may not be sustainable because it has relied too heavily on contractors – but Guggenheim claims that it has been successful in reducing corruption, improving transparency and ensuring far better participation of women than in the past. Judged a success, the KDP model was soon being replicated across Asia.

The 'success' of KDP has been questioned by Li on a number of grounds, the most serious being the bypassing of the state and formal civil society by working directly with 'communities', as if they are the real custodians of effective development. She considers what they assume about 'community' (2005). They see it as 'traditional' and 'natural' but in need of improvement. While the way to improve communities in the 1980s was through participatory rural appraisal, or the formation of groups in the 1990s, Guggenheim's approach centred on governance – restoring local communities to be the backbone of an invigorated civil society. So this is, like many programmes these days, a mixture of traditional and modern.

Their ideas of 'social capital', although well intentioned, justified an extremely intrusive intervention that aimed to inculcate habits of transparency, accountability, efficiency and the rule of law in communities through World Bank-devised ideas about what these communities needed. For example, they decided that corruption was partly a problem of culture that needed correction (Guggenheim 2006: 18). So there was the contradiction between arguing that communities needed stronger social capital to sort out their own problems and solutions but also doing so only in ways prescribed by World Bank experts. As Li writes 'the team positioned themselves as experts who knew the optimal forms that empowerment should take' (2005: 33). She suggests that what is really going on here is an example of government or rule, in Foucault's sense of the word. This is not about government in the sense of the state but about the World Bank social development team trying to shape how people behave, 'the habits, aspirations and beliefs' (*ibid.*: 3). They do this by creating a 'technical process' for managing people with manuals, checklists, categorisation, training and rewards for good performers. As an Indonesian critic said, they overlooked the 'fact that democracy, public participation, accountability and social and economic rights are all historically tied to the outcome of struggles of social forces and interests … the product of grinding social change over centuries, colored by often violent and bloody confrontations, not least between social classes' (*ibid.*: 34–5).

Anthropologists are increasingly trying to explore the hegemony of globalising forces but also how they play out in different ways in various places, institutions and times. In discussing governance and politics we move continually between the global and local. One globalising area that is receiving increasing attention from anthropologists is the nexus between security, militarisation of aid and development. Donor governments have stepped up their investment in security, redirected some funds to the war on terror and diverted aid to countries that are seen as partners in the 'war on terror', especially since the 9/11 attack on the USA by al-Qaeda[23] (Beall *et al.* 2006: 55–6). The impact that this has on different countries varies. While countries that are perceived to contain threats – such as Iraq and Pakistan – receive far more aid, others like Colombia stand still even though faced with high levels of violence (*ibid.*: 62–3). Keenan argues that the US 'security' work in the Sahara has fabricated terrorist incidents and even created armed rebellions where none existed before (2008). Christian Aid has pointed to the dishonesty in pretending that when aid budgets are spent on the war on terror this benefits the poor. As Beall *et al.* argue,

> a central question regarding the security-development nexus is *whose* security we are talking about. Failure to adequately distinguish between terrorism and other forms of violent conflict contributes to the vagueness of statements about 'security' being furthered by development and vice versa. While it is of course undeniable that states ravaged by internal conflict will face substantial development difficulties, this is a very different issue from using 'development' to make donor country citizens feel less insecure at home in the North. All too often the development-security nexus exists to manipulate development for 'them' with the ultimate purpose of enhancing security for 'us'.   (*Ibid.*: 25)

Global partnership: them and us

Sitting in a beautiful drawing room in front of a fire in Lima, a Peruvian banker asked Emma Crewe the following question: "I understand why my wife does charity work, she comes from a poor country. But why do you, someone from a rich country, worry about the poor in countries such as ours?"[24] At the time I spluttered, shocked that it – doing development – had to be explained. But did he have a point? Why had Emma – along with tens of thousands of European and US aid workers – displaced herself from home rather than doing development in her own backyard? He might have put the question rather more harshly as follows: "What gives you the cheek to take money from rich people in the name of the poor, decide how it should be spent, travel around the world, and keep some for yourself?" A possible answer chimes less with the banker and more with a Muslim community leader that Emma met in Ethiopia. When she asked whether he worked with all the children in his locality or only Muslim children, he replied: "You have come from England to help Ethiopian children. Children in Ethiopia are a common issue for us. Christians and Muslims are like brothers and sisters – our children are Ethiopian not Muslim or Christian. It is unthinkable to differentiate."[25] People in any location are a common issue for all of us. But is it really that simple?

First, we have seen so far in this chapter that people belong to institutions with different pressures, interests and ideas. People are socially grouped. They are socialised into 'moral communities', as Mary Douglas put it, with their ways of classifying, their representations of the world (including what is sacred and what is profane) and their ascription of identity to members (1987: 27). Such communities come together to create public good. Such behaviour cannot be dismissed as self-interested calculation. Despite its huge influence on economics and political science, Douglas shows how limited rational choice theory is in her book *How Institutions Think*: 'Our intuition is that individuals do contribute to the public good generously, even unhesitatingly, without obvious self-serving. Whittling down the meaning of self-serving behaviour until every possible disinterested motive is included merely makes the theory vacuous' (*ibid.*: 9). Nevertheless, generosity acknowledged, people practice hierarchy within, across and between institutions as much as they do in other corners of society. NGO workers tend to see members of staff in the World Bank as morally suspect; government officials see NGO activists as naive; and national development workers often resent expatriate so-called 'experts'.

Secondly, there is, surely, a political distinction between working permanently in a country within organisations that have national or local accountability systems, and satisfying some principle of national sovereignty, as opposed to working as an itinerant worker for an agency with no local accountability and who is no longer present later to answer to stakeholders when things might have gone wrong. This is made even more complicated by the prevalence of expatriate aid workers from former colonising powers visiting former colonised societies where race, ethnicity and nationality still have powerful effects on social relations.

One of the ways in which racism can be manifested in development encounters is in the creation of hierarchies of knowledge and capacity (see Chapter 6). Whether it is nations, organisations or individuals in aid-receiving countries, the widespread implication is that 'they' are weak, corrupt or even incompetent. Most interventions have some element of 'capacity development' of local or national agencies either to ensure delivery during the project or, for those thinking longer-term, to ensure more sustainable and effective development by those with some legitimacy. The assumption that effectiveness is necessarily weaker in the South is worth scrutiny. To give an example of such hierarchies of capacity, a manager working within a European donor agency said to Emma Crewe in 2004: 'we have two research programmes managed by organisations in the South and they are both a disaster. I mean, it is nothing racial, it is just that they don't work at that analytical level … We need an expatriate for the conceptual thinking, then the local consultant can do more of the running around for you.'

This highly experienced manager was not expressing racism in the sense of antagonism or hostility to the 'other'; but his assumptions about analytical thinking, and his denial of the relevance of race, are predicated on the idea that Europeans are apparently capable of a higher level of abstraction than 'locals'. Although both black and white development professionals tend to avoid talking about racism, when you explicitly ask about it in development encounters you get varied responses. White professionals will hotly deny it or look embarrassed, while a few vigorously agree. Black and Asian professionals will tend towards the opposite – mostly explaining that it is highly significant but that it is expressed in different ways by and towards different nationalities. Interpreting when inequality is caused by racism, rather than another form of difference, is not easy. An international institute located in India that employs both national (entirely Indian) and international staff (mostly white European and North American) provides housing in separate areas. The latter earn hugely more than the former so this partly reflects different housing standards. Similarly when the World Bank employs locally hired specialists local rates are paid while expatriate specialists earn Washington-based salaries. But is this a system of racial apartheid or economic inequality? Perhaps both, even if the racism is unintentional, but it is significant that the 'internationals' tend to view the rule as economic, while many nationals perceive it to be racist (Crewe and Fernando 2006: 4).

It may be the unthinking articulation of deficits and flaws in the 'other', and the easy trust established with people in your own group, that betrays racism in development encounters more tangibly. When Emma heard a European NGO worker cry out with some exasperation, 'What is wrong with these people? Why can't they meet deadlines? Is it laziness, incompetence, what?', he was referring to people in NGOs in Asia (conversation betweeen an aid worker and Emma Crewe, 2008). The same person found it tiring to socialise with staff in partner organisations in Asia due to the social distance between him and 'them'. For others the perceived deficits in agencies within the South would be politely attributed to resource constraints or unreliable IT, but even they would still surmise that the agency lacked capacity in the round (rather than specifically in its speed of communication). If racism consists of essentialising groups of people on the basis of cultural or biological difference, then is this racism? Since similar deficits are identified in Eastern European NGOs run by white people, these discourses are not inevitably racism. But in the context of post-colonial Africa, Asia and South America, it is arguably constructed with that unspoken tradition underlying it.

To identify gender as a feature of development has become uncontentious, but race is scarcely mentioned by Europeans or Americans in the literature or practice of development (White 2006: 53).[26] That it plays a role in representations of people is self-evident, but its shape and consequences are far from easy to pin down. For example, within bureaucracies employment opportunities are greatly enhanced for aid workers if they can present their experience as international, rather than local to one country, and this often benefits white people from aid-giving countries. In other contexts 'international' is even a euphemism for 'white' or 'western', as a British woman who worked for over two decades in India reveals when she says that in the early days there were no other 'international' (meaning white and foreign) women at her place of work, even though there were lots of US citizens who were originally from India.

Evolutionary schemas do not merely exist at an abstract level: they are communicated in relationships between real people who each have their own history which comes out of their own experience of their social and political world. Expatriates involved in the development constellations – whether in governments, multilateral agencies, or NGOs – represent 'them' (as opposed to 'us') in strange ways. Sarah White points to the white European disparagement of Bangladesh and all things Bangladeshi by expatriates in Dhaka (White 2002: 409). It gets more specific than black versus white and intersects with nationalities, religions and ethnicities. Crewe and Harrison (1998: 30) give examples of how development discourses often problematise 'locals': their characters ('Nepalis are friendly but lazy'); their morals (generalisations about corruption in the Third World and blindness to it in Europe and America); their traditions ('Muslims are anti-women'); and their knowledge ('locals lack know-how, capacity and technology'). Creating images of the 'other' is universal to all cultures. So Indians have been known to complain that Africans are unreliable as workers; Tanzanians say that Kenyans are materialistic and unable to speak proper Kiswahili; Nigerians are corrupt, according to many other Africans; and equivalent generalisations are made within all nations about different social groups.

The director of a small but highly effective environmental activist organisation in the Indian state of Uttarakhand offered Richard Axelby a series of revealing insights into the ways race may be used instrumentally to promote particular agendas. For several years the organisation had been fighting the cause of a group of buffalo-herding nomads called the van Gujjars. The establishment of a National Park had resulted in the eviction of many of these van Gujjars from their traditional grazing grounds. At the organisation's headquarters a particularly striking van Gujjar 'tribal leader' was on hand to represent their case to visiting officials, journalists or, indeed, anthropologists. 'We are not a threat to the forest. The city people take the trunk of the tree and without trunks there is no longer a forest. We van Gujjars only take the leaves from the trees. And leaves will grow back.' But it soon became clear from this tribal leader's permanent availability at HQ that he himself had long since abandoned his traditional nomadic occupation to settle down to town life. Furthermore it was the Director of the activist organisation who coined the term *van* (meaning 'forest') Gujjar in an effort to establish their residence in the National Park and distinguish them from other Gujjar communities of northwest India. While claims to 'tradition' and 'locality' might be supportive of their cause, often these arguments were clearly exaggerated. But race was used for more than the staking of local claims. Offering to accompany him on a walk to the market, the Director told Richard that being seen in the company of a white foreigner would make him and his work seem more important to the people of the town.

There may be patterns but forms of racism vary wildly. Stereotypes about people are further broken down by gender; assumptions made by British whites about British black women (e.g. hard-working) differ markedly from those made about British black men (e.g. fun-loving, aggressive). Meanwhile a Dane claims that 'as a result of the guilt, which characterises Danes and Swedes in our obvious psychological need to see a victim from above, we end up being not only the world's biggest donors of foreign aid, but also easily the most paternalistic racists' (Holdt 2003). Whether such statements are true, or partly true or false, will depend on whom you ask. But it is clear that it is not just race that makes up identities and it is not only white people who create them.

Furthermore, any simplistic assertion that the development industry consists of racist whites dominating oppressed blacks collapses when you consider who is involved. Take the example of 'expatriates'. The international development industry relies on huge numbers of itinerant professionals. Although the majority of 'expatriates' working in large development INGOs are white, increasingly, a large number in other global institutions are not (especially in the UN system and the World Bank). Those who do not fit neatly into a particular category – such as non-white expatriates and diaspora groups – provoke revealing reactions: a British Asian development worker working in Africa was recently told by a West African (to her annoyance), 'You have a white brain.' Parallel assumptions often get made within bureaucracies about what kind of competence is needed with the result that some agencies tend to be disproportionately dominated by white people, especially at senior levels.

White points to a possible paradox in the link between race and gender. While there appear to be a large number of feminists in the small group of development observers raising the issue of race, early gender and development debates were critiqued for their cultural imperialism (2006: 58–9). For instance, Mohanty pointed out in her seminal article that western feminists write about 'Third World' women as if they are homogeneous and passive (1988 and see Chapter 4). White summarised some of the black feminist, and especially North American, critiques of gender and development (GAD) perspectives since the 1980s: that binary inequalities, such as black versus white, are only a part of black women's experiences – they can only be understood in terms of gender, class and race; that men and masculinities have to be studied (as much as women) and alliances forged with men; that paid work does not necessarily bring women liberation; and that family and labour at home can be humanising (White 2006: 61). These critiques at least partly account for the more sophisticated, context-sensitive GAD rhetoric that currently prevails even if in practice gender mainstreaming

in agencies continues to be more about including some women in some programmes than about tackling gendered inequality (Chant and Guttman 2005:
240–9). GAD continues to dominate social development policy, at least in its
tame, technicalised form within planning and evaluation processes, while race,
class and other differentials remain in the background. And yet anthropologists
have shown that this flies in the face of people's experiences.

To give an example of these different identities at play simultaneously in people's
lives, when anthropologists Rutherford and Nyamuda set up a night school for
farm workers in Zimbabwe, the difficulties they ran into can be understood only by
seeing the multiple hierarchies involved. Men and women joined but also dropped
out of the school for different reasons. While some of the students were permanent
farm workers, most of the men were interested in job advancement; others were
female casual workers studying numeracy in a bid to avoid being short-changed
and to have the chance to take part in public life (2000: 847). However, the single
women were assumed to be prostitutes so married women were forced to drop
out in case their reputations would be ruined by proximity. Although Rutherford's
whiteness enabled the establishment of the school, including approval from the
authorities, Nyamuda's Shona identity made local elites ('vanhu vakuru' or big
people) suspicious. Perhaps they suspected he would use his association with the
white man to undermine their authority. Either through subversion or neglect, they
brought about its closure (*ibid.*: 849–50). The story of this project is shaped by the
gender of the students and the race of their teachers running in parallel. So clearly
the conversations and conflicts between inequalities take different forms according to context. Their meaning, social significance and impact cannot be predicted
in advance. But also, it is clear that whiteness is as relevant as blackness. Both the
race and gender often become invisible in the grip of power, as Loftsdóttir points
out, so that being white and male goes unremarked. But since development for
some (in the case of her research Niger pastoral nomads) belongs to white people,
and white people are assumed to be wealthy and a source of presents and money,
whiteness should be part of the study of race just as much as male identity is part
of understanding gender (2009: 5–7).

However complex it may be, race, gender and class (as well as other dimensions) all have roles to play in the development encounters within global partnerships. If you take a close look at the relationship between INGOs and NGOs,
hierarchies are becoming subtler but more profound. What INGOs mean by
partnership has changed drastically over the last twenty years. International
NGOs once presented themselves in far more political ways as part of an international social movement to challenge elites, inequalities and injustices. Now,
the 'capacity-building' of Southern CSOs is an apparently technical process that
is merely a means to achieve impact on 'beneficiaries'. The transition from solidarity to functional arrangements, all under the same rhetoric of participation
and partnership, is rarely talked about openly. It is taken for granted. The director
of an Indian NGO that Emma Crewe worked with was rare in expressing this
change explicitly in an email during a negotiation over plans:

A funder (even if the term 'Partner' is used) cannot have a status equal to an agency in the south which has actually conceptualized the programme even if the funder is the provider of funds ... Donor agencies are also called on to have a relook at their own roles vis a vis their donnees, particularly at a time when several south-south partnerships are emerging which are naturally on a different plain. These partnerships need to be respected and promoted and thus a good beginning would be to start making a distinction while using the word 'Partner' and for clarity refer to the funding agency as a 'Donor Partner'.   (Pers. com. 2008)

Pickard points out that after the Second World War the relationship between Northern and Southern NGOs was paternalistic, even neo-colonial but moved into a more collegiate phase of 'commonality of action and commitment' during the 1970s, 1980s and 1990s. Their shared aims were to oppose an unjust, undemocratic and exclusionary status quo in their societies (2007: 578). Since the late 1990s partnerships have shifted their emphasis towards hierarchy once again. As 'back-funders' and Northern NGOs have aimed for a quantifiable impact on 'poor' individuals rather than political change, so Southern NGOs and their staff have often been demoted. They are no longer social change agents but recipients of funding, technical expertise or capacity development (*ibid.*: 580). Crudely put, what was an alliance over class conflict has become a hierarchy based on race and nationality, with Southern NGOs colluding in a bid to access funding. This bold claim deserves rather more explanation.

A rhetoric of equality within the North-South partnership is surprisingly common and Southern NGOs often reassure their NGO funders that they buy into these representations, knowing it gives the appearance of full cooperation. In a meeting between Christian World Service and a Sri Lankan partner organisation, one participant claimed, 'it is not a meeting ... with people who give us aid. It is a meeting of equal partners who are together because they are committed to the task' (Gould 2007: 1). But the idea of 'partnership' glosses over the inequality inherent when funds are given, almost always from North to South. Partnership is an ambiguous concept implying that there is a sharing of resources. As Stirrat and Henkel point out, such relationships nearly always involve a transaction of money from North-based agency to South-based agency and such gifts are never free. If they are unreciprocated then they are symbolically good for the giver but bad for the receiver (1997: 73). So this type of relationship is not about sharing, but about asymmetrical patronage, and the strangest aspect is that it is taken for granted or even denied by some practitioners.

Back-funders do try to limit the amount retained by Northern NGOs. Some grant-makers and donors fund Southern NGOs directly and many in the UK (including DFID, Big Lottery Fund and Comic Relief in the UK) make sure that the majority of funding goes to the Southern, rather than Northern, NGOs by limiting the amount of money that can be spent in the UK (typically about 10 per cent). At the same time many bilateral donors have shifted funding away from state and parastatal organisations to working with NGOs directly, as part of a process of liberalisation where civil society mitigates some of the costs of cuts in public services and delivers donors' goals. Rather than support Southern NGOs to enable them to resist being co-opted by donors, some Northern INGOs have responded by creating their own branches, offices or sister organisations in the South at least partly to access more funding or retain more funds for their own organisations. Although usually established with a remit to strengthen local civil society, and often genuinely motivated by the aim of achieving a better impact on the poor, they often meander into direct service delivery, greater interference in planning, implementation and evaluation, or more contracting to national CSOs. In others this has led to circumventing partnerships with national NGOs altogether. This retention of more funding for INGOs displaces talented staff from local/national NGOs to better-funded international ones who pay higher salaries. But it is part of a broader displacement of national NGOs by INGOs who effectively take control of decision-making, representations and ownership.

Wallace *et al.* argue that the imposition of a managerial approach on Southern NGOs by both donors and INGOs ignores cultural diversity and power relations (2006). It is worth asking whether it is particularly the INGOs with a local presence that exacerbate this through greater interference. Northern-based NGOs have been known to make decisions on their behalf, use them as subcontractors to fulfil their own objectives rather than those emerging from the South, fail to be accountable to them, and treat them with disdain and disrespect. As the intermediaries between donors and Southern NGOs, they are in a position to design processes to control the language (mostly English), timing and key spaces for decision-making. Consultation with 'stakeholders' – in theory those affected by an initiative – can often be no more than a ritualised series of encounters that reinforce rather than challenge hierarchies (Crewe and Fernando 2006: 8–12). And Northern NGOs often ignore the intellectual property rights of their Southern partners and claim their ideas, as well as the right to disseminate them, as their own. Southern NGOs often put up with so little control, and comply with the conditions attached to grants, because potential sources of funding are so few and unpredictable.

An anthropologist working in development, Mary Ann Mhina, told a story about a Scandinavian grant-maker.[27] They found an accounting irregularity with one of the partners and sent in auditors. Then they emailed all the INGOs that they thought might be working with them, or might be in the future, and told them the results. They suggested sharing findings in the future in an email (abridged to preserve their anonymity):

> X Foundation … give grants to organisations that are run by people with disability or that are run by parents of children with disabilities … In Tanzania until last November, we also had another partner organization called Y. Unfortunately, we had to terminate our partnership with Y due to mismanagement and misuse of funds. We had commissioned an external audit, which brought these facts to light. Also with Z (*their other partner*)

we are facing challenges in terms of good governance and we are in the
process, together with ... (*other INGOs*), to find suitable solutions on how
we could best support and complement our efforts for sustainable improvements at Z ... Such cooperation would also help when doing background
checks on new applicants or partners, or when looking for possible references or contacts etc.   (Pers. com. 3 October 2010)

Such cooperation might sound benign on the surface, but Mhina objected to this
idea of sharing information about partners among INGOs in secret: from the
perspective of Southern NGOs it could be seen as enhancing the INGOs' mechanisms of control. The irony was that this foundation was, according to partners,
the least transparent donor.

Mhina provides another example of hierarchy. An Australian woman visited
an African country, did a little research, wrote six or seven documents and got
funding from USAID (and then DFID) to set up a local NGO. She needed a
UK NGO to be involved but the one she had in her sights pulled out so she
approached Mary Ann who was surprised firstly that this woman wanted to set up
a new NGO working on disability in this country when there are already so many,
but also that USAID/DFID chose to give her funding rather than national agencies. 'Was it just because she was foreign, white and they knew her?' she asked.
On being asked whether racism was involved in the donors' views, she replied,
that she had often felt that it was, often in subtle but nevertheless damaging ways.
She agreed with a colleague who recently said to her: 'The reality is that the aid
world is often racist. We can't get away from ourselves.'

But all is not hopeless. Some INGOs are concerned about power inequalities at all levels of international development and seek to do something about
them by radically restructuring their institutional arrangements. In recent years
ActionAid has chosen to subject itself to such a reorientation – giving greater
emphasis to accountability to beneficiaries rather than to donors – with all the
challenges of undergoing organisational change in a large INGO with offices
worldwide and over 1,700 staff. They have decentralised, moved their head
office to South Africa, and introduced an 'Accountability, Learning and Planning
System' that shifts from linear planning to participatory review and reflection.
Those involved are admirably self-critical about the huge tensions and cultural
and practical challenges that this new way of working entails, not least being
the need for coherence despite a decentralisation of power. Donors, including
DFID, under pressure themselves to report on achievements, apparently continue
to put ActionAid under pressure to return to more conventional approaches and
some individuals do return to 'business as normal'. Whatever the setbacks, their
innovations are beginning to influence others in the sector and could be useful
beyond measure as long as sufficient time and resources are given to such transformations (David, Mancini and Guijt 2006).

The pressures on INGOs, and on their back donors behind them, should not
be underestimated. At a meeting held for UK NGOs to discuss the economic

downturn in early 2009, and how to survive it, nearly all the participants talked about their reserves, their fundraising, how to collaborate with other UK INGOs (or even merge if necessary) and better articulate 'our added value'. Emma Crewe suggested at the meeting, 'surely the challenge is to maintain our integrity and ensure that we continue to serve our Southern partner local organisations? The financial pressures and incentives are to increase our own income, but now more than ever we have to ensure we are not deflected from our central purpose, that is, to contribute to the strengthening of capacity in the global South.' But people were mostly too anxious about their own fundraising needs to pay much attention or reply. The funding of aid for civil society means that displacement of local/national NGOs is the easiest way for INGOs to ensure their own survival.

Organisational boundaries

The attachment of labels to the institutions that make up Development World serves particular organisational structures and define roles, aims and objectives. Such labels are used instrumentally. Internally, they steer staff in clear directions and channel their activities into particular ways of working. However, as we have seen, organisations are complex entities in which tensions and divergent interests may undermine claims to internal unity. Labels are also used to define relations with other organisations. The boundaries between agencies and groups of actors may become blurred and relationships shift over time.

Organisational ethnographies have done much to tell us about how categories within development are constructed and how they help institutions to make sense of themselves and of others. An anthropological approach demonstrates how actors use organisational categories to bolster their expertise, to enforce their claims and to justify their own particular ways of working. In the following four chapters we examine some of these claims and the assumptions that underlie them.

Challenging questions arising from this chapter

What are the key agencies involved in aid and development and what are their roles?

How are people in Development World socially and politically organised?

What is the new aid architecture and what difference does it make and to whom?

Is Development World racist?

What are the moral and political problems with the governance of aid?

Who are beneficiaries of development?

How has the partnership between INGOs and NGOs changed in the last twenty
  years?
What is the shape of aid?
How might development institutions be reoriented to meet the needs of the poor
  more effectively?
What changes in attitude, behaviour and instructional organisations are needed?

4   The elusive poor

The reduction of poverty has come to be understood as the key object of the development enterprise. It is one of the taken-for-granted, 'silent traditions' (Bourdieu 1977: 167) of development professionals that the goal of international aid and development is to free the poor from poverty. But who are the poor? What defines them? And who gets to decide?

Key points covered by this chapter

- Predominant perspectives in development bureaucracies characterise poverty as absolute (rather than relative), such as living on less than $1.25 per day.
- Populist accounts advocate that poor people should be listened to, their knowledge should be respected and their participation encouraged. However, these accounts can be naive when it comes to the subject of power hierarchies.
- Both Marxist and feminist theories move beyond blaming the poor for their exploitation. The structural power relations explain poverty and need to be reversed.
- Anthropologists have been influenced by all three of these traditions, but add their own dimension. They have a relational, historical perspective that sees poverty as embedded in culture, ideology and politics.
- These various perspectives are underpinned by different ideas about the characteristics of poverty but also 'the poor'. Such ideas about poor people fit within broader classifications of people, and the representation of their interests, that often deserve to be questioned.

Development professionals have invested hugely in describing the characteristics of poverty and determining how it can be measured. In this chapter we will explain these various attempts at identifying the elusive poor and how anthropologists have critiqued them. The idea of development depends on the existence of groups of people in need of assistance. In this sense 'the poor' are an imaginary group fashioned out of the needs and practices of those who hope to develop them.

Some approaches implicitly blame the poor, or their ignorance, for their economic position, while others point the finger at elites and decision-makers.

Anthropologists try to convey a more relational and contextual approach, which locates the problems in relationships and structures rather than individuals or groups of people. When anthropologists are trying to understand poverty and economic relations, they consider representations and practices in context and from both *emic* (the social actor's or informant's view) and *etic* (outsider) perspectives before rushing to moral judgements of specific groups. Anthropologists take informants' views extremely seriously but do not treat them as simple conveyors of absolute truth. People they speak to when doing research disagree with each other and say what they say for all sorts of reasons (e.g. to make an impression, to make sense of the world, to deal with emotions), and take much of their ideology for granted. In order to understand what they articulate, anthropologists have to understand people's moral and ideological constructs, rules – both explicit and implicit ones – and how these relate to practices and individual histories. So we will probe the conceptual and moral assumptions underlying approaches to poverty that often go unnoticed: how 'poor' people are categorised, ideas about why poverty comes about and how it is sustained, and why it is tolerated by society. We will consider the extent to which the association between poverty and misery, or wealth and happiness, are universal or culturally produced in different ways. And whether this might pose any challenges for those working in development. Finally we will comment on how these social categories used by development professionals are part of a broader cultural construction of identity.

Defining and measuring poverty

During the 1970s the World Bank, under its then head Robert McNamara, began to take poverty more seriously as a focus of development and aid. Other donors followed suit. Since the 1980s there has been a growing consensus among policy-makers that development needs to address poverty reduction, but there has also been plenty of disagreement about what poverty is, how it should be measured and what should be done to reduce or eradicate it. Pre-1980 neoliberal economists battled ideologically with Marxists or post-Marxists. But since the end of the Cold War, neoliberal ideology has had such an overwhelming influence on international and national policy-making that virtually all governments abandoned socialism and those with neo-Marxist or Marxist perspectives were pushed to the margins. Meanwhile feminist theories of politics and economics, including the nature of poverty, have been moving towards the mainstream. But the extent of their adoption or co-option in superficial forms is a matter of debate (to which we return later in this chapter).

Poverty is described by international institutions in terms of a series of deficits experienced by categories or statistical groups of individuals. The World Bank stated in 2010 that poverty is hunger, lack of shelter, sickness, illiteracy and lack of power.[1] The neoliberal agenda assumes that development and poverty reduction rely on economic growth and that, in turn, is only possible with low tax rates, minimal subsidies, limited protection in relation to foreign investment, privatisation, deregulation and legal security for property rights. Growth in enterprise and increased income at the top of society will trickle down to the poor through employment and wealth creation, so neoliberal theory goes. The 'structural adjustment' programmes of the 1980s and 1990s were the means to reduce the role of the state in the economy through privatisation, cuts and deregulation. The resulting increase in trade, foreign investment and employment should have created growth, jobs for the poor and higher levels of income and consumption. In more recent versions social exclusion, risks and vulnerabilities will be reduced, while access to services and social capital are strengthened. In this internationally dominant view inequality means disparities in the poverty or wealth of individuals rather than the way that relationships between groups are economically or politically structured.

The final critical piece in neoliberal descriptions of poverty, and one that reveals much about the assumptions underpinning them, concerns measurement. To make comparisons within nations as well as between them, and to evaluate different poverty reduction strategies, donors and governments need a comparable method of measurement. The one that fits with their view of poverty, with its emphasis on the economic status of individuals rather than groups or categories of people, is to create an absolute 'poverty line'. The current line, or minimum level considered necessary for satisfying basic needs, is $1.25 a day. Thus, the MDG on poverty entails halving the number of people living on less than this per day. On the basis of this form of measurement, the World Bank claims success: 'poverty estimates released in August 2008 show that about 1.4 billion people in the developing world (one in four) were living on less than $1.25 a day in 2005, down from 1.9 billion (one in two) in 1981'.[2]

Both explicit and implicit critiques of neoliberalism are abundant, even if mostly ignored, and the milder ones have contributed to its refinement. The evidence of the painful consequences of structural adjustment programmes (SAPs) was overwhelming and even some of its architects, such as Joseph Stiglitz and Jeffrey Sachs, joined the criticism (Edelman and Haugerud 2005: 8). In recognition of the impoverishment caused by SAPs, the Bank added social investment programmes for poor people and debt relief for 'heavily indebted poor countries'. SAPs were then replaced with Poverty Reduction Strategy Papers (PRSPs) by international financial institutions at the end of the 1990s. In theory, aid-receiving governments produced these after nationally owned processes of planning determined their approach to combating poverty. However, critics have claimed that the national ownership is weak and PRSPs are just another means for international donors to impose their doctrines by rewarding those plans that have neoliberal ideas at their heart. Freeing the market to allow individuals to escape poverty remains paramount. An examination of thirty PRSPs by Stewart and Wang reveals no fundamental difference from the policy advice attached to structural adjustment programmes (2003: 19–22). They conclude that while civil society may have been marginally strengthened by PRSP processes, national governments may been somewhat weakened, while the position of donors has hardly changed (*ibid.*: 27). After all, the national plans still require endorsement by the World Bank and the IMF.

The more fundamental criticisms of neoliberalism question the idea that we can find significant economic success in statistics about the regions of Asia and Africa as a whole. They counter the claims of the international donors with their own statistics, showing how malleable they can be. If you take $1 a day as the poverty line then poverty fell between 1981 and 2001 but if you take $2 a day, then it increased. While East Asia has reduced poverty on these measures dramatically, it doubled in sub-Saharan Africa during the last two decades of the twentieth century. Regional disparities are disguised with the simple global claims of the international financial institutions.

Absolute measures of poverty can be superficial. When the World Bank says that one-fifth of the world is poor because it lives on $1.25 day, they are labelling the poor in absolute terms. In contrast, *relative* poverty draws attention to structured relationships between groups; women's ownership of property is far lower than that of men, for example, and to understand this inequality you have to consider how inheritance, violence and control over resources are gendered. If you measure poverty by household purchasing power then you completely miss out on questions of how income is distributed unevenly within households. Relative poverty is about the unevenness of poverty between and within groups.

More damaging still, the very premises upon which neoliberal theory sit are flawed. One strand of criticism points to the failure of sweeping economic theories to take account of the views of 'poor' people themselves. Robert Chambers, in his well-known book – *Rural Development: Putting the Last First* (1983), casts doubt on the assumption that poverty can be measured by compiling national statistics based on household surveys and gross national product to assess levels of economic deprivation. He challenges the positivist paradigm of rational decision-making that underpins mainstream development policy and produces easily digestible constructs such as the poverty line. Chambers writes about development tourists who are arrogant, biased and uninformed and recommends more participatory ways to find out about people's poverty, vulnerability and powerlessness. He maintained that we need to change our attitude to 'poor' people and recognise their hard work, knowledge and capacity for changing their situation. A veritable industry grew up promoting community-based development with methods for targeting, consulting and empowering the poor (such as participatory rural appraisal (PRA), Methodology of Participatory Assessments and Community Action Planning). For some of the challenges in decentralising power to communities, see Box 4.1.

Other populist approaches, in part informed by Chambers, have spawned ideas about sustainable livelihoods as a more rounded way of tackling poverty. As Scoones put it, a sustainable livelihoods (SL) approach asks, 'given a particular context (of policy setting, politics, history, agro-ecology and socio-economic

Box 4.1. Does community-based and community-driven development work?

Two World Bank economists, Mansuri and Rao, have undertaken a literature-based review of projects that aim to strengthen community participation (2004). Despite the increasing popularity of community or local participation, and the potential gains in theory of reversing power and economic hierarchies in communities, the impact on poverty has been limited. The reasons they suggest for this disappointing record are partly conceptual and partly flaws in implementation.

1. The concepts – especially participation, community and social capital – are idealised; the costs of consultation are underestimated, the harmony and homogeneity within communities are overplayed, and class and power are ignored.

2. The processes of targeting the 'poor' are often partial or subverted by elites, resulting in, for example, the selection of poorer districts but richer households within them or the exclusion of the very poor by the use of criteria that make their participation difficult (such as a financial or time contribution). They point out that social planners and community members can have different ideas of about poverty and fairness. Using the example of a food distribution project in the Sudan, they ask the critical question, 'whose preferences should count?'

3. Community involvement does not necessarily improve service delivery; the outcomes are a mix of positive and negative. A meta-analysis of fifty-two USAID funded projects concluded that participatory projects were more successful in 'developed', as opposed to less 'developed' economies, and smaller, less complex ones fared better. Community participation made no difference in some projects, but improved outcomes in others.

4. Prospects for sustainability can be strengthened by community involvement but conversely a lack of support from external agencies, including the state, imperilled others.

5. Support for collective action often fails to take account of the barriers faced by poorer households, especially when inequality is relatively more pronounced. Elite domination is inevitable in most participation projects to some degree and in many (but not all) cases this restricts the benefits to poorer people.

6. External agencies tend to be under pressure to produce quick results and lack in-depth knowledge of specific communities; both damaging to community-driven development.

7. If the state exploits rather than supports community-based development, then the process becomes authoritarian. In the case of a Javanese project, the combination of an autocratic state and ideas of self-reliance amounted to a form of forced labour.

8. Attempts to replicate local community development projects, with 'a mechanical application of best practice guidelines, without attention to local context', lead to poor projects (Mansuri and Rao 2004: 27). Successful scaling up depends on good monitoring, learning by doing, a gradual approach and downward accountability.

conditions), what combination of livelihood resources (different types of 'capital') result in the ability to follow what combination of livelihood strategies (agricultural intensification/extensification, livelihood diversification and migration) with what outcomes?' (1998: 3). His team in the Institute of Development Studies (in the UK) assume that a livelihood is sustainable if it can recover from setbacks, maintain its assets and capabilities and avoid undermining the natural resource base (*ibid.*: 5). In a series of working papers by the Overseas Development Institute, sustainable approaches were reviewed in the early 2000s. They found in India, for example, that SL had its uses, most importantly giving poor people themselves a stronger voice in design, but that impact was constrained for institutional reasons. The state governments had their own frameworks, priorities and institutional pressures; one of the Orissa design team compared the SL approach to a wish list that raises expectations but is politically and institutionally impossible to fulfil (Turton 2001: 25).

The ideological populism of Chambers and his followers has been eloquently critiqued in turn by anthropologists, including Olivier de Sardan: 'Ideological populism paints reality in the colours of its dreams, and has a romantic vision of popular knowledge' (2005: 9). In his view ideological populism is not, in practice, so romantic. It is nothing new for intellectuals from rich countries to want to fight for the rights of the oppressed, but 'development has become a profession, the development world a "market". However, within this profession and in this market, the populist ideology is far from marginal. It is currently institutionalised. Populism has indeed succeeded in selling a certain type of product on this market' (*ibid.*: 114).

Populist rhetoric has become a new orthodoxy, at times trotted out in unthinking ways for huge consultancy fees and sometimes used very superficially. Even the more thoughtful versions of ideological populism can be simplistic about the politics of development. The complaint that poverty should not be reduced to simple global econometric measures is well made, but the populists' alternative – participatory needs assessment by the poor – can be politically naive. 'The poor', 'beneficiaries', or the 'people' are often treated as a homogeneous and harmonious group, as if easily represented by a select few, say, women, men, elderly and youth (children are often excluded). This flies in the face of the conflicts of interest and hierarchies that anthropologists and others find at all level of society. Despite the respect accorded to the knowledge and resources of the poor, it is still assumed that the deficits belong to their communities (vulnerabilities, lack of capital, backward knowledge, AIDS, etc.) and escape from poverty requires their empowerment. But this too contains political naivety. Empowerment, 'bottom-up' development or grassroots-led poverty reduction mean that the main agents of change are the 'poor'; the role played by the medium and top receives less attention.

Partly in response to critiques, politics has been injected into many conceptualisations of poverty but not necessarily enriched our understanding as much as anthropologists might like. In 1990 the World Development Report treated poverty as if it was about income and the absence of safety nets, where the 2001 Report reported on multidimensional aspects of poverty including powerlessness and exclusion. And in the 2010s the role that politics plays has taken centre stage in global aid policy-making with the focus on good governance and attempts to enable more decentralised political ownership of poverty reduction. For example, the PRSPs[3] have the idea of participatory processes of consultation at their core. But, in addition to criticism that it is too donor-driven (see above), an anthropological perspective would point to the fact that it continues to rely on absolute rather than relational representations of poverty and these representations are rarely grounded adequately in history and social realities from the perspective of people themselves. Partly as a consequence of the continued absolute macro approach to poverty, gender mainstreaming within PRSPs tend to lack substance.

The development theorist who has done more than any other to broadcast the importance of distribution is the economist Amartya Sen. In his hugely influential book *Poverty and Famines* (1982) he argued that hunger is not simply a lack of access to food due to low production – it is unequal distribution and lack of entitlements, for example to work, that accounts for extreme poverty or famine. His ideas about people's capabilities, and the entitlements approach which looked at ownership and exchange of goods rather than just access to goods, have been instrumental in shaping policy in most of the major donor institutions. Some of his followers have developed theories about how social institutions define entitlements in structural ways – for example, to work and resources – and deduce that investment in social networks is important to poverty reduction. Others have used the idea of entitlements within gender frameworks, even if using the concept in different ways from Sen. Kabeer illustrates from research in Bangladesh how entitlement inequalities are gendered. Women, along with children, are classified as dependent minors and have less access to resources, physical security, mobility, services, property (including capital), work opportunities, social status and decision-making. She quotes from women trying to obtain credit from a bank: 'If we go alone, who will listen to us? We don't know who to meet, what to ask for. People are rude to us, they think we are dirty and talk to us badly. They don't try and explain anything to us.' Even their entitlements in food distribution are weaker than those of men, culturally justified by references to ideas about female self-sacrifice and altruism and enforced by male violence (Kabeer 1994: 143–4). In an attempt to take on board some of Sen's ideas about poverty, and measure poverty at the national level in a more rounded way than poverty lines, UNDP developed the Human Development Index. They assessed the extent to which individuals within a country could (a) lead long and healthy lives, (b) become educated, (c) have the access to resources needed for a decent standard of living, and (d) participate in the life of the community.[4] Building people's capabilities by expanding their choices is seen as key.

However, there is still much left unexplained by many entitlement and capability approaches. Appadurai points out that Sen has widened the idea of welfare to go beyond narrow economics (2004), but he does not look carefully at culture (which we will come back to later in this chapter). And what remains unsaid in entitlement approaches is troubling – the idea that a capability or entitlement deficit causes poverty and exclusion can be seen as perpetuating the familiar blaming of the poor. The poor are conceived of as individuals; socio-political inequalities at all levels (household, local, national and global) remain out of his gaze. As the development economist Devereux puts it, 'Without a complementary social and political analysis, the entitlement approach can illuminate only a small part of a very complex phenomenon' (2001: 259). Sen fails to recognise how individuals are embedded in households, communities and states and that famines can be political crises as much as economic shocks or natural disasters. For example, recent famines in the Horn of Africa, where assets are transferred or destroyed by conflict or war, require historical and political understandings not just narrow economic ones (*ibid.*: 248). As De Waal points out, in the Sudan people were not choosing to starve – as Sen claims they do in famines – but choosing to go hungry to preserve their way of life (as quoted by Devereux *ibid.*: 249). Critics have pointed out that choice (or lack of it) is made in a context of inequality; thus, it is those with the least power and greatest dependency who tend to die first in famines. De Waal also concluded that what may have been true in South Asia, the source of Sen's research, does not necessarily apply to Africa. Previous famines in Bengal and Bangladesh saw the poorest households suffer the highest mortalities, whereas in the Darfur famine poor water, sanitation and overcrowding killed people irrespective of income. The health crisis was a result of social disruption and not just economic crisis. Sen's individualistic approach in its work on famine, with its focus on private property, fails to explain collective patterns across the world. Devereux's conclusion that twenty-one out of thirty-two major famines in the twentieth century had adverse politics as their primary cause tells us more about what underlies hunger (*ibid.*: 256). So in the next section we consider adverse politics in more detail.

Class and gender

Theories of economic development in the international aid industry have been significantly, but unevenly, influenced since the 1960s by Marxist ideas and since the 1970s by feminism. In traditional Marxist theory, class inequalities result in low wages, job insecurity and exploitation for the working classes and, in contrast, accumulation for those owning the means of production. Marxists writing about the Third World have had to adapt Marx's observations about industrial capitalism to rural settings. So, for the majority of those facing poverty in rural areas it is unequal ownership and access to land and low prices paid for agricultural products that are part of what makes poor people exploited. Uneven capitalist transformation of production in agriculture concentrates wealth in the hands of the few and makes the majority more vulnerable to risk. Poor farmers and their dependents often have to migrate to survive. The adverse incorporation of poor rural people into urban labour markets then entails various forms of bondage and exploitation.

At the level of the world system in unequal exchanges between developed and underdeveloped, peripheral countries replicated a similar pattern of, for example, low prices paid to the latter and high profits for the 'core' countries (Gunder Frank 1966). While dependency theory has been criticised – for failing to account for differences between poor countries or explain class inequalities within them – Marxian theories have grown in sophistication and complexity. To take one example, Harriss-White's analysis of nine processes within capitalism that create poverty – including unemployment, war, global environmental destruction and the creation of social enemies – point to how the actions of the state can create variation (1997).[5]

One of the assumptions of many anthropologists using Marxian theories has been, as Mosse puts it, that all economic relations are social relations but not all social relations can be reduced to economics (2010: 2). The political and cultural dimensions have to be relied on to explain why poverty and inequality persist so stubbornly. If you look at poverty as social relationships that could be changed, then you have to wonder, why does anyone tolerate such suffering? As Green and Hulme (2005: 872) ask, why do some societies tolerate suffering for certain groups and not others? In different contexts those deemed second-class citizens will vary – whether it is widows in India, street children in Brazil or Palestinians in Israel and the Occupied Territories. And what about the exploited people themselves; why do they ever comply with relatively little protest? Marxian anthropologists have followed in the tradition of Gramsci, who propagated the idea of hegemony as a form of ideological oppression, and have expressed this in increasingly subtle explanations of the relationship between power, ideology and culture. On one level, poor people are politically marginalised and so their voice is weak and their concerns are not tackled within political agendas.

Others claim that there is more protest and resistance than is immediately apparent to elites. Many anthropologists have pointed to the resistance to subordination by the poor, most famously James Scott in his seminal work *Weapons of the Weak* (1985). Within an aid and development context, the embezzlement of funds, lying about what is really going on in projects and keeping silent about developments that may be unpopular could be seen as the weapons that relatively powerless people resort to when pushed around by donors or development workers holding the purse strings.

However, viewpoints that overstate either domination or resistance in relationships of power can be reductionist. This can entail explaining the behaviour of the powerful (e.g. those controlling resources) in terms only of the consolidation of their power, while others are seen as either complying with or resisting such domination. This can oversimplify human motivation and put the 'oppressors' too much in the centre of things. Such binary oppositions have fallen out of fashion in the analysis of class relations.

While class inequalities have been highlighted by those interested in political economy, including many anthropologists, but sidelined in mainstream development discourse, a form of gender analysis has become obligatory in development planning. Evidence of the gap between women's and men's economic and political positions is not hard to find: women represent two-thirds of the world's illiterate adults; women hold only 15.6% of the elected parliamentary seats and receive 78% of the wages paid to men; and in some parts of the world women provide up to 70% of the agricultural labour and 90% of food (Lopez-Claros and Zahidi 2005: 2–4). According to the UNDP, of the 1.3 billion people living in poverty in 1995, 70% were women and men own a far greater proportion of land and other assets. Gender inequality begins in childhood – far more girls than boys are out of primary school; more girls suffer malnutrition; and girls work longer hours. Such claims about the feminisation of poverty are well established in policy arenas. The more challenging questions are how did it get like that and how does it relate to politics, ideology and culture?

The basic premise of feminism is that gender is a lens that is necessary in order to understand the social, economic and political fabric of society and not just the position of women. Feminist debates within anthropology rose to prominence with Rosaldo and Lamphere's *Women, Culture and Society* (1974), which pointed to the invisibility of women in ethnography. Ortner's much cited chapter claims that it is culture and the way that women's nurturing roles are seen as being closer to nature that lead to the subordination of women (*ibid.*). In her bid to overthrow biological determinism, she ushers in a universalising cultural explanation. McCormack, Strathern and others (1980) challenged this idea; the separation of 'culture' from 'nature', and their association with men and women respectively, are cultural constructs that are not universal, but are specific to western societies. In other cultures or societies the culture/men vs. nature/women polarities do not have the same meaning.

It was not until the 1970s that feminism began to have an influence on development debates. Esther Boserup was a pioneer in the field when she wrote about the negative impact of economic development on women (1970). Women's experience of colonialism, industrialisation and modernisation was one of exclusion – men tended to reap the benefits of technology and the move away from family-based labour. More education for women and their incorporation into the workforce were the solutions, it was claimed. Boserup, and liberal feminists who followed her, encouraged aid agencies to understand more about the costs of development for women. The UN declared International Women's Year in 1975 and 1976–85 was UN Decade for Women.

While aid agencies did take on what have been called the 'efficiency' arguments for considering gender – that is that better progress will be made in reducing poverty, stimulating economic growth or protecting the environment – feminists took the argument further. Unequal gendered power relations were manifested in the relationship between domestic and wage labour, patterns of violence, political representation and control of resources. Molyneux distinguished between strategic and practical interests of women (1985).[6] Aid agencies tended to focus mostly on women's practical interests, that is, addressing their immediate needs for water or childcare to make their lives easier. What is needed, she argued, for greater gender equality is to address women's strategic interest in challenging gendered relations through, as examples, better political representation or a more equitable division of labour (*ibid.*). So gender policy in aid agencies shifted (at least in its rhetoric) from 'Women in Development', which was about trying to advance the position of women, to 'Gender in Development', with its attention to relations between women/men and girls/boys. Gender mainstreaming became an aim for many organizations, especially donor aid agencies and INGOs, with an emphasis on improving the access of women and girls to services. However, arguably gender in development remains poorly conceptualised in bureaucracies. For example, Jackson points out that gender and poverty became conflated so that gender programmes have been largely focused on getting women above the poverty line – missing the point that women and men experience poverty differently (1998: 39–64). A far broader conceptualisation of gender is needed.

Many ideas promoted by western feminists, and taken up within aid agencies, do not hold up to scrutiny when you study the lives of women and men in multiple cultural contexts. The overused ideas of women's inherent closeness to nature, their incorruptibility, their aversion to risk and their solidarity with other women are all unconvincing as universal claims when you consider women's real lives. Since the late 1980s western feminists were criticised by Third World feminists, most notably Mohanty (1988), for portraying Third World women as both passive and homogeneous, a symptom of their powerful and blinkered position. Some have been influenced by postmodernist debates – stressing the diversity of gendered relations around the world – and others criticise western feminism for failing to acknowledge the significance of post-colonial racism, Third World women's movements and post-development perspectives (Lind 2003). Anthropologist feminists from the West (while not immune to such criticism themselves) have been sympathetic to the more thoughtful critics partly because most have worked in different cultural contexts. They agree that much gender work is ethnocentric and myths about women persist (Cornwall *et al.* 2008).

Global political and economic changes continue to have an impact on gendered relations. The increase in power of the multinational corporations and the search for cheap labour in the South has led to the feminisation of low-paid labour, often in the informal sector. Cuts in public services have hit women (and children) harder than men. Male migration and environmental degradation have combined to increase women's (and children's) unpaid household and agricultural labour. What is the response of aid agencies? Gender mainstreaming has been established as a technical area across the industry – with the requisite toolkits, training courses and (often western) experts – rather than the political struggle and strengthening of democratic spaces that is needed (Byron and Ovnemark 2010). Although the World Bank spent $1.2 billion in the last ten years on the rule of law and gender equality project, only $7.3 million was allocated to gender equality (UN Women 2011: 15). The power has been taken out of women's empowerment (Batliwala 2007). So the more political struggle for structural change is left to social movements whether unions, the anti-globalisation movement or local-level protests, but as Mohan and Stokke point out, relying on the local and underplaying the role of the state and transnational power holders is dangerous (2000). And as the first report of the new coordinating UN agency for women – UN Women – makes plain, states are failing women (2011).

Both feminist and Marxian accounts portray poverty as caused and perpetuated by relations between people and resources rather than through the actions (or inaction) of individuals. As Mosse has argued, a relational perspective on poverty does two things: (1) it takes account of history – that is, how this set of economic and political relations develops over time in this place; (2) it rejects individualism and rational choice models and emphasises the importance of social process and relations of power (2007). The two traditions have had an uneasy relationship as Hartmann and Bridges warned back in 1975, 'the "marriage" of Marxism and feminism has been like the marriage of husband and wife depicted in English common law: Marxism and feminism are one and that one is Marxism ... [e]ither we need a healthier marriage or we need a divorce' (as cited by Chincilla 1991: 291). Both felt that their cause was primary and the other had to be tackled second so as not to dilute their own. And yet gender and class (and age) cannot be understood except in relation to each other. Women are subordinated by a combination of exploitation, dispossession and lack of representation in different ways in different locations and at different ages, but with patterns. Women, as well as men, in their turn exploit children. In general the unpaid work of women (and children, especially girls), is a form of exploitation within resource-poor households across the world. But the way in which social relations in households are gendered is quite different according to class and age. For example, richer households in much of South Asia rely on the exploitation of domestic workers – often children, and sometimes poorer kin, rather than their own female household members – to undertake work in the household. It is a mark of their higher social status that their 'own' women do not work. Poorer women do not usually have this choice, however, and have to fulfil household labour obligations at any age as well as seeking work in the labour market. When poverty is conceptualised within a relational perspective, gender, age and class have universal relevance even if their formation can only be discerned by a careful study of the context.

Obliviousness to gender and class has caused untold harm. Development benefits do not 'trickle down' (or 'up') to women or other subordinated groups and the reasons are political rather than environmental, technical or economic in a narrow sense. In order to be effective, solutions have to be political and concerned with social relationships and wellbeing as much as economics in a narrow sense. This means questioning an even more fundamental tenet of development – that more money automatically makes individuals happy.

Money, culture and happiness

According to Sahlins, 'money is to the West what kinship is to the Rest' (1976: 216). The suggestion is that relationships in Europe and the USA are shaped by economic class and material wealth, but in other societies what matters to most people are ties of blood or marriage. Such a neat division does not sound particularly convincing – class, kinship and money are all relevant to all societies – but in his seminal book *Stone Age Economics*, Sahlins brilliantly unravels some of the assumptions made within materialist theories. He wrote about how some societies under-produce, under-exploit resources and limit the amount of labour they put into production because they are not interested in accumulating large surpluses. Women consistently work harder in these societies, but he gives examples of men only working four to six hours a day. Citing the case of Australian Aborigines who do not distinguish between 'work' and 'play' (1972: 64), Sahlins argues that this is not because they are lazy but rather that there are other things more important to them than the accumulation of material wealth. In some societies it is only important to gather wealth in order to give it away. He gives the example of the north-west coast Native Americans for whom accumulation in any quantity is socially unacceptable unless it is for immediate redistribution (*ibid.*: 211).

Not surprisingly, people's experience of happiness, money and aspirations vary because they are embedded in culture. But cultural values are also connected in complex ways. Keith Hart points out that money and language are the two main ways that we make and share collective cultural meaning; money is earned both separately and together so that it acts as a symbol of our individual relationship with our community (2005). Some meanings are shared and others are specific to certain social groups. So, for example, Kabeer suggests that the women she interviewed in Bangladesh want to have enough money to acquire food, clothes, shelter, and so on, but not just for their own sake but also because providing those for their children is crucial to their self-esteem and a well-fed husband means they are less likely to be beaten (1994: 139, 144). Poverty is not just about goods or materialism, it affects people's status – it is socially *stigmatising*. In general poor people are not accorded respect. Since they are well aware of the stigma associated with poverty, an increase in income and changing economic relationship with others is bound up with social status as far as they are concerned. Beck found that in West Bengal forty-nine out of fifty-eight poor people living on the edge of survival valued self-respect more highly than food when asked to rank them (1994: 141). This challenges the widely held assumption that it is only the better-off that worry about status and self-esteem; the desire to escape poverty is at the least highly likely to be social as well as material.

To give another example of the embeddedness of money in culture and social relations, take the principle of reciprocity. Mauss's book *The Gift* explains how reciprocity has its place in all cultures; it sets up powerful social obligations that are not easily ignored. An understanding of the force of the gift – and why it has to be repaid and the way that it structures social relationships – is only possible

---

Box 4.2. The meaning of money in development

Development projects rarely consider the cultural meaning of money before embarking on, for example, income generation projects. When Emma Crewe did research in Sri Lanka in the late 1980s with potter communities, she found that the consequence of greater wealth caused considerable upset. One of the aims of the programme was to generate more income for lower-caste potter communities. The ethos of this 'family' of potters that stretched across Sri Lanka, all owners of their own enterprises with virtually no waged labour, was egalitarian between households (if not within) until they got involved in this project.

The 100 or so potters initially involved in the project became significantly richer than their neighbours by producing new products introduced by the project. This provoked huge resentment among both other potter households and higher caste families. No longer indebted to local elites, they stopped providing free services for them to the fury of the higher caste farmers and satisfaction of now richer potters. However, as they accumulated wealth and started employing other potters – especially younger men and women – as waged labourers, anger mounted from within their own communities as well. Neighbouring potters sabotaged the production process while products were being fired and attributed the breakages to evil spirits who disapproved of the project.

But eventually this new set of relations between those incorporated into the project and those left outside became part of the new social landscape. The poorer potter households either copied the new products, struggled economically or took up other professions. So the simple idea that generating income for potters was morally good, can only be morally judged if you look at the wider impacts on the whole community and different groups within it.

(Crewe and Harrison 1998: 125–8)

---

if you conceptualise reciprocity within the context of 'total social phenomena' ([1923] 1990: 1). Gifts, and all economic transactions, are anchored in their social and moral context; in many cultures to give a gift of greater value implies your social superiority, while only in some is it acceptable to ask a relative for money, to ask about people's incomes, or to give cash (rather than presents) to your lover (Bloch and Parry 1989). Money derives its meaning from the many cultures and social relations found within the world of development whether localised (see Box 4.2) or globalised or both.

Anthropologists try to understand poverty and economic relations within the wider context of history and socio-politics (including culture, class, gendered relations and moral assumptions). However, these anthropological perspectives are rarely taken up in planning debates and policy-making processes. Social relations, economics and politics are still treated as separable rather than interlinked issues; when planning a project designers are supposed to consider the potential environmental, economic, social and political impacts separately rather than seeing economic and political relations as part of society and culture. They might include something about 'culture' – usually as a barrier to poverty reduction – in the context of a plan or as a set of beliefs to change but it is not the overarching context within which people are making sense of their world, as it is for anthropologists. Culture is either something out there – a set of customs and beliefs – or a type of creative activity that includes art, theatre, poetry, music and performance. Consider a statement by UNESCO: 'development is not synonymous with economic growth alone. It is a means to achieve a more satisfactory intellectual, emotional, moral and spiritual existence. As such, development is inseparable from culture.'[7] But anthropologists will point out that that culture is something that people *do,* not something that they *have* – it is a process not an object. That process entails making sense of the world and shaping our relationships with each other. This point has yet to permeate into development discourse.

Anthropologists are yet to convince development planners of the relevance of reflexivity. When theorising about poverty, our own cultural constructs – derived from our experience and moral assumptions about money, 'the poor', and social change – influence our own thinking, whether we are planners or anthropologists. Certain assumptions about poverty have permeated across development bureaucracies and these are socially constructed. Space is needed for other conceptualisations of poverty, wealth and the future. As Appadurai suggests (2004), people's ideas about the future are culturally embedded and not just the simple products of material circumstances. This challenges the notion that the study of culture can only be concerned with looking back to 'traditional' forms. Anthropologists are interested in culture, but culture is about the future and the present as much as about the ways in which we are bound up in the past. Appadurai questions economists' prominence in Development World by pointing out that economy and culture are not opposed in people's lives. Thus, both your economic experiences of life, and the meaning you attach to them and to your future, are culturally produced and nurtured. The relatively rich and powerful have a more fully developed capacity to aspire, because they have more experience of the links between material goods, opportunities and options, so a new logic for development might be to develop poor people's capacity to aspire as well as tackling the adverse politics that makes it so hard for them to realise their aspirations.

Anthropologists point out that development decision-makers need to consider not only poverty in relation to individuals or selected groups, but socio-economic relations through time and place. On the one hand, anthropologists stress contextuality – simple universal explanations of poverty are bound to fail. Decision-makers need to examine how poverty is experienced in specific contexts, specific situations and specific relations (Hagberg 2001: 107). On the other hand, others argue that socio-political patterns can be found on a highly analytical level. A better understanding is needed of broader processes of accumulation, dispossession and exploitation in relation to gender, class and age and how to respond to them. Honesty about how views on poverty are culturally embedded would be useful. And decision-makers need to address questions about how development can root itself in more diverse understandings – by constituency groups in localised sites as well as development workers – about the relationship between wellbeing and poverty.

But an interest in wellbeing should not entail a neglect of people's material poverty; furthermore, there is the danger of co-option of ideas of wellbeing by those uninterested in structural poverty and focused on individualism (White 2010: 166–7). The promotion of wellbeing could become a project not to change the world – with all its inequities – but merely to change how you feel about it (*ibid.*: 167). However people feel about it, it is social relationships of exploitation and stigmatisation that cause poverty and it is relationships that need to be challenged. To do so naively can cause more harm than good. For example, it has become fashionable to promote social 'capital', in the sense of strengthening the connection between poor people and others in their social world – kin, neighbours, employers or other networks. But aid and development workers can be naive about the nature of the connections. The reality is that social networks tend to be characterised by inequality and exploitation. To be poor, as Mosse points out, is not to lack social contacts or networks but to engage with them in adverse ways because you owe your patron money, or are exploited by richer landowners, or are a women who can only be married off with a dowry (2007). Poverty is both an individual and a social experience, a form of structural violence embedded in culture. Thus, as Bourdieu claims, it is symbolic violence against people that constrains them into acting against their real interests (1977). Ignore any of these elements and it is all too easy to perpetuate the status quo, while nevertheless wishing to change it.

We have considered how aid professionals conceptualise, measure and try to reduce poverty. Their assumptions about poverty reveal much about how 'the poor' are seen: as deficient, individual, homogeneous but often female or young. Green elaborates: 'Marginal, excluded, vulnerable, unwell, illiterate and often indigenous and female, the poor predominantly live in remote rural areas and urban shanties, with few assets and weak social networks', while much less is said about the rich and how they create or maintain their wealth (2006: 1111, 1113). The images of the poor are charged with moral judgement. For the most marginal, their only asset is their bodies and it is their sales of themselves in prostitution, bondage, slavery and the sale of human organs that attract particular disrespect (*ibid.*: 1124). Thus, Green points to the value in reflecting not just on how poverty is viewed and reproduced but what labels are given to those in the category of 'poor'. 'Poor' is not the only way in which people are labelled in the world of development – although it may be the most widely used label. But before we consider other labels, based on rights in Chapter 5 and knowledge in Chapter 6, it is worth explaining what is entailed in the cultural process of labelling and classifying people's identity.

The politics of identity and politics in identity

The core assumption of anthropological accounts of identity is that while the lived-experience of identity is held to be natural or self-evident, in reality the classification of people is inevitably socially or culturally constructed. Every social group classifies and categorises people in different ways with moral and political consequences and the institutional cultures of development bureau-cracies are no exception. Development bureaucracies work to classify people and order the sets of relationships that link them together. Through acts of label-ling and ordering, sameness and difference are bestowed onto categories that are loaded with moral and political content.

Aid and development agencies often organise and describe their work as if catching the essence of people's identity is easy. And as the aid industry becomes more bureaucratised and interconnected these classifications become more overlapping, pervasive and influential. Beneficiary categories are subjected to essentialist and negative treatment: poor, disadvantaged, excluded, marginal-ised, children, the disabled and vulnerable. The pressure to define and count beneficiaries and to stress their terrible singular circumstances is exerted by almost all donors and grant-makers. The more bureaucratised they are, the more they are inclined to be impressed by the prevailing rhetorical classification and language.

Essentialist identity labels are not just negative in Development World; often they defy people's experience. In everyday life people's identities are multiple and changing: every individual has various markers of identity and they change as their circumstances shift (e.g. they change occupation or get divorced) and as they age. Social development academics and practitioners tend to hone in on gen-der, age, race, sexuality, religion, nationality, class, (dis)ability, occupation, mari-tal status, health, and so on. Although often presented as a list, they are far from identical: some have a basis in the cultural construction of physical biological difference (e.g. sexual attraction, race, being ill), while others are socio-political (class, religion, ethnicity). Furthermore, everyone has more than one identity and both individual and groups identities intersect. As Gedalof points out 'women's identities are constituted as much by race, nations and other categories of iden-tity as they are by sex or gender, and ... both symbolically and strategically, the "active management" of Woman/women seems, in turn, to play a key role in determining the "truths" around which these identities are constructed' (1999: 200). To give an example from Colombia, gender, class and race are mutually constituted by residents of Santa Ana. If you break with behaviour appropriate to your gender – for example by sharing alcohol or dancing as a woman or failing to provide for your family as a man – then you are considered to be like a 'black' and lower-class person. Older residents refer to the rich as 'blancos' and the poor as 'negros'. Thus, in everyday life race is embedded in both class and gender dis-course (Streicker 1995: 54, 57–8, 67).

As we have seen in relation to poverty, acts of categorisation are commonly used to define project beneficiaries, often using markers such as gender, class, caste, residence, indigeneity or ethnicity. Identity categories are created, such as 'below the poverty line', 'scheduled tribe', 'dam oustee', 'forest dweller', 'dalit', 'other backwards caste', 'orphans and vulnerable children', 'people living with AIDS', 'street children', 'pastoralists', and so on, each of which relates to an apparently appropriate official response. These classificatory systems, and the assumptions underlying them, place people within multiple, explicit and implicit hierarchies. Through the constructed categories and moral hierarchies that circulate around the world of development, and the exercise of power at all levels of society, relationships are created or reproduced in complex ways. Buying into these reductive categories and definitions runs the risk of manipulation by the state or other bodies; for example, in India the campaigns for social justice by dalits and other low caste or tribal groups have, according to opponents, been reduced into a narrow discourse of job reservations for the 'creamy layer' of a privileged few.

A recent report by DFID's Research and Evidence Division claims that public participation is constrained by 'dominant power relations' and elite capture but then reduces this to 'embedded cultural inequalities and styles of debate' when making recommendations (2010: 57). The proposals for supporting women's participation include building confidence, creating linkages and addressing barriers. Within these barriers they make no mention of gendered inequalities, violence and injustice but suggest 'working with men on their restrictive attitudes and behaviours ... to understand why it is good that women are taking part in these spaces' (*ibid.*: 63). This example of a donor falling back on depoliticised approaches to identity politics is familiar.

Even the representation of subordinated groups in formal political systems tends to have the power dimensions subdued within aid and development initiatives. UNDP assumes that women will only lift themselves and their children out of poverty if they are adequately represented. Self-representation of the poor, including women, is assumed to be necessary to advance their interests. The third of the Millennium Development Goals aims for gender equality and the empowerment of women. One of the three key measures of the extent to which this ambition is realised (along with access to education and share of wage employment outside of agriculture) is an increase in the number of seats held in parliament by women. But it is one of the poorest performing indicators with women parliamentarians in single or lower chambers at less than 20 per cent in January 2011. This numerical approach to women's representation (or girls' education for that matter) is superficial. Even where women are well represented in parliament the assumption that policy outcomes will favour women is not borne out in practice. It is widely assumed that to promote their gendered interests women parliamentarians require a critical mass of at least 30 per cent in parliament. However, when you consider specific cases, this numerical approach might be questioned. In the Rwandan parliament women have held over 48 per cent of the seats since 2003 (and over 56 per cent since 2008). Many deputies describe themselves as promoting feminism but it remains difficult to make space for gender issues and the impact on policy has not led to greater gender equality (Devlin and Elgie 2008). A more convincing line of enquiry would be to consider gendered relations within parliament, including the diverse interests of women as well as men's resistance to change and links with wider society. In general, gendered power hierarchies mean that women parliamentarians do not get the necessary support from political parties, the media or the public and, linked to this, male-dominated structures remains unchallenged. These are usually related in varying ways to the specific histories and hierarchies that interest anthropologists and that have to be understood when exploring specific locations. For example, in Afghanistan women were constrained in representing their gendered interests by locally specific processes such as a hostility towards quotas, a powerful politics of ethnicity that overrule ideas of gender equality, systems of patronage and corruption, and unhelpful international assistance (Wordsworth 2007). The creation of women-only spaces, for example, meant that women were less present in general spaces, such as the library, and gender-training workshops were seen as being only for women. In the words of one woman Afghan MP, 'international organisations do not know how to build the capacity of MPs. Sometimes they have experience of their own mature democracies and this does not match with our system, and so their advice is like a book, it is not reality, we cannot use it' (*ibid.*: 37).

Definitions of poverty are driven by the needs, wishes, interests and capabilities of developers; the perspectives of those that are categorised as poor are overlooked. This is a reminder that it is both easy and dangerous for aid and development workers to make assumptions, rather than reach understandings through in-depth dialogue and interpretation, about the realities of others. The policies and practices of poverty reduction continue to be based on ways of categorising, governing and reorganising people as if they were things with no complex, conflicting and localised thoughts of their own. Not much has changed since Adrian Adams wrote angrily in 1979 that in the name of 'development' expatriate experts behave as if poor people do not really exist except in their imagination (1979: 474).

Challenging questions arising from this chapter

Who are the 'poor'?
Who defines poverty and how?
How has the status of 'poverty reduction' as a goal changed since the 1970s and why?
What are the different understandings of poverty and approaches to poverty reduction?
What are the anthropological critiques of neoliberal, neo-Marxist, feminist and populist theories of poverty?
What is a relational understanding of poverty?
What are the relationships between economic poverty and power at different levels?
Are there different kinds of poverty or just one?
Is poverty an ethnocentric idea?

5   Human rights and cultural fantasies

Key points covered by this chapter

- Universal Human Rights have become an influential organising principle for government, development and aid.
- Within development agencies certain aspects of identity are accorded priority. These aspects of identity are recognised in certain ways and take on particular forms within a framework of human rights.
- Anthropologists have problematised the idea of universal rights through listening to the diversity of perspectives, and dynamism of life experiences, of various rights-holders.
- Through an examination of child rights theory and practice, we show how assumptions underlying rights can ignore context, specificity and dissent.
- Child protection projects provide a case study of the limits to rights frameworks, including their bias towards individuals rather than groups.
- The way that communities are constructed, by development agencies but also by communities themselves, reveals that they and their rights are cultural and contestable, rather than natural and beyond dispute.

In the mid 1990s the international donor community realigned their policies to place a new emphasis on the promotion of globalised human rights. No longer were human rights an *indicator* of a certain level of development; now rights were seen as a *device* that could be used to actively promote development. The interlinking of human rights with development and poverty reduction aims has now been adopted by multilateral agencies, such as the UNDP (1998), and bilateral agencies, including SIDA (2001) and DFID (2000). USAID includes the advancement of human rights and freedom as the first bullet point in its vision.[1] At the UN 2005 World Summit, member states made a commitment to integrate the promotion and protection of human rights into national policies. Even the World Bank, having initially sheltered behind the 'non-political' clause of its articles of agreement, has recently moved to include guarantees of civil and political rights within its poverty reduction strategies. National and local-level non-governmental and civil society organisations have been mobilised to advance claims to particular rights. The practical impact of this new fashion has been a repositioning of goals away from 'welfare and wellbeing' and towards 'rights and responsibilities'. Development is no longer to be seen as a gift to be given; it is a right that must be claimed.

Much of this new discourse on rights in development has centred on the relationship between citizens and states. Political liberties are viewed as a necessity for the achievement of sustainable development. A central idea is the post-Cold War emphasis on good governance, civil society and popular participation. It can be understood as part of the global drive to increase transparency, support democracy and civil liberties, and build 'liberal' states (Grugel and Piper 2009: 82–3). Rights entitle citizens to make demands on their governments and to hold them to account. As such the human rights agenda holds the potential to empower poor people to take decisions about their own lives. Different dimensions of rights – civil, cultural, economic, social and political rights – are viewed as mutually supportive. Rights to education, healthcare and to an adequate livelihood cannot be accessed if the poor cannot make their voices heard. In turn, democracy, transparency and good governance promote the improved provision of healthcare and education.

But is the relationship between human rights and development as simple as it is sometimes presented by rights activists? The gaps between international and national human rights legislation and its realisation in practice remain huge. In this chapter we consider how rights-based agendas have been enacted in diverse localities. Our argument moves from a theoretical consideration of the universal values of human rights to the examination of how these ideals are translated into official policy and the ways in which they are shaped and reformulated within development encounters. The view from anthropology encourages us to question the assumptions in human-rights frameworks. Anthropology's tradition of cultural relativism has long problematised the universal applicability of shared human rights partly because universal declarations of rights do not derive from a common consensus but are the product of particular sets of cultural influences. We will consider how and why forms of identity are conceptualised in development bureaucracies. We recognise supposedly 'natural' principles of abstract human behaviour as being culturally produced and are able to examine how commitments to such 'ideals' are creatively shaped according to local contexts and forms. Ideas of identity and rights are caught up in the dialectical relationships that exist between states, non-governmental development organisations and the wider society. A detailed examination of the United Nations Convention on the Rights of the Child (UNCRC) shows the difficulties, compromises and varied and unexpected outcomes that have resulted from well-intentioned legislation. The chapter concludes by considering the creative attempts of the particular communities to make claims on land and development rights through claims to 'indigeneity'.

The universality of human rights

The framework of international law upon which human rights rests was constructed in the aftermath of the Second World War. Representing 'the collective will of the international community' the Universal Declaration of Human Rights was adopted by the United Nations General Assembly in December 1948. Civil and political rights are at the centre of the UDHR but also included are a range of economic, social and cultural rights (see Box 5.1). All of these rights are said to share the characteristics of indivisibility and universality. *Indivisibility* means that the violation of one right will affect other rights (e.g. denial of access to education affects political participation). In other words there is no contradiction between the different rights and their application will be of benefit to all. *Universality* suggests that the basic rights enshrined in the declaration are a natural product – they represent a cornerstone of human existence, moral absolutes that stand unaltered across time or place. With all signatories committed to this set of legally binding international standards, the principles of the UDHR were intended to provide the basis for establishing rights at the national level.

The Universal Declaration is built on the principle that 'all human rights are for all people'. But anthropology's emphasis on cultural variety, dynamism and historical and social contexts means that the notion of 'universal rights' or 'shared values' is problematic for many within the discipline. As Richard Wilson (1996) points out, the 'universalist' position uncritically accepts the notion of a stable, unified and knowable conception of human essence. This contrasts with the anthropological notion that existence itself is culturally constructed as are ideas of the relationship between an individual and the wider society. The notion that there is a core set of shared human values is hard to sustain when you consider, as anthropologists tend to, the wide variety of human social experience. The diversity of global experience reflects a lack of agreement on the concepts and institutions that shape ideas of justice (see Box 5.2); cultural relativism – not judging a culture by the standards of another – recognises rights and entitlements as the products of particular sets of historical and social contexts.

International agreements on rights that are neither natural nor based in fact result from global inequalities that allow for the beliefs and concerns of certain nations and cultures to be prioritised over others. The basis of much human-rights discourse derives from the liberal enlightenment tradition and, in particular, from a distinctive concern with the freedom of the individual. But such a view overlooks alternative views of rights and justice. And the focus on atomised individuals ignores understandings of rights as invested in the group. Locating the construction of ideas of morality firmly within the collective, anthropology denies the possibility of rights as universal concerns identified solely upon the individual.

Anthropology has proved effective in highlighting the ethnocentric bias of the UDHR. But this is not to dismiss the idea – or importance – of human rights altogether. Rather the UDHR should be seen as the product of a particular culture and time; but these ideas have been transformed and adapted as they are applied in new social and historical settings. Making a commitment to the broad ideals contained within the document, signatories were expected to ratify the convention in ways appropriate to their own national situation. While the UDHR

Box 5.1. The collective will of the international community

Proclaimed as 'a common standard of achievement for all peoples and all nations', the *Universal Declaration of Human Rights* was adopted by the UN General Assembly in December 1948. Declaring that 'all human beings are born free and equal in dignity' it asserts that 'everyone is entitled to all the rights and freedoms set forth in this Declaration, without distinction of any kind, such as race, colour, sex, language, religion, political or other opinion, national or social origin, property, birth or other status'.

The rights in the Declaration extend to thirty articles. Civil and political rights guarantee to individuals the following freedoms:

- the right to security, recognition as a person before the law, nationality, and a fair trial or hearing before a tribunal;
- the right to freedom from discrimination, slavery and servitude, arbitrary arrest, detention or exile;
- the right to freedom of movement;
- the right to peaceful assembly and association and to take part in government, directly or through freely chosen representatives;
- the right to freedom of religion, opinion, speech and expression.

Economic rights are also recognised:

- the right to own property alone as well as in association with others;
- the right to a standard of living adequate for health and wellbeing including food, clothing, housing, medical care and social services;
- the right to form and join trade unions;
- the right to work, equal pay and to just and favourable conditions of work as well as to leisure;
- the right to social protection in times of need, especially for mothers and children.

Others are cultural:

- the right to marry and to found a family;
- the right to privacy, honour, freedom of thought, conscience and religion;
- the right to education that develops personality and promotes tolerance;
- the right to freely participate in the cultural life of the community, to enjoy the arts and to share in scientific advancement and its benefits;
- the right to the protection of the moral and material interests resulting from any scientific, literary or artistic production of which he is the author.

The Universal Declaration was followed by nine major conventions that set out in more detail what these rights mean (with some having optional protocols dealing with specific concerns):

International Convention on the Elimination of All Forms of Racial Discrimination (1965)

International Covenant on Civil and Political Rights (1966)

International Covenant on Economic, Social and Cultural Rights (1966)

Convention on the Elimination of all Forms of Discrimination against Women (1979)

Convention Against Torture and Other Cruel, Inhuman or Degrading Treatment or Punishment (1984)

Convention on the Rights of the Child (1989)

International Convention on the Protection of the Rights of All Migrant Workers and Members of Their Families (1990)

International Convention for the Protection of All Persons from Enforced Disappearance (2006)

Convention on the Rights of Persons with Disabilities (2006).

For details about international law generally, see the Office of the High Commissioner for Human Rights, www.ohchr.org, and for the international treaties, optional protocols and treaty bodies responsible for monitoring them, see www2.ohchr.org/english/law/index.htm.

centres around the relationship between states and their citizens in terms of civil and political rights, more recent international agreements have widened this basis to encompass economic and social aspects and extended their attention to non-state actors. The very existence of new conventions and treaties subsequent to the UDHR further highlights the flexibility of the human rights agenda over time. Nor should it be assumed that different actors in the development field will understand or operationalise rights identically. As Cornwall and Nyamu-Musembi (2004) suggest, significant differences exist in the ways development organisations have come to approach the integration of human rights into their operations. While some conform to the narrow civil and political rights intended to reform the state and promote good governance, others take a wider view that includes social and cultural rights and recognises the importance of ensuring that rights are appropriate to different social settings.

Of course the proclamation of a right does not necessarily lead to it being fulfilled. Rights legislation may be passed but the benefits are left unclaimed because services do not exist, because of a lack of awareness, because the cost of accessing them is too great for those living in poverty, or because social discrimination makes such claims impossible. Despite the centrality of the rhetoric of poverty reduction, within which social protection for poorer groups became mainstream during the early 2000s, chronic poverty and inequality persist. Social protection has involved cash transfers, pensions, minimum wages, school feeding, the establishment of social services, or social empowerment – depending on the approach. But partly due to the severe limits placed on public spending by aid donors, the impact of social protection programmes has been minimal. Furthermore, on their own they

---

Box 5.2. The right to marry and found a family

Article 16 of the UDHR enshrines in international law the right of the individual to marry and to found a family.

UDHR Article 16. (1) Men and women of full age, without any limitation due to race, nationality or religion, have the right to marry and to found a family. They are entitled to equal rights as to marriage, during marriage and at its dissolution. (2) Marriage shall be entered into only with the free and full consent of the intending spouses. (3) The family is the natural and fundamental group unit of society and is entitled to protection by society and the state.

But this definition is based on a limited and arguably an out-dated and ethnocentric understanding of concepts such as 'marriage' and 'family'. There is an implication that 'family' is created by the marriage of two adults who then have children, whereas in many cultures family consists of a larger group (for example, of related adults, their parents, spouses and children) or a smaller one with single parents and their children or unrelated, sometimes homosexual/lesbian, adults with or without children. In child-headed households you will find no adults.

So the membership of *family* is hard to define but even the possibility of a meaningful universal definition of *marriage* has been questioned by anthropologists. It is traditionally assumed to be the union of a man and woman that legitimises the status of their children. But the Nuer of Sudan allow women to act as husbands in some circumstances, children have rights (e.g. to support from their father) even when their parents are unmarried, and same-sex marriage is now legal in some countries. Both polygamy (when a man marries more than one woman) and polyandry (where a woman has more than one husband) continue to confuse the idea of marriage containing two adults. It is legal for children under 16 years old to marry in some countries so it is not even confined to adults. Marriage is clearly about economics, sex, children and domestic living but so are civil partnerships. Neither requires all of these and there is no one essential ingredient.

Some have questioned the implication that family is natural or should be protected. Feminists have described it as the site of women's subordination, fraught with violence and inequalities, while Leach saw it as 'far from being the basis of the good society, the family, with its narrow privacy and tawdry secrets, is the source of all our discontents' (1967: 44).

So what appeared to be a straightforward Article in the Declaration of Human Rights, becomes difficult to implement when you consider the diversity of people's kinship, family and marriage in different cultures and law regimes.

---

could not address structural inequalities. As Tania Li puts its, 'across Asia, from the viewpoint of urban elites, the dispossessed are out of sight and out of mind, and the elite has recourse to discursive practices that operate at scales from the household to the nation and beyond to make abandonment seem necessary, and acceptable.'[2] Societal interests, norms and values within households and communities may block or alter the realisation of human rights agendas just as effectively as a lack of governmental capacity or will. Human rights should not be understood as simple universal ideals; if people are to be empowered through ideas of rights it is important that the wider contexts in which they exist is fully understood. And the ideals themselves will not bring about a decent life for all.

Charges of 'cultural imperialism' overlook the extent to which, in Wilson's words, 'human rights doctrine has been adopted by many people to whom it was once foreign' (1996: 9). The recognition that key terms and definitions of international law are not necessarily reflected across the diverse cultures of the world, including within the category of 'western', has not prevented individuals and communities from actively engaging with these legal provisions to secure forms of advantage. We argue that, while often couched in terms of universal applicability, human-rights commitments are merely the starting points for lengthy and often unresolved processes of negotiation between governments, development organisations and the wider society.

Anthropology has shown the relevance of its approach with respect to human rights through its ability to trace the manner in which vague ideals and abstract principles are materialised as they are put into practice. Taking account of diverse historical and social contexts, anthropology is well placed to examine how legal processes and institutions affect people in their everyday lives. As part of this process objective human rights develop a subjective social life as they are infused with varied meanings and serve different purposes according to the situation in which they are introduced. Contrary to the arguments made, respectively, by the universalist or cultural relativist camps, it is necessary to recognise that ideas of morality vary both *between* and *within* cultures. Political choices are central to decisions on how rights should be used. Quoting from Wilson again: 'If human rights reports strip events free of actor's consciousnesses and social contexts, then part of anthropologists' brief is to restore the richness of subjectivities, and chart the complex fields of social relations, contradictory values and the emotional accompaniment to macro-structures that human rights accounts often exclude' (1996: 15).

In the remainder of this chapter our attention turns to anthropological examinations of how cultural ideas as well as social groupings have been created, transformed and translated through contact with the new wave of rights-based development policy.

Rights and childhood

Certain categories of rights-holders are recognised as being in greater need of protection. But what is it that gives these particular categories their significance? The numerical size of their membership? The degree of discrimination against them? The extent to which they need help in the eyes of others? Answers vary according to context but it is clear that within development certain markers are privileged above others. Policy statements by donors or NGOs often reveal the prominence given to certain groups, for instance by emphasising the importance of focusing on women or, more broadly, 'on the rights of women, children and disabled people'.[3] Diversity may be acknowledged; for example by paying attention to the ways in which gender differences take on different meanings as they are cross-cut by class, race, caste, ethnicity, age, marital status or family position. Doing so allows for policies, programs and projects to address the differences in experiences, interests, needs, roles, resources and situations. But on the whole the nature of reinforcement is rarely explained and the other markers play supporting roles only at best.

One consequence of processes through which certain forms of identity are prioritised is the emergence of shallow understandings of lived experience and essentialised notions of needs. And while some categories receive undue prominence, others are marginalised. In the public statements by agencies, class (as relations between groups rather than just measurements of poverty) is rarely explored and little mention is made of sexuality or racism. For reasons already examined individual rights usually receive greater attention than the more complicated and politically loaded notions of communal rights. Holding simplistic visions of a limited range of possible beneficiaries, promoters of universal rights struggle to cope with the diversity and complexity of social reality.

We will examine this struggle in relation to a category that receives substantial attention from aid agencies, but far less from development studies scholars and all but a small group of anthropologists: children. We do so by looking at cultural constructions of childhood, how they have influenced the United Nations Convention on the Rights of the Child, and what happens to children's rights in practice in diverse contexts.

The United Nation's Convention on the Rights of the Child (UNCRC, 1989) is the most widely signed treaty in the world. According to many, it is also the most poorly implemented (see UNICEF 2009). As we have seen, many anthropologists question the validity, or at least usefulness, of universal frameworks. The first question that would strike most anthropologists exploring the value of the UNCRC would be the following: What are the assumptions about people that underpin this treaty? UNICEF introduces it as follows:

> The Convention sets out these rights in 54 articles and two Optional Protocols.
> It spells out the basic human rights that children everywhere have: the right
> to survival; to develop to the fullest; to protection from harmful influences,
> abuse and exploitation; and to participate fully in family, cultural and social
> life. The four core principles of the Convention are non-discrimination;
> devotion to the best interests of the child; the right to life, survival and devel-
> opment; and respect for the views of the child. Every right spelled out in the
> Convention is inherent to the human dignity and harmonious development of

every child. The Convention protects children's rights by setting standards in healthcare; education; and legal, civil and social services.[4]

Critics charge the UNCRC with simplifying and misrepresenting the lived reality of children's lives. Even the idea that 'children' or 'youth' can be easily defined in terms of age is problematic. The Convention states that people are children up to the age of 18 but ideas about when childhood stops are culturally constructed and vary greatly across and within locations. In some places, age identity is linked to status – for example, whether or not you are married or have had children – while in others to biological age, with some believing people remain children until they are variously 16, 21 or 30 years old. Within many cultures, you only become an adult after undergoing rites of initiation. A treaty that sets out the rights of such a diverse group, including babies, schoolchildren, soldiers, parents and full-time workers, is ambitious to say the least. The implication is that 0 to 18-year-old people share enough in common to make it a meaningful group in terms of planning and intervention. But the capability and life experiences of a 16-year-old and an adult will usually have more in common than a 3-year-old and a 16-year-old, especially if the 16-year-old is married or even a household head.

Generalisations are made in the UNCRC, despite the diversity of ideas about childhood, about how children should behave and what adults should do to protect them, across cultures and nations. The Convention rests on the idea that childhood is supposed to be 'carefree, safe, secure and happy' and should not be polluted with experiences associated with adulthood, such as work, sex, fighting wars or travelling alone (Boyden 1997). But to what extent are such notions merely western cultural fantasies? In his history of childhood, Philippe Aries (1962) shows the commonly accepted universal idea of childhood to be a relatively recent European creation. Though strong attachments exist to nurture and protect the young across all cultures, the meaning and form such notions take vary partly owing to variations in economic and socio-political environments, and partly because ideas about childhood and adulthood are culturally constructed, and transmitted and reformed across generations. The distinction between adult and child and the socialisation of children are both gendered. As Nancy Chodorow (1999) has shown, in some contexts, girls' childhoods are shorter than boys', because their economic contribution begins far earlier and girls often have to be socially responsible, and are expected to marry and become parents themselves, earlier than boys. It is not just the learning of roles that is gendered, but also the learning of morality and value systems. In Vietnam, for example, honour and reputation are embodied in boys because they are thought to be born with it, whereas girls have to learn the appropriate feelings, such as self-denial and helping others in order to embody honour (Rydstrom 2001).

Clearly, the ways in which children are thought about and treated varies within and across cultures. But we should also note that children are not passive receivers of culture – 'empty bottles' into which culture is poured (Montgomery 2005:

Box 5.3. Child soldiers as social and political actors

The idea of children as soldiers tends to fill development professionals with moral panic. However, Finnstrom's research with young rebels in Uganda illustrates that when you talk to children or young people themselves about their experiences assumptions get turned upside down (2006). Child soldiers were neither simple victims nor wild and out-of-control deviants; they were navigating youth and childhood and trying to engage in politics.

The Ugandan government, INGOs and the media could only see children being abducted by rebels – this reaction completely overshadowed the politics that arise from the north and east of the country being only peripherally included in the nation. In the northern region 63 per cent of the population is below the poverty line, compared to a national average of 38 per cent, so its young people feel disconnected from their country's development and let down by their elders. The media – including the BBC and CNN – reported that the rebels were driven by Christianity and the biblical Ten Commandments; those coordinating the reintegration of child combatants also failed to appreciate the politics. But when you listen to those involved they differentiate between two dimensions – the spiritual and the political, moving between these elements and separating the brutal violence from their hopeful aspirations so that they can deal with the apparent contradictions.

Others have also pointed out that children are portrayed as passive innocents forced into conflicts, whereas in fact they are responding to growing up in a war zone where they see no positive place for themselves in society (Wessels 2006: 3). Violence can be a way to challenge and try to replace the existing political order and fight for social justice in their minds. Or children sometimes join or stay with a militant group because they are like a family or because they feel a sense of power and respect or because they conclude that it is the best way to survive. Furthermore the idea that child soldiers are automatically worse off than any other children in a war zone is refuted. They sometimes have better access to food and protection and some, including girls, have even expressed their experience as soldiers as being liberating and empowering (Rosen 2007).

This is not to say that children's involvement in war is anything but horrible – these writers are not romanticising – but anthropologists have pointed out that even children in extremely dangerous situations have views, take decisions, make sense of the many contexts they inhabit and exercise agency.

475). Ethnographic research has shown that they are active participants in social interactions, making meaning and modifying norms and practices. Children are shaped by culture but, in turn, cultures are partly changed by children. For example in fighting against Apartheid in South Africa, they engaged in social movements and, at the same time, were being active agents in their own socialisation (Honwara and de Boeck 2005). Or as soldiers children can be navigating danger and politics in ways that should not be simply reduced to victimhood (see Box 5.3).

Inevitably some of the assumptions of the UNCRC fail to take account of diversity while others duck controversial debates about relationships within the family and children's agency. Rights frameworks cannot be applied in the same way in different countries. Since the UNCRC is based on a largely western 'protective view of childhood', rigid adherence to rights frameworks arguably infantilises the South (Pupavac as quoted by Bentley 2005: 117). So what happens when the UNCRC, or related rights frameworks, are used in interventions? In the next section we will explore some of the difficulties of using universal frameworks by looking at how international civil society organisations have responded to children's rights to protection.

Protection for children at work

Article 32 of the CRC states that children should not engage in work that is harmful. Similar assumptions about benign and harmful work have a history of several decades and have led to a determination to eradicate child labour outside the home through prohibition. In 1992, two policy regimes started to have an influence – the International Labour Organisation's (ILO) International Program for the Elimination of Child Labour and the US Child Labour Deterrence Act that banned products made by child labourers. During the 1990s development agencies, and activists in the global North and South, took up the challenge of eradicating child labour with mixed results. In some cases prohibition of children from factories has led them to resorting to more abusive forms of labour. The Bangladesh Garment Manufacturers and Exporters Association released 40,000 children from employment at a single time. However, after being forced to leave factories without alternatives many then had to resort to working on the streets, rag picking and prostitution (Rahman, Khanam and Absar 1999). In other cases it was small producers who suffered. In Nepal O'Neill writes about how the Nepalese carpet industry has declined as a result of anti-child labour rhetoric (2003). The larger exporters removed children from their factories but the informal factories still employed children, often in a system of debt bondage and extremely low wages. An NGO called Rugmark responded to the problems caused by abruptly forcing children to leave factories and set about returning them to their families. But to set the numbers in some proportion, they brought about 243 family reunions out of a total of 407 children under their care. They did not reach the hundreds of thousands of other carpet weavers or the estimated 2 million children working (mostly) in agriculture. Rugmark also introduced a system of labelling, with the result that carpets with no label – which tended to be produced by smaller producers – were devalued and so their sustainability was diminished. Many small enterprises closed. Child protection action, in this instance, stopped child labour but harmed an industry and arguably, increased poverty. Furthermore, when the children themselves were asked, many expressed a preference for working in carpet factories above household work (Johnson *et al.* 1995). Other have had more success at getting children out of labour – even its most abusive forms – by adopting an intensive approach that focuses on the longer term.

Currently NGOs working in Africa, Asia and South America are ranged along an ideological continuum with those at one end insisting that immediate eradication is imperative, while those at the other end arguing it is a long way off and we should respond to children's demands by improving conditions.

Anthropologists have suggested that a much subtler analysis is needed of children's work and labour – one that requires an examination of each context. Nieuwenhuys points out that stopping child labour in societies has become a measurement of modernity (1996); modern societies do not, apparently, have child labour. This implies that apparently 'modern' societies, such as those found in Europe, abolished child labour as a result of moral outrage and concern for children's welfare. It is the case that industrialisation led to an increase in the exploitation of children's labour and that in the nineteenth century there was an outcry against it. But some have argued that eradication was not due to moral panic but rather to enable the greater mechanisation of industry, protect society from the potential political instability of a very young working class, and ensure compulsory education (Boyden 1997). This was the best way to ensure that the future workers were trained and shaped in ways that would ensure their compliance.

The ways in which different kinds of work are evaluated point to further contradictions in attitudes to child labour. State legislation initially in Europe and the USA, and then internationally through the policies of the ILO, has tended to define child labour as *waged* work only. On the other hand, *unpaid* work is largely ignored or viewed as morally acceptable and useful for learning skills. The idea was that waged labour for strangers was exploitative whereas what happens within households is benign and non-exploitative. Nieuwenhuys quotes an ILO report: 'We have no problem with the little girl who helps her mother with the housework or cooking, or the boy or girl who does unpaid work in a small family business ... The same is true of those odd jobs that children may occasionally take on to earn a little pocket money to buy something they really want' (1996: 239).

The ILO sets age limits for appropriate types of work. Fifteen years old is the minimum age for full-time work, 13 years is the minimum for light work and 18 years for hazardous work (including combat roles in the armed services). Such an approach ignores different cultural ideas about appropriate ages for different types of work and the strangeness of applying the same rules to children of the same age even in child-headed households or when some have dependents (whether children of their own or siblings to care for).

What is noticeable is how little attention is given by development agencies in all sectors to children's labour within households, whether within their own family or those of relatives or strangers, and in agriculture. And yet if we take the example of India, around 10 per cent of children living in poverty are formally employed, while the remaining work in agriculture, informal sector businesses and households. Girls, in particular, are trained to internalise the feminine ideals of devotion to the family (*ibid.*: 243) and the value of their work is treated as if it is even lower than boys. As long ago as the 1970s, Mamdani wrote about children's contribution to household economies (1972). Just as women's unpaid work plays a role in reproducing households, and can be seen as a form of exploitation, children's work does the same. Why is it less harmful because it is unrewarded? Whether children – and particularly girls – are collecting water and fuelwood, or doing agricultural work, why should the status of their work be seen as so different from women's, that is, exploitative if excessive (in children's case relative to their age) and as denying them other opportunities?

The emphasis of the UNCRC, and civil society initiatives focused on rights, is to eradicate *paid* child labour – whether slowly or abruptly – and to get children into school. The reality is that children often try to combine labour with school, and struggle because they are exhausted but also because they are stigmatised by their poverty and labour. They do not always want to stop working completely but they want respect and consideration of their circumstances. Even when governments or NGOs tried to address these problems, they tend to leave untouched the social systems that perpetuate children's exploitation in domestic and public domains and their assumed inferiority as social actors.

Protection for children on the move

A group of children that has received a disproportionate amount of attention are children without parental care (including street children, migrants and those working for others). The UNCRC gives parents, or legal guardians, primary responsibility for the care of their children (article 18). If deprived of their family, the state assumes responsibility. However, the reality for many children is that the ideals of the UNCRC are an elusive fantasy. The image of children migrating from rural areas to cities, especially in Asia and South America, and then living on the street has elicited emotive public concern, on the one hand, and fear of wild, untamed criminal youth in dangerous spaces, on the other. A large number of 'street children' agencies rose to the challenge in the late 1980s and 1990s. However, simplistic definitions of children who have migrated to 'the street' quickly unravel when closely examined. The 'street child' category gives the impression that all street children are in similar circumstances – as if they are all living on the street, homeless, ruptured from their family, isolated and migrant from somewhere else (Panter-Brick 2002). In fact this describes a tiny minority. Girls, boys and youth are present on the streets for all kinds of reasons and in many different ways; they are often still in touch with their relatives or they might be on the streets during the day to earn money and then sleep at home. UNICEF and others tried to distinguish between 'of the streets' and 'on the streets', the former meaning more permanently living on the streets, but children defy those categories by switching between the two. Children only talk about themselves as street children if they are seeking access to development projects and they have discovered that access depends on that category. As Hecht puts it, the street is the venue rather than saying anything about their character (quoted by Panter-Brick *ibid.*: 151).

Such categories give the impression that you are catching the essence of that person. Defining people simply as 'street children', 'farmers' or 'cooks' misses out everything else that they are – any of those might also be 'traders', 'child carers', 'healthcare users', 'orphans', and so on. They are labels that are useful for development agencies who want to meet targets in relation to specific issues rather than being meaningful for the children concerned. Referring to 'street children' also often obscures gendered differences between boys and girls away from home. Girls rarely live permanently on the streets, because of the perceived high risks of sexual abuse, but are more often employed as domestic workers and in sexual exploitation than boys. Finally 'street children' is viewed as a pejorative and demeaning label in most societies. Although negative labelling is useful for securing funding support, it can perpetuate the stigmatisation of particular groups, including 'street children'.

Rights for children within the framework of the UNCRC are centred around a belief that children have a right to and a need for the protection of a home and family. Implicit in this assumption is the idea that children are too young to look after themselves or to make decisions about their lives. However, against the idea of 'protective' and 'nurturing' family environments, we are faced with a reality in which families are sites of inequality and conflict. With stability, protection and education not guaranteed in the home, many children consciously choose to leave and may have very good reasons for doing so.

When designing interventions for runaways it is important to understand why they have been forced or chosen to leave. Development workers tend to attribute single causes to migration: poverty or family breakdown, AIDS or abuse. The pressure to pick the cause that is more fundable can be overwhelming. Agencies tend to privilege poverty for a donor that is interested in promoting sustainable livelihoods, abuse for those prioritising child protection and AIDS for those investing in orphans. But anthropological research points to multiple causes (even for individual children) and diversity across locations.

Accurate information about the diversity, fluidity and complexity of child migrants and children on the move is essential for those working out how to support them. Confirming the importance of in-depth investigations and holistic understanding, Conticini and Hulme report on why children migrate to the street in Bangladesh (2007). They point out that one-off surveys often do not get to the bottom of the matter – you have to build a relationship of trust with children to find out about the mix of circumstances that led them to leave. Their research points to the breakdown of social relationships rather than economic poverty, as the main cause of child migration. Similarly, Taylor found that child migration from rural Thailand to Bangkok was not driven in a simple way by poverty or lack of education (2005). It is not the poorest or least educated families that send their girls to Bangkok to earn money. In fact, birth order has a bigger role to play as families tend to have one child working with them in the fields with parents, one in education and one in Bangkok. Gender is also important – oldest daughters are usually expected to look after their younger siblings at home, while last-born children often migrate to work in sexual exploitation as one of the strategies of providing for families. Dorte Thorsen sheds further light on why straightforward causal lines cannot be drawn between children migrating and negative circumstances (2006). Children in rural Burkino Faso migrate to renegotiate their social position – migrating to town is associated with freedom and higher social status – not simply to run away from violence or because they were sent away by parents facing poverty.

Simplistic answers to questions about why children migrate essentialise complex processes, and ignore often-substantial differences between children. We may assume in the West that children get less and less dependent on adults as they get older, but that dependence (or even adulthood) can shift forwards and backwards depending on circumstances and obligations. Hashim reveals that as many as a quarter of seventy child migrants from one area of Ghana moved to gain access to education, while some of those who migrated to gain an income did so because they wanted to spend it on their education (2007). This challenges the idea that children migrating, especially into fostering situations, always disrupt their education. We are not saying that migration is a positive experience, but just that we should re-examine our assumptions about how and why children migrate. Rather than trying to stop migration, agencies might then make it less risky and work to improve child labourers' rights, working conditions and pay.

Some organisations take a more sophisticated approach to migration. For example, the Organization for Child Development and Transformation found links between child marriage, family breakdown, poverty and migration and is working on community-based advocacy to address the multiple causes (see Box 5.4). But it is far more common to find NGOs or governments focusing on singular causal links with less impact. All too often attempts to help children are based on flawed understandings of their histories, their needs and their agency. In an effort to meet the desires of their funders, those running orphanages, schools, clinics, and so on take too little account of children's perspectives.

Tobias Hecht writes about various schemes established to help street children in the Brazilian city of Recife (1998). He recognises three commonly occurring components to these schemes centred around ideas of outreach and informal education; vocational training; and moving children off the streets and into refuges. The central idea being promoted here is that children can be 'remade', that is, their childhoods are reclaimed by disassociating them from the street, drugs, sex and crime. The element of salvation from the hellish environment of the street with its death squads is clear, often in the hands of heroic figures. Hecht wrote, 'reduced to something to be cured, street children become objects in a distant debate among adults' (*ibid.*: 188). So, why are many development agencies so negative about children's experiences of migration and involvement in the street? They aim to work with children who are suffering. If undertaking research with

Box 5.4. Using anthropology to understand street children by Girmachew Adugna

An anthropological perspective has helped me to gain a deeper understanding about children's everyday lives, while carrying out research to assess the causes and patterns of children's migration to the city and when I worked as a development practitioner in a child-focused organisation in Ethiopia.

To begin with, anthropology helped me to understand the seemingly distinct but fluid categories of street children, the interrelated and multiple causes of child migration, the role and nature of social networks in (re)structuring migration and survival strategies, the multiple and changing identities, reciprocity, power relations and hierarchies among street children and other social actors, and most importantly, linking children's migration and street work to the situation of rural households which are located in hundreds of kilometres away from the city. The latter can be seen in terms of remittances, livelihood diversification and children's education and family welfare. Moreover, it helped me to see the notion of childhood beyond the western perspective and the conventional depiction of the 'lost childhood' of marginalised children. The available research and most development actors operating in Ethiopia provide narrow definitions and often victimise working and street children. This understanding is often drawn from shallow quantitative summaries that fail to take into account the children's own experiences and perspectives. This mainstream approach overlooks and obscures children's resilience and agency, which has a significant implication for development policy and practice.

Taking anthropological perspectives means a focus on children's agency. You gain a better understanding of what resources children have, how they pool these resources and how they diversify activities to survive and reduce risks. You learn how children construct and reconstruct the cultural value of mainstream society and produce or reproduce it in their street-based activities. Moreover, it helps to gain insight into how children interact with different social actors, institutions and networks (the police, churches, mosques, NGOs, shopkeepers, hotel staff, etc.) over the range of issues and concerns that constitute social life. Exploring social networks means understanding gender, intergenerational relations and how children gain access to resources and jobs, and pursue their livelihoods.

But anthropology can also have an important role in development practices and not just research. While working for a child-focused organisation in Ethiopia,* I found anthropology vital in our attempts to address issues of child protection, risky migration, education and health through community-based interventions. It was essential for identifying and defining the problem under question and embedding locally grounded development interventions in a way that ensures sustainability. For example the participatory monitoring and evaluation mechanisms we designed reflected local realities and gave us a deeper insight what was really doing on in the project. However, this is not without challenges. Working with children raised ethical dilemmas – about my own position as a researcher but also how research or development can reproduce power relations created as a result of age and other social and economic differences – as well as challenges in living with the stories that get printed on your memory.

* The Organization for Child Development and Transformation (CHADET)

the children involved in development projects that aim to help vulnerable children, it is hardly surprisingly they rarely hear happy beginnings. This is part of a wider problem; globally agencies often rely on the perspectives of those already in their interventions rather than doing research with members of the wider community, partly because funding tends to be more forthcoming for researching and tackling social problems rather than positive aspects of life.

The creation of negative, essentialised and separate identities is damaging in other ways also. While development agencies neglect the positive in children's lives, they also ignore the negative for children in programmes intended for others. Barlett points out that although child-focused agencies have improved wellbeing for many girls and boys, children are not taken into consideration in more general community development projects (2001). It is assumed that 'what benefits communities will also benefit children in these communities' (*ibid.*: 64). So development agencies' attention to children cannot be measured simply in terms of total funding allocated to children's programmes, and promoting their rights within those programmes, but ensuring that the interests of boys and girls are a factor in all decision-making in relation to all development programmes (*ibid.*: 69). Arguably, by separating children's rights from those of adults and by essentialising children's diverse experiences and needs under a single banner, the UNCRC obscures the links between groups' interests and conflicts of interests. On the one hand promoting women's rights can harm children (e.g. creating employment for women can lead to neglect) and, on the other, championing children's rights with no regard for their families can do harm to other members.

Concerns have been raised about the way that certain identities and certain kinds of right are more amenable to states and development organisations. As we have seen, street children and child labourers are given special attention and, based on often simplistic understandings of their situations, priority is given to the particular forms of intervention. However, these interventions tend more towards alleviating problems ('saving children') rather than addressing the kind of underlying causes that led to Juma's death (see Box 5.5). The dramatic and the extreme inevitably attract more attention than the commonplace: 'the public's attraction to scandals and exaggerations of abuse have drawn attention from political questions and the role of inequality and poverty in the adverse situations of many children. The shift in priority (from child survival to children's rights) may have had a negative effect on child mortality rates' (Einarsdottir 2006: 195).

If agencies were serious about tackling violence on a far larger scale, they would go beyond the street to the violence children suffer at home and the structural violence of poverty that make street life attractive. In fact too great a focus on street children can deflect attention from the far larger number of children and youth in rural areas, urban slums and in low-income communities that are subjected to the 'quiet private death that is hunger and disease' (Panter-Brick 2002: 152). To put it another way, children facing poverty and violence may need social protection more than child protection in a narrow sense.

Box 5.5. Individuals and structural violence: the case of Juma

The UNCRC stresses the protection of children as individuals rather than as seeing how the whole group is affected by wider political and economic relations. The anthropologist Chris Lockhart writes about street boys in East Africa (2008), probing the relationship between individual histories and macro structures. Most street children have lost at least one parent to AIDS; there are close to 2 million orphans in Tanzania alone. Rather than their sexual practices (as is often portrayed in the media), ultimately people are made vulnerable to AIDS by the everyday structural violence of poverty linked to privatisation and neoliberal policies.

Lockhart tells the story of how one boy, Juma, was affected by national and international economic policies. Juma's uncle's family moved in with Juma's family after being evicted when a Canadian mining company bought the land on which they lived. When Juma's father died of AIDS, this uncle claimed the land and threatened Juma's mother, so she and her children moved out. After resorting to sex work her health deteriorated. Meanwhile Juma was taken out of school and began interacting with boys on the streets. He became part of a gang and did what was necessary to be seen as tough. This included forcing sex on younger boys. Juma was caught by a group of militia, handed over to the police and put in jail, where adult prisoners raped him. He was released but could not afford medical care when he tried to get treatment and was then beaten by hospital guards. He died as a result of his injuries.

Juma's horrific death, Lockhart argues, needs to be considered against a larger backdrop of everyday violence. This context included:

- economic stress caused by shrinking land base, decreasing price of cotton, increasing costs of agricultural inputs, debt to traders and lack of state support;
- AIDS, which tends to be more prevalent in poorer households, especially in areas of forced migrations;
- subordination of women – in this case Juma's mother, whose land was grabbed by her late husband's brother – and their exclusion from development, including job opportunities, which forced her into prostitution, and led to her death by AIDS; and
- the neglect of children by the social service sector, which allowed Juma to become involved in a violent street-based life and be beaten to death.

To isolate Juma as a street child and imagine how he might have been saved as an individual would ignore the need to tackle various interconnected inequalities arising out of global and national economic policy, unequal property based on gender, class and age, and the tolerance of violence towards women and children. Understanding patterns at many levels – local, national, global – and taking account of diversity makes development work far harder than just understanding the needs of individuals. It is much easier to deal with innocent children and cruel adults, simple categories, single causes and straightforward generalisations whether framed in terms of needs or rights. But they defy real life and the stories that real people tell you so the easy route is doomed to fail.

If these examples tell us that protecting children requires attention to the diversity of both context and their perspectives, then where does that leave the idea of universal child rights and global instruments such as the UNCRC? Clearly (as maintained by cultural relativists) it casts doubt on the idea that a statement of rights can be straightforwardly applied to children in vastly different contexts and circumstances. But that was never intended by those who drafted the convention. Despite the problems of defining childhood, the UNCRC may provide an inspiring vision for policy-makers and practitioners about what is good and bad for children – and a list of commitment by states that they can be held to account for – but only if room for negotiation and manoeuvre is left and acknowledged by all. When designing interventions, hard political choices have to be made, for example, about when children should work or marry; the rights and responsibilities of families versus the state; and how resources should be allocated. In making these, negotiation between children and duty-bearers should be part of the process and they need the space to take contextual diversity into account.

Some anthropologists have attempted to assess the overall impact of the UNCRC. An extensive study by Harper and Jones concludes that progress on child poverty is mixed. Numbers of child deaths may be falling but, in many countries, levels of child poverty are stagnating, or even worsening (2009a: 1). Harper and Jones argues that the Millennium Developments Goals (MDGs) focus on health and education means that other aspects of children's lives are ignored. Child protection systems in the global South are weak with many states able to do little to prevent or stop abuse and exploitation or take children's view seriously (*ibid.*: 4). In their view it is the failure to implement the UNCRC, not the idea of rights, that is to blame. Not surprisingly UNICEF claims that 'the treaty has inspired changes in laws to better protect children, altered the way international organisations see their work for children, and supported an agenda to better protect children in situations of armed conflict', and offers a few examples of new laws, systems and plans. Harper and Jones conclude that the UNCRC provides development agents with a valuable alternative to welfare approaches which may fulfil children's needs but do little to change attitudes, laws and structures (Harper and Jones 2009b: 2). The value of the UNCRC is that it encourages agents – and gives them the confidence – to think about systems and links between different aspects of children's lives.

However, it remains all too easy to ignore children's voices. Despite all the rhetoric about children's participation, they did not participate in drafting the Convention and the UNCRC treats the rights of participation and protection as if there are no contradictions between them. Categories imposed by adults and formalised into international law actively deprive children of agency. Not only does the UNCRC hold to a narrow definition of children requiring protection and nurturing, there is an inevitable lack of clarity about when and how children attain the capabilities needed to decide how to protect themselves or other children. This is mirrored in efforts intended to 'save' children whether from life on the street or working in exploitative conditions. A strong tendency exists for children's identities to be restricted to that of victims, while more complex versions of socio-political reality are ignored. UNICEF is the UN body that champions the UNCRC but even in their own handbook for staff they fail to recommend that children should be consulted when responding to emergencies. The occasional suggestion that staff should try to understand 'the population's own perceptions, priorities and capacities' seems tokenistic and half-hearted.[5] In cases where anthropologists have set out to meet children and learn from them about their experiences, a different picture tends to emerge. While paying attention to the structural difficulties that constrain choice, more rounded understandings are also capable of recognising children and young people as active agents able to navigate a path through difficult and dangerous terrains.

Rights and community

We have been arguing that a focus on the needs of 'the child' encourages the development of individualised needs assessment rather than an analysis of how inequalities are structured by age, gender, class and other differentials. But at the same time, despite and alongside this individualism of rights-based projects and initiatives, development interventions are designed to meet the needs of 'communities'. It is taken for granted that communities are easily defined and developed. Decades of anthropological investigation challenge these simplistic assumptions.

Within the framework of rights discourse, the idea of 'community' has come to assume a growing importance. But what does 'community' mean? When dealing with 'communities' development bureaucracies tend to imagine harmonious groups of people holding common interests and whose separation from other groups of people is self-evident. It is not unusual to confuse a statistical category with a social group. But, after initially supporting such notions, anthropologists came to recognise that boundaries of community and identity are socially constructed rather than existing in a concrete sense. And agreement often varies about where the boundaries of community actually lie: ideas of identity clash, overlap and coincide between and even within cultures. Contrary to the rather static picture of communities held by many development professionals (and by structural-functionalist anthropologists pre-1970s), it is clear that people leave communities or particular groups or belong to several at the same time and social relations and identity are in a constant state of flux. Ideas in development about 'community' say more about the way people see the world than they do about how people live. People do (and do not) belong to 'communities' but not in any neat or fixed sense. Communities are conceptually created: their boundaries shift and people are put (or put themselves) in different or several communities depending on context.

Within development encounters 'community' has become a way of referring to groups of beneficiaries irrespective of whether they see themselves as a symbolically bounded community or not. As such it can be said that communities are actively created through development interventions. However, it is not just development bureaucracies alone that shape identities. People with whom development agencies and professionals interact actively create and live with their own cultural construction of identities. Prospective beneficiaries are often successful in presenting themselves in ways that bureaucracies are keen to recognise. And this may be done to gain access to rights. Divisions and disputes within 'communities' can be disguised and areas of agreement emphasised along with certain salient aspects of identity.

Where geography, administration and kinship meet, multiple dimensions of classification are overlaid on the top of identity. Development bureaucracies allocate people into households, communities, districts, nations and regions. Working 'at the national level' tends to mean working with the state or public sector as it tends to be only the institution with reach across whole countries, although some unions, social movements and NGOs develop substantial networks. Operating at the grassroots means usually through 'communities' or 'community-based organisations' and these are treated as if they are easily defined groups of people even if the boundaries are implicit rather than explicit. Communities in development discourse are usually a mysterious mixture of geographical residence, place of work and kinship. But real life is a messy social map of intermarrying lineages, clans, tribe, caste, race and class where people only sometimes define themselves clearly into 'communities'. When development agencies and agents seek to recognise self-evident 'communities' to which can be assigned 'rights', questions should be raised about the actual and natural existence of either.

'Community' as a concept suffuses project proposals, often with no explanation at all. But recognising this, we should also be aware that people may display considerable savvy in classifying themselves to external agencies (see Box 5.6). The 2007 United Nations Declaration on the Rights of Indigenous People[6] both reflects and encourages such creativity as the following examples taken from southern Africa demonstrate.

The 'indigenous' population of the Kalahari Desert in Southern Africa have various been termed *San*, *Sho*, *Koi*, *Basawa* and simply 'Bushmen'. But these terms are externally derived and carry pejorative connotations: in the nine different languages and dialects spoken in the Kalahari no word existed that conveyed a sense of shared identity. Furthermore, the immediate group of known relatives and associates was commonly considered as the sole reference point for identity – even in cases where language was shared (Aglaja Kempinski, pers. com., 2011). Existing as hunter-gatherers without recognisable political structures, the lifestyles of the people of the Kalahari has proved incompatible with dominant 'western' systems of rule which seek to categorise land and community. Dismissing the Bushmen as nomads lacking in even the most basic 'tribal' institutional structures, the prevailing logic of the colonial and post-colonial states denied them the right to formal land ownership. Unable to hold title to land and rigorously restricted in their movement, over the course of the twentieth century

Box 5.6. Communities claiming their rights in Orissa

Beneath the earth of the Indian state of Orissa is to be found one-eighth of the world's untapped bauxite. Promoted as a means to attain development, for both state and national government, mining has become a highly lucrative source of revenue. But controversies have arisen over how the costs and rewards of mining operations should be distributed. In making claims to rights, notions of indigeneity have been forwarded.

In 2004 a subsidiary of the British registered mining giant Vedanta Resources proposed the opening of a bauxite mine and aluminium-smelting refinery in the Niyamgiri Mountains of Central Orissa. Vedanta promoted their plan with the claim that mining would bring economic prosperity and development to one of the most deprived areas of India. But after the State government granted permission for the mining operations, an international campaign was mobilised against the predicted despoliation of an environment deemed sacred by the Dongria Kondh, a tribal group native to central Orissa.

In India the classification of ethnic populations as 'tribal' stretches back to colonial times. The image of the primitive *adivasi* (original inhabitant) making a subsistence living in the forest has long been romanticised. Verrier Elwin, Christian missionary turned anthropologist, argued that tribal peoples were the custodians of unique cultural traditions that were not just distinct but superior to both the Indian and European mainstream culture (1954). For groups like the Dongria Kondh, a powerful, symbolic attachment to land has becoming a central feature of their contemporary self-representation and identity.

The cause of the Dongria Kondh was taken up by the campaigning NGOs Survival International and ActionAid who amplified their claims to the land: 'to be a Dongria Kondh is to live in the Niyamgiri Hills in Orissa state, India – they do not live anywhere else'.[7] And the Dongria Kondh's very existence was threatened: Vendanta was 'forcing people out of their homes and damaging the forests and streams that have been the lifeblood of these tribal groups for thousands of years'.[8]

For the 2009 Vedanta AGM, Dongria Kondh representatives were taken to London as symbols of their endangered 'culture'. The following year, protesters from Survival International dressed as blue, alien-like *Na'vi* characters from the Hollywood blockbuster *Avatar* to publicise the case of the Dongria Kondh. But ultimately it was the idea of 'rights' that forced Vedanta to withdraw their proposals to mine the Niyamgiri range.

Also known as the Scheduled Tribes and Other Traditional Forest Dwellers Act, the Forest Rights Act (FRA) of 2006 restored to forest-dwelling communities the rights to land and other resources that had been denied to them through the continuance of colonial forest laws. For the first time local tribal groups and other forest dwellers were given a decisive say in decisions over the diversion of the lands for dams, mines and industry. On 24 August 2010, the government of India rejected Vedanta's plans to mine on Niyamgiri on the basis that the Dongria Kondh's traditional and customary access would be extinguished if the area were transferred for mining.

Though acclaimed as a victory for the Dongria Kondh, the Vedanta case raises a number of concerns. Representing the Dongria Kondh as a distinct cultural whole essentialised their identity and simplified the issue. The cause became reduced to one of environment vs. development; tradition vs. modernity; Dongria Kondh vs. Vedanta. With the Dongria Kondh fixed as an unchanging part of the Niyamgiri environment, no space was left for the expression of alternative voices or development possibilities. More disturbingly the provisions of the Forest Rights Act extended only to the tribal communities. Non-tribal inhabitants of the area were unable to claim the Dongria Kondh's distinctive ethnicity; though many were desperately poor, they were denied the protection of rights as a result because they did not fit into the narrow and arbitrary categories defined by the Forest Rights Act.

the Bushmen were allocated the role of second-class citizens. But this shared history of marginalisation and dispossession has served to unite the Bushmen around a common identity for the first time.

Using the 'western' concept of rights to deal with 'western' concepts of land ownership, groups describing themselves as indigenous have played with notions of identity and heritage to make claims to traditional lands. Following research in South Africa's Northern Cape and Northern Provinces, Steven Robins (2003) has written of how farmers have sought to challenge the privatisation of communal grounds in terms that are at once both modern and traditional. Elsewhere, Robins recounts how two groups of Kalahari San Bushmen reconstituted themselves as a 'traditional' community in order to get benefits from development projects. In this case their identity was complicated by the fact that one group was made up of settled farmers, while the others were the descendants of traditional hunter-gatherers. The 'war of representation' to access donor funds involved drawing on genealogies, livelihood strategies, indigenous bush knowledge, language and dressing to look 'like a proper bushman' (2003: 13). Robins concludes, 'by participating in NGO and donor-driven projects, indigenous groups such as the Kalahari San are drawing on the modern institutions and resources of a global civil society to reconstitute themselves as a "traditional community"' (ibid.: 14). Deploying hybrid and highly selective responses to development interventions, actors employ what Robins terms 'indigenous modernities' to redefine the terms of their engagement with the wider world.

Complex rights and creative claims

In this chapter we have seen how development organisations work to shape ideas of identity and community within the promotion of human rights. Complex, overlapping, fluid and variable forms of identity are defined, delimited, fixed and formalised as a function of bureaucracy. Bureaucratic interventions require that real identities are simplified. Development bureaucracies and the social groups that they interact with each possess distinctive cultures that label and judge each other in unspoken ways. 'Rather than seeing their own ideology as a product of history, their thinking is oriented by it. Ideology is automatically imbued with a character of objectivity for insiders' (Bourdieu 1977: 167). According to this silent tradition aid helps beneficiaries. The essence of beneficiaries is caught and either privileges certain groups (women, children, etc.) or remains vague (the poor). Many of the targeted groups have international treaties demanding attention to their universal rights. The social construction of identity-marking categories is informed by implicit assumptions and then, dialectically, has a significant influence on assumptions made about groups and people's relationships with each other. Both the representation and the reality of living within these categories are loaded with content. Inequalities tend to be structured by such markers and they are clearly in conversation with each other.

Development involves a process of political struggles in which different groups mobilise in attempts to determine priorities and access resources. Human Rights frameworks may provide a structure by which marginalised groups can make such claims, but the ability of such groups to do so will vary widely. All of this is not to dismiss or undervalue the immense efforts of those people around the world who struggle to fulfil the ideals of human rights agendas. Indeed we fully recognise that support for human rights can be an invaluable weapon in the arsenals of those who seek to combat discrimination and poverty and to promote social justice and development. The point we have made is that such rights should be recognised as variable cultural constructs. Inevitably they will take new and varied forms as they enter into the world of application and practice. Only where there is mutual respect and understandings between the promoters of rights-based frameworks, and the norms and ideals of the wider society, can such agendas hope to achieve their full potential.

Challenging questions arising from this chapter

How do right-based approaches differ from other development approaches?
How and why have human rights been globalised?
What are the gaps between rights regimes at different levels?
Who constructs rights and for whom?
Why do anthropologists question the universality of rights?
What are the differences between women's and children's rights?
How has the position of children changed in the last twenty years?
In what ways do communities have rights and how do they claim them?
What difference do rights make and to whom?

6   Hierarchies of knowledge

The creation and application of new ideas and technologies entail complex and open-ended processes. Anthropologists probe how the production, use and evaluation of technology are socially situated. This means critically examining the cultural meanings that attach to varied knowledge forms, the social systems within which they are embedded and the impacts that new technologies have upon constellations of social relations. In short, since technology is never value-free or neutral, it is highly likely to have significant political and economic consequences shaped by varied local settings.

Key points covered by this chapter

- Within the many cultures that exist within the development industry value judgements are made about knowledge and technology.
- We consider: What is technology? What is the relationship between technology and society? How does culture influence technological innovation? And how does technological development influence culture? What role does technology play in development?
- In contrast to the technological determinism of mainstream science, anthropology recognises all forms of knowledge and technology as being embedded in social systems.
- As a challenge to the ethnocentrism of many orthodox approaches, anthropological perspectives see knowledge as being contested, recognise and respect its many different forms and promote hybridity.
- Some anthropologists working in development aim to assess local needs and resources and ensure that externally originating technology responds to each context. Others critique the way that political processes are seen as knowledge deficit problems requiring technical solutions.

In Development World we find that science, and its applications through technology, have been treated as being the bedrock of progress. If low levels of development are identified by the presence of poverty, hunger or disease, then certain forms of scientific knowledge and advanced technology can symbolically represent a higher level of development. They are also a large part of the means by which it may be achieved; science has been seen as synonymous with, or at least required for, technological advancement and human progress. In some contexts and agencies development is even understood as the appliance to human society and government of the scientific principles of rationality, empiricism and enlightenment. And central to the development project of modernisation is the practical application of scientific knowledge in the form of technology.

Science and technology are panaceas for more than economic problems; they have been more recently applied to social and political domains. Whether it is the technology of governance in the form of electoral systems or improving social relations with technical toolkits to educate people about gender and rights, technical solutions are central. One of the responses to a perceived failure of aid is to improve the rigour of evaluation, which for an increasing number of institutions involves using scientific methods. As examples, in October 2010 DFID and AusAid (the Australian government's aid agency) joined with the International Initiative for Impact Evaluation (3ie) to promote 'evidence-based policy' and more scientifically valid evaluation, while in August 2011 the International Labour Organisation was looking for consultants with skills in econometric analysis to carry out quantitative, statistically robust impact evaluations of child labour interventions.[1] Since science allows us to understand the world better, it is also assumed that advanced technology and specialist technicalised expertise give us the means to change and measure it.

As we saw in the previous two chapters, anthropology looks at the way culture is constructed within the development industry through the classification and labelling of *people*. This chapter extends this focus to consider the ways in which we commonly understand, classify and attach meaning to *ideas* (mental constructs) and to *things* (inanimate objects). But things do not sit in splendid isolation; anthropologists are interested in the relationship between things and people. In this chapter we reveal some of the common assumptions about things, knowledge and expertise that shape the way that development is practised. Within the development industry certain ideas about science and technology have gained the status of orthodoxy – as naturalised and incontrovertible fact – whereas we find in practice that science has many forms and is used alongside other systems of knowledge in all societies.

Science and the promise of modernity

The idea of transference of science and technology from 'the West to the rest' has been central to the mainstream development paradigm; it was once explicit but it remains in implicit forms. Evolutionary frameworks of technological hierarchies are the basis of much mainstream development thinking. In this view it is the appliance of science that explains the productivity and prosperity of the 'developed world' and emerging economies, and its absence underlies the presence of underdevelopment elsewhere. Science is seen as capable of curing poverty, of alleviating hunger, promoting capacity and of bringing people and resources to fully productive use. Through the collection of evidence science can also measure progress towards the attainment of these goals. But what is meant here by 'science'? How does scientific knowledge translate into development? And what form of development does this mode of thinking promote?

Central to science is its promise of objectivity and universality. Such claims are founded on the empirical basis of scientific data, its logical reasoning and rigorous testing. In its classical form, the ideal of scientific objectivity suggests an absolute separation from subjectivity, whether the distorting push and bias of political and economic pressure or the numbing stasis of custom and tradition. Uncontaminated by subjective influences it is suggested that science is able to uncover the true and universal nature of reality. Scientific knowledge is not only neutral it also makes claims to universality, that is, it applies regardless of time or context. Thus the world can be rendered predictable with the concomitant promise that it can be transformed for the benefit of all. Part of the perceived superiority of science rests on its power to address a range of environmental, social and even political problems. As anthropologists have long argued, what are counterposed as other knowledge systems, whether 'indigenous' or 'traditional', are dismissed as static, backward and culture bound (Hobart 1993; Crewe and Harrison 1998; see Box 6.1).

The idea of 'western science' is no longer convincing. In the globalised world of the last few decades, with its new centres of science and industry in India, Brazil and China, science is no longer 'northern' or 'western', but does remain concentrated in particular urban settings. A technical elite – urban-based and university educated – is assigned the mantle of expertise and, as possessors of advanced knowledge, these experts accept the task of directing and transforming local systems of production. The apparently passive beneficiaries are waiting to be educated and development remains of mostly external origin – those marginalised at the periphery lack capacity and are apparently incapable of producing knowledge or initiating progress on their own. These hierarchies of knowledge take material forms with advanced urban (and once 'western') goods and knowledge situated at the apex and locally produced technology or ideas at the base. Underdeveloped is synonymous with simple or 'low' technology and cultural beliefs, while progress is achievable through the introduction of advanced 'high' technology or knowledge. Aid projects are supposed to speed up the natural process of technological evolution whereby people move in a simple, linear fashion from the use of simple tools to complex machines. Thus, development becomes a form of technological Darwinism with new and better ways of thinking and doing being created, standardised and disseminated around the world, replacing those inferior forms that precede them.

However, even if globalised, to what extent is science a uniquely separate and homogenous set of beliefs and practices? The claims of science to objective separation from wider influence and to the universal applicability of its findings are undermined by differences found between and even within various disciplines over time. It is only in a banal sense that science is a unitary system of knowledge

Box 6.1. Farming and politics in South Africa: an interview with anthropologist Dan Taylor

Dan Taylor first studied commerce at the University of Natal, South Africa in the 1970s and then worked as an auditor and financial accountant for two years. Bored with accountancy, he became interesting in farming and studied agricultural management at the same university. On graduating in 1978, he spent a year as a locum farm manager, but concluded that the exploitation of black farm workers that characterised white agriculture was untenable. He then decided he would prefer to work *with* black farmers rather than *over* black workers. To gain further agricultural experience before getting involved in agricultural development work, he travelled to New Zealand and Australia where, for two years (1980–1) he worked as a tractor driver, stockman and lambing shepherd and also on organic farms. On returning to South Africa he joined the KwaZulu government (1982) as an agricultural advisor but his critique of the government's attitude to Black African farmers made him persona non grata and he was forced to leave their employ.

Dan's next employment was with the University of Zululand's Centre for Social Research and Documentation (CSRD) at the University of Zululand, as Agricultural Research Fellow and as a coordinator of one of its projects (1984). The Centre consisted of a cadre of progressive development workers who understood that development was a political activity, which countered the prevailing wisdom that it was a technical enterprise. During this time, 'I was amazed by the agricultural knowledge embedded in local farmers' practices and began to observe and study how systems of agriculture that embraced polycultures, rather than monocultures, made use of agroecological niches and were both eclectic and resilient in the face of climatic uncertainties." He began to collect and document farming practices and local seed varieties used. After three years of working in a remote area in relative isolation he decided to study further and undertook an MBA (1987) to improve his administrative abilities, noting that development work required a wide range of generalist skills. For almost two years after that he worked in the informal settlements that surrounded Cape Town and 'coloured' rural areas, providing loans for small entrepreneurs.

He returned to the University of Zululand in late 1989 and soon thereafter created the Centre for Low Input Agricultural Research and Development (CLIARD) as an NGO linked to the university and became its director. Realising that black farmers lacked resources and political clout, rather than skills and knowledge, this organisation became part of a coalition of NGOs and CBOs with a progressive agenda that sought structural and political change in South Africa. Development, and agricultural development in particular, was recognised as a political project.

The projects that CLIARD supported had many dimensions. They were built on the foundation of farmers' rich knowledge. Rural people were encouraged to form farmers' organisations that were economically secure and to aim for environmental sustainability, good health and nutrition, employ appropriate technology and to view development as empowerment. In contrast to the analysis on both the political right and left – that black African farmers were hopeless, hapless and technically incompetent – CLIARD relied on farmers' expertise and agency. While the Apartheid regime was stamping out the entrepreneurial potential of black farmers, emphasising their otherness and using ethnicity to divide and diminish, CLIARD acknowledged that cultural difference underpinned people's identity but sought social inclusion for all within a broader South African context. Development for CLIARD was a process in which people were mobilised: no upper limit was set as a target neither were numbers of participants predetermined. The ability to work with freedom and to innovate contrasts with the current audit culture that permeates our society.

In 1994, after the first free elections, Dan applied to UCL to do a PhD in anthropology, looking at the local knowledge of resource-poor (black) South African farmers. No academic in South Africa at that time was interested in 'indigenous agricultural knowledge', so he decided to study abroad.

After the first year of study Dan joined Find Your Feet (FYF) and continued to research and write up his thesis, since FYF was working in South Africa. But without South Africa government support, small-scale agriculture was doomed to remain marginalised and Dan, in time, decided that FYF should withdraw from South Africa. The current policy of the ANC government assumes that small black African farmers would emulate white farmers, and appears to see no role for small-scale agriculture.

It is this concern for the poor that drives Dan, and the understanding that development is a politico-cultural struggle of the poor against their domination. This political process is being forgotten once more by INGOs. But, Dan explains, 'politics is being ignored once again. Despite INGOs espousing political advocacy development is being reduced to technical transfers and capacity building.'

That is not to say that getting results is unimportant. In an article written with CAPS Msukwa he has argued that projects would be more efficient and effective if managed like funerals, that is, if participatory development practices were embedded in people's everyday lives rather than imposed in alien ways from outside (Msukwa and Taylor 2011).

So has anthropology made any difference to Dan's approach to development? He saw the world through a political lens in any case, not surprisingly as he was brought up in Apartheid South Africa. Why did he think differently from the majority of white South Africans? Perhaps it was because at an early age an elderly Zulu man who worked for his parents – a headman of his locality – used to berate him for speaking Zulu badly and who constantly warned him – sometimes jokingly, sometimes wishfully – that the Zulu army would return to drive the white population into the sea. Perhaps being Jewish gives him a fuller understanding of what alterity means. So he did not need anthropology to teach him about difference, racism or politics, but he did need anthropology to teach him to look harder and further and seek greater understanding, particularly regarding the politics of cultural difference and the uses to which this was made – both positively and negatively by different vested interests.

But he also became more reflective and less certain: 'I was never certain about the correctness of my actions but doing anthropology made me even less certain … It is not about trying to look at the truth, but the reality beneath the superficial representation, the message that underlies the common discourse. For example, development is becoming all about funding. NGOs have become so opportunistic at times, that development processes are utterly subverted. The pressure to appear successful leads to untruthful representations when the truth is different. I tell this story to illustrate.

I went to meet people involved in a seed saving project. In the evaluation one woman had said that she put two children through university as a result of being given seeds. I asked this woman whether she said that to the evaluators. She said yes. I then asked, "do you take me for a fool?" "No, why do you say that?" "Because I know that a few seeds could not bring this about." She laughed her head off. There was collusion between the INGO, the local NGO, the evaluators, the woman and the funders – it suited them all to believe that the seed project had resulted in such a positive outcome. But it just wasn't true. Yet, this happens all the time.'

Anthropology may not reveal absolute truth, but it is good for exposing untruths.

(Interviewed by Emma Crewe on 26 January 2012)

when you take account of how theories and methods evolve and vary (Kuhn 1962). Before we explore further different systems of knowledge, we will consider the *application* of knowledge and the domain of technology development within 'Aidland'.

Technology development, exchange or destruction

'Technological determinism' suggests the influence of new technology on societies is inherent and uniform. Innovation proceeds as a one-way flow of ideas and artefacts produced by engineers moving into production and then being delivered to consumers as if unchanged. This orthodoxy has influenced the international development discourses that underlie policy unevenly over the last fifty years. After a lull in the 1990s and early 2000s, during which the primacy of science and technology receded to some extent with the popularity of the participatory movement, the economic crises has provoked a panic about creating and proving 'results' and evidence of them at the same time. A former DFID official, Owen Barder, explains how in the 2000s a large number of technical specialists were employed by the UK government to improve the generation of evidence and build the capacity for the collection and analysis of statistics in 'developing countries' (2007). So new technology hardware is no longer seen as central to economic development as it once was, but technical expertise remains an essential component of international development policy. One of the ways this is manifested is in the investment into pilot projects that are expected to create 'best practice' models, which are evaluated and then replicated in other settings, with various actors 'adding value' along the way. It is as if such processes can be standardised, simple and received neutrally to the benefit of many; in reality, the distribution of new techniques and technologies has not proved to be so straightforward.

Contrary to the optimistic expectations of advocates of technology transfer, the effects of technology have strayed from original intentions and caused harm as well as benefit. In agriculture, Green Revolution technology provided significant increases in agricultural production but these gains were concentrated on a narrow range of agriculturalists, regions and crop varieties. Though supposedly scale-neutral the introduction of high-yield crop varieties led to increased landlessness and, it has been argued, rural immiseration (Miller 1977: 193–5). Communities with longstanding claims to use and ownership have been dispossessed so that governments and corporations may exploit the forest resources growing on the land or the mineral wealth underneath it. Large dams, beloved of central planners as a means to provide power to an expanding industrial sector, have displaced residents as homes and fields are flooded. Irrigation opens up new areas for cultivation but is linked to increases in malaria, soil salinity, siltation and the drying up of rivers. Thus, introducing new technology to stimulate economic growth can lead to the exploitation of groups already facing chronic poverty, whether migrants, women or young people.

Descriptive critiques pointing to the significant detrimental social and environmental consequences of science and technology are plentiful; as examples Illich (1976) wrote a seminal book on the harm caused by medicine and the UN Environment Programme lists damage that technology does to the environment.[2] This is part of a long tradition that emphasises the destructive nature of science, pointing to evidence of pollution, increased poverty, landlessness, environmental degradation and human inequality. From this perspective science is viewed not as a positive benefit but as a system of control. The process of systematic documentation that underpins western science orders knowledge and facilitates exploitation. Making knowable the resource wealth of the global South opens it up for extraction. The idea of unproblematic technological progress is increasingly questioned. A broad alliance of activists and academics argue that it would be a mistake to attempt to foster the values and methods of western science onto other cultures with their own ways of thinking and doing.

Vandana Shiva is amongst the best-known proponents of this critique of the scientific basis of development. In a series of books (e.g. 1988; 1997; 2000; 2001) that combine feminism with environmentalism Shiva documents the threat to culturally specific production systems in the face of expanding scientific universalism. Attempts to modernise agriculture through mechanisation and the extension of new seed varieties ties farmers into production for commercial markets, limits their understanding of their own production methods and deprives them of control over their livelihoods. Particular ire is directed at the use of patent laws that are used to impose Eurocentric notions of property over the products of indigenous knowledge. Knowledge is privatised (1997), while multinational companies gain intellectual property rights over life forms and previously commonly accessible knowledge. Shiva argues forcefully for the promotion of biodiversity and that control over ecosystems should be vested in local communities.

Against these views it could argued that the rejectionist approach can be as unhelpfully reductionist as those that promote science as a simple panacea for all the world's ills (Jackson 1992). Shiva is inclined to portray western science as unvaryingly exploitative, extractive and destructive of local practices. This is in

Box 6.2. Biotechnology: 'frankenfood' or the solution to world hunger?

Intervening in natural processes for centuries, farmers have selected, crossed and bred to improve the quality of crops and livestock. While traditional methods involved the mixing of thousands of genes, genetic modification allows for single genes to be inserted into a plant in order to engineer its properties. Debates about the Genetic Modification of food crops epitomise attitudes to science and illustrate the politics of agriculture. In his review of the risks and potentials of GM technology, Herring (2007) describes two polarised and deeply entrenched reactions.

To supporters, GM crops have the potential to eliminate the problems of poverty, hunger and famine. New varieties can be developed to combat the problems of disease and pests and to expand the frontier of production possibilities. With seeds being a scale-neutral, divisible technology (i.e. they cost poor farmers no more than rich ones), biotechnology offers the promise of technology to feed a hungry world. This optimistic narrative fits easily into the standard view of science with the spread of advanced technology from the laboratories of developed countries out to peasants' fields of the Third World.

But not everyone is convinced of the positive potential of GM technology. In India, opponents of transgenics have labelled them as the 'seeds of death' (Shiva 2000). This opposition centres around the monopoly control of seeds by large multinational corporations. First of all, it is argued that research will be driven by the needs of the wealthy and to the tastes of consumers in developed nations. There is little private incentive for biotechnology producers to orient their activities away from large-scale commercial agriculture and towards small-scale, subsistence farming. Secondly, GM critics argue, Malthusian arguments for GM misdiagnose the problems of hunger and famine as stemming simply from inadequate supply. Rather, as Sen's (1982) work on famine theory proposes, it is poor distribution rather than a lack of food that creates hunger. The production of GM crops would do little to alter the ability of rural and urban poor to access adequate food. Far from being rescued from poverty and hunger, it is precisely the most vulnerable people who will be most disadvantaged by the introduction of the new technology. 'Poor farmers, in this view, will be crushed by bondage to multinational monopolists, re-subordinating poor nations to neo-colonial control' (Herring 2007: 4). Particular outrage is reserved for the way in which multinational companies commit acts of 'bio-piracy': plundering the genetic resources of indigenous peoples and poor nations to make corporate property out of them (e.g. Shiva 2000, 2001). Biotechnology and increased supply would be of little use where the problem is one of demand rather than supply – the role of redistribution in alleviating food insecurity is overlooked.

Herring views these two polarised positions as unnecessarily reductionist:

A global debate reproduces cleavages introduced by Prometheus and Pandora: between camps that believe the genomics revolution to be more like fire – a source of human progress, entailing risks but amenable to control and wise use – and those who believe it to be more like Pandora's jug, set to unleash unimagined evils on our species and others from ecological disaster to bioterrorism. Divergent claims to knowledge reflect and justify widely varying, socially conditioned distributions of risk aversion and risk acceptance. (Herring 2007: 2–3)

As the moral reactions to technology show – and especially to the new technologies that rearrange well-established ideas and relationships – technology is not neutral, and we need to look at how it is applied and ensure that benefits are directed to those that need and deserve them, which are political processes.

Addressing market failures that produce human misery is a central legitimisation of development policy. The standard narrative thus converges on redirection of biotech research and development as necessary conditions for reaching the poor. Getting the institutions right is then a necessary condition for purposive pursuits of poverty-reducing outcomes. (Herring 2007 : 9)

opposition to the marginalised and oppressed subaltern entity: 'community', 'the poor' and 'women' are presented as unitary entities with common experiences and interests. A return to (imagined) traditions of local autonomy and common resource use, though romantic, are likely to prove inadequate to meet the needs of expanding populations.

Conventional extension models of technology transfer are under question by other social scientists in a more measured way (Crewe and Sarkar 2006: 31–5; Hall *et al.* 2005). The standard approach of scientists helping farmers is to generate a solution through scientific research, hand it over to the government extension services or NGOs and for the latter to transfer the technology to farmers through training and technical assistance. This process often fails. Two of the main shortcomings of this approach are that research can be remote from the needs of marginalised or small-scale potential users and the research system is too slow to react to change. Hyderabad, India, witnessed an attempt to move beyond technology extension to innovating within a coalition. Since the early 2000s, social scientists at the International Crops Research Institute for the Semi Arid Tropics (ICRISAT) have been trying a different approach. They established that sorghum had not reached its market potential and that the institutional links between different stakeholders in the marketing chain were weak. In 2002 they established a coalition of five organisations – ICRISAT, a university, a crop farmers federation, a poultry farmers federation and a private-sector organisation selling poultry feed – to create new marketing opportunities for poorer farmers in Andhra Pradesh. The technical idea was to use sorghum in poultry feed. These five organisations jointly planned the project and, in the words of one, developed a 'feeling of a win-win situation for all the partners' (*ibid.*: 32). After only two years, the coalition generated four clear benefits to farmers and manufacturers:

1. they established that sorghum could be used in poultry feed without impairing its quality and convinced poultry farmers and feed manufacturers of this;

2.   the farmers and feed manufacturers worked together to ensure the quality of the grain was high enough;

3.   the dealers who bought grain from the farmers and sold it to the feed manufacturers were being made redundant, thereby increasing the profit to both farmers and feed manufacturers; and

4.   the direct link gave the farmers the incentive to operate collectively, which increased their bargaining power and reduced marketing and transportation costs.

The key question is: to what can we attribute this success (for the protagonists, at least)? The members of the coalition achieved various institutional innovations in their working practices: clear roles and responsibilities kept the need for complex communication to a minimum; they focused on excellent communication and relationships to establish trust; and they recognised the need for different forms of validation for the different groups. While scientists relied on their traditional scientific methods, they respected farmers' assumptions that 'seeing is believing' and reports from farmers are more reliable than those of outsiders (including scientists). Rather than classifying data and codifying their knowledge, they emphasised the need to test the innovation in their specific settings and facilitate learning within a community of practice.

This approach allowed them to make use of various technical innovations successfully, especially when demonstrating that, contrary to popular opinion, if sorghum replaces maize the quality of the feed is just as good (i.e. the level of tannins and toxins remains low). They developed the methodology for the poultry feed trials, whereby chickens were fed grain with a high sorghum content to see if it impaired their health, as a collective to ensure that all had confidence in the results. The poultry scientists conducted tests according to their traditional scientific methods: they adjusted the energy content of the poultry feed to ensure that it was equal in each, thereby making sure that the experiment was not affected by other variables. But the poultry farmers and feed manufacturers do not use computers, which are necessary to calculate the energy content when formulating feed, so they wanted to know what the effects were without changing the energy content. In a second test the scientists agreed to repeat the experiment with a simpler method: part-by-part replacement of sorghum in place of maize and then assessment of the differences in quality of the feed. A feed manufacturer's mill was used to conduct the second test so that non-laboratory conditions were replicated. The scientists also agreed to repeat the tests on different breeds, as the poultry farmers were all concerned about whether different breeds would react differently. Although previous research informed the scientists that they would behave in the same way, they agreed to repeat the tests – at their own cost – knowing that the success of the project depended on poultry farmers believing the results rather than scientific validation. The quality of feed was the same for sorghum and maize, and for all breeds, and confidence in the results was achieved on all sides. It seems highly probable that without the coalition either the cost of this research would have been far higher (with a long gap between repeat tests if they had been done at all) or the innovations would not have been adopted. But it does not finish there. The coalition was aware of the need to influence government to make sure their policies support the marketing of sorghum, but while the project was small, they knew it would be difficult to make an impression. With the scaling up of this initiative, they plan to involve government – especially at the district level in India – making the most of the private sector's participation because the government listen more readily to the well-organised industrial lobbies than they do to farmers (Crewe and Sarkar 2006).[3]

The social and cultural consumption of technology

The dissemination of knowledge and technology, in common with other forms of development intervention, often involves acts of displacement. Technology is abstracted away from the context of its creation while, at the same time, intended beneficiaries are separated from the 'expert' promoters of new ideas and hardware. Anthropological approaches stress that all forms of knowledge and technology are the product of social and cultural contexts; their introduction and use can only be understood when proper attention is paid to these wider settings. As well as being visible, tangible and material, technological objects can also be regarded as cultural artefacts that provide insights into the nature of the particular society in which they exist.

A central assumption of the prevailing 'standard view of technology' sees scientific solutions developed in direct response to needs (Pfaffenberger 1992). There is an expectation that problems and needs can be simplistically identified and technical answers will be found in reaction to them. In this view, the form taken by any response will be directly determined by its function resulting in a tool or technique that that can be widely applied. To borrow a phrase, necessity proves to be the mother of invention. Anthropological perspectives suggest that material progress does not take place in a vacuum and that new tools and techniques should be recognised as products of very particular historical, economic and political contexts. As Pfaffenberger argues, 'culture, not nature, defines necessity' (1992: 496).

While proponents of technological determinism argue that technology shapes human action, alternative approaches recognise the role of human action in shaping technology. Technology fulfils a double role: it is at once material in terms of utility but also cultural through the communication of symbolic meaning and the value attached to it. Function and form are thereby intertwined. Various nonmaterial factors combine to predispose people to react to technology in certain ways. Instead of viewing machines in isolation we need to see the social, cultural, organisational, political, technical and psychological conditions that shape how they function. This can be demonstrated by the example of the motorcar. The rise of motor vehicle use in America took place alongside developments in

Box 6.3. The politics of climate science

Man-made climate change represents one of the greatest threats faced by our species in the twenty-first century. But what insights into this global phenomenon might anthropology provide?

One avenue fruitfully pursued by anthropologists is to consider how communities observe, interpret and respond to local impacts of global warming. Crate and Nuttall's (2009) edited volume draws on case studies from Alaska to the South Pacific that illustrate how understandings of ecological change are culturally grounded and locally produced. In turn, anthropologists are able to observe the ways in which the physical manifestations of climate change are socially negotiated and the effects that ecological disruption has on social relations.

Peter Rudiak-Gould points to the limitations of such approaches, which, he suggests, often maintain an artificial distinction between 'indigenous' and 'scientific' knowledge. To Rudiak-Gould it is important that anthropology should consider 'the local' alongside 'the global' (2011). Arguing that few people are now unaware of scientific discourses on climate change he points to the interplay of global and local knowledge to understand how climate change is produced as an *idea*.

Rudiak-Gould's research in the low-lying Marshall Islands documents a society in which scientific discourse is a crucial influence on perceptions of climate change. But this is not the case everywhere; cultural and ideological reasons inform choices of whether to trust or distrust scientific discourses on global warming. In some cases the weight of scientific evidence is dismissed, not because of contrary observations but because the solutions offered are deemed unacceptable. Disagreements arise over where to place the blame for climate change, over the means to reduce emissions and over who should pay the price. In the absence of agreement on these fundamental questions, climate change sceptics question the scientific data in ways that weaken the political will to implement the far-reaching economic and social changes necessary. Objective measurements that indicate the existence of a problem are insufficient when the ethical debates over solutions remain unresolved. Meanwhile carbon emissions increase and average global temperatures rise.

mass production and standardisation in industry based upon the mobilisation and control of labour and resources. Consumption was underpinned by the development of capitalist markets and the encouragement of individual consumerist desires. Resulting forms saw a standardised model of the family car designed to seat two up front and two behind conforming to, and in turn serving to promote the notion of the ideal nuclear family. In order to play a role beyond the purely symbolic, a motorcar requires a support network of transport infrastructure – roads, petrol stations, mechanics, car parks, traffic lights, and so on. Increased air pollution, the disruption caused by road building and vehicle noise and the deaths and injuries caused by accidents are judged to be acceptable prices to pay for individualised mass rapid transport. Without widespread political support new ways of doing and being are unlikely to be accepted (see also Box 6.3 on the politics of climate change).

Technology transfer or choice involves complex and often clashing social and political choices being made by different groups. Science and technology are framed within larger cultural and political value systems and successful adoption, at least for some, requires that these are taken into account. And once technologies are accepted and disseminated their resulting form and impacts will vary according to the socio-political contexts in which they exist. For example, as a cultural artefact the motorcar is likely to be understood and used very differently in New York, New Delhi, Mogadishu or Nairobi.

To give another example of how cultural values attach to technology, consider houses. When working for the international NGO Practical Action (then called Intermediate Technology Development Group), Emma Crewe visited a housing project in East Africa in the early 1990s. Housing specialists had identified problems with the so-called 'traditional' oval wattle and daub houses and designed low cost rectangular brick houses for a particular community of settled Maasai pastoralists. It was obvious that the new brick houses were uninhabited. When asked about this the owners explained that the brick houses were colder in the winter, warmer in the summer, get smoky if you use wood or charcoal burning stoves, and are not as good at preventing theft. The oval houses have a passageway with a bend as the door so that people coming in can be heard before they appear, making it easy to defend yourself against burglars. When Emma asked whether they preferred the oval or rectangular houses they replied: 'We may be Maasai but we are modern Maasai. Of course we want modern rectangular houses.' However, they continued to live in the wattle and daub houses; the newly built rectangular ones were employed for ceremonial occasions or for receiving visitors. They valued the associations with modernity that the new houses communicated to visitors, that is, their symbolic capital rather than their more mundane use-value as a place of residence (Bourdieu 1997). Such symbolic capital confers status and the impression of power, and therefore the potential for real power, on the owner. So the most significant value of a rectangular brick house for the Maasai owner was not its use-value as shelter, but its symbolic value as an expensive and modern asset. In a similar way organisations and governments put up or build what Amity Doolittle calls 'shrines to modernity', signs or posters or monuments declaring that this village or community or group is no longer backward but is developing or modernising and making progress (2006: 64).

Different societies receive change in different ways with existing sets of social relations – along lines of class, gender, age or ethnicity – guiding who gains access to new technologies and how they might use, adapt or produce them. Inequalities are often exacerbated as the benefits of new techniques and knowledge are channelled to those groups deemed most deserving of them (as determined by the values of the disseminator) and intercepted by those best placed to do so in the receiving community. In particular, gender is a major fault line. If societies were equal then technology might be value free, but the vast majority of social relations exhibit dynamic inequalities and hierarchies including those based on gender. It is supposed that scale-neutral, high-yield seeds varieties may

---

Box 6.4. Unequal gendered access to and use of technologies

Some of the reasons for women's limited access to technology include:

Men tend to dominate technology education and design. Men tend to be seen as designers, developers and creators partly due to women's under-representation in science, technology and engineering courses and professions, but also because women's technical innovations in rural, work situations are unrecognised or undervalued.

Women and girls bear a disproportionate burden of household and community maintenance work, including cooking, healthcare, cleaning, fuel/water collection and care of children and the elderly, as well as food production.

They lack access to technologies that are relevant to them, including household technologies, and the investment in making these accessible to those facing the greatest time and economic poverty is insufficient.

Gendered and age inequalities tend to mean that men have greater control over technology choice but also the property, capital and income that give people access to technology.

When technology or knowledge designed for women or young people and becomes particularly lucrative, then it is often co-opted by men.

(*Source:* Gill *et al.* 2010: 7)

---

prove socially divisive because small farmers (and indeed rural labourers) are unable to access the accompanying chemical inputs and increased irrigation that their adoption requires. The widening of economic inequality and landlessness that results from attempts at agricultural extension illustrate the extent to which technological impacts are political. If women produce 50 per cent of the world's food, as the FAO estimates,[4] and technology inputs into farming increase gender inequality, then the harmful impact of agricultural technology for women is on a colossal scale (see Box 6.4).

The introduction of technology to bring about change cannot be reduced to a simple equation of cause and effect. Though the acceptance of a new technology may be determined by existing sets of social relations, in turn, social arrangements can be transformed in this process of adaptation. The introduction of new technologies may act to alter the relationship between the various social groups within recipient communities. The nature of a technology interacts with the particular sociocultural norms of the societies within which it is innovated or into which it is introduced. Through these processes the questions of *who* might use the technology and *how* they do so are answered. Such processes challenge the simplistic one-way transfer of technology that supposes the unaltered flow of scientific knowledge and progress southwards from the technologically advanced centres of the developed world.

Anthropologists have long championed context specific and culturally appropriate forms of development. Within development projects a role thus opened up for anthropologists as two-way communicators at once able to express local needs to technological innovators and to ensure the local appropriateness of externally generated plans and technologies. The work of anthropologist Stephen J. Lansing illustrates the importance of paying attention to existing social and religious systems when introducing new technologies. Lansing's study of the role played by religious authorities in coordinating agricultural activities on the Indonesian island of Bali shows why the idea of interplay works better than simple determinism (1991).

Bali was one of the first targets of the Green Revolution – an attempt from the 1960s onwards to modernise agriculture and increase agricultural productivity by replacing existing rice varieties with high yielding hybrid varieties that needed chemical fertilisers and pesticides. In many places the Green Revolution has proved successful in increasing agricultural yield. But such successes may come at a price – the supposedly scale-neutral technology has been famously critiqued for making richer farmers richer, excluding poorer farmers including women, and damaging the environment.

What happened in Bali and why? First, what was there already? Balinese water temples were connected to each other in a regional system – the main ones defined the rights and responsibilities of subsidiary shrines and their associated rice-producing collectives. Across the island, temple priests employed complex ritual calendars to coordinate cycles of rice growing. Temples served as a focus for the systematisation of knowledge about local ecology. Through this system the water temples effectively ensured the cooperation necessary for distributing water and guaranteeing that land was left fallow – essential for pest control and fertility. Social units were symbolised by holy water from different parts of the system. When the water from another social unit was used by farmers to help production this was far from a trivial matter. It symbolised that the whole ecosystem depended on social relationships constructed by the water temples.

The planners of the Green Revolution did not notice these systems. The only question for them was whether or not the traditional system was going to resist modernisation. The changes introduced, including continuous cropping with no fallow and the removal of power from the water temples, resulted in an explosion in pests and chronic water shortages. The water temples were seen as traditional and, therefore, backward. But stripping them of power led to the collapse of the management of irrigation. Green Revolution scientists had assumed that improved technology would work its magic irrespective of social relations.

Lansing recognised that the water temples as a 'system of ecological management with deep historical roots in Balinese culture' (1991: 116); for the Balinese agriculture was a social as well as a technical process. To prove his thesis Lansing devised a computer-generated model that demonstrated the efficiency of temple irrigation systems to Public Works Department officials that were being undermined by their interventions. It was interesting that Lansing's expatriate status, and the use of computer modelling with quantitative data, was needed to persuade the officials to value indigenous knowledge. It was even more ironic that officials requested the computer programme to improve their knowledge of farming yields in order to estimate better the levels of taxation.[5]

It appears that some forms of knowledge and technology that are apparently highly successful in North American and Europe have failed, or are received completely differently, when exported or tried elsewhere. One aspect relates to the nature and limits of scientific understanding itself. While certain forms of science have been extremely adept at concentrating on the impact on a single, isolated variable, it proves less successful when faced with certain forms of complexity. (Newer forms, such as complexity sciences, aim to do exactly the opposite.) In its more linear forms, other variables and externalities can be overlooked. James Scott applied this idea to the example of agriculture. In relatively stable and optimal environments agricultural outputs may be raised through mechanisation and the introduction of chemical inputs. However, a sharp focus on immediate farm inputs and corresponding crop yields leaves out related long-term side effects, which may negatively impact upon soil structure or water quality. 'The potent but narrow perspective' of what Scott terms 'high modernism' is, he writes, 'troubled by both certain inevitable blind spots and by phenomena that lie outside its restricted field of vision' (1998: 263). So it is supposed that universal modern technology developed in the global North often fails to fit to the often marginal and unstable environments found in the global South. Local soils, local landscapes, local labour, local implements and local weather are not taken into account in pre-packaged projects (see Box 6.5).

It is not only in terms of the production of knowledge and technology that science's universality and objectivity may be questioned. The forms of consumption of new knowledge and technology also demonstrate the limits to the technological determinism model. Given the negative impacts often associated with external interventions, it is understandable that scientific knowledge – and the claims of its superiority – is not always received uncritically by proposed beneficiaries (e.g. Riedmann 1993). At times the assistance of technocrats, professionals and development specialists has been underutilised, reworked or outright rejected by so-called local people. Rather than writing this off as cultural conservatism or resistance to modernity, anthropologists have explored how and why technology means different things to different people in different cultural settings (Crewe and Harrison 1998: 132–7).

Alternative approaches to technology

Since the late 1960s, as awareness grew of the disappointing uptake of transferred technologies, alternative systems of knowledge and technology were re-evaluated. Development agencies increasingly sought to tailor programmes of change to particular social and physical environments. Amongst the best-known proponents of this approach is Practical Action, founded in 1966 by

---

Box 6.5. Systems of knowledge in their social context

Despite its critics, western science sees itself as superior to other systems of knowledge. Scientific thought is logocentric, according to Derrida, in the sense that it relies on culturally constructed binary oppositions (subject/object, mind/body, nature/culture), where one element is defined as the absolute absence of the other element. Irrationality is what is not rationality.

In relation to a case study of smallpox in India biomedical science defined it as a disease with a single cause, whereas in 'non-modern' India smallpox is the Goddess Sitala, both the absence and presence of disease. The colonial and then Indian government promoted vaccination with cowpox matter and outlawed other methods – variolation or inoculation combined with rituals in honour of Sitala – which entailed the use of human smallpox matter.

The imposition of vaccinations led to resistance, which was political and cultural in nature not superstition as the health authorities assumed. Vaccination was associated in people's minds with the government and foreign rule. Even after the end of colonial rule, vaccinators were technically inefficient but also callous and authoritarian in their approach to people. The more the programme failed, the more aggressive they became, feeling justified in their behaviour because they believed themselves to be representing a vastly superior form of knowledge.

It was only once they realised the need for public support for the campaign – and with the help of anthropologists guiding on information flows – that vaccinators showed more respect for the Goddess Sitala and had more success. Smallpox was wiped out in 1977 but only at high political and cultural costs and the loss of other forms of knowledge.

(*Source:* Frédérique Apffel-Marglin 1990: 102–44)

---

the economist EF Schumacher. Recognising the limitations of the then pervasive model of exporting large-scale technologies to developing nations, Schumacher suggested a shift in emphasis towards the promotion of what he termed 'intermediate technologies'. 'Helping them to help themselves', intermediate technology works to harness the existing resources and skills in a community in direct response to their expressed needs. They promote mostly local knowledge and technology that is both environmentally sustainable and socially just. From an initial focus on food production, Practical Action today also helps poor communities to develop appropriate technologies in renewable energy (small-scale wind power, improved stoves, solar power and biogas), food production, water and sanitation, agro-processing, shelter, small enterprise development, climate change adaptation, disaster risk reduction and communications.

This kind of move from top-down 'transfer of technology' to bottom-up learning from the locals involves a challenge to the orthodox assumptions about 'project beneficiaries'. While most aid projects are designed on the assumption that 'local' people have a capacity deficit, the kind of populist participatory technology development promoted by Practical Action sees them as canny and confident social actors possessing considerable resources of knowledge and skill. 'Alternative' development approaches seek to harness this knowledge and skill and to learn from other cultures.

The particularistic, contextualised, sympathetic, empirical, organic, holistic, and practical character of indigenous knowledge is contrasted with the rationalistic, reductionist, theoretical and abstract basis of modern western science. In its highly specific appreciation of local environments and the long-term aggregation of historical experience, indigenous knowledge may provide insights that western science lacks. Supporters of appropriate technology, such as Schumacher, suggest that a combination of indigenous 'know-how' and observation and modern scientific techniques, with their complementary strengths and weaknesses, could achieve together what neither could alone. The quantitative basis of hard science requires a qualitative bedding of soft local knowledge if it is to function. Utilising local autonomy, skills and materials a system of genuinely sustainable development will emerge, it is assumed. And drawing on local understanding results in technology that is more appropriate and, therefore, more likely to be adopted.

Attempts to ensure that external development interventions are appropriate to local circumstances have heralded the value of indigenous knowledge as separate from, but not necessarily inferior to, orthodox scientific understandings. However, the re-evaluation of indigenous knowledge is a two-way process. By challenging widely accepted models and concepts the cross-cultural study of knowledge could advance scientific understandings. As Sillitoe notes, 'the heretical idea is gaining currency that others may have something to teach us' (1998: 227). Remote and isolated communities may be familiar with plant varieties unknown to science or, over many generations, used selective breeding to produce improved agricultural seed varieties. Integrating indigenous knowledge has become mainstream (see Box 6.6). In 2000 the World Bank and others have even produced a set of guidelines to help agencies to integrate indigenous knowledge into project planning and implementation.[6]

The valorisation of indigenous knowledge extends to measuring, systematising and storing such knowledge. UNESCO has even published a register of 'best practices on indigenous knowledge' for different regions.[7] The term 'bioprospecting' refers to attempts to take advantage of the genetic resources and indigenous knowledge and technologies of remote and marginal communities. However, aside from the difficulties of ensuring that benefits are shared fairly, attempts to communicate local specificities, needs and interests and to record local knowledge and practices are not unproblematic.[8] By orthodox definition indigenous knowledge is small-scale, geographically localised and culturally specific. So important questions remain: should indigenous knowledge be assessed according to scientific criteria and who owns it?

The act of translation inevitably involves distortion. In development, problems arise from the often unspoken and even unconscious (non-cognitive) basis of all

Box 6.6. UNEP on indigenous knowledge in natural disaster reduction in Africa

In Africa, local communities had well-developed traditional indigenous knowledge systems for environmental management and coping strategies, making them more resilient to environmental change. This knowledge had, and still has, a high degree of acceptability amongst the majority of populations in which it has been preserved. These communities can easily identify with this knowledge and it facilitates their understanding of certain modern scientific concepts for environmental management including disaster prevention, preparedness, response and mitigation ... a blend of approaches and methods from science and technology and from traditional knowledge opens avenues towards better disaster prevention, preparedness, response and mitigation.

Globally, there is increasing acknowledgement of the relevance of indigenous knowledge as an invaluable and underused knowledge reservoir, which presents developing countries, particularly Africa, with a powerful asset in environmental conservation and natural disaster management. Specifically, from time immemorial, natural disaster management in Africa has been deeply rooted in local communities that apply and use indigenous knowledge to master and monitor climate and other natural systems and establish early warning indicators for their own benefit and future generations.

In the traditional African worldview, environmental resources (land, water, animals and plants) are not just production factors with economic significance but also have their place within the sanctity of nature ...

Regarding land-use conservation, shifting cultivation was a traditional practice in which land was never over used or repeatedly cultivated season after season and year after year. Land was left to rest and covered again with plants and leaves to enable it to accumulate vegetable manure. Mixed crop cultivation practice enables leguminous crops to restore nitrogen in the soil for other food plants. Knowledge of when to expect long or short rainy seasons enables the farmers to plan appropriately which crop is suited for a particular season. Traditional indigenous knowledge terminologies of types of soil and their reaction to water enables the people to use each type of soil appropriately by planting the correct crops ...

These examples underscore the importance of harnessing indigenous knowledge not only as a precious national resource but also as a vital element in environmental conservation and natural disaster prevention, preparedness and response.

However, despite the prevalent application and use of indigenous knowledge by local communities, it has not been harnessed to fit into the current scientific framework for environmental conservation and natural disaster management in Africa. As a result, there is a general lack of information and understanding of the need to integrate or mainstream indigenous knowledge into scientific knowledge systems for sustainable development in the continent. To achieve this integration would require a blend of approaches and methods from science and technology and from indigenous knowledge.

(*Source:* extracted from an article by James Kamara, Acting Chief of the Disaster Management Branch of UNEP's Division of Environmental Policy Implementation, www.grida.no/publications/et/ep3/page/2608.aspx, accessed 20 August 2011)

knowledge. Embodied practices – acquired through observation, experience and imitation – prove difficult to explain verbally or write down. When asked to evaluate the qualities of soil in a particular location, Paul Sillitoe relates how highlanders in New Guinea will inspect it and handle it before offering their opinion. If subsequently asked to explain their judgement they are likely to look bemused: 'one just knows; one is not used to being asked what or how' (1998: 229). (The same could often be said of those using science.) This relates to a wider point about the holistic settings in which knowledge is contained. Specific areas of information cannot be extracted from wider cultural contexts as if representing some independent technical fact; as we have argued, all knowledge is a construct that can only be understood as part of its own sociocultural environment.

On the question of exactly *which* knowledge is to be translated and *who* is the holder of that knowledge, Agrawal suggests that 'because indigenous knowledge is generated in the immediate contexts of the livelihoods of people, it is a dynamic entity that undergoes constant modifications as the needs of the community change' (1995: 428). Faced with diversity scientists try to essentialise what is necessarily complex and dynamic.

Though undoubtedly an improvement on simplistic technology transfer models, the ideals of proponents of 'alternative' development have, to some, proved to be overly optimistic. The suggestion is that the problems that arose from technology transfers were merely a matter of inadequate communication. Limited to attempts to communicate local needs and context, the appropriate technology movement tended to ignore the long-term impacts on social structures created by change. Furthermore they have often failed to overturn long-established and entrenched power inequalities that support hierarchical evaluations of knowledge and technology.

Knowledge and power

The history of technology development, whether through conventional or alternative approaches, unpopular or popular, raises questions about the way we view not only technology but also knowledge. We have already argued that technology is never neutral and the introduction and use of technology are overtly moral, cultural and political processes. In this final section we will return to how knowledge is conceptualised and then consider its relationship with power.

As we have already seen, across Development World a conceptual contrast is commonly made between 'universal' science and 'local' or vernacular knowledge forms, even if the relative evaluation of each is more varied. Anti-development 'neo-indigenistas' value local knowledge but they still remain committed to the same kind of dichotomous classificatory scheme as the modernisation vision held by modernist economists and engineers. On one side we have the global reach of 'modern scientific knowledge' and on the other 'indigenous' or 'traditional' knowledge that is locally rooted and produced. Some homogeneity is assumed within each form of knowledge and absolute differences between them (Agrawal 1995: 421). But when you look more closely at the fundamental assumptions underlying the divide, the idea of two simple, unified types unravels.

The multiple terms used to denote 'indigenous knowledge' hint at some confusion: traditional knowledge, local knowledge, folk knowledge, folk-science, ethno-science, and so on. Whether the key distinction is between the technical and popular, the external and the indigenous, or the modern and the traditional, these terms are united only in the manner in which they are placed in simple opposition to 'modern scientific knowledge'. While science is abstracted and global, advocates of indigenous knowledge suggest (or imply in the subtler forms) an essentialised and romantic picture of 'primitive' cultures embedded into their environments but incapable of the advanced analytical reasoning necessary to transcend relatively closed systems of knowledge.

Why is this picture unconvincing? By definition, there can be no single global indigenous knowledge: the context-specific designation of indigenous knowledge means that it defies one category. Rather than constituting a homogenous category any knowledge takes many different forms, utilises different dissemination methods and is based on different rationales. Indeed, homogeneity of knowledge does not even exist within a specific community. Although often romanticised as democratically shared by a 'community', anthropologists recognise that forms of knowledge may be stratified, contested and unequally bounded by class, gender, age or occupation.

Context-bound local knowledge is seen as being purely practical – that is to say that wider theoretical conclusions cannot be drawn from it. The reach of such knowledge and the reasons for its production are therefore limited. Anthropologists would argue, however, that science has no monopoly on theoretical abstraction – all knowledge exists within wider theoretical frameworks, as the US physicist Kuhn and anthropologist Bloch have pointed out (Kuhn 1962; Bloch 1991).

Though indigenous knowledge is often conflated with 'tradition' it does not follow that it is in any sense static; just as traditions change, so do technologies and worldviews. Indeed all knowledge and practices – whether those of a farmer or scientist – display considerable dynamism based on ongoing empirical experimentation and enquiry. These characteristics of empirical investigation and truth searching are usually credited as central to science. But the everyday practice of making sense of the world, whether for practical work purposes such as cultivating land or spiritual exploration of mysterious questions, relies on the construction and contestation of theories.

Scientific knowledge in its cruder form presents itself as distinct from and superior to other forms of understanding. The recognition of subjectivity within science by chaos theoreticians does not appear to have permeated to all branches of science, with many scientists (and some social scientists) still seeing themselves as relying on rational empiricism and independence from personal or cultural influences. But it is worth noting that scientists have a vested interest in claiming that their methods generate objective knowledge. While it would be unhelpful to attribute the hierarchy of knowledge to a conspiracy of scientists competing for and protecting their status, funds and legitimacy, it is relevant to understand the pressures within the worlds of science and the cultures within it. Those who practise science occupy a dual identity – as does anyone searching for universal truths – being at once both scientists striving for objectivity and also politically influenced, culture-bound human beings.

Scientists are not the only group claiming objectivity. Latour is well known for his brilliant portrayals of the cultures of technology and science – showing how engineers (1996) and scientists (1987) are social actors responding to the world around them – but has also completed an ethnography of the making of law in France (2010). Both scientists and lawyers see their objectivity and detachments as superior to the other, but the way they produce and communicate knowledge is different. While scientists are experimenting directly with the material world and aim to suppress the subject (e.g. their own influence), legal objectivity is produced by the mental ability of the subject (the lawyer) but not by its object. 'Scientists speak inarticulately about precise objects, lawyers speak in precise terms about value objects' (Latour 2010: 236–7). Scientific journal articles contain passion and challenges to existing theory, whereas lawyers are measured and meticulous and the legal process gives the impression that fact, theories and truth are constant. Science prizes innovation whereas law aims to create stability (*ibid.*: 243). So scientists and lawyers seek objective truth but for different purposes and in different ways.

'Science' is an on-going dynamic *process* rather than a fixed and established set of incontestable *facts*. What we now think of as modern science had its roots in European folk knowledge systematised through Enlightenment philosophy. Thus the systematic study of botany emerged out of horticulture, chemistry from alchemy and physics from practical mechanics. Science can be said to have its origins within a distinct cultural and historical milieu and some of these cultural understandings are still apparent in its practice today. What was once western scientific knowledge is no less culturally located than other knowledge traditions and its development is no longer literally located in the 'West'. So there is no basis in the evolutionary framework that contrasts a single notion of advanced scientific knowledge in simple opposition to a single indigenous form that is locally produced and rooted. All knowledge is a hybrid product used in specific contexts.

In an age of globalisation when change is pervading all human societies, the conceptual divide between western and other forms of knowledge collapses. It would be more revealing to explore similarities between forms of both globalised and localised knowledge, and differences within them and the new hybrids, rather than attempting to categorise each form as separate and distinct. Sillitoe (2002) suggests a shift from the continuum model (a flat, one-dimensional model that invites discrimination) to a model of a globe that is more inclusive and points towards the dynamism of the global integration of knowledge. From this perspective all knowledge is both local and global and all societies hold both modern and traditional views. This model of the globe is also able to better account for the multiplicity of actors and networks working within Development World. Translation is possible if we move away from the idea of 'pure' and 'homogenous' forms of knowledge and recognise the ways in which actors may access multiple frames of meaning. These are themselves in a constant state of flux as they encounter others creating complex processes of syncretisation, blending, incorporation, integration as well as hybridisation. Thus, it is not possible to mark or fix any piece of knowledge as uniquely 'indigenous' or 'western'. If we recognise that the two knowledge forms are not completely different or even distinct, then we must ask whether ultimately science is merely a very successful and powerful form of indigenous knowledge. In that case, the distinction and evaluation of distinct knowledge traditions would appear to be more about differences in power than differences in what is known.

The old adage 'knowledge is power' may be true sometimes, but it is not necessarily so. Access to knowledge does not automatically change an individual's or group's position of power, but the knowledge of powerful people tends to be taken seriously. So power can appear as wisdom. When you look at the political and cultural systems of evaluation of knowledge and technology, power is more relevant that utility. These evaluations are accomplished by decisions about the methodology for evaluating knowledge and who is qualified to make these decisions. Though practitioners of development present their behaviour as objective, the pretence of neutrality is a useful disguise for political decisions that silence certain voices and exclude alternative forms of thinking. By suggesting objectivity the blank face of modern knowledge, expertise and technology can be seen as a mask that disguises political processes.

The separation and categorisation of so-called 'indigenous knowledge' from 'scientific knowledge' involves acts of power that create or reproduce hierarchies of relative superiority and inferiority. These hierarchies mirror relations of power between aid-giving and aid-receiving countries and even within them at all levels. The supremacy and resurgence of 'scientific' knowledge within development discourse reflects its dominance within the more prominent aid bureaucracies. Science differs from other types of knowledge mainly in its ability to force its reality upon others. Culturally rooted evaluations determine which goods are accorded high status and which are dismissed as primitive and inferior; uncovering these cultural beliefs reveals the ethnocentric bias apparent in many development institutions and initiatives.

How do these cultural systems of evaluation influence development practice and what roles are played by class, nationality and gender in determining the value of technology? The attribution of expertise is revealing. Rather than any objective superiority, it is the creation and careful maintenance of subjective hierarchies of knowledge that underpin the 'rule of experts' within development (see Box 6.7). 'It appears that technical knowledge is not measured and valued

Box 6.7. INGOs, technical capacity development and toolkits

UK-based International NGOs have a demanding range of partly technical functions to perform. They deliver services and provide technical assistance direct to national NGOs or governments and/or act as intermediaries channelling funds from donors to national or local actors. Part of their 'adding value' is to monitor progress, advise on effectiveness and develop the 'capacity' of their partner NGOs, networks or government departments. This capacity development, assumed necessary owing to the deficit of skills and organisation within the local or national agencies, is provided through technical assistance, training or provision of materials.

The pressure to claim technical expertise and publish toolkits or manuals that document this specialist knowledge can be overwhelming; securing funding depends on it. Many donors will even directly ask INGOs to write about their added value, the technical assistance they will bring or the technical outputs they will disseminate in funding proposals The manuals can relate to conventional technical areas – such as renewable energy – but also to re-ordering social relationships in the form of, for instance, 'gender mainstreaming' or managing people within communities or organisations. As Mowles puts it, 'many capacity development handbooks draw heavily on systems theory and optimisation. The field of capacity and organisational development is awash with grids and frameworks that purport to help analyse and assess the state of the "whole" organisation, usually comparing it with an idealised organisation towards which it can be optimised' (2009: 13). The reliance on systems theory in understanding organisations is too mechanical and simplistic and this approach to capacity development by outsiders takes ownership away from the insiders.

Within INGOs, staff feel obliged to overstate their technical expertise in virtually every funding proposal. To give evidence of 'added value', they typically claim that partners will be trained by the INGOs' technical experts when visiting projects. The availability of a toolkit produced by the INGO is evidence that they are leaders in that field. When visiting partner NGOs in Africa, Asia and South America, the reality tends to be, however, far more modest. UK Programme Managers are knowledgeable but often less expert than the managers of national NGOs implementing programmes in their regions. In practice, and despite the elevated claims in funding proposals, Programme Managers mostly ask questions, do a little monitoring and offer advice, which is frequently ignored.

by so-called experts according to utility for users when put into practice; its value is predetermined by its source and the social context from which it emerges. In effect, it is the inventor who is valued rather than the invention, and the evaluator will rank the inventor according to the power relationship between them' (Crewe and Harrison 1998: 104).

Defining certain people as 'expert' confers on them the ability to decide the future. The attribution of expertise on a specialist minority necessarily excludes the great majority of people from participating in deciding the direction of development initiatives at critical points. Just as a culture of expertise within development works to promote certain interests, it also serves to exclude others. Crucially the ascription of expertise relies on subjective evaluations that repeatedly promote the expatriate, and often but not always white men, and the technician over the local and the non-technician. Again processes of negative evaluation work on a number of levels. As we have already seen indigenous technology is denigrated by being classified as cultural rather than technical in character. Similarly local knowledge is labelled as traditional and assumed to be deficient, while some people are assumed to be more 'traditional' than others. Innovation by those labelled non-expert may be overlooked or dismissed and the poor, the indigenous and the non-educated are not deemed capable of producing improved or sophisticated techniques or tools. When Emma Crewe saw one potter in India show a development engineer his brand-new design for a sawdust-burning stove, the engineer asked, 'do you make any other traditional stoves?' But all new stove technology generated in laboratories is modern, irrespective of when it was invented; it seems that it is the identity and location of the inventor rather than the invention that is ranked on the modern/traditional continuum. In this worldview, modernity is not about newness.

Similarly, cultural ideas about gender dictate that women's innovation and expertise are undervalued. In development interventions it is common for women to be labelled non-technical with the self-fulfilling consequence that they are unlikely to be included in technological extension efforts and their own practices, needs and knowledge overlooked. In this way, the imposition of western technology and expertise reinforces or exacerbates inequalities. Other knowledge forms, and those that hold them, are hidden and silenced. The promotion of expertise is perhaps less about the exclusion of indigenous *knowledge* from development discourse, but rather the exclusion of indigenous or local *people* from participating. A feminist perspective of technology has broadened its definition to encompass women's technical innovation from a narrow focus on material forms of technology to the organisation of both tools and knowledge to achieve a task (Bush 1983: 155). This means that women's technical innovations, which tend to be more about small-scale technology and knowledge, would no longer be conceptually excluded from technology development (Appleton 1985).

These debates about the nature and meaning of knowledge and technology are far from new but have yet to inform fully development practice. Technological determinist models of knowledge and innovation as linear in evolution and neutral in impact continue to promote simplistic technological extension models. Not only are these expensive but they carry a high risk of failure. If standard models are often unworkable then there is a strong argument for considering the practical implications of alternative understandings of technology as socially embedded and requiring different approaches.

Anthropology offers a holistic picture of the creation, dissemination and consumption of information and material artefacts. Innovation, learning and transfers of technology must take full account of the social dimensions of innovation. It is not enough to 'get the technology right'; proper attention must also be paid the politics of transmission and use. New technology should by flexible enough to offer new adopters the chance to creatively enhance its functionality and ensure it is appropriate in the widest possible variety of settings.

Questioning the notion of scientific knowledge as unique and inherently superior, or even inherently different from other systems of knowledge, anthropology has done much to promote a positive re-evaluation of culturally appropriate and contextually sited forms of knowledge. Different knowledge forms rooted in different cultural contexts can be seen to share common methodological and epistemological frameworks. Anthropological perspectives suggest not a binary opposition between fixed and locally rooted understandings but rather a fluid process of mutual interaction in which knowledge is continually translated, interpreted and recreated in new, hybrid forms. These processes deserve to be given due recognition. Promoting alternative forms of evaluations may lead to a democratisation of ideas and expertise. By dismissing the sterile dichotomy between indigenous and scientific knowledge and seeking bridges between what are seen as opposing knowledge forms, Agrawal argues that we might initiate a productive dialogue that safeguards the interests of those whose needs, interests, views and understandings have been marginalised (1995: 433). We need to move away from the model that dictates that knowledge and technology flows unvaryingly from North to South or from laboratory to field. Knowledge is everywhere and we should create spaces for contestation and communication rather than systems of transfer.

Challenging questions arising from this chapter

Does technology development respond to need or culture?

What value is attached to different types of knowledge and technology? What does this reveal about the people who judge and are judged?

What is wrong with the opposition between so-called 'modern scientific knowledge' and 'traditional indigenous knowledge'?

How is knowledge socially constructed and embedded?

What impact have technology and science had on people, society and the environment?

What is the relationship between technology development, poverty and inequality?

How and why does technology transfer work or fail?

What different roles do science and technology play in international development policy and practice?

7   The moralities of production and exchange

This chapter examines the notion that development is promoted through integration into national and international capitalist markets. In these terms development is an economic process of global interconnectedness making trade and trade policy vital tools in attaining development objectives. Over much of the past half century international development policy has been premised on a belief in the freedom to pursue individual economic interests as the solution to the problems of poverty and hunger.

Key points covered by this chapter

- Contrasting the agricultural producers of developing economies with the financial powerhouses of global capitalism, this chapter examines the distinct positions and perspectives of varied buyers and sellers, producers and consumers.
- Recognising markets as more than simple arenas of economic exchange, anthropology traces the social relationships and cultural norms that underpin the workings of markets.
- The globalisation of production and exchange is driven by political relationships as much as economic ones; outcomes are shaped by moral, historical and social contexts.
- When differing interests and aims are incorporated into global systems of exchange, inequalities can be deepened. We review the possibilities for achieving more equitable impact.

To many policy-makers, development requires the expansion of trade. The argument runs as follows: greater exposure to global competition lowers prices for consumers, promotes specialisation and raises productivity among producers. Inclusion into the expanding global market furthers the diffusion of new techniques, products, ideas and capital and permits people and nations to trade themselves out of poverty. But the broad narrative of market integration and economic growth may conceal other possibilities. From US$59 billion in 1948, the total volume of good, services and merchandise traded internationally in 2009 was valued at US$12.421 trillion (WTO 2010: 11).[1] The global movement of goods and produce, capital, information, technology and people suggest a world that is

157

increasingly interconnected and interdependent. Yet, over the same time period, Africa's share of world merchandise exports has fallen from 7.3% to 3.2%. For Central and South America the figures are from 11.3% to 3.8%. Economic globalisation is clearly progressing more quickly in some regions than in others. However, statistics are malleable. The champions of economic globalisation still present the history of global exchange and consumption as an inevitable progression towards greater interdependence and shared prosperity.

Against the quantitative data that informs economic theory, anthropology's longstanding interest in production, distribution, exchange and consumption offers different understandings. Broadening the field of vision allows us to consider the alternative rationalities that drive production, the rituals that shape exchange and the symbolic meanings that lie behind consumption practices. This is not to suggest that all anthropologists approach 'the market' in the same way – as we shall see, significant differences exist. But, anthropology's empirical basis warns against generalisations; and never more so than when assessing the direct impacts of integration into a single global market.

Paying special attention to agricultural production and the distribution and consumption of food, this chapter investigates how political interests, cultural beliefs and social norms shape economic practices. Thanks to low labour costs and plentiful natural resources developing countries should enjoy a comparative advantage in exporting raw materials and agricultural produce. And yet, in a world that produces enough to feed everybody, millions find themselves unable to obtain adequate levels of food. While recognising that markets are an undeniable part of all of our lives, anthropological research concludes that we do not all enter into exchange relationships in the same manner or with the same results. It is suggested that the drive to fuller integration into global markets will not be uniformly beneficial to all; for those experiencing poverty, hunger and malnutrition, 'the market' may be as much a cause as a solution.

The pure and natural market

From farmers' fields to supermarket shelves an international infrastructure coordinates trade by linking producers and consumers in a global chain of exchange. Coffee planters in Columbia, cocoa growers in Ghana and wheat farmers in Bhutan must orientate their activities towards the demands of buyers from transnational corporations. In Bangladesh and Malaysia migrant labour is attracted to manufacturing centres that are funded by foreign investment. In factories and sweatshops raw materials are transformed into finished products for export. As a growing class of urban, middle-class consumers push up the price of meat, swathes of rainforest are turned to pasture. In the cargo-holds of container ships and jumbo jets, billions of tonnes of produce are shuttled around the world every day: tulips from Kenya, chicken from Thailand, cucumbers from Spain. Meanwhile commodities traders in the City of London, Frankfurt and on Wall Street finance investment, insure against risk and speculate on future prices. Collectively these points of connection constitute a single global market-place composed of multiple interconnected mini-markets. But behind these connections across countries and regions lie internationally agreed policies that are grounded in economic theory that suggests a universal rationality in how we engage in exchange.

Updating the classical economic template, 'neoliberalism' describes a set of market-driven approaches to social and economic development. Simply stated, neoliberal economics emphasises the fundamental superiority of 'the market' as a way of ordering production. A theoretical model of 'perfect competition' demonstrates the logic of the free market as follows:

- individual actors are free to enter and exit the market and to buy and sell from one another at will;
- all actors possesses a complete ('perfect') knowledge of the other actors in the markets, the products which they sell, and the prices of these products;
- each actor makes rational choices about buying and selling that maximise their individual utility; and
- with no single actor able to dictate to the market, the impersonal interplay of supply and demand determines price.

With these conditions met the optimal allocation of resources is achieved – the right quantity of production at the lowest possible cost. Furthermore, in a perfect market, so the theory goes, free competition and the uninterrupted flow of market signals lead to outcomes that are optimal not only *economically* but also *socially*. The ideal market model establishes a self-regulating harmony of interests. Extrapolated to the level of an entire economy, it follows that the free market is the instrument through which the distribution of goods and services is best determined.

Advocates of neoliberalism suggest that the 'free market' ideal is a condition to which all societies naturally progress. Conceived in this way, economic globalisation is a linear process of development by which 'they' (poor, traditional, subsistence producers) can be made more like 'us' (rich, modern, specialists) through incorporation into a single arena of exchange. Integration into the global market is simultaneously a measure of progress and the means through which it is attained. At national and international levels, it follows that institutions and policies should be shaped to promote 'the market' as the driver of development. With the market credited as being fundamentally benevolent, it follows that anything that interferes with its free operations is likely to be bad. Corrupt, cumbersome and inefficient, the state sector is identified as a distorter of market signals and therefore an impediment to economic growth. The core principle of neoliberal economics is that *more market* requires *less state*.

These ideas are far from new; Adam Smith (1723–90) coined the metaphor of the 'invisible hand' to illustrate the self-regulating nature of the marketplace in a 'system of perfect liberty'. Others, notably Friedrich Hayek (1899–1992) of the Chicago School of Economics, promoted free-market capitalism as the best means by which the interests of producers and consumers could be communicated and satisfied. Revived for the end of the twentieth century, and boosted by the fall of communism, supporters of neoliberal doctrine sought to unleash the creative power of the free market.

From the early 1980s a broad consensus has developed among mainstream academic economists, politicians and policy-makers that recognised market liberalisation as key to economic growth. Subsequently international development policy has been increasingly oriented to promote the primacy of the private sector. How did these economic and moral assumptions attain their current dominant position? The chronic economic problems that afflicted many western industrial nations in the 1970s undermined support for state-led attempts to manage the economy. Across the developed world the role of the state was curbed through deregulation and privatisation in the belief that this would unleash the creativity and drive of the private sector. And what was good for the rich world was felt to be good for the poor. Applied to the developing world the 'Washington consensus', that is, the broad agreement on neoliberal economics across the world's dominant governments, defined policy-making within the IMF and World Bank.

By the decade's end, limited returns from state-led programmes of modernisation left nations across Africa, Asia and Latin America struggling to meet the debt repayment obligations. Unable to borrow from private sources many governments were forced to turn to international donors for assistance. International financial bail-outs of these heavily indebted states were made conditional on their accepting a range of neoliberal policy prescriptions. World Bank and IMF-endorsed programmes of 'structural adjustment' include a range of measures such as the abandonment of price controls and subsidies, the scaling back of the civil service and drastic cuts in government spending levels (especially on social protection for those living in poverty). With privatisation 'rolling back' the state, programmes of deregulation removed controls on the operations of financial markets. More recently a modified 'post Washington consensus' has recognised a role for government in facilitating the operations of the private sector; but again the market remained central to this model of development.

Market integration is presented as a solution to the problems of poverty and underdevelopment. 'Getting prices right' supposedly allows the objective forces of supply and demand to reflect the true rewards and risks of production. With regard to food it is suggested that liberalisation creates a globally efficient food production system characterised by low production costs, reliable supply and low food prices for consumers.

Neoliberal theory has been translated into policies that constrain the scope of operations of governments in poorer countries and restructures the relations between these countries and the rest of the world. The failure of the centrally planned economies of the communist bloc at the end of the 1980s further entrenched the notion that integration into a single capitalist market system

was inevitable. The following decade saw renewed efforts to reinforce a global architecture for international trade and to promote the flow of goods and
services across national borders. Created in 1995 to replace the earlier General
Agreement on Trade and Tariffs (GATT), the World Trade Organization (WTO)
is tasked with stabilising world trade through the negotiation and enforcement
of international agreements. Under the tutelage of the WTO the idea was promoted that trade should proceed unhindered by the influence of governments or
other bodies. In recent decades measures designed to support local producers
have been abandoned, controls on imports and exports reduced or eliminated and
restrictions on the movement of capital lifted. The prevailing orthodoxy is that
nothing should get in the way of the operations of the free market.

How did the global economic recession of 2008 affect the neoliberal hold
on international policy-making? It might be expected that the coordinated governmental response to this crisis of global finance would temper some aspects
of free market fundamentalism. But, a brief flirtation with coordinated stimulus
packages was soon replaced by the austerity measures, budget cuts and sweeping
programmes of privatisation that remain the standard IMF-endorsed prescription
for malfunctioning economies. To do otherwise would be to risk the wrath of
financial markets.

The former World Bank consultant and Goldman Sachs economist Dambisa
Moyo writes in her polemic *Dead Aid* that the economic benefits of trade have
attained the status of a generally accepted truth (2009: 115). Moyo denies the
need for assistance in the form of aid on the grounds that it corrupts fiscal discipline. For many people, salvation from poverty and underdevelopment continues
to be found in the simple mechanics of the market; not only is economic integration seen as inevitable it is also held to be a good thing.

The view from the farmer's field

A 'formalist' approach to economic decision-making suggests that,
given a certain level of abstraction, everyone makes choices in the same manner.
Against this, the 'substantivist' position argues that exchange in pre-industrial
economies is based on notions of reciprocity and redistribution (Polanyi *et al.*
1957). With cultural and social factors pushed to the fore, it follows that conventional economics is poorly equipped to examine the basis of economic life in such
societies. Neoliberal arguments about the efficacy of markets might have attained
considerable influence among donor governments and within the World Bank
and IMF. But against these optimistic models the view from the farmer's field
can look very different. Describing how markets work in practice, anthropology
provides a useful corrective to abstract models of how they work in theory.

A strong bias towards the 'modern' urban economy has been identified in
state efforts to promote development. Not without basis, it is claimed that policies designed to favour urban workers and the middle classes systematically

discriminated against rural populations (Lipton 1977). By 'shifting the terms of trade towards agriculture' (World Bank, 1981;[2] 1986[3]) free-market reforms might improve the position of small-scale cultivators and landless labourers. In theory integration into market systems would permit poor farmers to move beyond subsistence production and out of poverty. Opening up markets might raise the profitability of agricultural production thereby increasing demand for unskilled rural labour and thus reducing rural poverty.

But efforts to improve the efficient functioning of markets have not always lived up to the predictive models on which they were based. The impacts of neoliberal trade policies have, at best, been varied and rarely conform to expect-ation. An example of this disjuncture between prediction and experience arrives from Mexico. Preibisch, Herrejón and Wiggins consider how rural households in the central highlands negotiated changes in agricultural policy (2002). Having adopted a neoliberal growth model in the early 1980s, the Mexican government targeted agriculture with measures intended to insert the sector firmly into the global marketplace. The implications for the production of maize, the most important food crop in Mexico, were dramatic. Government subsidies for the production of staples were abandoned at the same time as the lifting of trade barriers opened up the Mexican market to cheap American imports. Between 1990 and 1998 maize prices fell by 48 per cent. And yet, in spite of the dras-tically reduced economic incentives for production, Preibisch *et al.* reported that in their study areas of the Toluca-Atlacomulco Valley the fields continued to be planted almost exclusively with maize. This was clearly 'contrary to the expectations of both Mexico's neoliberal technocrats and some of their critics' (*ibid.*: 68–9). Cultural preference and gender politics explain the community's continued determination to produce their own grain. Growing one's own maize provides farmers with the security of a supply of high-quality grain with which to make tortillas, the country's dietary staple. The consumption of homemade tortillas was 'a source of pride for *campesinos* and *campesinas* alike'; imported maize was considered 'dirty' and store-bought alternatives were a poor substitute for the 'real thing' (*ibid.*: 72). Gender norms also played a part; by improving availability of wage labour (and leaving women dependent upon their husbands for cash), the reforms benefited men disproportionately. But decisions about the consumption and sale of maize remained firmly under the control of women. The independence and security this provided was not to be lightly abandoned. Price alone played only a small part in household decision-making about maize production and consumption in Toluca-Atlacomulco Valley; extending beyond narrow economic considerations allows us to appreciate the influence of cultural values, social roles and gender norms.

The adoption of neoliberal policies for agriculture in Tanzania produced a dif-ferent set of outcomes. Stagnation in Tanzania's agricultural sector led to the adop-tion of a series of programmes of economic liberalisation beginning in the early 1980s. The abandonment of protectionist measures offered new opportunities for Tanzania's farmers to sell their produce internationally. Currency devaluations improved the competitiveness of exports, while the removal of national price controls increased the profitability of agricultural production. However, a close analysis of Tanzania's agricultural performance since liberalisation suggests that the results have been mixed at best. Some farmers have undoubtedly benefited, typically the larger landowners who were already closely integrated into systems of transport infrastructure and able to orient mass production to the specifications of international buyers. But overall, the expected boost to agriculture proved elusive and did little to improve the lives of the rural poor.

According to Skarstein (2005), agricultural GDP grew no more rapidly in the post-liberalisation years in Tanzania than in the so-called 'crisis years' from 1976 to 1986. In order to understand why this might be so, he examined how farmers responded to the price incentives that liberalisation created. Farmers were expected to specialise in export-oriented crops, but many opted to diversify their activities. For some this involved withdrawing from commercial production and re-establishing a subsistence base; others sought alternative sources of income in petty trade, petty transportation and the brewing of beer (2005: 359). Why might they have chosen to act in a way contrary to the logic of neoliberal market theory? The answer lies in different evaluations of risk and reward. The opening up of new market opportunities resulted in higher prices for cash crops overall but these prices were subject to considerable volatility: in times of plenty prices dropped; when there was shortage they soared. In the face of a higher degree of exposure to the vagaries of the market both 'income diversification' and 'subsistence fall-back' are rational responses to economic instability. For many Tanzanian farmers the long-term security previously provided by low but constant prices was preferable to the uncertainty of higher rewards.

example of traditionalism beating capitalism

In Malawi the consequences of liberalisation were more severe. As elsewhere in sub-Saharan Africa, low agricultural productivity was attributed to high levels of government interference, mismanagement and corruption. At the centre of this system were the monopolistic marketing enterprises known as *parastatals*. With one hand these government-run bodies subsidised farming with inputs of pesticides and fertilisers; yet with the other hand they took away by buying produce at below market price. Such double interventions – simultaneously distorting supply and demand mechanisms – were seen as a serious impediment to the workings of the free market. In combination with bilateral donors, the IMF and World Bank sought to curb this arrangement. Over the course of the 1980s and 1990s state intervention in agriculture was gradually reduced. With agricultural production incentivised, economic liberalisation was expected to raise output and increase incomes for farmers and rural labour. Official control of maize prices was eventually abandoned in 2000. Little more than a year later a major famine resulted in a death toll that extended to tens of thousands (Devereux and Tiba 2007: 145).

liberalism is trouble during times of hardship

With different explanations hard to disentangle from one another, the causal factors behind famine deaths are rarely simple (see Chapter 4). But in the Malawian case, the liberalisation of the economy certainly contributed to the collapse in food security experienced by many households. One significant trigger for the crisis was a decline in maize production in 2001. Yet Malawi had faced instances of food shortage before without succumbing to famine: in 1997–8, for instance, total maize output was approximately 360,000 tonnes *less* (a full 27 per cent) than in the crisis year of 2001–2. The difference in outcome can be partly explained by the increased vulnerability and food insecurity of many rural people that resulted from liberalisation. As in Tanzania, a relatively minor shortfall in production translated into major shifts in commodity prices taking basic foodstuffs out of the reach of the poor. Smallholders who had previously been able to survive shortages were now left dangerously exposed. In previous instances of food shortage massive intervention by the Agricultural Development and Marketing Corporation (ADMARC) had been effective in maintaining adequate levels of provision. But the liberalisation of the agricultural sector meant that by 2001 many of the official mechanisms for intervention in food markets had been abandoned and those that remained proved largely ineffective. Exposed to the unpredictable whims of the global market, and with the safety net of state support withdrawn, malnutrition, hunger and starvation were visited on the people of Malawi.

These three cases illustrate how people and communities do not necessarily conform to the narrow predictions of neoliberal economics. In Mexico women farmers in the central highlands ignored supply-side price incentives. Smallholders in Tanzania sought alternatives to the higher rewards offered by the export of produce. The Malawian case demonstrates why people might choose to reject the logic of the market. Economic reforms sometimes have unadvertised side effects in the form of increased inequality, poverty and insecurity. Just as social norms and political interventions can restrict and stifle individual endeavour so too can they be positive and supportive. Focusing on the narrowly individual ignores the importance of the communal and the networks of solidarity and mutual aid that reduce risk and provide a safety net in times of hardship. Anthropologists point to the manner in which cultural and institutional contexts shape 'individual' economic acts in unexpected ways.

Harnessing the power of the market and individual enterprise produces winners, but there are losers also. The above examples illustrate that for many rural dwellers neoliberal promises of an end to poverty are unlikely to be fulfilled. First they undermine the broad claim that market liberalisation promotes economic growth; second, even if this were so, it does not follow that economic expansion reduces poverty. But it required a systemic crisis of global proportions before the basic tenets of neoliberal belief came to be seriously re-examined. The financial crash of 2008 saw trillions of dollars wiped from the values of the banking sector and the global financial system brought to the brink of meltdown (Gillian Tett, a financial journalist with a background in anthropology, follows this process in her 2010 book *Fool's Gold* – see Box 7.1). As might be expected this crisis soon manifested itself in the wider economy. Across the world the

Box 7.1. An anthropologist among journalists

An in-depth understanding of marriage rituals in Soviet-era Tajikistan may not seem immediately relevant to financial journalism, but this is exactly the leap that Gillian Tett made when she went from a PhD in anthropology to covering the capital markets for the *Financial Times*. From an interview with the *Observer* newspaper: 'Finance is not just about numbers,' she says. 'It's absolutely about social systems and political fabric. For me, learning about finance and the economy was like learning Tajik: they both need to be decoded in some way.'[4]

In her book *Fool's Gold* Tett follows a 'small tribe' of bankers at the US powerhouse JP Morgan to explain the roots of the global financial crisis that broke in 2007–8. She draws on Bourdieu's *Outline of a Theory of Practice* and the concept of mental and structural *silos* to explain what went wrong. For Tett 'bow-tie days' in the office and brainstorming retreats at which golf buggies are raced around hotel lawns are as relevant to the story as the invention of the credit default swap.

'Back in the 1990s, when I first started working as a financial reporter, I used to keep rather quiet about my "strange" academic background. At that time, it seemed that the only qualifications that commanded respect were degrees in orthodox economics, or an MBA; the craft of social anthropology seemed far too "hippy" (as one banker caustically observed) to have any bearing on the high-rolling, quantitative world of finance. These days, though, I realise that the finance world's lack of interest in wider social matters cuts to the very heart of what has gone wrong. What social anthropology teaches is that nothing in society ever exists in a vacuum or in isolation. Holistic analysis that tries to link different parts of a social structure is crucial, be that in respect to wedding rituals or trading floors. Anthropology also instils a sense of scepticism about official rhetoric. In most societies, elites try to maintain their power not simply by garnering wealth, but by dominating the mainstream ideologies, both in terms of what is said, and also what is not discussed. Social "'silences" serve to maintain power structures in ways that participants often barely understand, let alone plan. That set of ideas may sound excessively abstract (or hippy). But they would seem to be sorely needed now. In recent years, regulators, bankers, politicians, investors and journalists have all failed to employ truly holistic thought – to our collective cost. Bankers have treated their mathematical models as if they were an infallible guide to the future, failing to see that those models were based on a ridiculously limited set of data. A "silo" mentality has come to rule inside banks, leaving different departments competing for resources, with shockingly little wider vision or oversight. The regulators who were supposed to oversee the banks have mirrored that silo pattern too, in their own fragmented practices. Most pernicious of all, financiers have come to regard banking as a silo in its own right, detached from the rest of society. They have become like the inhabitants of Plato's cave, who could see shadows of outside reality flickering on the walls, but rarely encountered that reality themselves. The chain that linked a synthetic CDO of ABS, say, with a "real" person was so convoluted it was almost impossible for anybody to fit that into a single cognitive map – be they anthropologist, economist or credit whizz' (Tett 2010: 298–9).

Box 7.2. Two worlds collide: when farmers and bankers meet

Commodity exchanges are financial instruments, which allow participants to agree a sale at a fixed price at a future date. For farmers commodity exchanges provide a useful role allowing them to hedge against risks such as bad harvests. Speculators who guarantee prices perform a useful role in providing liquidity.

In 2008 and again in 2011 global commodity prices rose sharply. Food inflation impacts most heavily on the poorest who spend a greater proportion of their income on staples such as rice, maize and wheat. With families struggling to feed themselves, these price hikes provoked riots and political instability across Africa, the Middle East and Asia. The factors behind the price rises are not easy to disentangle. Climate change and related periods of drought or unusual hot or cold temperatures impacted negatively on the supply side. Rising demand for meat, sugar, cocoa from the emerging middle classes of China and India also accounted for global food inflation. Oil price spikes caused by instability pushed up the cost of processing and transporting commodities. But these underlying fundamentals are also subject to speculation on commodity exchanges. Promoted by complex financial instruments which allow bets to be placed on future prices, over the past decade speculation on prices of basic commodities has increased greatly. The billions of dollars in new capital that have been invested in agricultural commodities play a significant role in the increased volatility and higher prices. In times of financial uncertainty investors seek out safe havens for their capital – food is an easy bet. But as inventors get rich, and speculative bubbles expand, food is taken out of the reach of the poor and families starve.

---

net effect of economic liberalisation had been to financialise both produce and people, transforming them into commodities that could be bought and sold. It also exposed them to the vagaries of international commerce. 2008 also saw a dramatic spike in global commodity prices particularly food goods. Far away from the world of high finance, decisions made in the offices of hedge funds and investment banks had very real implications for the ability of millions of people to feed themselves and their families (see Box 7.2).

Neoliberal views of globalisation promise that inclusion into world markets will charge economic growth. Progress is envisaged as movement towards a common shared future, of becoming a part of a united and prosperous global society. But, as we have seen, the variety of local experiences suggests neither linear convergence and homogenisation nor uniform economic development.

As well as documenting the varied impacts of neoliberal policies, anthropology is a discipline well suited to examining the reasons behind their failure. Actual markets differ from the neoliberal theorised markets in two major respects:

- *Diversity.* People engage in exchange relations in different ways, motives vary as do interests, rationalities and aims.

- *Power.* Actors do not engage with one another on equal terms. Exchange is rarely carried out entirely freely – certain interests, rationalities and aims are privileged over others.

Economic globalisation, as Haugerud, Stone and Little point out, should be seen as 'an uneven and contradictory set of processes that takes on very different forms in particular places' (2000: 3). We ask whether notions of the existence of a single global market can really be maintained.

One market or many?

Mainstream economics seeks to reveal universally applicable truths through the analysis of abstract formal models. This approach holds that economies and economic processes are comparable and therefore that all markets are fundamentally the same. In so doing economics mimics positivist science. But 'just as physics has its point masses, frictionless surfaces and pure vacuums', so too positivist economics conjures up 'cost-less transactions, rational actors and perfect knowledge' (Carrier 1997: xi). These universal, stylised and formalistic visions of the operations of the market are undermined once they come into contact with reality.

The idealised workings of the 'free market' are quite distinct from how people interact when they buy and sell. An article published by the anthropologist Timothy Jenkins considers the practices involved in buying and selling cattle in south-west France. In the Pyrenean region of Béarn each town holds a market on a weekly or fortnightly basis. Jenkins describes market day as an occasion when peasant farmers descend from the surrounding countryside 'to shop, to do business, or simply to meet friends and to talk' (1994: 435). Business revolves around the cattle market where the professional livestock dealers are to be found. Wearing black smocks as a mark of identity these dealers regularly travel long distances to reach a wide circuit of markets. In reviewing the interaction of peasant producers and professional dealers, Jenkins describes a distinct market culture that is not simply reducible to the economics of exchange: 'The market place has its own forms of language, its vocabulary and figures of speech: the actors speak largely in banalities on preordained topics … The business of selling, the transaction between peasant and dealer, is also a ritual controlled by the moral code of each group' (*ibid.*: 437).

Other opportunities to trade livestock exist. If economics alone determined exchange, then farmers would opt to sell directly to slaughterhouses in the regional capital. Yet, despite improvements in transport and communication links, the larger weekly markets held in towns around Béarn have continued to survive and even flourish. The social element of the game of buying and selling counts for more than price alone. When sizing up an animal there is a sequence of gestures that are performed. The buyer must consider the health and age of the animal, estimate the potential yield and weigh up what the fat and kidneys might contribute. Both buyers and sellers acknowledge they are involved in a contest of wits in which one may deceive the other by employing underhand techniques to improve the appearance of the animal. Such deceptions might be expected to result in hostility between the two groups. But, as Jenkins reveals, it is not the negotiation of price that causes antagonism but rather instances where one or other of the parties fail to properly observe part of the ritual of exchange through which the market is socially constructed (*ibid.*: 436). Here we see exchange as not just an economic act, but a social one also. As Hann and Hart point out: 'self-interested calculation *and* moral norms are present in all economies; what matters is their variable interplay' (2011: 85).

The free market model used to justify neoliberal trade policies is based on a series of simple (and arguably simplifying) assumptions. In this idealised scheme actors are autonomous individuals able to enter into utilitarian exchange with other similar individuals. There are no barriers to entering or leaving a market and all users possess perfect knowledge about that which is being bought and sold. The market thus conceived is 'an aggregate of strangers' (Berthoud 2010: 80). Just as actors are seen as being freed from social constraints as they enter into the market, so too do the subjects of trade become commoditised as objects detached from symbolic or spiritual meaning. The function of the market is to facilitate communication between buyers and sellers that allows them to weigh accurately costs and benefits. Each actor seeks to maximise his own utility, narrowly defined in economic or material terms; she or he is entirely selfish and the utility of others does not enter into her or his calculations.

Anthropologists approach ideas of markets in ways that are manifestly different to those of most economists. While neoclassical economics tends to neglect all forms of human activity that are not specifically economic, anthropology views markets as constructed out of and within networks of social relationships. From this perspective participation in markets by individual actors is not autonomous but rather is bound up in the values, norms, rituals and beliefs that constitute social and cultural life. For the peasants of Béarn the weekly market offers an opportunity to meet, talk and socialise. These farmers and the buyers with whom they trade combine into complex and shifting social groups, their transactions structured by shared rituals and understandings. They are not simple 'utility maximisers' but complex social beings with varied aims, interests, rationalities, desires and knowledge.

Reducing transactions to economic dimensions alone reduces products to their simple material state – quantities are measured without regard for qualities. In emphasising the economics of exchange, social relationships and the cultural attribution of value are hidden. But, as Appadurai argues, far from being 'private, atomic or passive', consumption is a set of actions that are 'eminently social, relational and active' (1986: 31). Things, like people, come to possess a 'social life' through the symbolic value and ideological knowledge that people attribute to them. Building meaning and memory into base material, anthropology re-centres the symbolic value of objects to reveal the richness, depth and complexity of economic exchange.

The ideal of the free market is here revealed as an illusion – markets are never truly free; nor are they natural. As Hewitt de Alcántara (1993: 6) points out, it is misleading to speak of a single, simple, universal integrated exchange environment: 'There is often more likely to be a network of micro-markets, sometimes only short distances apart, in which local power structures define the terms of trade, as well as the channels through which resources pass from lower to higher levels within the broader economy' (ibid.: 7). The politics of production and exchange operates alongside the economics at all levels. Moral economies are intertwined with material ones; 'marketplaces everywhere and at all times are regulated through political, cultural and legal conventions' (Pottier 1999: 101).

How do such understandings help us to comprehend the kinds of changes that result from the incorporation of local exchange relations into wider, even global, economic systems? Anthropologists argue that the particular ways in which market incorporation manifests itself in different locations cannot be attributed to 'the forces of global capitalism' alone. External influences are continually reinterpreted through particular historical, social and cultural contexts; micro-struggles at the level of the community or household determine the peculiarities and limits of market interaction. Resulting forms are shaped in complex and competing ways by social and political determinants that stretch from the immediate (within the household), to the local (community, village or district), to the national (the role of government and non-governmental institutions) to the international (the terms in which countries are integrated into global economic systems).

This leads us to question orthodox conceptualisations of economic globalisation. With no single way of conducting exchange, how are we to understand economic globalisation? Clearly it is not a process of homogenisation in which all forms of exchange converge into an identical capitalism. Nor are responses to this process reducible to accommodation or resistance. Instead we see a variety of hybrid forms emerge as new exchange relationships are established to link individuals, institutions and communities in complex chains of production, exchange and consumption (see Box 7.3). It is important to understand how economic ideas are produced, but also how they travel. In this way globalisation can be seen as the interaction and co-production of complex forms of exchange in fluid, ongoing processes that span the local, the national and the international.

What happens when different cultures of exchange come into contact with one another? Departing again from orthodox abstract economics, anthropology recognises that exchange rarely takes place between equal individuals possessing similar knowledge, resources, interests and capabilities. Markets function because of difference: this is the basis of acts of exchange. And it is social as much as economic norms that dictate the practice of exchange: *how* you trade is determined by *who* you are. Power and particularly the power to determine value

Box 7.3. Commodity chain analysis

Commodity chain analysis follows the passage of a given commodity or set of related commodities from initial raw material production through processing/packaging, shipping, marketing and consumption. The steps in the chain may be simple or complex depending on the product.

As an example, a takeaway coffee begins life with the beans harvested by farmers and sold on to local dealers. The beans are passed on for processing before exporters arrange their transportation overseas (large coffee estates and plantations often export their own harvests or have direct arrangements with transnational coffee processing or distributing companies). Importers accept large container loads of coffee and break them into small orders, which are delivered to roasters. The coffee can now be processed, ground, standardised and packaged. Coffee finally reaches the consumer through a wide variety of cafes, supermarkets and other retail outlets.

The analysis of commodity chains can take a number of forms. Economists calculate the value of rents imposed at different points along the chain. Untangling the differing elements that determine the final sale price reveals the level of profit extracted by different actors at various stages. And knowing *who* profits allows us to investigate *how* they extract value from a product. Focusing on the political and social relations of organisation it is possible to reveal the uneven distribution of power among strong and weak links in the chain.

As well as physical material flows, commodity chains can be understood as interconnected discursive forms. By examining the social, cultural and historical factors that shape exchange and consumption, anthropologists present a fuller picture of a commodity. Considering the ways in which particular characteristics are attributed to particular products (Apple computers, German cars, diamonds from Sierra Leone) this approach helps explain how we select certain goods, while rejecting (or even boycotting) others. Seeking out meanings attributed to food we complete the final link in the chain by moving from the supermarket shelf to the dinner table.

cannot be ignored. The next section considers how it is decided who gains and who loses from market integration.

The view from the banker's window

Looking down from the upper floors of an office building in the metropolitan heart of global capitalism, it is easy to suppose that the trading of bonds, stocks and shares conforms to the perfect ideal of free-market competition. Equipped with an array of up-to-the minute data, individual speculators engage with one another without ever necessarily meeting. With the global flow of trade captured as a series of numbers on a flickering computer screen, the narrowly economic is firmly separated from the physical and the social. Abstract trades are made with the push of a button: traders are isolated from the material reality in which they deal.

Box 7.4. An ethnography of the Shanghai stock market

In *The Trading Crowd*, Ellen Hertz's describes the early stages of development of the Shanghai stock market. A period of ethnographic fieldwork carried out in the early 1990s allowed Hertz to document the moment in China's experiments with economic reforms when a 'capitalist mechanism' was first promoted on a large scale. She describes how a political contest over the meaning of this economic experiment was visible from the start. Western commentators painted the reforms as part of an inevitable embrace of western capitalism, a view that Hertz summarises as follows:

> Economic 'reality' had led the Communist government to adopt the world's only functional development model – that of Western capitalism ... [i]t followed that it is impossible to organize a stock market along other than Western lines; the only real stock market is a Western stock market, and the Chinese will have succeeded in their experiment to the extent that they mimic this model. (Hertz 1998: 10–11)

China's central government was equally insistent that the Shanghai exchange was a stock market 'with Chinese characteristics' and was therefore compatible with a 'socialist commodity economy'. Hertz confirms that the Shanghai market operates along different lines, with different structures, different rules and a different ideological dynamic from the international market (1998: 13). But this is not to say that the Shanghai stock market conforms to the image forwarded by Party ideology. To determine the nature and degree of the Shanghai stock market's 'Chinese characteristics' Hertz recommends us to recognise that a distinctive 'native point of view' is informed and influenced by dominant 'global' discourses of capitalism. But discourses shift and dominant ideas don't last forever. How long will it be before we talk of 'Chinese socialist commodity economies' with 'European characteristics'?

Influenced by the substantivist position, anthropology has had much to say about systems of exchange as practised in small-scale, non-western and subsistence based societies. Where anthropology has, until recently, provided less illumination is with regard to the production and function of the global capitalist system itself. But to make sense of Development World, we need also to understand the sites in which neoliberal theories of economics are most strongly held.

In seeking to understand economic relations in small-scale societies, Polanyi's substantivism presumes a categorical distinction between 'traditional' exchange arrangements and those to be found in 'modern industrial societies'. But separating 'the West' from 'the rest' places 'pre-capitalist' systems of exchange against an abstract and idealised capitalist model. The presumption here is of a monolithic capitalism as a static system of internal consistency. Challenging such polarisation, a number of anthropologists have set out to identify the social and cultural elements – ritual, symbolism and meaning – that are embedded within the supposedly most advanced capitalist settings. In doing so, they follow Hertz's injunction that the study of the stock market should not be left to economists (1998: 16; see Box 7.4).

Empirically grounded studies of high finance reveal the 'personalities, private perks and little interest groups, prestige, [and] imagination' that underpin the workings of investment banks, hedge funds and stock markets (Miller, cited in Ho 2009: 32). Invisible in the abstract modelling of conventional economic analysis, these aspects of everyday life are immediately relevant and amenable to anthropological investigation. Situating the supposedly abstract market in sites possessing distinctive institutional cultures, anthropology offers a convincing counter narrative to notions of economic globalisation as an inevitable and natural process.

In her ethnography of Wall Street, Karen Ho shows us that the economic practices of major financial institutions are as much cultural products as the activities of subsistence farmers or hunter-gatherers. Having previously worked as an internal management consultant with a Wall Street investment bank, Ho returned to conduct detailed ethnographic enquiries into the everyday practices, lifestyles and career paths of her former colleagues, the networks that they formed and the attitudes that they held. Deconstructing the concept of the market in western culture, Ho demonstrates the extent to which market ideology in the West is intimately tied to British and American notions of 'individualism, property, and neoclassical economics' (2009: 33).

But Ho goes beyond the recognition of the existence of specific values and norms inside Wall Street's investment banks to consider how these sensibilities are transplanted onto the wider world. Financial elites do not simply describe and analyse the operations of markets, they also work to perform and produce them. Ho describes the 'world making influence' (2009: 31) that key actors and institutions have established over the global economy and thus the lives and livelihoods of all those it touches. Wall Street imposes its own cultures of risk, reward, disposability and flexibility upon other settings. Above all, this culture promotes itself by celebrating the 'the market' as the ultimate realisation of individual economic freedom, unbound by subjective values or ties of social obligation. Extending beyond the world of finance, these ideas have attained a level of prominence within political and academic circles in North America and western Europe and in the upper echelons of the World Bank and IMF. Thus, financial institutions outside and inside Development World are connected.

The set of beliefs described by Ho become truly 'world making' when applied to aid conditionality. Market-led globalisation has been forcefully promoted by powerful donor governments and the major international financial institutions in ways that leave developing countries with little option but to conform. As powerful external forces alter the balance of relationships of production and exchange, global economic integration promotes new forms of alienation. Certainly the inability to participate in a marketplace, whether through marginality or discrimination, represents a form of deprivation. But, as individuals, families, communities and nations are drawn into wider economic systems whose values and interests run contrary to their own, it becomes apparent that inclusion on unfavourable or unequal terms is not necessarily any better.

Far from the seamless capital movements and the uninhibited operations of the market promised by neoliberal logic, what we see is the establishment of new constellations of wealth and power which link the local to the national and the global. The enactment of neoliberal policies involves the construction of complex networks stretching from the executives of foreign companies to the representatives of national governments and an array of state and non-state actors at regional and local levels. Recognising the socially constructed nature of markets highlights the role of power in determining possibilities and outcomes of exchange. In a system of perfect liberty, goods and resources may be optimally distributed as all actors are assumed to possess similar interests and to benefit equally from shared ties. But this ideal ignores the existence of asymmetries whether in physical resources or in the ability to enter freely into market relations. Rhetoric about privatisation and marketisation assisting the poor repeatedly masks a reality in which the already wealthy and privileged benefit disproportionately. At all levels it is differences in power that rigs markets against the many and in favour of the few. Power determines whose interests are recognised and whose are denied, who gets to eat and who goes hungry.

Socialising the economic: alternative approaches to trade

So far the policy recommendations emanating out of neoliberal economic theory have been explained in terms of a rebalancing of the relationship between the public and the private sector. As the state is rolled back, the newly incentivised market is assumed to fill its place. We now go on to consider the ways in which a third set of actors – aid agencies, civil society movements and advocacy campaigns – have responded to these changes.

We have seen how varied models of exchange relations are brought into contact with one another through economic globalisation. New systems of exchange emerge and are shaped by the interaction of a range of actors with varied needs, interests, rationalities and goals. The range of possibilities stretch from exploitative forced inclusion through to perfect incorporation. We would argue that the usual outcome is somewhere between these extremes: benefits from inclusion are not evenly distributed; but nor are participants unable to shape their engagement with wider market forces. We now examine three attempts to influence positively the manner and mode of integration. In different ways each seeks to empower either financially or politically, those that suffer from disadvantageous incorporation into local, national and global economic arenas.

From Bangladesh to the world: micro-credit

The story behind the creation of the Grameen Bank has been told so often that it has almost passed in the realms of development legend: an origin myth for micro-credit. It runs as follows: frustrated by the inability of conventional economics to alleviate hunger and poverty, in the mid 1970s Professor Muhammad Yunus left Chittagong University to spend two years learning about the lives of his fellow countrymen and women in rural Bangladesh. Yunus made two inter-related discoveries. First he realised the importance of self-employment, from which many Bangladeshis, and particularly women, earned a significant por-tion of their income. His second discovery was that the ability of the rural poor, and especially women, to generate income through self-employment was ser-iously curtailed by a lack of access to credit. Obstructed from borrowing except at extremely disadvantageous rates of interest, many were forced into cycles of debt repayment that left them unable to raise themselves out of poverty. Though the nationalised banks were officially required to lend without concern for gen-der and class, in practice a series of institutional biases within the banking sys-tem meant that those most in need of credit were least able to get it.

The norms and procedures of mainstream banking institutions discriminate against women in a number of ways. Form filling requires basic literacy as well as time and effort. Women's enterprises are generally small scale and deemed less creditworthy owing to the comparatively higher administrative costs required to process small loans. Banks located in urban areas are inaccessible to rural people. When gender norms deny female ownership of material assets (especially land), women will lack the security and collateral needed to secure loans. Though less tangible, the obstacle of social distance separates educated, middle-class and typ-ically male bank officials from poor women seeking loans. Of the latter Kabeer writes (1994: 238): 'Their clothing and general appearance, combined with their general lack of experience and confidence in the public domain, ensured that poor rural women were unlikely to obtain entry into mainstream banking institu-tions, assuming that they attempted it.'

Professor Yunus set out to prove that the exclusion of poor women from access to credit is not only unjust but is also bad banking. Rather than expecting the poor to conform to the norms, practices and beliefs of conventional banking institu-tions, Yunus insisted that the structure and practices of his bank were designed to respond to the lives and needs of the people who were to use it. Against precon-ceived notions that poor, rural women are not creditworthy, Yunus countered that it was the banks that were not 'people-worthy'.

The belief that a bank should meet the needs of the people, rather than the people having to fit into the inflexible operations of conventional banking institutions, led to the foundation of the Grameen (Village) Bank in 1976. Experimenting with organisation structures and procedures and involving borrowers in the decision-making process, Yunus reoriented the conventional structure of a bank towards the needs of the poor. The basic unit of the Grameen Bank was established as a group of five members all drawn from similar socio-economic backgrounds. The idea was that the members of the group should feel comfortable together, know and trust each other. Though loans were made to individuals, it was the respon-sibility of the other members to analyse the feasibility of each member's loan proposal and to ensure that it was repaid. If a borrower were to default, then the other members of the micro-credit circle would know that this could jeopardise their own chances of receiving future loans. Depending on the application of peer pressure and peer support, the use of joint liability did away with the need for material collateral required by conventional banks.

The system of micro-credit pioneered by the Grameen Bank has been presented as an unequivocal success story. By the mid 1990s the Grameen Bank was operating in over 35,000 villages throughout Bangladesh and had in excess of 2 million members. Micro-credit had by this time attained the status of a development panacea, a magic bullet able to solve material poverty and empower people to take charge of their lives. The operating model of the Grameen Bank was exported globally including to countries in the developed world. Kofi Annan praised micro-credit as being a critical anti-poverty tool that empowered women: 'to improve not only their own lives, but, in a widening circle of impact, the lives of their families, their communities, and their nation' (cited in Young 2010). Professor Yunus was awarded the Nobel Peace Prize in 2006.

But the Grameen experiment also has its critics. Standard evaluations of micro-credit programmes calculate success through the measurement of total value of loans or rates of repayment. But these quantitative measures tell us little about the social effect produced by the loans. Anne Marie Goetz and Rina Sen Gupta (1996) went beyond the narrowly economic to consider the likely impact of women's lending circles on household and community gender relations in rural Bangladesh. Asking 'who takes the credit?' they found that although women were able to gain access to loans, it was often their male relatives who determined how the money was invested and spent. Micro-credit might be effective in integrating women in the banking system but it does less to promote the position of women in the wider society.

The widespread support for microfinance reflects, in part, its compatibility with a neoliberal conception of market salvation. The problems recognised by Professor Yunus – the systematic discrimination of mainstream banks and the gender norms of rural Bangladesh – are viewed as cultural baggage preventing poor, rural women from realising their full entrepreneurial potential. Grameen's goal of improving the terms of access to markets for poor women fits neatly into the neoliberal ideal of individual entrepreneurship and free competition. Capacity-building schemes seek to draw marginalised producers – often women or small-scale farmers – into systems of market exchange; whether inclusion will be of long-term benefit goes unquestioned.

Though effective in challenging institutionalised forms of discrimination, Grameen has had less success in tackling forms of inequality that exist within the household and also beyond the village. Increased earning power provided by micro-credit does little to challenge inequitable markets or increase participation within social and political spheres. Certainly, there is a role for small-scale credit programmes within a balanced development strategy but micro-credit alone is not equipped to challenge relative poverty and inequality. Other approaches offer a more holistic strategy that seeks to challenge assorted aspects of discrimination.

Collective cooperative opposition

The Self-Employed Women's Association (SEWA), like the Grameen Bank, has roots in South Asia in the 1970s. Though recognising similar problems, the two organisations adopted distinct approaches to challenge the biases in exchange relations. For SEWA micro-credit is only part of an approach that improves the bargaining position of poor women, not just in the economic sphere but also in social and political arenas.

The origins of SEWA lie in the women's wing of the Textile Labour Association (TLA) in the Indian city of Ahmedabad, Gujarat. Historically the TLA focused on social work among the wives of union members. But this approach neglected the reality of the lives of many of these women, specifically those involved in productive activities. Keith Hart (1973) drew an important distinction between formal labour recruited on a permanent and regular basis for fixed rewards, and informal labour that is irregular, uncertain, unregulated and under-represented. The majority of female workers in South Asia are concentrated in the informal sector, where they undertake productive activities, ranging from the hawking and vending of goods as street traders, to home-based production as weavers and garment makers, to manual labour in construction and agriculture. What unites female workers in this diverse range of activities is their exclusion from representation. Conventional labour unions such as the TLA negotiate with employers to secure the rights and incomes of members. But such a model is organised around a definition of employment that assumes a single, clearly defined employer.

SEWA was formed in 1972 to look after the interests of women workers whose activities lay outside formal employer–employee relationships and who had been overlooked by mainstream trade unions. The spark that led to the formation of SEWA was a delegation of 'head-loaders' who approached Ela Bhatt, the leader of the Women's wing of the TLA. Paid to carry loads of cloth between the wholesale and retail markets, the women complained that the cloth merchants were routinely cheating them and wanted to know if there was anything the union could do about it. Realising that these women needed not welfare but organisation, SEWA was established to pursue a range of activities based around the interests of poor women workers. In contrast to the Grameen Bank model of microfinance, which aims to improve the income-generating possibilities of individuals, SEWA pursues a collectivist approach to challenge exploitative economic relationships. One aspect of SEWA's work has been the establishment of working women's production cooperatives. By organising collectively women have been able to gain a degree of control and ownership over their production. Depending on their productive activities, these cooperatives provide members with a means of collective representation, whether it is in negotiating with suppliers of raw materials or involvement in the marketing of finished products. Renegotiating exploitative exchange relationships or dispensing with them altogether, SEWA memberships provide leverage for women to gain fairer rewards for their productive activities. The formation of cooperatives also works to bring women together, allowing them to identify common problems – economic but also social and political – and to organise against them.

The examples of Grameen and SEWA offer two distinct possibilities for producers to tackle obstacles that prevent equal engagement in exchange relations. The Grameen strategy locates itself at the level of the individual to provide access to credit, empowering women economically and promoting entrepreneurship. In contrast, SEWA harnesses the strength of the collective to confront wider forms of inequity at all levels. Both are producer-led and as such, both are essentially organisations of the poor and of the global South.

The next case study shows globalisation is not simply a process by which producers and consumers are connected by economic ties. New ties and relationships may also manifest themselves in the establishment of transnational cultural and political ties. Mission-driven NGOs, other types of civil society organisations and social movements have emerged around the promotion of human rights and environmentalism and the promotion of fair exchange relations.

Reintegrating morality: connecting producers and consumers

The shift from subsistence to market-oriented production entails a conversion of longstanding social and cultural norms and relations into new, externally determined commercial relationships. Entering into systems of market exchange transforms the fundamental *qualities* of produce into *quantities* measurable in monetary terms. Literally and metaphorically, market-oriented production alienates producer from product. The act of consumption also reflects this estrangement. Consumers are distanced from producers by standardised and uniformly packaged produce that reveals little about the paths they took to get there or the conditions under which they were produced. Critics of unfettered capitalism perceive this as problematic. By cutting the distance between producers and consumers the alternative trade movement suggest a possible means of overcoming the dual alienation. Organisations such as Cafédirect combine direct support for producer cooperatives with marketing drives that seek to orientate consumption around notions of fairness and justice. In providing information for consumers, Fair Trade certification works to re-embed commodities in the circumstances of their production and to re-establish human connections between producers and consumers.

The inequalities of international trade have led many to question whether conventional pricing arrangements are a legitimate, or at least appropriate, means of valuing commodities. One of the best-known attempts to develop alternatives to conventional systems of pricing is the broad coalition of producer and consumer groups brought together under the umbrella of Fair Trade. Critiquing the narrow 'economic' determination of pricing, the Fair Trade label raises moral questions about global trade. Actors aligned to Fair Trade work closely with producers to organise supply, build capacity and guarantee secure prices. The typical arrangement that Fair Trade buyers establish is to pay producers a minimum price when

the market falls below a predetermined level plus a premium on top of market *futures*
rates when the price exceeds this floor. Guaranteed rewards immunise producers *& markets?*
against the uncertainties of global commodity price movements. It also challenges the logic that price alone determines consumption choices and that decisions are made solely to maximise self-interest.

Mirroring networks of economic exchange, Fair Trade schemes promote a
transfer of knowledge that provides consumers with an awareness of the social
and environmental conditions under which goods were produced. Knowledge of
provenance is central to the Fair Trade image, with consumers informed about
the product, the producer and the conditions of production. Produce bearing the
Fair Trade label can be marketed as an ethical choice, and, as such, the Fair Trade
label allows consumers to differentiate between otherwise similar products on
factors other than price alone.

Combining aspects suggestive of local resistance and global protest with
reformist alternatives to capitalism, the Fair Trade movement is partly a civil
society organisation, partly an NGO, partly an advocacy campaign and partly
a commercial enterprise. But how well do these elements hold together? And
what happens when alternative trading arrangements break through into the
mainstream? In order to answer these questions, the anthropologist Peter
Luetchford conducted research on the formation of coffee producers' cooperatives in Costa Rica. The early 1990s saw a conscious effort by a consortium
of NGOs to enter the mainstream coffee market. Teaming up with producer
cooperatives in Costa Rica allowed the Fair Trade labelling scheme to differentiate their brand from non-ethically sourced competition. Gaining awareness of
similarly disadvantageous conditions both geographical (being situated away
from the principal coffee-producing areas) and economic (few members have
more than 10 hectares of land), a number of producer cooperatives affiliated
themselves into the Coocafé consortium. Coocafé offered small and marginal
farmers the technical assistance, capital and credit that they needed to improve
the quality and quantity of production and to adopt the new techniques that
had transformed coffee production in other parts of the country (Luetchford
2006: 130). Above all, the formation of the consortium provided a means to
improve the negotiating power of small-scale producers. By collectively marketing their crops farmers significantly improved their position vis-à-vis traders and exporters.

Though the extension of Fair Trade labelling schemes to Costa Rica provided
an answer to the problem of unequal participation by coffee farmers, Leutchford
discovered a number of difficulties stemming from the way the ideals of the
scheme were mediated through 'social practices, moral ideas and commitments
at the local and regional level' (2008: 7). His analysis of the political economy
of coffee growing 'lifts the lid on the simplistic representation of small farmers working for themselves on their own land' (*ibid.*: 10). The catch-all category of small producers or smallholders overlooks the significant differences
in livelihoods and options facing the farmers who make up a cooperative. More

disturbingly, in concentrating on members alone such a focus fails to acknowledge 'the invisible reserve army of landless poor, women, children and migrants
who harvest coffee yet often lead the most precarious and marginal existence
of all' (*ibid.*: 4). It is suggested that this paradox of Fair Trade reflects a tension
between two essential aspects of development: on the one hand is the desire to
promote welfare (the 'altruist paradigm'); on the other is the imperative of technical and economic progress (the 'modernist paradigm').

While Fair Trade cooperatives may have improved business practices and even
led to benefits for those who usually gain least from global businesses (such as
small producers or workers), many activists, academics and NGOs have argued
that such efforts are negligible compared to the fundamental structural change
that is needed to make business fairer. Indeed, moving from Luetchford's Costa
Rican farmers to the campaigners who promote the Fair Trade schemes, related
critiques have raised questions about the extent to which Fair Trade is a genuine
departure from conventional systems of trade. Laura Raynolds points out that
the market success of the Fair Trade label is tied to the deployment of industrial conventions rooted in formal standards, inspections and certifications (2002:
411). Alternative Trade Organization (ATO) certification is the gift of distant
bureaucrats working to regulate and certify. '[Fairtrade Labelling Organization]
certification represents a form of control, linked to formal standards and inspections. Like other certification and labelling systems ... Fair Trade certifications
reflect North / South power relations and industrial monitoring practices' (*ibid.*:
418). This echoes Luetchford's account: he records managers and farmers in
Costa Rica feeling powerless to question decisions taken abroad. They relate
this experience to 'neo-colonial attitudes' in ways that suggest that Fair Trade is
no more than an exercise in governmentality, a more subtle form of domination
(Luetchford 2006: 141). Again alternative trade organisations, such as Fairtrade,
are only a partial answer to the logic of orthodox economics. In implying that is
possible both to consume more and to consume ethically, Fair Trade only partially tackles the basis of global capitalism.

Retaking markets for the people: anti-capitalist protests

We all need markets. Exchange is part of what it means to be human.
But we should not accept exchange as an unquestionable good. The three
approaches described in the latter part of this chapter offer a partial corrective
to the extreme prescriptions of neoliberal utopian economics. Each is successful in effecting change at the level at which they operate, but ultimately their
function is to smooth down the rough edges of the market model rather than to
challenge its foundations. Attempting to temper or correct the inequities that are
inevitable within the systems of social relations on which markets are currently
based, these efforts try to reinstate the primacy of the 'human' into the economic. Recognising the negative impacts that result when diverse interests are
incorporated into global systems of exchange, with an anthropological lens we

have reviewed possibilities of overcoming some of these problems and of making trade, if not perfect, then at least less imperfect.

But is this enough? The UK's Trade Justice Movement points out that though international trade is worth $10 million a minute, poor countries only account for 0.4 per cent of this trade – half the proportion that they had in 1980.[5]

David Graeber sees anthropology as being well placed to study, analyse and catalogue alternative social and economic structures around the world and to translate them into alternatives to an existing system that privileges the 1 per cent at the expense of the rest of humanity.[6] Graeber has become well known for his direct and indirect involvement in political activism, including the Occupy Wall Street movement. Such ambitious (and at times subversive) campaigns aim to redress the inequities of trade rules or even, at their most extreme, overthrow the global capitalist system. At its most formally organised, civil society – NGOs, trade unions and religious groups – can point to the injustice of the current rules and practices. They arrange rallies and lobby decision-makers. They encourage their members to try to persuade, as examples, the World Trade Organization to reform the rules that protect rich countries and European countries to stop forcing unfair deals on former colonies. Anti-globalisation activists are even more ambitious. They are taking on what Graeber has called the 'first genuinely planetary bureaucratic system' and its neoliberal agenda (2009: xii). Ranging from the hugely famous Zapatista movement in Mexico to the groups that gather to protest at World Economic Forums – such as the one held in Seattle 2004 or Davos in 2011 – for some anthropologists these developments are promising (see Box 7.5). Graeber argues that the value of the loose movement of activists challenging neoliberal ideas and creating new forms of democracy is that it is not a well-oiled authoritarian machine aiming to seize power (*ibid.*: 11).

Multiple markets for exchange

In this chapter we have suggested an anthropological approach that is capable of explaining how markets function and also how they fail. Contrasting the agricultural producers of so-called developing economies with the financial powerhouses of global capitalism, we have examined the distinct positions and perspectives of buyers and sellers, producers and consumers in a bid to understand the social basis and cultural norms through which markets work. In emphasising the social and cultural aspects, the view from anthropology differs fundamentally from the narrow fixation on the economic that has dominated policy-making in recent times.

The approach we take is not intended as an attack on the discipline of economics per se. Instead we have traced the reasons why particular theories and models have proved most acceptable to key actors in international finance, governance, trade and development. We suggest that, consciously or otherwise, key

Box 7.5. Anthropologists and the Zapatista movement

On 1 January 1994 Chiapas made international news when armed guerrillas occupied several towns in Mexico. The leaders – including subcomandante Marcos of the Zapatista Army of National Liberation (EZLN) – told the press that they were fighting 'for humanity and against neoliberalism' and more specifically the privatisation policies of the government of Carlos Salinas (Gledhill 2008: 491). The Zapatistas identified themselves as indigenous people with women's empowerment as an important part of their agenda. The government's counter-offensive backfired because the rebels managed to marshal considerable support from across the globe through NGO networks and the Internet, so the government was forced to negotiate. Twelve years on, the movement has lost some of its support in Chiapas, thanks to the Mexican governments' military counter-insurgency war but also subtler manipulation dividing communities with social development programmes (*ibid.*: 494). But they have become famous as an anti-capitalist movement that operates at both local and global levels.

Political anthropologist Gledhill explains, 'the EZLN secured an unusually strong grip on the global activist imagination as a demonstration of the possibilities of challenging capitalist globalisation from below, developing more profoundly democratic societies, and truly empowering indigenous people. To a great extent it retains that global significance and still cannot be regarded as a totally neutralised force in Mexican national politics, almost a decade and a half after the original rebellion' (*ibid.*: 484). What is unusual is their determination to change the world through their critique rather than by seizing power.

Anthropologists such as Gledhill greatly enhanced our understanding of the Chiapas uprising. But their relationship with such movements is complex. As Gledhill puts it, 'The problem facing anthropologists in this, as in so many other contexts in which situations of profound oppression and social injustice are being contested, is the gap that tends to emerge between the relative certainties of an activist formulation of what is at stake and the more complex and ambiguous realities that emerge from our fieldwork' (*ibid.*: 484).

policy-makers choose to select certain ways of understanding the operations of markets, while rejecting or ignoring others. It is political relationships as much as economic ones that drive the globalisation of production and exchange. The dominating influence of elements of neoliberal economics has little to do with knowledge and much to do with power.

Over the last thirty years, neoliberal beliefs have shaped the ways in which globalisation is understood and have formed the institutions and practices that promote it. But this is not to conclude that there is anything inevitable or imperishable about this model. Like the long boom that preceded it, the global economic crisis that commenced in 2008 was intensified by the mobility of capital and absence of regulation promoted by neoliberal beliefs in the efficacy of the free market. Discredited (but not necessarily abandoned) neoliberal thinking can no longer be regarded as a natural product, still less as Fukuyama's 'end of history' (1993).

With the precepts of market fundamentalism coming into question in the heart-
lands of liberal capitalism, alternative ways of thinking about trade and development are coming into view. The emerging economies of the global south provide
new possibilities for transnational trade and cross-cultural connection. The model
of capitalism practised in India is distinct to that offered by the USA or Europe;
and it goes without saying that free-market neoliberal capitalism differs greatly
from the new engagement in international commercial exchange being pioneered
out of China. As urbanisation and the growth of a global middle class shift us
away from simple South–North material flows, we move into territory that is
more varied and diverse.

What unites all forms of exchange, and what are likely to continue, are the
inequalities that mean that not all benefit equally from engagement in market
activity. Differences exist in knowledge, in the ability to deal with risk, in the
form and extent of engagement permitted, and in the degree of bargaining power
held by different actors. While alternatives to market exchange remain thin on
the ground, or at least limited in impact, creative opportunities to challenge the
inequalities of the market and to resolve its negative effects, are found in multiple, mutually reinforcing forms. Anthropology provides a perspective for recognising and promoting these.

Challenging questions arising from this chapter

What is neoliberal theory, what are the assumptions underlying it and why does it
   have such a potent influence on development policy?
How are anthropological perspectives on economic development different from
   those of conventional economics?
To what extent does the behaviour of farmers and consumers conform to neoliberal
   theory?
How does the formal sector differ from the informal sector? What implications
   does this have for employment policies?
What has been the impact of neoliberal economic policy on poverty and inequality
   around the world?
What are the alternatives to an unfettered market and how do they fare?

8   The politics of policy and practice

Key points covered by this chapter

- Delving beneath the surface of Development World, this chapter looks at various ways that socio-political relations are created by development ideas, policies, rules and encounters.
- The main ordering processes are: the creation of rules and policies; simplification and measurement to tame the unruly; mechanisms of separation and exclusion; and temporal and spatial displacement.
- While ordering processes suggest convergence, they are often contradictory, contested and transformed within different sites. Divergence and convergence coexist.
- We make the case for going beyond 'power functionalism', whereby all action is seen as either a strategy to consolidate or resist power, and stress both the importance of understanding specific social relations but also the moral aspects of politics.

Anthropology often starts with the views of the people involved in a particular world. Applied to the world of aid and development, anthropologists have worked to understand the perspectives of farmers, traders, slum dwellers, nomadic-pastoralists, street children, migrants, the poor, marginalised and excluded. Increasingly, they have also tried to understand the culture of development professionals. But to do so is harder than it sounds for a number of reasons. First of all, these groups, and individuals within them, hold highly divergent views of the world; even individuals express endless contradictions, and ambivalent or ambiguous perspectives. Secondly, people's articulation of their views cannot be read as a mirror of their reality, because what they say can be spoken through a filter of self-publicity, wishful thinking or politeness. Thirdly, what people say they do or think is usually completely different from what they actually do, as anthropologists find out through observation. So to get beneath the surface appearances of social life, anthropologists have to interpret and make sense of multiple perspectives, often trying to look at the way people organise themselves from a more detached, and sometimes lateral, or analogous angle. In this and the next chapter we take a step further away from (or underneath) the emic perspectives (see Chapter 4) on development ideas and practices and explore them through a different lens.

Taming the unruly

Much anthropological work on development – and on social organisation more generally – looks for the ways that social actors make sense of and order their social world. In aid and development settings anthropologists have found that the relationships, ideas and practices are formalised in policies and plans in ways that give them the appearance of order. However, the reality of practice is not as tidy as it looks in documents or other forms of representation. While the study of 'social order' once entailed looking at persistent social structures, institutions, rules and practices, it now means giving almost as much attention to the discontinuities, tensions and contradictions.

Partly to make Development World (and especially poor people within it) more manageable, bureaucracies create systems of simplification, separation and measurement. The resulting mechanisms of exclusion pervade all political situations and development is no different. Development work is packaged into 'policies' and 'projects' within which intended beneficiaries, problems and solutions are tightly defined and other people or possibilities excluded. The makers of plans, whether in donor organisations or national NGOs, close down alternatives and blinker themselves to 'anything lying outside its sharply defined field of vision' (Scott 1998: 47). As explained in Chapters 5–7, poverty reduction, human rights, the transfer of technology and economic growth are defined narrowly so as to diminish the possibilities for thinking about collective wellbeing, interconnected rights, hybrid forms of knowledge and limits to consumption. Time and effort is spent constructing or conforming to these representational models. The purpose that bureaucratic rules actually serve and whether they are in fact necessary are left unexamined.

In order to defy mechanisms of exclusion, actors continually redefine people and ideas to fit within prescribed categories, as two examples will illustrate. When Emma Crewe was seeking funding for a project in Ethiopia, she wondered how to present it. The 'reality' in their own words was that the Organisation for Child Development and Transformation (CHADET) had persuaded funeral societies – community-based organisations that collect money from their members and then spend the funds on organising their funerals – to collect and disburse money for the most vulnerable children in their locality. The funeral societies also organised a system of community volunteers to visit these children to assess their needs, find ways to keep them in school (or get them into school) and make sure they have a safe place to live. Many were orphans. All were at risk of various problems: no access to services, taking to the streets or lacking adult care. When there was a gap in funding Emma studied various grant-makers' funding rules and criteria and submitted three separate proposals for the same project:

- one proposal portrayed the children as 'at risk of being street children';
- one proposal described the project as a child protection and education initiative;

- and a third proposal framed the project as an innovative way of responding to orphans.

These descriptions were all true, but they were also creative ways to bend representations to please the donor and overcome mechanisms of exclusion.

When Jessica Hodges worked with street children in Delhi, she found that they endlessly redefined themselves as they visited different NGOs in a bid to make sure they were eligible for services (2011: 12). As she puts it, 'interactions between street children and development institutions always involve a specific, not generic, street child choosing between an array of different development organisations, among other options' (ibid.: 16). Children compare notes on different organisations – which ones are good for food, for sleeping or for playing – and make choices about where and how to present themselves. In a bid to protect their independence from adults, but access benefits when they want them, they modify their names and tell stories that fit with the NGO's agenda (Christian, health-oriented, for orphans or whatever). But these untidy, subversive actions are rarely acknowledged by development agencies, especially to their donors or supporters.

People of Gujarati origin living in the English town of Wellingborough also illustrate the point by creating multiple 'communities', and therefore facets of identity, for different purposes (Crewe and Kothari 1997: 18–23). When soliciting donations from Indian Hindus to build a temple they presented themselves as the Hindu Association. The 'New India League' was abandoned because it sounded too political and it was easier to get charitable status as a religious organisation rather than as 'nationalist' one. They were part of the Wellingborough Black Consortium and the Racial Equality Council when advocating for more equal treatment within health and education services. They were also 'black' when they set up residential care for elderly Asians, and later for Afro-Caribbean people, and they got money from the Housing Corporation on the grounds that white Housing Associations are discriminatory. They were Pravasi Mandal – or the Asian Group – when they wanted funds from the County Council to establish day care services for elderly people.

Moral taming of the unruly through simplifying and standardising is not just a process in development but can be found, once again, in most bureaucratic systems of rule. This tendency has exploded in popularity across the globe. Marilyn Strathern and others point out that a global audit culture with 'rituals of verification' has been created with the apparent aim of improving accountability (2000: 1–4). These audit practices that derived originally from financial management take on different meanings, and can become coercive, when taken up by other sectors (Shore and Wright 2000: 58). 'Audit is essentially a relationship of power between scrutiniser and observed: the latter are rendered objects of information, never subjects in communication' (ibid.: 59). Thus, as Power points out, the 'audit explosion' has a depersonalising effect by which individuals, relationships and institutions are reshaped according to the image demanded by the inspector (as cited by Shore and Wright *ibid.*: 72). Audit cultures aim to identify and punish failure. But 'failure', the definition of which is always highly subjective, is more often measured by appearance rather than reality. As a result time and energy is redeployed from achievement to looking busy and measuring that appearance of hyperactivity, the precise opposite to the intentions of policy-makers. With scrutiny provoking insecurity, commitment and loyalty can be undermined to such an extent that relationships and quality of work suffer, rendering the whole process counter-productive. Michael Power alerts us to how auditing the focuses on good controls and the management of risks, rather than demonstrating good teaching, caring, manufacturing or banking (1994: 19).

There is a paradox between the low level of trust placed in professionals that has led to the perceived need for auditing and the high level of trust that attaches to auditors and evaluators. In the context of international development, every donor-funded project requires an *external* evaluation to check progress – on the assumption that an outsider will be more impartial – but the recipient is trusted to recruit the evaluator. The evaluation involves judging whether and how the project has met objectives or not, so the donor may ask that the evaluator has no relationship with the recipient organisations on the assumption that closeness may incline them towards a favourable view. But they rarely look into how the ritual of evaluation produces knowledge. Evaluations usually involve visiting beneficiaries to collect their opinions, but trips are often organised by the recipient agency with plenty of opportunity to ensure that more positive stories come to the forefront. Beneficiaries become as expert as development workers in representing projects as success stories (see Box 6.1). Thus, auditing is a mix of coercion, compliance and collusion that ensures that the funding keeps flowing within established patron–client relationships.

The rhetoric states that development should achieve results or outcomes and these then have to be measured so that we can convince supporters – whether taxpayers or grant-makers – that their money has been well spent. Checks that funds have been spent on planned activities have become de rigueur. But these have extended far beyond the financial audits that have been a feature of organisational accountability for many years. As Harper's study of the IMF shows, economists use numbers to make projections about the future and to re-orientate policy (2000: 39). He describes IMF staff rushing around having meetings with key informants – people from whom they knew they could get reliable information – until they were ready to present a picture of the economy to key officials. The process of turning these raw numbers about an economy into the information upon which policy can be formed is not a mathematical sum and analysis. It is a moral transformation (*ibid.*: 47). IMF staff used figures during meetings to claim moral authority: that they were the experts and it was 'their assessments that counted, their assessments of what was the right way of doing things that mattered' (*ibid.*: 49). The authorities accepted the numbers and policy changes was a reflection of the power positions of all those involved.

When grant-makers require applicants and grantees to count beneficiaries they shift between believing that these numbers reflect reality and recalling that they are symbolic. A grant-making manager said to Emma Crewe a few years ago, 'I can't understand why NGOs make such a fuss about counting beneficiaries. It can't be that difficult.' Emma explained,

> It is easy if you run an orphanage because your beneficiaries are all present. But most of the work you fund is more interesting than that – a mix of service provision, advocacy, attitudinal change and activities where you don't know how many people you are reaching. You can make a very rough guess. But then that guess contains all those affected and does not distinguish between those benefiting and those losing out.

These numbers become symbolic justification for the project. In the social context of his committee he forgets the nature of the work that he chooses to fund – because he knows most of his committee would prefer to give grants for tangible results and services – and he forgets the symbolic nature of this counting. In the social context of talking to NGOs, he remembers how difficult counting can be and colludes in a process of wild guesswork. Thus, even one person's memory understanding can shift in the different social situations he finds himself in.

Adams points out that the practices of auditing have been neglected by anthropologists when you bear in mind how the life of development professionals is dominated by the concern to spend and account for funds (2009: 7). As bureaucratic regimes become more restrictive and demanding, the accounting creativity of grant-receiving agencies grows. Most NGOs receive money to spend on specific projects and lack 'core funds' to pay for their general running costs (rent, non-project staff, organisational audit, publicity materials, and so on). Supporters prefer to give money to what they see as the 'real work' rather than administration. To cover these core costs they put a proportion of non-project salaries (e.g. for the guards or the director) and administration into project budgets as 'overheads'. Some grant-makers cap this at somewhere roughly between 8 and 15 per cent, knowing that beyond that amount supporters or committee members may start to ask awkward questions. As Adams writes, 'spending in aid is an art that operates in grey areas, and the practitioner's challenge is to apply the rules in a conventionally appropriate way while at the same time finding the room for manoeuvre required to incorporate the "hidden transcripts" of various actors' (*ibid.*: 17 and see Table 8.1).

Good politics and bad policy

Policies are a taken-for-granted aspect of administration and governance both nationally and internationally. But the process of policy-making has many layers and serves many purposes. Communicated through a range of linguistic devices, whether in manifestoes, speeches or statements, policies have

Table 8.1. *A typical but imaginary three-year participatory health project budget by a UK-based INGO to a UK grant-maker*

Item	Amount (£, $ or €)	'Hidden transcript' – what is really going on behind the numbers
Local NGO		
Computers	2,000	Although the narrative describes these as project equipment, the computers will be used by the whole organisation. It will waste resources and cause resentment if only some project staff have use of the equipment.
Head of Programmes (10%)	6,000	This person might spend 10 per cent of her time on the project but the total amount distributed across projects is 150 per cent so her post is over-funded to help cover the cost of the Director.
Project staff salaries	60,000	Most of the staff are working on project activities but a few will be occasionally deployed on other tasks if other projects fall short of funding.
Community education and sensitisation on issues of health	25,000	This is really a series of workshops and meetings with the community. Since you have had no funds to do any consultation yet you don't know where this will go so, if you can, you keep this as broad as possible. You might hazard a guess about what topics might be covered (e.g. malaria, violence, AIDS or whatever) and then negotiate for variance.
Training of communities in communications	18,000	Training in communications really means getting communities to campaign for health policy reform. But the grant-maker will not fund 'advocacy' or 'campaigning' for fear of supporting any political activity. Thus 'training' is the preferred term.
Mid-term review and external evaluation	12,000	Two local consultants will be employed to undertake these ritualised processes of auditing.
Monitoring costs	9,000	This is to undertake a baseline and then periodic monitoring. However, you don't actually know what the real content is yet because the consultation with the community has yet to happen. Also you have some doubts about the value of a 'baseline' – after all the communities are not starting at zero. So you don't put much cost here because you know that monitoring will be done by the communities themselves at a fairly low level.

Communications	1,200	You often have no idea what type of communications you will embark on so this is a wild guess.
Overheads – rent, audit, HR, finance etc.	11,000	General running costs are never sufficiently covered within project budgets. Usually you put in whatever amount to think you can get away with.
Total for local NGO	144,200	

UK INGO

Technical assistance by UK experts	10,500	This might be calculated by putting in as many days as you think you can and charging a daily rate that is relatively little for a small NGO (far more for a large one or a research institute). Or you charge a percentage of the experts' time. Or you put whatever you think you can get away with and work backwards.
Monitoring and evaluation by the UK NGO (including travel and subs)	8,500	In reality you are likely to do technical assistance and monitoring during the same trip to the local NGO. One or two trips a year are typical. In theory you are an impartial participant checking the monitoring and evaluation by the local NGO and the external evaluators. In reality you have conversations with a sample of all those involved and the extent to which you find out what is going on depends on the quality of your relationship with the partner and the extent to which they are in a position to be open and honest.
Total for INGO	19,000	This is quite a large percentage – more than 10% – so you will need to argue hard to prove your 'added value' in the narrative.
Total	162,200	

economic, legal, cultural and moral implications (Shore and Wright 1997: 3, 7). Raymond Apthorpe explains how the language and writing of policy functions as power in various ways (1997). Policy language can achieve a symbolic force by being 'plain' but not 'clear'; you can get support from a wider range of conflicting and competing groups if concepts are fudged. 'Goal' policy language garners support either externally or internally. Finally policy can function as power by reassuring people. For example keywords – like community and participation – tend to be scattered through planning and policy documents to soothe readers. The interesting thing about these political terms is that they have no valued opposites and cannot be empirically tested, which is extremely useful if you do not want to be to be exposed to censure. Apthorpe adds, 'persuasive power in the public text is strongest where descriptive power is weakest' (*ibid.*: 54).

Concepts underlying policy are not necessarily positive. For example, following the August 2011 riots in England, Prime Minister David Cameron bemoaned the moral breakdown in Britain's broken society and partly blamed human rights legislation. His attempts to build a 'Big Society' with responsible citizens are, thereby, given additional justification. But former Prime Minister Tony Blair commented,

> In 1993, following James Bulger's murder, I made a case in very similar terms to the one being heard today about moral breakdown in Britain. I now believe that speech was good politics but bad policy. Focus on the specific problem and we can begin on a proper solution. Elevate this into a high-faluting wail about a Britain that has lost its way morally and we will depress ourselves unnecessarily, trash our own reputation abroad and, worst of all, miss the chance to deal with the problem in the only way that will work.[1]

Despite the numerous examples that point to an opposite pattern, policy-makers are under constant pressure to present policy as data-driven or 'evidence-based' – as if policy flows in simple unfettered ways from research. But policy, just like any other form of language, is embedded in social processes, cultural values and moral systems. The claim that policy determines practice, and rests upon 'proof' is, of course, comforting to those who seek order and certainty. When the UK government awarded grants to UK-based INGOs in 2011 they employed the auditing firm KPMG to undertake 'due diligence' to ensure that the organisations had the capacity to manage the grants. They assessed the organisations' governance, financial health and capacity, technical skills in the programme area, systems and processes (mainly compliance with policies, laws and regulations), environmental risk management, value for money (mainly procurement processes and administration costs), and measurement of results. They had two main methods:

1.   they required each agency to submit fifty-three bundles of documents – either policies or 'evidence' – ranging from HR policies to finance manuals, evaluation procedures, CVs for trustees and staff and so on. It ran to thousands of pages; and

Box 8.1. Success and failure in policy and practice

A DFID-funded project in India promoted rain-fed agricultural development with tribal people. This project started in 1992 and was seen as very successful initially. VIP visits were an important part of ensuring that DFID officials were impressed (Mosse 2005: 63). Development success was not 'objectively verified' but socially produced: Mosse called it a magico-religious system within which it was important to build a large community of believers who then represent the project in the right way. They developed a thorough participatory approach and the objectives in the logframe changed from being about impact on people to being about attaining participation.

But a mid-term review was highly critical. The evaluators questioned not the *implementation* of the project but the *idea* that participation was so important. They asked about its cost in relation to other choices and dismissed the idea that it would necessarily lead to good impact. The evaluators were responding to a new aid regime within DFID that prioritised impact on poverty. Also, DFID was shifting its policy focus from improved rain-fed farming and productivity to sustainable rural livelihoods and strategies for the poor (*ibid.*: 180). In response to the review the project shifted and redesigned its framework around livelihoods and planned for a huge scale-up from 75 to 275 villages. This did not make much different to practice, except that staff were massively overstretched. By 1998 it was the jewel in DFID's crown; everyone loved it once more.

However, in 2000 it had one of the most critical reports ever written about a DFID project. When Mosse reviewed it in 2001 he found the practice on the field level was much the same as some years earlier. The management had changed in response to demands for greater efficiency, targets that could be met and plans that were much more ambitious. It was all about command and control; staff got sacked if they did not cooperate or get things done fast enough. But the practice and how farmers experienced the project remained constant. He concludes that the public or official judgement about success or failure is not focused on implementation, practice or impact but about the interpretation of it through a lens of policy and rhetoric. The truth is that you nearly always find both success and failure in development projects.

2.   they carried out interviews spread over two days during which the KPMG auditors filled out a fifty-four-page standardised questionnaire on their laptops.

These assessments allowed no scope for discussion, nuance or taking account of diversity of the organisations; it was simply a matter of deciding whether or not they could tick each box or not. There was no concern for the most important question for judging whether INGOs do good development – the quality of their partnerships with organisations in Africa, Asia and Latin America. And there was an assumption that good policy leads to good practice.

For an illustration of the problems with the assumption that policy drives practice, take the example of equal opportunity policies. Development agencies, like most charities and public bodies, are expected to have an equal opportunities policy with grand statements about respect for diversity on the assumption that moral rhetoric will prevent discrimination. In many UK-based INGOs it is considered 'best practice' to draw up a list of questions when recruiting a new member of staff and pose them exactly as drafted, and in the same order, to all candidates. It is then permissible to ask 'follow-up' questions, for example if specific concerns arose out of their CV. But, this policy, however well intentioned, does little to address covert, unconscious or institutional discrimination. It does not allow for different questions emerging from people's different backgrounds, experiences and understandings or a more sensitive dialogue that can take account of the differences between people. By dictating such a rigid methodology, and giving interviewees so little room for manoeuvre, there is little space to allow interviewees – in all their diversity – to push the method of assessment in a direction that suits them, whether more informal, discursive or exploratory. Finally it does nothing to address the conclusions that interviewers jump to about different candidates based on their identity, whether related to their gender, race, age, appearance or other ascribed characteristics. Proposals for explicit discussion about underlying assumptions about the identity of each candidate are never mentioned in equal opportunities policies. As Scott puts it, 'anyone who has worked in a formal organisation – even a small one strictly governed by detailed rules – knows that handbooks and written guidelines fail utterly in explaining how the institution goes successfully about its work' (1998: 253).

Mosse's (2005) ethnography about a project in India describes in detail how policy does not drive practice, it legitimises it (see Box 8.1). But it does even more than this.

1. Policy maintains political support and legitimises rather than orientates practice.
2. Interventions are driven by the exigencies of organisations and the need to maintain relationships.
3. Projects have to maintain themselves as coherent policy ideas and systems of representation as well as operational systems.
4. Projects don't fail or succeed; they are failed or deemed a success by wider networks of support and validation.
5. Success and failure as policy-oriented judgements may obscure project effects.

These propositions can be seen at work in relation to household energy projects. Household energy for people living in poverty is mostly about developing, improving and selling fuel-burning stoves. Half the households in the world use stoves to burn biomass (wood, charcoal or organic residues), principally for cooking. The oil price hikes of the 1970s together with growing alarm about the depletion of resources (e.g. Meadows *et al.* 1972) combined to create the perception of a 'woodfuel crisis'. Misplaced assumptions about household or domestic energy, deforestation and biomass fuel were accepted by many international development agencies (Leach and Mearns 1988). 'Experts' mistakenly thought that people routinely cut trees to get fuel for domestic consumption and, therefore, deduced that a decrease in domestic fuelwood consumption would reduce the rate of deforestation in areas of scarcity. The orthodoxy also stated that domestic fuelwood consumption increases proportionately with population growth and that both are directly related to deforestation (Cline-Cole *et al.* 1990: 514). National governments and international agencies decided that the existing stoves, most commonly three stones arranged in a triangle, were wasteful of fuel. Something needed to be done.

The answer was better stoves. In twenty years up to 1990 about $100 million was spent on improving stove technologies. But initially uptake was slow. Africa, Asia and South/Central America were littered with rejected models; their unpopularity was attributed to the cultural conservatism of its users. In any case, even if used, they would not have reduced deforestation because timber-logging, land clearance for agriculture and charcoal-making were all far more significant as causes of tree-cutting than wood-fuel consumption. Just as the donors realised this, and began deleting improved stoves programmes from their priorities, a series of design and marketing breakthroughs led to a pronounced surge in acceptance of new stoves. By 1993 over 165 million improved stoves had been installed in kitchens worldwide, mainly in China, India, Sri Lanka and Kenya (Crewe 1997: 112–13). The popularity of these stoves with purchasers was not based on dubious assertions about saving forests. Rather the stoves were safer, cleaner, saved cooking time, required less supervision, reduced fuel collection time and generated less smoke. But it was too late. Just as the users decided they rather liked these better models, the donor agencies decided that improved stoves were worthless and withdrew their funding.

But this is not the end of the stove story. Today remnants of the improved stoves programmes are still to be found. They continue because a few dedicated 'stovies' have been able to re-present their benefits in health terms. Improved stoves can reduce indoor air pollution, which in turn mitigates respiratory diseases, so their promotion has become possible again. It is not their popularity with users, or use value, that ensured the survival of improved stove programmes, it was the efforts of 'stovies' to reinvent their representation to fit with other policies that meant stoves have stayed on the agenda.

So, in relation to these stove programmes, how should success or failure be judged? Most energy experts in donor agencies claim that stove programmes have failed because they have no measurable beneficial impact on national economies, forests or levels of global pollution. Meanwhile, gender analysts claim that stoves have failed because they do not challenge gender inequalities – time-saving stoves may reduce women's unpaid work and improve well-being, but they do not lead directly to more equal control over resources on the basis of gender. On the other hand, many African and Asian energy experts in national NGOs have argued that stoves can generate income, relieve the pressure on biomass resources, alleviate women's workload and point the way to an alternative, more environmentally sustainable energy strategy for their country (e.g. Davidson and Karekezi 1993, Asia Regional Cookstove Program 1995). Some producers have become significantly wealthy through participation in many stove programmes, while millions of users signify their popularity by buying them. Plainly stove programmes have both succeeded and failed in different ways and from different perspectives at the same time. The same is true of most development intervention; there is, therefore, no such thing as pure success or failure.

Displacement in time and space

Displacement is a process that is commonly found in political realms. Displacement means that hierarchical social relationships are reproduced and people are governed with the minimum of fuss and the maximum appearance of control for aid-givers. When considering the time and space patterns created within Development World, it becomes obvious that development encounters are no exception. In this book we have seen how through processes of displacement poverty may be ordered, rights are granted or denied, technology disseminated and economic policies justified.

Development policy and practice is constructed on unreliable memories of the past and vivid dreams about the future. Simplified representations of prior achievement (as evaluations, audits, reports, face-to-face accounts or film) are deployed to prove and champion results. Similarly, representations of the future (visions, business plans, policies, procedures, proposals, log-frames, methods for effectiveness, training) serve to motivate support and gain access to funds. This constant shift of attention forwards and backwards prevents actors from having to deal with the messy and uncertain reality of the present. This does not contradict David Lewis's argument that development agencies fail to explore and take account of the history of their contexts, ideas and practices and live in a perpetual present (2009). The failure to look at history means that projects are rarely designed or managed with a thorough understanding of what has taken place economically, politically, institutionally, technologically and culturally within specific locations. But our emphasis here is slightly different. The deflection of people's time from taking action in the present (preferably with a well-informed understanding of the past) to *performing* the past and *imagining* the future in order to summon support means that development actors, like politicians, are rewarded for showmanship and spin rather than changing the status quo.

A second type of displacement activity is equally prevalent in Development World. Alongside temporal displacement we find a related process of spatial displacement. Whether by villagisation, migration, famine, conflict (or the desire to work in international development) the world of development depends upon a profound restlessness to rearrange and order people in space. Coercion by displacement within development is significant and pervasive.

The possibility that these processes are brought about by the way Development World is organised is worth examining.

Temporal displacement

In the last twenty years the proportion of time office-based development workers spend focused on the past or future seems to have grown significantly. Their work is increasingly about the representation in documents of what *has* happened or what *will* happen. Fixed into texts, numbers, diagrams, charts, photographs and films, the lived reality of the present is reduced to depictions of the past and predictions for the future. The experience of development as interactions between people in the present has declined.

Part of the process of the bureaucratisation of aid entails the package of development work into projects, programmes or national plans. For officials in donor or recipient agencies, in Johannesburg or Washington, the documentation required by the 'project cycle' has proliferated, with some donors demanding quantities of paperwork about the future and past which have a substantial cost in time. Applications stating your plans, or reports on what has happened in each year and at the end of the project, can run into hundreds of pages and hundreds of budget lines. Although every donor has its own bureaucratic requirements (and therefore a multiplicity of forms to be filled), the pattern of project cycles[2] tends towards the following:

> *Imagining the future:* the plan. The first stage of a 'project' entails research, needs assessment or getting into a dialogue with stakeholders about context, problems, needs and solutions. Whether or not these conversations concern their past, present or future is usually fudged; intended beneficiaries are supposed to live in a perpetual static state. They are displaced from their realities of endless change into a pretence of stasis.
>
> Ideas will be translated into plans that can then be documented in the form of an application. These applications must follow the bureaucratic requirements of the donor that include their policies, rules and requests for information. For all large donors and grant-makers, that will entail filling out a specific form. Only a few progressive grant-makers avoid using cross-comparable, standardised forms to aid their decision-making and allow applicants to develop proposals in their own way. The standardisation of applications permits grant-makers to compare and manage the ever-increasing burden of requests. As the Internet has made the schemes of public donors and grant-makers accessible to all, and the representation of the past/future has become a specialist professional skill with most applicants producing impressive documents, the task of choosing between applicants has become far harder. Increasingly applicants, and especially international NGOs, pore over the policies and criteria, and twist the framing of a project into the donors' language and boxes so that they score as highly as possible. The required buzzwords[3] of participation, partnership, gender, environment, evaluation, learning, outcome and added value are liberally scattered throughout the document.

In addition to the form a planning framework is often required – a business plan, logical framework and/or theory of change – to explain how the impact will be achieved over 3–5 years. These forms and frameworks address the same questions – what is the problem, what is the solution expressed as a goal, how many people will benefit, how will it be achieved, how will you prove that you have achieved it, who was involved in developing this plan and what will happen after the grant has finished? Each goal must be related to a hierarchy of causally related aims/outcomes, outputs, inputs and activities. It is vital to give the impression that, on the one hand, the plan was the result of long and intense discussions with a range of stakeholders and, most importantly, the intended beneficiaries. On the other hand, if this initiative has not yet attracted any funds (the typical situation) then it is extremely difficult for such processes to be affordable. In reality the plan is a guess about the future, based on previous engagement with groups of people and maybe some potential beneficiaries, that tends to feign ease, agreement, certainty and consensus. Conflict is displaced out of reality in favour of harmony and cooperation. Although different groups want different things, have different priorities, and no one knows what the outcomes of activities will be or what everyone else, including the government, is going to do next year let alone in five years' time, imaginative fictions have to be presented as concrete plans.

The present: implementation of the plan. For some donors or grant-makers implementation – the period when people meet, persuade, exchange money, build wells or teach – is required to take place with little variance. The more experienced recipients become experts in the levels of flexibility and variance that different donors will accept. Some tolerate very little whereas others are reassured by some deviation from the plan because they know that in reality you have to continually adjust to changing circumstances if you are being responsive to people. As long as you learn, and 'capture your learning' by documenting and disseminating, then variance is not necessary forbidden. The British government's DFID tolerates it as long as permission is sought for changes, for example. Thus, even in the present you are looking over your shoulder at the future reporting demands.

Individuals working within grant-makers know that variance is inevitable especially if the process is genuinely participatory. Even so grant-makers are not in a position to allow unlimited flexibility. The political support from their committees, trustees or senior management has been gained for a particular set of goals so diverging from those goals challenges their control over the grant-making decisions. They claim that it is their stories of success about those goals that allow grant-making organisations to seek political support from their own supporters, whether public or governments, or even their committees. But of course the latter are interested in stories about helping beneficiaries, rather than evidence of organisations' skill at predicting the future, so this is a weak justification for the bureaucratic demands they impose on recipients. The emphasis on adherence to plans is about control (or at least the appearance of it) rather than quality or fundraising.

The recent past: reporting during implementation. Agencies are expected to constantly monitor during implementation to check progress, adjust activities and gather data to be used for evaluation and reporting. The precise reporting demands vary across grant-makers and donors but the general rule tends to be that projects lasting longer than a year require an annual narrative and financial report. Each donor has its own rules and forms for reporting, meaning that some aid recipients can consume huge proportions of their time translating their own narrative and financial reports into the specific formats that are required, especially if they have several donors for different aspects of one project. There is an assumption that high-quality reports are an indicator that the project is achieving substantial benefits. It is through skilful reporting that variances are either disguised or explained.

The distant past: evaluation. At the end of the project (and sometimes in the middle too), it has become obligatory to have an evaluation by one or more 'external' evaluators. 'External' means outside the project on the grounds that this person will be more impartial and objective. This is often a two- to three-week exercise of interviewing and reading documents so that an evaluator, or a team if the project is larger, paints a rough sketch of whether goals and objectives have been met and whether a sustainable impact is likely or not. Those deemed outside the project are rarely consulted, processes not packaged within the predetermined goals can often be left out and the value of the goals themselves are rarely questioned. It is essential for the project that the evaluation says objectives were met because the next grant may be affected by its findings. This is more influential than any interest in finding out what happened to the people affected but not 'targeted'. In theory the evaluator has access to monitoring data that reveals what changes have taken place for different stakeholders; in practice, monitoring usually either generates very little information about change for people but plenty about whether or not activities have been carried out.

The need to prove results has become the core activity of development. This applies equally to aid-giving governments who must persuade their publics that money is not wasted, or charity fundraisers who must demonstrate their competence. Proof for some requires objective and scientifically valid evidence. For those in the field of medicine and some development economists, proof is only truly obtained by randomly selecting people to take part in a scheme and then comparing change (or lack of it) for intended beneficiaries in an intervention against change for a control group. Once effectiveness is proved, then the intervention can be replicated elsewhere without the need for such rigorous evaluation. The use of randomised control trials for measuring social change has been criticised on methodological and ethical grounds, even by some of its proponents (Barrett and Carter 2010). But it is gaining popularity for political reasons; its results can be portrayed as more valid and rigorous and, therefore, gain its users greater support and access to funding. Since cost is prohibitive, such trials are likely to fall out of fashion.

To secure political support and access to funding, development initiatives are represented as 'projects' with these project-cycle phases and a system for managing inputs and outputs to achieve aims/outcomes and goals/impacts. The different groups of participants are dependent on each other and are organised in a system that is apparently designed to achieve efficiency. Rather than guiding performance, 'goals' within such systems are used instrumentally to generate support and gain funds.

Many have complained that planning tools are a blueprint approach reflecting a positivist worldview in which development is characterised by a linear causality that few have faith in any more. Despite the attempt at greater efficiency and 'professionalism', taking ideas of causality from the physical sciences may give the appearance of being in control of the future, but scientific assumptions about causality have moved on from the mechanistic determinism of Newton. Chaos theory tells us that most physical systems are non-linear, small changes in one part of the system can lead to large-scale, complex effects elsewhere and observers can affect results. The latest developments in the physical sciences have yet to percolate into business planning models or even into the social sciences that aspire to be scientific.

These outmoded planning models have been criticised for leaving little room for unintended effects or change, which are difficult to measure (Wallace *et al.* 2006: 36). In practice, one action does not lead to another in a predictable, even or linear way, particularly when people are aiming to be creative (see Box 2.2). Gasper explains that planning tools such as the logical framework ('logframe') have a hierarchy of objectives converging on a single goal according to a predetermined time-frame. Proceeding on the assumption that change is largely controllable and could be achieved by a single organisation, they encourage an audit style of accountability that serves to block participation, learning and innovation (Gasper 2000). When criticised, proponents of these planning models tend to say that it is the way they are used rather than the tool itself that is problematic. But as Gasper notes, logframes often become 'lockframes': although in theory they can be revised it rarely happens because people do not find this a useful way of reviewing their plans. Such planning tools simplify complex processes and relationships and give the false impression of consensus between all the groups involved.

Across the globe some development bureaucrats and planners favour the use of logframes: they see them as a way to encourage clearer direction and discipline in the work or they love the opportunity to make their ideas look professional. Others react against the rigidity and lack of flexibility and point to how easy it is for those in charge of the logframe to take control of decision-making about the future. The search for alternatives is a viewpoint that coexists with the increasing dominance of logical planning and auditing, as a project in Sierra Leone reveals (see Box 8.2).

Disagreement and contestation between people is not expected to fit within the prevailing methods for imagining the future and representing the past (i.e. planning and evaluation processes). Quarles van Ufford illustrates this in relation to a development project in Indonesia where two contradictory needs were in operation – the need to spend large amounts of funds and the need to uphold a participatory bottom-up approach (1993). When an evaluation team wrote a report saying that the farmers' organisations that had a big role were not representing

Box 8.2. When the present diverged from the imagined future

In a project in Sierra Leone, the national organisation managing the project – Help a Needy Child International – aimed to reintegrate conflict-affected children with their families. The grant-maker awarded over £800,000 for a series of activities that responded to conflict.

During the civil war (1991–2002) girls and boys became caught up in the violence in different ways. While boys became soldiers, girls were abducted by rebels and became 'bush wives' (or sex slaves). Those who fell pregnant were rejected by their families and communities when they tried to return home and received no aid assistance because it was conditional on handing in a gun.

They were turned away by parents partly owing to the shame of their association with rebels but also due to becoming mothers out of marriage, even if as a result of rape. Schools refused them re-entry again because unmarried child mothers were not allowed to attend. They were deemed to be a bad influence on other children. So this part of the project evolved unplanned community-based advocacy to change school policies and parental attitudes towards children who have babies out of marriage in the context of an extremely religious (Christian and Muslim) society and pronounced gender/age inequalities. Through lobbying local leaders and chiefs, getting the priests and imams on board, using the radio to enable the girls themselves to voice their views, and a poster campaign, gradually attitudes towards these girls shifted. They were forgiven and given respect. In the words of one young mother, 'I used to feel shame earlier, even to walk with my son. Now I feel proud to go anywhere with my child. I know I can be somebody in the community.'[4] Schools changed their policy and allowed schoolchildren to attend even if they had children themselves.

This advocacy was the only way to achieve what the girls asked the staff to do but it was not in the plan. The project staff had to keep reporting about the consequence of the war – and how the project was changing attitudes towards child soldiers and girls abducted by rebels – because the grant came under the donor's 'conflict' theme. The more permanently significant policy and attitudinal change to the position of unmarried girls/younger women was mentioned in passing but not as indicators of success. There were no lies; rather project staff just compartmentalised aspects of the work and drew attention to the processes that were actually less important to the girls but more relevant to the bureaucratic needs of the donor.

whole villages – that is, they were making sure that the benefits of irrigation reached their family and friends – the project staff and even the donor agency staff buried this report. The appearance of success was vital for the project's survival but also to generate 'evidence' that bottom-up approaches work. By keeping up appearances and protecting reputations, the project made sure that certain people and representations were kept separate and compartmentalised.

In order to maintain success, you have to displace failure. Aid projects achieve compartmentalisation partly due to the organisation of time but also by maintaining geographical separation between people; for example the work of INGOs can

Box 8.3. Working with disabled people in East Africa: An interview with anthropologist Mary Ann Mhina

Mary Ann taught English in Zimbabwe during her gap year. She was horrified by what she saw of the way INGOs behaved and was appalled that she was expected to teach English to children, given that she had not had any teacher training. It was as if gap-year organisations, at the time, believed an untrained 18-year-old foreigner was good enough for 'them'. She studied anthropology and learned Swahili; she realised that unless you know the local language you don't really know what is going on.

She began her career by working for Basic Needs. They were planning to start work in Tanzania. She advised them to change the model that they had developed in India for working with people with mental illnesses. In India there were plenty of services for mentally ill people – thousands of psychiatrists, for example – whereas government services were minimal in Tanzania. She interviewed lots of people, including mentally ill people, and recommended how they might adapt the model. Did anthropology make a difference in that work? 'Yes, anthropology gives you an attitude. It tells you not to assume you know better than the people you are working with. You get values from anthropology. In contrast the prevailing mind-set is such that many people working in development – even perfectly "nice" people – reveal their attitudes when they say things like, "Africans can't get things done".'

Mary Ann then went on to be Director of AbleChildAfrica (ACA). She learned about good development from partner organisations in East Africa.

'When I started at ACA I felt the pressure to learn about strategic planning and accounting as if that is the only way to run an organisation. But I realised by looking at various different local organisations that that wasn't true. In fact too much planning makes it harder to do good development. Policies and procedures don't produce results. You need some governance and some structure, but not in standardised ways and what you need depends on what you are trying to achieve.'

Mary Ann also learned more about the social model of disability, and rights approaches, from East African NGOs staff but also disabled people, including children. People are disabled by society and attitudes within it rather than by their own 'deficiencies' or lack of ability; there is no such thing as a physically 'normal' person. Mary Ann developed a social approach partly by listening but also because of anthropology. Anthropology confirmed the value of a social model with its emphasis on social constructions, power and representations.

She went on, 'anthropology does other things too. It helps you to see the complexities. But how much does this help you to do good development? It does not help with getting funding. It is nearly impossible to get money for sharing experiences and South-to-South learning. It's too complicated and risky for a funder. Funders want to put you in a box and be able to judge whether you have done what you said you'd do or not.' So Mary Ann translated what partners wanted for donors in ways they would find acceptable. She defended partners.

The reality is that partners can be experts in producing logframes but then don't necessarily follow them. They may present their work if it is innovation but actually there are continuities, that is, they keep doing the same thing because that was what was needed, but spend more or less in different districts even if that varies from the plan. Balancing the budget is impossible because in real life you have to spend on more urgent things and you cannot anticipate them. 'Partners in Africa get hauled about by other INGOs, asking "what have you done with that £500?" And forcing them to do what they don't want to do. If I had lots of money I would give it to people to do what they wanted to do. If they had a good idea, I would invest on trust. There is plenty of research that the current existing model – with its planning, logframes and so on – does not work, so why does it continue? You need to look like you are saving the world.'

(Interviewed by Emma Crewe on 8 August 2011)

be more easily accomplished because of huge geographical distances between relevant groups of people. This brings us to a different form of geographical displacement – the physical shifting of people in the name of development.

Spatial displacement

In this section we will look at how citizens have been physically displaced by the state. Physical displacement is not always involuntary. Voluntary migration from rural to urban areas, or even to another country, usually has a complex series of interrelated causes behind it; as examples, one or many of the following – running away from persecution, violence, poverty or family breakdown; moving to find better access to services, like education, a job or food (especially in times of crisis and famine); or seeking a better, more 'modern' life. Often migration is a mix of voluntary and involuntary, positive and negative, pull and push. Forced displacement is also the product of a range of political, economic and social circumstances, ranging from the trafficking of women, girls and boys into prostitution to the imprisonment or exile of political opponents, but is rarely positive. It can also be the most extreme example of the coercive nature of development, as cases from Tanzania and Israel/Palestine will demonstrate.

James Scott, in his book *Seeing Like a State*, explains how the settlement of Tanzanians into villages between 1973 and 1976 involved the displacement of at least 5 million people (1998). He is interested in this case not because it was the most brutal – Soviet collectivisation and removals in South Africa during apartheid were far more destructive – but because what began with a promise that no one should be forced to move soon descended into coercion and sometimes violence (*ibid.*: 223). The increasingly coercive element came about because officials, donors (including the World Bank and USAID) and, most influentially, Nyerere (Tanzania's then head of state) shared a 'quasi-religious faith in a visual sign or representation of order' but also the view that the ignorant peasants did not seem to realise what was good for them (*ibid.*: 225, 231). The visual aesthetic of progress meant that 'proper' villages should be tidy, clean and ordered, with houses placed in straight lines along the roads, while farming plots should be individual, growing one crop and more easily accessible to the government's extension officer (*ibid.*: 238). Villages had cells, with a cell leader, made up of ten households. In this vision, agricultural productivity would increase and it would be simpler to provide people with services such as healthcare, water, education and the rule of law.

For Scott, 'the thinly veiled subtext of villagisation was also to reorganise human communities in order to make them better objects of political control and to facilitate the new forms of communal farming favoured by state policy' (*ibid.*: 224). While the subtext may have worked, with Tanzanian officialdom consolidating its position, the main text – development for Tanzanian citizens – was an abject failure. The designers forgot 'the most important fact about social engineering: its efficiency depends on the response and cooperation of real human subjects' (*ibid.*: 225). Their resistance was well founded. With regard to agriculture, farmers refused to go along with the formerly generic colonial solution to soil erosion, ridging, and it turns out that they were right: ridging creates larger erosion gullies in the rainy season, dries out the soil in the dry season and attracts ants to attack the roots (*ibid.*: 227). Planners wanted a standardised model of cultivation, with the same crops and techniques, irrespective of household size, their other occupations, gendered division of labour and farmers' preferences. With the exception of the government's over-funded showcase pilot projects, the more farmers were incorporated into their model, the more disastrously they fared whereas those who stayed outside the scheme, although seen as disorderly squatters, did reasonably well (*ibid.*: 228). Huge imports of food became necessary from 1973 to 1975. Officials blamed the farmers for the failure: they were lazy, traditional in outlook and unwilling to change.

As far as settling people into villages was concerned, those who were reluctant to move were told that famine relief would only be given to those who moved peacefully. The militia and army compelled people to comply and burnt the houses of those who refused (*ibid.*: 235–6). Some evaded the policy, for example, fleeing the new village as soon as they could, and some areas were scarcely touched by officials, arguably those particularly well represented by the bureaucratic elite. They designated existing villages as new planned villages and, therefore, gave the appearance of compliance by both the state officials and the villagers but actually moved no one in to these re-designated villages. However, most resettlement caused havoc with people's lives, by exiling them from their homes, disrupting social relations and even increasing cholera. Scott concludes, 'what a neutral observer might have taken as a new form of servitude, however benevolent, was largely unquestioned by the elites, for the policy sailed under the banner of "development" even if its origins can be found in colonial history' (*ibid.*: 246).

When citizens have been displaced within their country by huge projects or modernising initiatives – such as dam or road building, clearance for agriculture or the settlement of pastoralists – the cost is often justified by claiming that they gain other benefits. Ovesen, an anthropologist who has worked as a consultant for a Norwegian company contracted by the Norwegian government (NORAD), tells a controversial story about losses and gains brought about by a dam in Laos (2009). In his assessment for a hydropower scheme in 1998 he concluded that it would reduce poverty so resettling some of the local population was worth it. He argued that, as a result of population pressure and the difficulties of expanding swidden agriculture, the population to be displaced would be better off cultivating paddy on the plains and their access to health, education and transport should improve (*ibid*.: 264–5). The dam went ahead although his was only one of many assessments that influenced the decision. He had less influence over the fate of the displaced villagers, as he discovered when he returned three years later. The project had ignored his recommendations and offered no electricity, planned development of paddy fields, irrigation or assistance in resettlement. Even so, he concludes, 'I happen to believe that hydropower development in Laos is a good thing … In the early 1990s, hydropower emerged as a realistic measure to diminish excessive logging and consequent environmental damage … I have seen my task as an anthropologist to do what I can to ensure that the local population in a hydro-power development area will get the best possible deal' (*ibid*.: 276). According to Ovesen, the anti-hydropower environmental lobby have failed to come up with an alternative. In the debate about the moral rights and wrongs of large-scale hydropower, for anthropologists as much as anyone else, clearly underlying the decision about whether the costs are worth it are ideas about whether dams (or any large-scale projects) are good or bad.

The next example is politically more complex because the borders of displacement are highly contested. The Zionist project to create a Jewish state took tangible form with the establishment of Israel in 1948. Many Palestinians were displaced from their homes, the majority forced into exile in the Occupied Territories, as they are now called, or neighbouring countries. The displacement of Palestinians outside the borders of the state (and their relegation to second-class citizens within it) was the result of Israeli military occupation and subsequent state policies. Benny Morris, one of Israel's 'new historians', documented this, but in 2004 he justified the displacement: 'A Jewish state would not have come into being without the uprooting of 700,000 Palestinians. Therefore it was necessary to uproot them. There was no choice but to expel that population.'[5] To deal with Palestinians in the present, he proposes, 'Something like a cage has to be built for them. I know that sounds terrible. It is really cruel. But there is no choice. There is a wild animal there that has to be locked up in one way or another.'

Israel's existential problem remains. As Israeli anthropologist Jeff Halper puts it, Israel can only achieve a Jewish character and control its own and occupied territory, if it is to 'relieve itself' of the Palestinian population (2009). 'Transfer', as the forcible expulsion of Palestinians is termed, is favoured by some extreme Zionists but is considered politically unacceptable by most of Israel's supporters who instead argue for a separate Palestinian state (*ibid*.: 31). Even so, for Israel's most important supporter, the USA, a separate Palestinian state has been more about protecting the Jewish state than recognising the rights of Palestinians. A letter from President Bush to Ariel Sharon in 2004 illustrates this stance:

> The United States is strongly committed to Israel's security and well-being as a Jewish state. It seems clear that an agreed, just, fair and realistic framework for a solution to the Palestinian refugee issue as part of any final status agreement will need to be found through the establishment of a Palestinian state, and the settling of Palestinian refugees there, rather than in Israel.   (As quoted by Halper *ibid.*: 74)

In addition to aid to the West Bank and Gaza, the USA gave nearly US$600 million to Israel in 2010, making it fourth in their league table of aid recipients.[6] A report to Congress explains that until 2004 (when it was overtaken by Iraq) Israel received military assistance of around US$3 billion a year, making it the biggest recipient of US foreign assistance.[7]

Overall, notwithstanding some rhetoric to the contrary, it has long been clear that the USA is prepared to tolerate Israeli settlements in the Occupied Palestinian Territories. Thus, successive Israeli governments have engaged in the corralling of Palestinians into secured areas separated from the network of Israeli settlements and roads. Bureaucratic and military actions are used to maintain segregation through the erection of a wall, checkpoints, identity checks, curfews, land confiscation and the demolition of Palestinian homes. 'They constitute collective punishment, not of a government, but of a people – in clear violation of Article 33 of the Fourth Geneva Convention', in the view of a UN Special Rapporteur (as quoted by Halper *ibid.*: 82). Over 650,000 Palestinians have been detained in the Occupied Territories since 1967 (*ibid.*: 33).

Meantime, the demographic time bomb for Zionism that still ticks away is the proportional increase of the Palestinian population relative to Jewish Israelis. Halper sums up the Israeli response to perceived threat of Palestinian population increase; 'to counter this trend, Israel actively pursues policies of displacement: exile and deportation of Palestinians, the revoking of residency rights, economic impoverishment, land expropriation, house demolitions and other means of making life so unbearable as to induce "voluntary" Palestinian emigration' (*ibid.*: 38–9) (see Box 8.4). Halper argues that what emerges is a picture of displacement by a state, whether it is bringing about an exodus of Palestinians from the country or confining them to reservations or 'Bantustans' that are similar to those created within apartheid South Africa (*ibid.*: 14, 31). Migration to find work would be even higher if the Palestinians could afford to leave for other countries or did not have the determination to 'stay put', as Bowman puts it (2007).

Israeli state rhetoric is that of defence; the actions against Palestinians, they say, including the imprisonment of those within 'the wall',[8] are necessary to defend the country against its enemies. The 'right of return' to their place of birth cannot be recognised for the Palestinians who fled in 1948 because their very presence in such large numbers would jeopardise the Jewish character of the state. Israeli governments justify what are seen as rights violations in any other

---

Box 8.4. An Israeli anthropologist resisting the displacement of Palestinians

Jeff Halper has established an NGO to resist the occupation. His entry-point is to stop the demolition of Palestinian houses, as he explains in his book *Obstacles to Peace*:

> The Israeli Committee Against House Demolitions (ICAHD) is a non-violent Israeli direct-action organisation established in 1997 to end Israel's Occupation over the Palestinians. ICAHD takes as its main focus, as its vehicle for resistance, Israel's policy of demolishing Palestinian homes in the Occupied Territories – over 24,000 homes destroyed since 1967. The motivation for demolishing these homes is purely political: to either drive the Palestinians out of the country altogether, or to confine the four million residents of the West Bank, East Jerusalem and Gaza to small, crowded, impoverished and disconnected enclaves, thus effectively foreclosing any viable Palestinian entity and ensuring Israeli control. In more than 95% of the cases the homes demolished had nothing to do with security: their inhabitants did not commit any acts of terrorism and, indeed, were never charged with any crime. (Halper 2009: 5)

A house serves more than a physical function; it is, Halper suggests, the centre of our intimate social lives and an expression of our identity and social status (*ibid.*: 53). To demolish a home is to destroy a family but the experience varies for different members: men are humiliated because they are responsible for providing shelter, women lose their main sphere of influence and have to live within the domain of other women, while children are traumatised (*ibid.* 54).

ICAHD's approach relies on understanding the Palestinian viewpoints at all levels – family, locality, as a population – and the connections between displacement of families, villages and whole areas through a mixture of state policy, coercion and violence. He unravels Israeli intentions and assumptions, presents empirical data in meticulous detail and offers an extremely convincing interpretation. Halper's representation of his status as an 'Israeli in Palestine' (as he titles one of his books, 2008) in itself challenges the dominant ethnic hierarchy. This is a clear example of anthropology applied in both theory and practice.

---

context partly by representing themselves as peacemakers and Palestinians as terrorists. To this day, the Israeli government makes the possibility of peace and a separate Palestinian state impossible by refusing to compromise over questions of borders, the status of Jerusalem, control over water and roads, and the rights of Palestinian refugees and Jewish settlers (Halper 2009). The Israeli government insists on 'security before peace', thereby ensuring a permanent 'interim' situation that achieves their purpose: the protection of a Jewish state. Security and development for Israel is incompatible with security and development for Palestinians.

To show how the Israel–Palestine case study concerns development, rather than conflict in the narrow sense, it is relevant to consider people's lived experiences and 'conditions of being' (Matar 2011: xi). Dina Matar's collection of oral histories, although extremely varied, illustrates how for Palestinians banishment,

humiliation, violence and poverty interweave. Khaled Ziadeh's story explains
how some of these connections are experienced:

> My Father grew up in the camps, but moved to Gaza City at the start of 1970.
> I was born in Gaza City and moved to the camp when the *intifada* [uprising]
> started ... We became politicised, talking politics all the time because of the
> brutal effect of the occupation. They banned us waving the national flag,
> playing national music, and reading books, all of which strengthened the
> politicisation of the community. The military government wanted us to be
> afraid and wanted us to forget that we had basic human rights as individuals
> and also as a community and this led us to look for ways to mobilise and
> organise against these attempts. The local economy was almost non-existent
> and youths and middle-aged men had to commute to Israel as cheap labour.
> Few people had the chance to be educated.   (As quoted by Matar
> *ibid.*: 169–70)

Since then the wall and tighter restrictions make it impossible for most Palestinians
in the Occupied Territories and Gaza to travel for work in Israel.

At the same time Israeli perspectives have common threads as well as variation.
Aronoff, another Israeli anthropologist, wrote about divisions within Zionism
but explains that they share a conviction in that Jewish people have a right to political sovereignty in their 'ancient homeland', and a shared history of persecution
and a distrust of non-Jews (1989: 156). But there are deep divisions about how
much the state should be based on religious or secular law as well as the territor-
ial boundaries of Israel (*ibid.*: 133). Those Israelis who reject both Zionism and
the rules of the political game in Israel 'tend to be dealt with by the police and the
military rather than through the regular political process' (*ibid.*: 141).

In exploring why Israelis can be indifferent to the suffering of Palestinians,
another Israeli academic, Nurit Peled-Elhanan (Professor of Language Education)
finds racism in school textbooks. Israel sees itself as a beacon of development
and democracy – a modern, well-organised and prosperous nation surrounded by
the chaotic and hostile Arab countries, of the Middle East. Here security, stability and development are conflated. Children are socialised into their worldview
by the state through their schooling. Palestinians are either absent from Israeli
schoolbooks or depicted as a problem. They are never depicted as professional
people but as stereotypes. Peled-Elhanan told a journalist:

> The Arab with a camel, in an Ali Baba dress. They describe them as vile
> and deviant and criminal, people who don't pay taxes, people who live off
> the state, people who don't want to develop ... The only representation is as
> refugees, primitive farmers and terrorists. You never see a Palestinian child
> or doctor or teacher or engineer or modern farmer.[9]

She claims that history teaches Israeli children that violence towards the
Palestinians was necessary for the creation and protection of the Jewish state.
But in an extraordinarily brave appeal published on the website of the Chicago

Chapter of Jewish Women for Peace, Nurit Peled-Elhanan resists Israeli demon-
ising of Palestinians:

> When my little girl was killed, a reporter asked me how I was willing to
> accept condolences from the other side. I replied without hesitation that
> I refused it: When representatives of Netanyahu's government came to offer
> their condolences I took my leave and would not sit with them. For me, the
> other side, the enemy, is not the Palestinian people. For me the struggle is not
> between Palestinians and Israelis, nor between Jews and Arabs. The fight is
> between those who seek peace and those who seek war. My people are those
> who seek peace. My sisters are the bereaved mothers, Israeli and Palestinian,
> who live in Israel and in Gaza and in the refugee camps. My brothers are the
> fathers who try to defend their children from the cruel occupation, and are,
> as I was, unsuccessful in doing so. Although we were born into a different
> history and speak different tongues there is more that unites us than that
> which divides us.[10]

By self-reflexively questioning the division between 'our' side and the enemy –
even though her daughter was murdered by a Palestinian – she goes to the heart
of political violence. By 'othering' Palestinians as dangerous and underdeveloped the Israeli State seeks to avoid culpability for creating and maintaining the
displacement that gives rise to poverty and violence.

Forced displacement

The forced displacement of individuals, groups and institutions in the
name of development – or its historical brother colonialism – is always coercive.
But the intentions behind it, and its impacts, might be plotted in quite different places on a moral compass. The forcible settlement of people in villages in
Tanzania, the Soviet Union, or Ethiopia are clear examples of state-controlled
displacement. All failed but to different extents and for different reasons. Even
so, their architects shared a quasi-religious or magical faith in development as
progress. Ethnic cleansing divides the world very differently in moral terms –
whether in Bosnia, Rwanda or Israel-Palestine – in that it does not even pretend
to offer development to the people being cleansed or displaced.

These examples are savage compared to the more subtle displacements created between development agencies and actors. In Chapter 3 and earlier in this
chapter (see also Box 8.5), we provided examples of INGOs bypassing NGOs,
NGOs taking over as service providers from states, and aid agencies displacing
both NGOs and the government by working directly with communities. This
does not immediately involve bodies being physically removed from homes, but
it does mean workers losing power, jobs and funds. Still more subtle is the displacement of development workers' attention from the present to the representation of the past/future. This form of displacement – including the assessment of

---

Box 8.5. Displacement in civil society: the instrumental use of national NGOs by INGOs

In a particularly poor approach to partnership, a local office of an international CSO (code-named HELP) had a good relationship with an African NGO – let's call them AfriAIDS – in the same country. AfriAIDS was implementing a child-focused HIV and AIDS project with funds coming from a UK donor via HELP. Due to a misunderstanding between HELP's headquarters office in Europe and their local office, in 2006 a member of staff at the HQ submitted a concept note to apply for core funding on AfriAIDS' behalf to a UK donor without even consulting or informing them. Core funds rather than project funds can be spent on an organisation's general expenses rather than on one particular prescribed project. The core funding would necessarily lead to a different type of relationship between AfriAIDS and both HELP and the UK funder: more intense monitoring of all their work, a commitment to frequent visits from both 'donors', and more complex reporting. The concept note reached the UK funder just as another ICSO submitted an application for the same type of funding on behalf of AfriAIDS, following six months of intense discussion weighing up the advantages and disadvantages and facilitating the development of their strategic plan. The UK funder was, unsurprisingly, unimpressed but fortunately gave AfriAIDS the benefit of the doubt, believing the explanation that AfriAIDS did not know about HELP's concept note. HELP's local office apologised and withdrew their concept note. But did they realise that by including the local NGOs – and satisfying the donor's demand for partnership with locals – but failing to tell the Africans (or better still ask their permission), they displaced them from having control over their own future? And if not, why not?

(Adapted from Emma Crewe 2007)

---

success versus failure – has increased with the explosion of planning, auditing and policy-making.

These temporal and spatial exclusions and displacements are connected, as we will briefly explain. There is a sense in which the centre of all people's experience of reality is in the present and wherever their physical body happens to be. Past and future, and 'elsewhere', even though elsewhere is someone else's centre, are peripheral to their vision. Administrators and rulers of others – whether in governments, non-governmental organisations or corporate agencies working in their own or foreign countries – are no different from anyone else in this respect; other locations, and the bodies within them, are peripheral to the way they perceive the world. So, when administrators organise people they prefer their compliance, but if compliance is in doubt then displacing them so that their attention (or even their bodies) goes elsewhere makes it easier to retain control. Beneficiaries that conform to the plan (street children for a street children fund) will be selected, while others that do not fit into the donor-defined category are treated as if they do not exist. Thus, Development World is made tidier and easier for its administrators to manage when people are displaced into nowhere.

These processes of displacement are the exercise of control over people by public institutions – the state or NGOs – forms of power that can range from subtle coercion through ordering people in time and space to brutal violence. But the state is not only about control and coercion. It can be benign, protecting and offering services. Furthermore, it is not only an instrumental system or collection of functions; it is an idea. As Spencer explains, we need to find, 'the link between the state as an institutional apparatus and the state as a space for political imagination. The link is provided by the semiotic capacities of violence, and its place in the configuration of sovereignty in the postcolonial world' (Spencer 2007: 119).

The state as ordered on rational principles, along the lines of Weber's ideas on bureaucracy, does not hold up. As Spencer explains in his book *Anthropology, Politics and the State*, the appearance of order and stability is never more than situational and ephemeral (*ibid.*: 101). Something similar is true in all agencies. Coercion is only part of the story – an important one in terms of immediate impact – but not necessarily the most intellectually interesting one for anthropology, or, significantly, the process that has the most powerful significance for people in the longer term. An even larger part of the story of Development World, we have tried to argue throughout this book, is collusion and compliance.

Scott elucidates that development has partly been produced by uncritical faith in high modernism but also by science, with its requirements for empirically verifiable evidence (1998: 4). High modernist projects – such as Nyerere's 'ujamaa' in Tanzania, a state's attempt to create rational order in aesthetic terms – are self-defeating partly because they fail to see what they take for granted and the contradictions in their approach. Anthropology helps us to understand the links between the layers and contradictions in Development World and the ordering processes of exclusion, displacement and moral taming of one group by another. Are they the exercise of power? If yes, then when you find people obstructing or finding alternatives, is this resistance to power? Before we answer these political questions from an anthropological point of view, it is worth saying a word about the history of political anthropology.

Traditionally political anthropology made a strict division between culture and politics and put the latter 'on an abstract plane where social processes are stripped of their cultural idiom and reduced to functional terms' (Fortes and Evans-Pritchard, as quoted by Spencer 2007: 34). The function of a political event or system – to create cohesion in a community or to consolidate power for the ruler – should be identified and everything is reduced to this function. Thus, even when people are trying to improve society – or do development – in a crude functionalist account, they would be following their self-interest. (Much of political science, currently more concerned than anthropology to appear 'scientific', continues to find a version of this – rational choice theory – convincing. People's rational choices involve weighing up options through the filter of their own self-interest leaving them inclined to follow the route that improves their status, income or position of power.) Up to the 1980s anthropologists portrayed politics through a functionalist lens, using formal models and typologies, taking all the culture and ritual out of politics and leaving them to be discussed within the study of religion. Anthropologists were separating and excluding phenomena, failing to explain the significance of things beyond their vision, just as the planners were doing in Scott's account of villagisation.

The reductionist aspect of functionalism began to be heavily criticised by the 1980s but what replaced it – resistance studies – maintained more functionalist tendencies than were explicitly stated. The idea of resistance partly came out of new versions of histories that showed colonised people rebelling against colonisers and partly out of Marxist accounts of resistance to the hegemony created by political-economic structures of power (Spencer *ibid.*: 38–9). James Scott's *Weapons of the Weak* (1985), the best known example, detailed the everyday resistance of peasants against local elites, while Escobar paints development as a polarised world of domination and resistance. However, as Ortner asks, when a poor man steals from a rich man, is it resistance or a survival strategy (as quoted by Crewe and Harrison 1998: 179)?

Although Monique Nuijten sounds as if she is heading towards a rather monolithic view of power when she describes discourses as the product of domination in society (2003: 195) – in this case of *ejidatarios* who temporarily borrow land from the Mexican government – she does emphasise inconsistencies and contradictions. For a start, the state as an idea is viewed in contradictory ways. It is a corrupt and violent enemy but it is also the benign provider of services such as water and electricity. The Mexican bureaucracy has an ability to continually overcome people's scepticism and bewitch them into fantasising about new projects (*ibid.*: 196–7). But she then retreats back into the idea that power domination is the key when she says that even the moral ambiguities are part of the process that constitutes power rather than a resistance to it. So, the reproduction of hope is part of the hegemony of the state. And the corrupt practices that are such an important feature of the relationship between citizen and state are the murky and shadowy set of rituals that confirm the mastery of the officials. Thus it is corruption linked to the nation's civil public order than forms the basis of power (*ibid.*: 203–4).

However, the contradictions in the relationships between citizens and the state could be interpreted in another way. For example, citizens do not mind paying large sums to officials if they get what they want and it is only when they are deceived that they complain about corruption (*ibid.*: 202). Furthermore it is clear earlier in the account that despite a lot of paperwork, the state is not exercising strong control over citizens. 'On the contrary, we find *ejidatarios* with great autonomy and freedom in their land transactions and state-bureaucracy with very little control over local land issues' and the power of state is 'to a great degree imagined and cultivated' by those same citizens (*ibid.*: 90, 118). So doesn't collusion sound more convincing in this case than the idea that these citizens are simply being duped? Finally – and this is surely the clinching argument against simple domination by the state – the membership of the bureaucracy continually changes so that most members of the middle class (or their relatives) have held political or governmental office at one time in their lives. So bureaucracy is not separate from society; everyone is part of the bureaucratic machine (*ibid.*: 154). The officials are doing their work and they have to believe in the new projects and programmes, the fantasies created by the hope-generating state machine, simply to do their work (*ibid.*: 174).

To highlight more of the problems with power functionalism, the idea of the state displacing people (or any other coercive act by an institution) unravels somewhat when you consider that the boundary between state and society is always blurred and porous (Spencer 2007: 111). Spencer gives Emma Tarlo's work on sterilisation in India as an illustration of this. In 1975 Prime Minister Indira Gandhi's policies of slum clearance and forced sterilisation were implemented by her son, Sanjay. Tarlo found evidence that slum dwellers were given new housing only if they agreed to sterilisation but also that what was described on paper was quite different from what actually happened. The trade of a new housing allocation in return for undergoing sterilisation did not preclude applicants paying someone else to have the operation. Rather than portraying this as coercion and resistance, Tarlo shows that bureaucrats and poor people cooperated and colluded in familiar ways: 'What happened during the Emergency was an intensification of dynamics and relationships already in existence' (as quoted by Spencer *ibid.*: 112–3).

Neither classical political anthropology nor more recent resistance studies, so influenced by Foucault, can explain some of the most interesting aspects of politics but maybe more recent imaginative and locally embedded perspectives can help us. So let us go back to what can be seen as interesting aspects of development – the exclusion of poor people from benefits of aid, the brutality of displacement or the moral transformations involved in auditing – and take another look at our question: what is going on?

If Spencer is right, then what is going on is what is always going on in politics. The political dimension is that 'morally unsettling space in which friend is differentiated from foe' (Spencer 2007: 180) and across all political realms power, antagonism, imagination and ritual are critical themes that we will take up in the final chapter. In this one we have argued that they take place within a backdrop of ordering processes and specific social relations – local, national, global – with a history that has to be understood before you can make sense of the politics.

The politics of development frequently work to displace the targets of interventions in time and space. As we have seen in this chapter, acts of social, physical and temporal separation justify in the eyes of the developers their own superiority and enforce order onto 'beneficiaries'. Anthropology is effective in revealing these acts of displacement and creations of hierarchy. Stressing the importance of context, anthropologists can act to firmly ground development in the here and now.

Challenging questions arising from this chapter

To what extent do major development institutions impose their ideas on aid-or loan-receiving countries in different situations?

How much do people contest the dominant ideas and rules of development and what effect does this have and for whom?

What is the relationship between policy and practice in development interventions?

What do success and failure mean to different people and why?

What is entailed in planning, evaluation and reporting and what relationship does it have to people's experiences in the present?

How and why does the state displace citizens? Is there a connection between different forms of displacement?

Is development coercive? What does this tell us about power and politics?

9   Imagining the future

This book is a collection of anthropological perspectives on development. Having introduced the multiple agencies and actors that inhabit Development World, we described some of the most significant and influential aspects of their thinking. The world of development is full of layers, tensions and even contradictions. 'Development' is, at different times, used as a synonym for 'poverty reduction', 'rights', 'science and technology', 'growth' and 'freedom'. Planned development takes place within a context of development in a broader sense – change brought about capitalistic expansion and globalisation. We need to explain why development can be so many things to so many people and how thinking is shaped by institutional practices. In this final chapter we will look at how the promoters of development create and make sense of the future and finally what anthropologists can contribute to our understanding of development.

The spaces between

> Someone once described music as the space between notes. Astronomers often see the universe in the pull of *total control* on the one side and *total chaos* on the other; economists look to the space between supply and demand to determine value and price. Should we not do the same?   (Severs 2001: 103)

Space is assumed to be unimportant and empty. But it can contain much of significance that is ignored; it is often the unexplained and unexplored between two points in time or place, between concepts or between layers of experience, within which social life is experienced. At the same time, the points or poles are not only culturally constructed, along with the space within and between them, but contested and continually so. This book has shown how anthropologists can uncover the relevance of 'the spaces between'. A fuller understanding of Development World is revealed when attention turns to the overlooked and unconsidered within and between gaps, layers and contradictions.

In theory, in development the moment when things actually happen occurs somewhere between the making of plans for the future and the checking and reporting of past events. However, as Strathern writes in relation to policy and audit, what is presented as two ends of a continuum – past → future – can be illusory (2000:

282). The simplistic version may be that plans are formed by policy and audit considers their execution, but actually policy and audit are also contained in each other. Planners and policy-makers usually have to include targets, key performance indicators and methods for evaluation and audit in their plans, while auditors or evaluators consider the effectiveness of the plans and policies. In a similar way people live not in the idealised states of traditional culture or modernised society but in a mixture of the two, refashioned in their own particular ways, within and between frozen old and innovative new, and contested between different groups. For both development professionals and intended beneficiaries, the lived experience of development is not summed up as either unqualified success or absolute failure but as a combination of positive and negative, judged (and argued over) according to the viewpoint of the observer and the shifting face of fashion. Development World is like any other world within which people are busily constructing and contesting culture. It is alive with endless idealised polar opposites (and the occasional conceptual triad or other configuration) that take on different meanings as they travel across contexts and within relationships between people. Our contention is that people actually experience development not within idealised states but in the spaces between categories. Contrary to discourses theorists, we suggest in this chapter that people's experience of these spaces is not merely determined by ideological constructs or power strategies. Ideology and power are important but they are not the whole story. We take up Spencer's challenge and explore how power, imagination and ritual all have parts to play (see also Chapter 8).

The study of development for anthropologists is partly about reflecting on the past in terms of historical practices and impacts of aid. Anthropology's empirical basis brings a focus to bear on what already exists – in a sense the future cannot be studied because it has not yet been created. And yet, the practice of development is partly lived in the future. Through visions, plans, proposals, policies and needs assessment exercises, the future is continually created and evoked. It is in the space between the future and the past, between a hope for happiness and despair at failure, that the most human aspects of development can be understood. By participating in the visioning processes people are invited to live in the future in their imagination and articulate what they see. Whether it is farmers explaining what problems they see in the coming year or social developers expressing their vision for solving poverty, during those processes there is a sense in which people are, at least in part, living in the future. In this section we turn to the content of these imaginations, what they mean and how they are created through various lenses. Hinting at how the future is constructed and the past reinvented through the use of rituals, symbols and ideas of self and sovereignty, we invite others to explore more fully the cultural construction of development.

Normally associated with religion rather than politics, ritual may appear irrelevant to aid and development. But as Kertzer points out, symbolism and the ritual context within which it is communicated pervade political practices the world over (1988). Bearing in mind that aid and development is inevitably political, it should not be a surprise to find that rituals and symbolism play a significant role in development encounters. Anthropologists have traditionally seen rituals as creating systems of shared meaning or enforcing/resisting hierarchies of power:

1. *Making meaning and allowing people to make sense of what would otherwise be a chaotic world.* Heterogeneous and dynamic, Development World can appear a particularly chaotic place. However, through ritual, areas of potential confusion can be smoothed over and conflicts of interest can be resolved. So the ritual of a series of Participatory Rural Appraisal (PRA) sessions in a community takes the complexity of participants' lives and enables them to select some priorities. Interactions are structured and prescribed by 'facilitators', through exercises in ranking or mapping, and symbols are used to communicate views or decisions. In reality, it is impossible to convey your view about anything complex (such as agriculture or advocacy). But through such ritualised encounters the views of a range of people may be symbolically represented on a series of 'post-it' notes or coloured stickers that show the ranking of priorities.

Or the power aspect is stressed:

2. *Reproducing, producing or contesting power relations.* Power is always expressed in both symbolic, as well as concrete, forms. Concrete expressions of power mean that, for example, some groups enter the labour market at a severe disadvantage and so are easily exploited, while others are over-represented in national or local institutions of governance. Symbolic expressions of power can involve, for example, words, objects and patterns that stand for something other than their intrinsic property. In the world of development, a logframe symbolises professionalism, while a concrete house symbolises modernity. In the case of PRA, 'facilitators' may shape encounters in ways that suit them; the power to decide is often captured by local elites in ways that reconfirm existing hierarchies (Cooke and Kothari 2001). Participation can mean going along with the external agendas set by the donor agencies, rather than the donor agencies participating in the agenda of local people and/or organisations. This also goes for the Poverty Reduction Strategy Papers (PRSPs) and the Millennium Development Goals (MDGs) about which there is considerable discourse at the international level but not much ownership among national development workers (see Chapter 3). The rituals of participation effectively mobilise the consent of those most affected by development, the intended beneficiaries, by allowing some of them to express their views but not allowing their realisation in practice.

But rituals and symbols can be seen in another way, which reveals more about neglected aspects of what goes on within development. Two stories of ritual will serve as our starting point. Both draw (but are not limited to) Emma Crewe's experience as Director of ChildHope. One is about management of staff – specifically how people in UK agencies (and elsewhere to different extents) do performance management – and the other is about envisioning the future as a collective.

Managing performance

The rituals of staff appraisal and performance management tend to follow similar patterns across organisations. Organisations create a cycle with a beginning and an end punctuated by ritualised events along the way. Such rites of passage start with the determination of objectives. Each member of staff identifies (or is given) individual objectives and targets that have to be specific, measurable, achievable, realistic and time-bound (or 'SMART'). These might be to raise £100,000 of funding, to influence a donor to adopt a piece of guidance, or to develop the staff member's skills in communications. The more elaborate the system, the more it requires some 'evidence of success' in order to judge whether a target has been met or information collected. Evidence might include the following: the organisation's financial accounts, which reveal funding income; a document from the donor confirming your success in advocacy; or a record of attendance at particular training courses. During regular supervisions (perhaps monthly, six-weekly or quarterly) the 'line manager' then monitors performance and the staff member needs to demonstrate how successful he or she has been. Any failures should be explained and discussed; if deemed the fault of the staff member, then the line manager should give advice about how to overcome difficulties. If this fails, then the line manager may have to set new objectives or, eventually if failure persists over time, go into a 'disciplinary procedure' which could end in dismissal with its own set of rituals (both face-to-face and in documents). Finally, at the annual or bi-annual appraisal performance against the objectives will be measured in more detail. The extent to which it is self-assessed versus the evaluation by the line manager varies across organisations. When performance is rewarded with bonuses (or 'performance-related pay'), the line manager has to have a bigger role as the judge of good or bad performance.

There are various interesting assumptions underlying these rituals of performance management that reveal much about the way change is viewed and the future is imagined. Change in the form of success and failure can be attributed to *individuals*. This is problematic for an anthropologist or any social scientist who sees 'success' and 'failure' as idealised categories that are socially and culturally produced. Even when someone's work appears extremely self-contained – a trust fundraiser working on their own, for instance – it is hard to know whether the level of income they raise is owing to their brilliance, the trust being hit hard by the recession, the quality of information they get from a programmes team or being poorly managed by their boss. When someone is working as part of a team, or running a whole organisation, separating their success from those around them becomes even harder. The variables are interconnected and can only be understood holistically.

The second assumption concerns *performance*. The idea is that you can improve people's ability to work well by setting targets for them and rewarding them (with praise or money) or punishing them (with harsh words or no bonus). So the view that people are primarily motivated by a rational assessment of their self-interest is alive and well within current thinking on management despite a critique from social constructionists, including anthropologists (e.g. Shore and Wright 2000: 64), that show it to be far from convincing.

Finally, it is assumed that working well is about motivation for individuals, rather than learning or understanding in groups or collectivities. It is by imagining the future through individual objectives – with the promise of rewards – that you motivate people as single and separable units to work hard and intelligently. But Emma Crewe's experience at ChildHope, and that of many similar organisations challenges this. Reforming the system of appraisal in ChildHope, she laid the stress on reflection rather than evidence. The results were encouraging. Staff members dropped the habit of promoting themselves or defending against mistakes – as if they were politicians spinning their performance on the radio – and moved into a different conversational mode. For the first time discussions between the line manager and member of staff, or within teams, on their work became grounded firmly in the present. They became self-critical, sometimes absurdly so, probing into why, not just whether, aspects of work were going well or badly and from whose point of view. They discussed their relationships, their struggles to learn complex skills, the obstacles to getting things done and the aspects of their work that they found truly exciting. This approach spilt into other discussions – ChildHope generally became more reflective and challenging of conventions. The rituals were still there – an annual appraisal and six-weekly meeting – but by changing the rules and guidance, a different set of assumptions created a different set of rituals. The questions on the form changed from ones about performance to ones about learning. The form no longer symbolised the rigidly defined evaluation of success/failure but served to provoke a sense of reflection and the communication of ideas.

Managing the future

A second type of ritual concerns envisioning. No self-respecting organisation is without a vision. Political parties have them and the struggle to say something different is becoming acute as they all tend to say the same thing. They write about the past to denigrate the deficiencies of opponents' performance in contrast to their own excellence. And they write about the future: about how, if they are (re-)elected life will improve for citizens. They reassure the reader about their abilities, make it clear whose side they are on and define their place in the world. Abstract words, such as excellence, value and fairness, are liberally scattered throughout.

Reassuring moral abstractions also form the cornerstone of corporate vision statements imagining the future.[1] As examples: 'McDonald's vision is to be the world's best quick service restaurant experience. Being the best means providing outstanding quality, service, cleanliness, and value, so that we make every customer in every restaurant smile'; and Amazon: 'Our vision is to be earth's most customer centric company; to build a place where people can come to find and discover anything they might want to buy online.' Most but not all aspire to be the very best but there are exceptions where global pre-eminence is not mentioned: Toys R Us: 'Our Vision is to put joy in kids' hearts and a smile on parents' faces.' Then you also have to have a 'mission', which says more about your aims as a business (or other organisation) and how you fit that into your image of the future: Disney: 'We create happiness by providing the finest in entertainment for people of all ages, everywhere.' These statements have a dual purpose in the rhetoric about the rhetoric: internally staff will feel incentivised and motivated and externally customers will be impressed and sales will increase. And mission statements are not restricted to political parties and corporations. NGOs and even governments produce similar visions, missions and theories of change (see Box 9.1 for an example). These days every self-respecting NGO, donor and aid agency comes branded with a visionary motto at the very least.

- 'Guided by the belief that every life has equal value, the Bill and Melinda Gates Foundation works to help all people lead healthy productive lives.'[2]
- Comic Relief: 'A just world free from poverty.'[3]
- 'US foreign assistance has always had the twofold purpose of furthering America's foreign policy interests in expanding democracy and free markets while improving the lives of the citizens of the developing world. Spending less than one-half of 1 per cent of the federal budget, USAID works around the world to achieve these goals.'[4]
- Fairtrade Foundation: 'Fairtrade is about better prices, decent working conditions, local sustainability, and fair terms of trade for farmers and workers in the developing world.'[5]

The envisioning rituals of development organisations vary according to the number of people involved and where they are located. But increasingly INGOs employ participatory techniques to ensure that a range of staff, partners or even beneficiaries feel a 'sense of ownership' over their vision, theory of change, mission and strategy. These are often tightly controlled by facilitators – sometimes internal and sometimes external specialists – who, having established the wishes of the organisers, tell participants when to speak and sometimes even what to say.

A typical visioning process might go like this. Proceedings usually start with an 'ice-breaker' and/or introductions. If you do not know each other, you might be asked to get into pairs, find out three things about your neighbour, and then explain them to the group. If you already know each other, the ice-breaker might entail a game that you play with your neighbour or will reveal something that

Box 9.1. Practical Action's vision for the future

The latest trend in the formulation of statements about the future is that they need to make explicit their 'theory of change'. Practical Action recently developed a narrative to describe theirs:

Since the economist Fritz Schumacher founded our organisation over 40 years ago, we have supported millions of people to transform their lives ... Schumacher's ground break-ing book 'Small is Beautiful' is as relevant today as it was in the 1970s. We are still living in a world where economic growth and technological advancements offers little for the two billion people living in abject poverty. And we still treat our planet as expendable – exploiting it beyond its natural capacity – with global warming being one such devastating result.

So we find ourselves in the twenty-first century in a world that is truly at tipping point. There is a very real danger that, unless we take radical action soon, the opportunity will be lost forever to secure a just and sustainable future for everyone on this planet ... For us, at Practical Action, our blueprint for this new world is based on three big, bold ideas that can inspire and bring about lasting change: equity, wellbeing and technology justice.

Greater equity is key to achieving a better world. The New Economics Foundation found that during the 1990s, for every $100 of economic growth, only 60 cents trickled down to people in deep poverty. But it doesn't have to be like this. Studies have shown that poor people living in countries that have a more equal distribution of wealth fare much better than those from more unequal societies – they get more share of the development cake. But, it's not just the poor in developing countries who benefit from a fair and just society. Developed countries which have less extremes of wealth also have less social problems. For example, crime is lower, communities are more cohesive, there is less bullying at school and life expectancy is higher, compared with countries that have big differences between the rich and the poor.

Our wellbeing is also an important indicator for a new world based on happiness. But what does wellbeing actually mean? Critically it's about people getting their basic material needs met. Our work in areas such as food security and access to energy and clean water are all key to improving material wellbeing. But wellbeing is also more than this. It's about the degree of control people have over their lives and the quality of relationships within their communities. What this means for Practical Action, is that it's not just what we do that's important, but also how we do it as well. People participating in decisions and taking control of their own development is a golden thread which weaves its way through all our work.

Finally, we believe technology justice is vital to developing a just and sustainable world. Technological advances have increased productivity and income, improved quality of life and raised life expectancy ... in the developed world. The truth is that technological innov-ation is focused on meeting the wants of rich consumers rather than the most basic of needs of poor people in the developing world. Every year 1.5 million young children die from water and sanitation-related diseases. This is technology injustice hitting you in the face. We have both the knowledge and technology to prevent these deaths. Technology justice must be a rallying cry across the world.

(For the fuller external version, see http://practicalaction.org/our-story, accessed 9 August 2011) people did not know about you. Then you typically have a presentation – perhaps an inspiring speech by the CEO about the achievements of the organisation and the opportunities for the future – with time for questions. This might be followed by a structured discussion in the big group, perhaps the facilitator asking a question and getting each person to respond, or, more likely, breaking people into smaller groups. The work set for smaller groups is normally in the form of an exercise: you collectively do a SWOT (assessing the strengths, weaknesses, opportunities and threats of the organisation); and/or you create a problem 'tree', and come up with solutions, and group the problems/solutions into categories; and/or you prioritise your solutions by listing them and getting people to vote or rank them (with ticks, coloured stickers or some other method). Another variation of small group work is called a 'bus stop'. Each group has a different exercise/topic/question and one moderator or facilitator picked from the group. Once a set period of time has passed, then all the other members except for the facilitator move to another group so that they have a chance to discuss another issues. A small group either writes their conclusions on a flip-chart and it is placed on the wall or, more usually, they summarise to the wider group. Questions might be allowed. Then some kind of discussion may take place with the wider group, usually by taking a range of views but not usually encouraging probing debate or discussion. Rather views are expressed as consecutive statements and the relationship between views can often remain unexplored and obscure. The facilitator warns people not to dominate discussion by talking too much or for too long because participation requires interjections by every participant, preferably with a roughly even distribution of speaking time consumed by each individual, making sure that women have an equal voice. This might go on for days but because the range of views is always diverse and complex, there is never enough time for discussion. The final conclusions are usually left up to the organisers.

So what is going on here? The question can be answered on many different levels. The ritual involves a series of events within which interaction is highly regulated. Individuals follow the rules because everyone believes in participatory planning and subverting them would be seen as arrogant. You would risk social ostracism or, at the least, negative gossip about you during the breaks. Performance in these rituals is premised upon the idea that as long as everyone speaks, the real diversity of views will be articulated and the whole view that emerges is meant to represent a consensus.

Chris Mowles – a complexity theorist specialising in management – makes the point that INGOs and private-sector organisations are increasingly similar in the way they take up values, including within such visioning processes. He argues that in both sectors managers ignore power relations and these processes encourage obedience and conformity and close down the possibilities of contestation and reflection on conflicting views (2007: 402).[6] So giving each individual the opportunity to speak without debate disguises the dominance of those with more power, confidence or charisma. Hannah Arendt throws light on this,

> The sovereignty of a body of people bound and kept together, not by an identical will which somehow magically inspires them all, but by an agreed purpose for which alone the promises are valid and binding, shows itself quite clearly in its unquestioned superiority over those who are completely free, unbound by any promises and unkept by any purpose. This superiority derives from the capacity to dispose of the future as though it were the present, that is, the enormous and truly miraculous enlargement of the very dimension in which power can be effective.   (Arendt, as quoted by Mowles 2008: 11)

This is powerful stuff since it can create solidarity between people and merges an enlarged sense of self with the sense of group so that, 'It can feel like an island of certainty in a sea of unpredictability, and it assumes a realisable future' (Mowles 2008: 11). The danger is that this feeling does not necessarily last for long because just as shared values are produced by social processes so they can only be renewed through continued social relations. People have to keep reflecting, discussing and negotiating but organisations often fail to create opportunities for collective renewal. There is another aspect of his theory of values that helps us reach to another layer. It is important to recognise that the outcomes of these processes – the manifestoes for the future – are impossible when the future becomes the present. And yet we go along with them. In one of these visioning exercises observed by Mowles, a CEO reminded her colleagues that the last strategy was a struggle but she demanded such ambition in the next one that it was as if only the impossible was sufficient (2007: 406). We know when we vote for a political party that much of their manifesto will be beyond reach. It is as if the capacity to aspire, in Appadurai's evocative phrase, goes mad in the political realm; only a capacity to aspire towards the impossible is good enough.

Surely this is dangerous? We are doomed to disappointment, which can lead to conflict. Schumacher counsels us to beware of false imagination:

> a man who uses an imaginary map, thinking that it is a true one is likely to be worse off than someone with no map at all; for he will fail to inquire whenever he can, to observe every detail on his way, and to search continuously with all his senses and all his intelligence for indications of where he should go.   (As quoted by Scott 1998: 342)

However, this is to assume that we actually *believe* in the visions we create. This confuses belief with rules and anthropologists have long since shown that gaps between what people believe, think or say they do, and what they actually do are part of the human condition (Crewe and Harrison 1998: 187–94). Rather than explaining this gap *in terms of* power in a conspiratorial way, it is clear that power resides in this gap in the sense that we collude with the status quo by forgiving past mistakes and joining in the exciting buzz of imagining the future. This it is not only about power; it is in the incongruities between belief and practice and between past, present and future that we experience the emotion, performance and spectacle of politics. It is in those spaces that we know alienation, solidarity, fear, hope, anger, excitement and frustration. To understand more about that is a challenge for future anthropologists.

Anthropology and development

We offer a recap on anthropological approaches to a general understanding of development as portrayed in this book. Conventional development depends upon hierarchies of aims, linear progressions and lines of separation to both describe processes of change and to organise practice. By paying attention to the silenced, the unofficial and the unreported, anthropology is uniquely situated to read between and across these lines and to identify the submerged meanings and practices of development. By adopting anthropological perspectives assumptions are busted, ethnocentrism highlighted, established explanations questioned, scepticism injected, outlooks challenged.

Over time 'expert consensuses' grow up in and around development. These dominant sets of ideas about poverty, rights, technology and economics have fed into particular policy prescriptions and institutional practices. Anthropologists show through multiple case studies that when such development policies are put into practice they are filtered through local power hierarchies, leaving elites with their power intact, consolidated or even strengthened. More unusually elites are challenged and/or new elites create themselves. Once in a while more egalitarian relations are established. But whichever result, development initiatives are always embedded in society with its gendered, class and age inequalities. And yet the increasingly bureaucratic management of change treats potential political change – promoting women's rights, for example – as if it were merely technical and often fails to challenge the status quo. Bureaucracy, with its auditing, rules and documents, is not the rational product that many assume, but a collection of social rules and practices. Anthropologists have described how experts are busy disguising the gaps between rhetoric and practice or even actively maintaining them so that people are organised, controlled or even coerced despite seemingly good intentions (Mosse 2011: 13). By considering alternative points of view, anthropology ensures that simplistic understandings are replaced by rich contextualisation, ambiguity, new outlooks and possibly even improved working practices.

What is it about anthropology that takes us in these subversive theoretical directions? Like most scholarship in the humanities since the 1970s, *deconstruction* has helped us understand culture and language. Culture within Development World (and any other world, for that matter) is created partly by endlessly assigning new meanings to language. Conceptual categories are created to signify places – 'Third World'; people – 'the poor'; institutions – 'the state'; or a period in time – 'the project'. People who use these categories in everyday life or work act as if they have real existence and hard boundaries around them, rather than being porous concepts that are necessary for ordering the world around us that

ANTHROPOLOGY AND DEVELOPMENT

will change over time. Some of them become treated as boxes into which more and more characteristics are thrown so that the label becomes hazy and easily misunderstood. 'Civil society', 'participation', and 'partnership' have become layered with multiple meanings and associations, which is why anthropologists are often inclined to 'unpack' such boxes and look hard at what is inside. It is not surprising that practitioners find the questioning of their cultural world unsettling. One's own culture is taken for granted as if it is fact. So anthropologists can create uncertainty.

Alongside deconstruction, anthropologists construct theories about what is going on in development by endlessly comparing the similarities and differences between different encounters. Early anthropological theories of politics and economics are now seen as reductionist in the sense of explaining whole systems in terms of one essential function or structure. Crudely put, the *function* of incest taboos was to create alliances between families or they are created due to the universal *structuring* of the world into binary oppositions (e.g. people you can have sex with and people you cannot). Or, as we saw earlier in this chapter, a structuralist might once have argued that rituals reflect the making of meaning, while a functionalist would point to the consolidation of power hierarchies. A structural-functionalist would have combined a mixture of the two. The construction of universal theories for all social relations, rules or rituals has been abandoned by most anthropologists as a fruitless exercise, with the result that ethnography is taken far more seriously once again. Rather than assuming function or structure, anthropologists investigate each specific context, with its own set of social relations and culture, building their theories from the specific upwards rather than the general downwards.

Plenty of disagreement between anthropologists persists and it partly revolves around history and power. All anthropologists agree on the importance of specific contextual history for explaining change – rather than simplistic grand theory – but disagree about how much and what kind of room there is for individual social agency. Within any group you find numerous, complex and fluid categories of people and endless different cultures and worldviews. They are almost always in hierarchies based on an intermeshed mix of status, wealth/poverty, and power. But the mix is not universally predictable. Since ideological constructs, rules, the realities that limit the room for manoeuvre and individual histories vary from locality to locality, individual agency can only be explained through the following: (a) broader analysis of explanation of power; (b) the diversity of practices that individuals engage in a specific location; and (c) understanding the dialectical relationship between the two. But what is meant exactly by this cliché of a *dialectical* relationship? Consider how it might work within the philosopher Stephen Lukes's theory on three facets of power: (1) the power *to*: when A has power over B and can get B to do something he would not otherwise do; (2) the power *over*: which means that A now has control of over the agenda and decides what can be discussed and what cannot; (3) the power *within*: A is not just an individual but a collectivity that has the power to share and control desires and beliefs even though they may be contrary to B's interests, for example, through the mass media or education. Within this broad theory it is then possible to allow room for manoeuvre; for example, development can be seen as many sites of power struggle but also contestation within which relations are reworked through grounded everyday struggles (Moore 2000: 673). For example, in the UK the government appointed the chairs of parliamentary select committees but this was changed by parliament, against the wishes of the government whips, in 2010. Furthermore, policies may be designed to put decision-making in the hands of one group (e.g. a donor agency by setting priorities for funding), but since practice is not determined by rules in an automatic way, such decision-making power only works at the level of representation. So to avoid a theory that is reductionist and determinist – reducing behaviour to one explanation or framework that leaves little scope for individual agency – the status of generalised theory has to be demoted to only a tentative and provisional part of the explanation. A universal theory can help to probe but often fails when employed to *define* power in specific sites. The diversity of practices within specific locations, and how they change over time, deserves at least equal weight.

A century after Malinowski's entered 'the field', anthropologists are still working to 'present facts, develop concepts, destroy fictions and empty phrases', even if so-called facts and concepts are endlessly contested. With their ability to recognise alternative perspectives, anthropologists are well placed to play a role in presenting development as a multi-production. The individual anthropologist cannot do all this alone. The real world of practice inevitably involves compromise and concession. Collaboration is essential and promotes the kinds of creative energy necessary to effect meaningful and sustainable change that can challenge orthodoxies and hierarchies. But this entails hard work in building relationships and coalitions, dealing with race, age, class, and gender differences as well as negotiating in the face of diverse and conflicting views. Development work is messy, emotion-laden and as stressful for anthropologists as any other professionals (Mosse 2011: 16). Expatriate anthropologists can find themselves at odds within groups of international development professionals – who tend towards parochialism, 'closed off from other epistemologies and ways of knowing' (Harper 2011: 136) – and, at the same time, be seen as outsiders by intended beneficiaries, especially if they are affiliated to development agencies.

Anthropology has been able to escape the impasse between theory and practice by breaking down the walls between the two. As examples, reflecting on their own activities anthropologist practitioners may theorise on their work, while academic anthropologists benefit from taking on employment as consultants in the short or long term. But, as Widmark explains in her article on short cuts in ethnographic methods, anthropologists are blocked from their bid to explain change over time in holistic and participatory ways because development is organised to map and count results against intentions in a ridiculously limited amount of time (2009: 292–3). To accept a role as anthropological broker then, you have to decide whether you share enough of the ethical assumptions and the politics of your employers and whether the practical constraints are bearable. Institutions are dynamic. The situation of anthropologists in the World Bank has surely improved in the last twenty-five years with their number increasing to 150 in 2004 (Mosse 2011: 83). But the marginality and limited influence of social scientists within the World Bank, the demand for simple off-the-shelf tools to solve complex problems and the protection of dominant paradigms continue to make the place unpalatable for many. The anthropological cry for taking account of local contexts tends to be ignored by development agencies working across the globe under pressure to simplify and standardise. The rich detail of their knowledge of place but also topics – work, irrigation, disease, conflict, poverty, pastoralism, farming, migration, identity, rights, the state, social movements, gender, technology, exchange, food, violence, environment, etc. – gets lost in translation.

Anthropologists working in development must accept that they operate under different time constraints and that their findings must be presented in ways that can be communicated, understood and acted upon. Judging when this becomes a harmful betrayal of diversity of views and contexts is part of the work of any engaged anthropologist. At the same time by paying proper attention to the politics, culture and morality of the institutional structures within which they are employed, anthropologists can hope to be better at both *understanding* and, possibly, also *doing* development. To make development better requires far more than anthropology but anthropological insight can assist in identifying new ways of thinking and doing. In this book we have offered plentiful examples of anthropologists doing just that.

So what about the insights that anthropologists generate: what do anthropologists have to say about specific ideas, policies and practices within development? They are ill at ease with the categorisation of people and countries. Developing versus developed hides too many flawed assumptions and First versus Third World are really euphemisms for similar judgements (see Chapter 3). While it is meaningful to use the categories 'aid-receiving countries' versus 'aid-sending countries', many nations fall into both categories (India and China are the obvious ones). It is only sections of those countries that receive international assistance or engage in development initiatives, principally state and NGO bureaucracies but also social movements, and large numbers of citizens are excluded.

Development takes place in every country whether by a welfare state, a voluntary agency, or a neighbourhood group, whether in Baltimore, Sheffield, Kisumu or Hyderabad. These are political worlds with the 'development' administered by government being the more formal and bureaucratised. There are both similarities and differences between development that receives no, little or lots of foreign funding. In all cases of development processes are ritualised, resources are fought over and success/failure are contested. But the USA receiving loans from China is clearly completely different from Mali getting grants from USAID – different countries have vastly different positions of power and room for manoeuvre. Despite the diversity, development and public policy is a feature of every country that has organisations aiming to improve the lives of its people. We can no longer use the old North–South division to describe the international exchange of ideas, technology, expertise and money. It is time to conceive of development as a genuinely universal phenomena at all levels of all societies – in and between all households, communities, and nations.

Development has always been about more than aid and planned intervention. Wider processes of socio-economic and political change have long been seen as being under the rubric of development. Development in the twenty-first century is a global phenomenon. It has been suggested that development in the sense of modernisation has been replaced with globalisation – whether it is the expansion of capitalism, the micro-chip revolution, the spread of the market, cultural hegemony, international treaties and rules or a social movement (Schuurman 2001: 63, 9).

However, Development World has become increasingly dominated by Aidland over the last fifty years; that is, what passes for development is increasingly about the transfer of aid. The shape of international Aidland has been called a machine, an industry and a system; but it does not really have such clear boundaries with predictable connections within it. At times development is treated as if it were synonymous (or nearly so) with its goals: rights for all; science for progress; economic growth for poverty reduction. But if development is about improving people's lives then it is curious that it is so easily squeezed into such narrow frames.

The governance of aid and development is undergoing dramatic transformations. The roles of state and civil society are blurring; public services continue to be privatised; and there is a greater reliance on the private sector, NGOs and other CSO agencies. The record of the different sectors for different tasks and services remains mixed and misunderstood, but corporate social responsibility has been investigated by anthropologists and they have found it oriented towards improving reputation rather than challenging poverty.

Within Aidland, most agencies rely on fundraising images, films and stories that focus heavily on the negative – pictures of starving children or videos of suffering and rescue – giving an impression that huge swathes of the world are mired in misery and despair. Even in dry proposals for funding, the portrayal of the terrible past and present and the promise of the future are exaggerated. The plans are massaged to meet the expectations or criteria of the potential supporter rather than stated in the unaltered words of the applicant. Funding usually comes with incredible demands, mostly paperwork and figures, so that some NGOs spend more time securing and reporting on money than doing the work. Planning draws people into various problems – setting unrealistic and inflexible targets and assuming a simplistic linear causality – while auditing can be superficial, distorting or even coercive.

Some development interventions have caused more harm than good – displacement, domination and coercion – and funds have been wasted or appropriated either illegally or legally. Some initiatives have benefitted those most in need of assistance. But whatever the mix of success and failure from different perspectives, no one would contest the need for improvement. This implies that quality will not be achieved by renewed policy, technical guidelines or bureaucratic rules but by greater attention to power, relationships and communication.

Anthropologists have written about the need for greater accountability downwards (or sideways) to beneficiaries and not just upwards to donors. Linked to this, it is assumed that greater effectiveness is only possible with more transparency about where aid comes from and what it is spent on. This will lead to less corruption, it is hoped. But as Olivier de Sardan's work shows, these processes go to the heart of professional cultures in bureaucracies and they will not be changed with rhetoric and conditionality. He shows us the value of giving enough time to the exploration of development before rushing to judge (2009: 101–23). Within his research in West Africa he found that the widespread corruption and disdain for users by civil servants is partly a product of the donors bypassing the state. In order to change the professional cultures found in state agencies in West Africa, he argues for reform from the inside rather than conditionality imposed by donors. We should support reformers within state agencies by exposing the everyday implicit 'practical norms' that govern corruption, whether commissions for illicit services or string-pulling, as well as the culture of impunity. So, in this and other development areas, probing everyday practices, identifying different voices and challenging linear assumptions anthropology may promote more positive forms of development intervention.

Anthropologists' proposals for attitudinal changes often stress contextuality, relativity and inclusion. Rather than conceiving of knowledge on a continuum (or in two categories) from science to indigenous, we need to see science as a form of globalised indigenous knowledge and shift to a more inclusive understanding of the integration of global/local knowledge. If we took better account of different localised ideas about a range of development goals – poverty reduction, wellbeing, growth, technology innovation, rights – it would lead to a reconsideration, and less rigid understandings, of these ideas. For example, anthropologists' questioning of 'universal' notions of rights looks at the problem caused by trying to standardise morality. International instruments, laws and policies lay down a range of rights – some relating to all citizens, while others are specific to particular groups (women, children, disabled people, indigenous people) – that are supposed to hold true irrespective of time, place and context. Anthropologists have critiqued rights frameworks for glossing over contradictions; focusing on individuals; failing to challenge localised and interlinked inequalities based on gender, age, class caste; and raising expectations without being able to fulfil them (see Chapter 6).

If we are right that Development World is a political and cultural domain – an international form of what happens in national politics – then we need a better understanding of antagonism, ritual, imagination and power than we have reached so far. Development is culturally constructed in bureaucracies, homes, on the street and in boardrooms, and through relationships, encounters, rituals, conversations and documents. Development professionals construct culture as much as farmers or activists – we are all making meaning, judgements, hierarchies and practices.

The richness of anthropologists' analyses of aid, planned development and social change – from the perspectives of a huge range of actors within endlessly changing constellations – seems to us beyond dispute. Anthropology has moved beyond simple functionalist, structuralist or discursive determinism; we now have postmodern deconstruction with some interesting and constructive patterns that surely help us understand what is going on. But anthropology remains obscure to others and depressingly critical of attempts to improve the world. Some have tried to create short cuts, translating anthropology into the language and priorities of Development World with toolkits, method tips and neat categories. But, in our view, our collection of research has shown that the potential for transformation is limited without more fundamental questioning and promotion of alternatives.

Challenging development policy-makers and practitioners remains a worthy task for anthropologists. One of the most useful jobs we can do is to probe the policies and practices of Development World by asking difficult questions. Development anthropology works best when, rather than closing down discussion, it opens up fresh areas for debate. For this reason we suggest some of the areas of questioning that anthropologists and others have posed, are posing and will continue to pose in the Appendix. Anthropology has done much to uncover the complex realities that lie behind simplistic representations. In this sense anthropology's role has been to complicate development, to reveal its tensions and contradictions, to acknowledge that it is difficult, to probe and ask questions. Development is not a simple process: it involves the convergence and divergence of different ideas, technologies, bodies of knowledge, actors and interests. Multiple points of contact and overlapping relationships promote possibilities for mutual advancement but also lead to new sources of tension, friction and conflict. In practical terms anthropology serves to identify points of friction and to subject them to scrutiny. As a discipline anthropology is well placed to offer understandings of social relations and practices and to assist with acts of interpretation and translation, to promote exchanges and to stimulate debate, many examples of which have been outlined in this book. The message of anthropologists is not singular and new insights keep emerging. Some of these insights may perplex people whose ears are closed to other voices but for those with an open mind, and a tolerance of ambiguity, the future is full of potential.

Appendix: challenging questions arising from this book

1. **Geography**
   (a) What purpose is served by the search for a global classification by geography and stages of development? Is it useful? Should it be abandoned? If so, what should it be replaced by?
   (b) What terms accurately describe the nations involved in aid and development? Can we generalise across geographical locations in ways that still take account of national/local complexity, diversity and local specificity?
   (c) Is it possible to identity similarities and universal patterns that do not collapse under close investigation or require significant caveats?
   (d) What advice should be given to planners, policy-makers, and advocacy specialists about what, when and how to generalise about locations and boundaries?

2. **Classification of people**
   (a) How should the people who populate Development World be represented?
   (b) Where do the inhabitants of 'Aidland' stand in contrast to those of Development World?
   (c) How do we cope with the cross-cutting of different forms of identity (e.g. farmers can be female/male, young/old, rich/poor, etc.) and multiple forms of identity (at the same time farmers, healthcare users, grandparent carers, etc.)?
   (d) If the donor demands that people are essentialised, which terms are useful and which are appropriate? Are these two sets of terms the same?
   (e) If you are a donor, how do you express your preference for certain types of beneficiary group? For what reasons have you chosen this set of beneficiaries? In what ways do you draw boundaries around these groups?
   (f) What meanings attach to the term 'beneficiary'? Is the term helpful? Do these meanings accurately convey the realities of the targets of development projects? Is 'constituency groups' any better?

3.   **History**
          (a) How can historical processes be understood? What can be
               learned from the past?
          (b) With staff turnover, simplified narratives and project funding all
               working against processes of historical learning, how can insti-
               tutional practices be reoriented towards engaging more fully
               with the past?
          (c) How do others understand these processes and what can we
               learn from them?
          (d) What would encourage greater self-criticism, reflexivity and
               in-depth analysis of the history of development at all levels?

4.   **Civil society and the state**
          (a) In what ways do civil society organisations contribute to devel-
               opment? What is the nature of the relationships that may develop
               between local, national and international agencies?
          (b) How can people involved in development strengthen existing
               structures, while also challenging inequalities?
          (c) Can civil society be strengthened without weakening the state?
               How can development policies, agencies and actors avoid under-
               mining the state?
          (d) What are the right roles for the state, private sector and NGOs in
               different contexts?
          (e) How can actors and agencies stop foreign agencies undermin-
               ing national NGOs and networks? How can foreign agencies
               support national NGOs and networks so that their capacity is
               enhanced and, as a consequence, their reach and influence is
               extended?
          (f) How are new donors – China, Brazil, India and South Africa –
               altering the relationships between states, development institu-
               tions, and beneficiaries?

5.   **The governance of aid**
          (a) How can aid and development be more accountable to the
               intended beneficiaries or constituency groups?
          (b) With vested interests deeply entrenched, what can be
               done about the everyday practices of secrecy, control and
               corruption?
          (c) How can aid and development be more accountable and
               transparent?
          (d) How can we understand and reform professional cultures with
               aid and development bureaucracies?
          (e) Should international agencies interfere with the governance or
               security of states receiving aid?
          (f) Should aid-sending states use development cooperation to
               improve their own security?

6.   **Knowledge**
        (a)   Can existing hierarchies of knowledge be challenged in ways that progress beyond a simple romantically inspired reversal?
        (b)   What happens when science is viewed not as a rational producer of facts but as a shifting and hybridised process of globalised indigenous knowledge?
        (c)   Are acts of translation or negotiation truly possible between different knowledge systems? What prevents the successful integration of local knowledge into scientific frameworks?
        (d)   How can knowledge systems, beliefs and values be rethought in ways that make them accessible to other systems of knowledge and worldviews? How can we integrate and value different systems of knowledge? What would be the impact on development policy and practice if a more inclusive integration of global and local knowledge were permitted?
        (e)   How can we ensure that marginalised (e.g. women's) knowledge is given equal value to dominating (e.g. men's) knowledge?
        (f)   How can we develop methods for research and learning that deepen our knowledge and generate more convincing explanations and more effective models?

7.   **Rights**
        (a)   In what situations are rights helpful or unhelpful, for whom and why?
        (b)   How can general human rights be promoted – including rights for specific disadvantaged groups – when resources are insufficient or unavailable?
        (c)   What are the contradictions between and within rights treaties?
        (d)   What impact have rights treaties had on rights-holders, including women, children and disabled people?
        (e)   How can critiques of rights be addressed by acknowledging challenges, making better links between rights treaties and rights-holders and prioritising when resources are limited?

8.   **Planning and evaluation**
        (a)   What is the impact of current planning and evaluation approaches?
        (b)   How can the ritualisation of processes be transformed so that they are more genuinely discursive and allow contestation rather than closing down contention?
        (c)   What information should be provided to grant-makers/donors to enable them to make good decisions and to account for the grant once it has been spent?
        (d)   How should the information be conveyed and substantiated or checked?

      (e)   How can approaches to planning and evaluation be improved? Who should design them?

9.   **Funding**

      (a)   Is it possible to garner support for aid without demeaning people or bending the truth?

      (b)   Are there other ways of raising support for aid and development that do not rely on portraying recipients as passive and needy victims?

      (c)   What arguments can be made for and against the need for bureaucratic reporting exercises to be attached to the provision of funds?

      (d)   When and how can the bureaucratic demands for 'business planning', proposal writing, and reporting be reduced?

      (e)   What conditions is it justifiable to attach to funding?

      (f)   How can grant-makers be persuaded to rely on trust, take more risks and tolerate failure if thoughtfully and self-critically explained?

10.   **Impact, quality and effectiveness**

      (a)   What is the impact of aid on different groups and what impact do those groups have on aid?

      (b)   How can we deepen our understanding of context, diverse perspectives and the dynamism of people's lives? Once we understand it, how do we deal with this complexity and diversity?

      (c)   How can international development become more respectful and less coercive?

      (d)   How can partnership between development agencies and actors show greater respect for the perspectives and knowledge of those that are usually marginalised?

      (e)   How can national governmental and non-government agencies, and the links between them, be strengthened in their capacity? How can community groups and social movements, the links between them and their influence on decision-makers, be strengthened? How can these agencies and groups be more accountable and transparent to those they represent or seek to assist?

      (f)   How can people be given opportunities to reflect, develop relationships and embed learning into practice?

11.   **Culture and politics**

      (a)   What are the cultures of 'Development World' and 'Aidland' and how do they relate to other cultures?

      (b)   How are aid and development political? Why and how are they transformed into technical processes?

      (c)   Why and how do aid and development often exacerbate inequalities, including those based on class, gender and age? How can these inequalities be challenged?

      (d)   How can we develop a better understanding of the morality, ethics and politics of aid and development?

12.   **Anthropology**

      (a)   What insights can anthropologists offer into development as process, theory, politics or policy?

      (b)   Which anthropological perspectives are most readily acceptable to development practitioners and which are more likely to be overlooked, dismissed or rejected as inappropriate?

      (c)   How can anthropologists communicate their critiques of Development World in ways that influence protagonists?

      (d)   How can anthropologists have more influence within development institutions?

      (e)   Under what circumstances, if any, should anthropologists compromise themselves methodologically and ethically in order to influence development practice?

      (f)   How can anthropologists behave ethically in a world where agencies and actors sometimes cause harm?

      (g)   How can anthropologists explain their approaches and methods in more accessible ways?

      (h)   How can anthropologists engaged in development support each other more effectively?

      (i)   In an increasingly global world, what role might anthropology play in examining and explaining cultural diffidence?

13.   **International 'development' and 'aid'**

      (a)   What is the difference between aid and development? What is the meaning of aid and development and should it be redefined? If yes, how?

      (b)   What are the similarities and differences between the range of various types of foreign assistance and funding?

      (c)   What is the range of development goals from different perspectives, why do they differ and how can we create more opportunities for debate?

      (d)   Why do the critiques of the meaning and goals of development make so little impact and how can alternatives get more credence?

      (e)   How can we reconceptualise international development to challenge inequalities at all levels, while recognising the specificity and diversity of local contests and conditions?

Notes

1   Introduction: hope and despair

 1   www.ids.ac.uk/news/ids-film-examines-how-british-media-portray-global-south. Accessed 9 February 2012.
 2   www.christianaid.org.uk/. Accessed 23 August 2011.
 3   www.savethechildren.org.uk/. Accessed 23 August 2011.
 4   www.oxfam.org.uk. Accessed 23 August 2011.
 5   *Ibid.*
 6   www.christianaid.org.uk/give/. Accessed 23 August 2011.
 7   *Source:* http://celebrityanddevelopment.wordpress.com/blog-and-progress and http://celebrityanddevelopment.files.wordpress.com/2011/09/getting-it-website-version1.pdf. Accessed 26 September 2011.
 8   For a more in-depth consideration of this point, see Schech and Haggis 2000.
 9   www.trumanlibrary.org/calendar/viewpapers.php?pid=1030. Accessed 26 August 2011.
10   For a fuller critique of Sen's approach, see Chapter 4.

2   Anthropologists engaged

 1   http://humanterrainsystem.army.mil/htsAboutBackground.aspx. Accessed 26 September 2011.
 2   www.baesystems.jobs/job_detail.asp?JobID=1790549. Accessed 26 September 2011.
 3   www.aaanet.org/issues/policy-advocacy/Code-of-Ethics.cfm. Accessed 14 February 2012.
 4   http://www.theasa.org/ethics.shtml. Accessed 23 May 2012.
 5   *Ibid.*

3   The social and political organisation of aid and development

 1   www.oecd-ilibrary.org/development/development-aid-total-official-and-private-flows-2011_aid-off-pvt-table-2011-1-en;jsessionid=1pds8em23f4nj.delta. Accessed 19 September 2011.
 2   Migration Policy Institute, http://www.migrationinformation.org/datahub/remittances.cfm. Accessed 20 December 2010.
 3   UN, http://icsc.un.org/sal_ss.asp, and Obama-Biden Transition Project, http://library.ias.edu/hs/ssstheme/20081212_aid3.pdf. Accessed 20 December 2010.
 4   www.bicusa.org/en/Institution.18.aspx. Accessed 27 September 2011.
 5   See IMF, www.imf.org/external/np/sec/memdir/members.aspx. Accessed 15 September 2011.
 6   See UN website, www.un.org/millenniumgoals.
 7   For more information see the World Bank's World Development Indicators http://data.worldbank.org/data-catalog/world-development-indicators or the UN Data's information about official aid http://data.un.org/Data.aspx?q=aid&d=WDI&f=Indicator_Code%3aDT.ODA.ALLD.CD.

8 See OECD website: www.oecd.org/dataoecd/57/60/36080258.pdf.

9 www.usaid.gov/about_usaid. Accessed 31 August 2011.

10 www.usaid.gov/locations/afghanistanpakistan. Accessed 31 August 2011.

11 Andrew Mitchell, speech at a BOND AGM, www.bond.org.uk/pages/andrew-mitchell-keynote.html. Accessed 23 December 2010.

12 http://et.china-embassy.org/eng/zgxx/t626101.htm accessed 28 October 2011.

13 www.guardian.co.uk/world/2007/feb/08/development.topstories3. Accessed 27 September 2011.

14 Axel Berger and Sven Grimm, 2010, *Opinion: Western aid and South-South Cooperation: learning together?* www.dw-world.de/dw/article/0,5980604,00.html. Accessed 23 December 2010.

15 www.foreignpolicy.com/articles/2011/06/17/2011_failed_states_index_interactive_map_and_rankings. Accessed 28 October 2011.

16 UK Office of National Statistics, www.statistics.gov.uk/cci/nugget.asp?id=407. Accessed 19 December 2010.

17 World Bank, 2005, *China Deepening Public Service Unit Reform*, Report no. 32341-CHA, www.cebc.org.br/sites/500/522/00000092.pdf. Accessed 19 December 2010.

18 www.unglobalcompact.org. Accessed 15 September 2011.

19 Deloitte, www.deloitte.com/view/en_GB/uk/news/news-releases/press-release/3fcf5ed790de4210VgnVCM100000ba42f00aRCRD.htm. Accessed 20 December 2010.

20 Dena Freeman, 2011, 'On corporate social responsibility', *Anthropology of this Century*, Issue 2. http://aotcpress.com/articles/corporate-social-responsibility/. Accessed 1 October 2011.

21 Tutu Foundation UK, founded by Archbishop Tutu, www.tutufoundationuk.org/index.php. Thanks to David Marsden for alerting us to this organisation. Accessed 5 August 2012.

22 Research for Development website, DFID, www.dfid.gov.uk/r4d/caseStudies.asp?ArticleID=50700. Accessed 23 December 2010.

23 Naomi Klein's Shock Doctrine argues security concerns and neoliberal policies are intimately linked in US foreign policy and go back to Milton Friedman, decades before 9/11.

24 Interview with Emma Crewe, July 2007.

25 Interview with Emma Crewe, November 2010.

26 A few exceptions can be found in *Progress in Development*, vol. 6, issue 1, where White's article appears.

27 Interviewed by Emma Crewe, 8 August 2011.

4 The elusive poor

1 The World Bank, http://web.worldbank.org/WBSITE/EXTERNAL/TOPICS/EXTPOVERTY/0,contentMDK:20153855~menuPK:373757~pagePK:148. Accessed 2 August 2010.

2 World Bank, *ibid.*

3 For research about the emergence of PRSPs, and what contributed to their adoption, see ODI working paper 216, www.odi.org.uk. Accessed 21 May 2012.

4 United Nations Development Program, http://hdr.undp.org/en/humandev/. Accessed 2 August 2010.

5 Barbara Harris-White (1997), *Poverty and Capitalism*, www.sed.manchester.ac.uk. Accessed 21 May 2012.

6 www.newschool.edu. Accessed 21 May 2012.

7 UNESCO, http://portal.unesco.org/culture/en/ev.php-URL_ID=35030&URL_DO=DO_TOPIC&URL_SECTION=201.html. Accessed 2 August 2010.

5 Human rights and cultural fantasies

1 USAID, www.usaid.gov/about_usaid/dfa/. Accessed 4 August 2011.

2 Tania Li, http://anthropology.utoronto.ca/people/faculty-1/faculty-profiles/tania-li-1/tania-lis-research-projects. Accessed 30 January 2012.
3 USAID, 'Our work', www.usaid.gov/our_work. Accessed 4 August 2011. HMG government website published by the Cabinet Office, 'The Coalition: our programme for government', http://programmeforgovernment.hmg.gov.uk/international-development/. Accessed 19 June 2010.
4 www.unicef.org/crc. Accessed 25 November 2009.
5 UNICEF, *Emergency Handbook*, www.unicef.org/lac/emergency_handbook.pdf; for example see p. 30.
6 www.un.org/esa/socdev/unpfii/en/declaration.html. Accessed 30 October 2011.
7 www.survivalinternational.org/tribes/dongria. Accessed 6 September 2011.
8 www.actionaid.org.uk/100926/the_struggle_to_save_niyamgiri_mountain.html. Accessed 6 September 2011.

6   Hierarchies of knowledge

1 For the International Labour Organisation's approach, see www.uneval.org/newsandup-date/newsdetail.jsp?news_id=590.
2 United Nations Environment Programme, Division of Technology, Industry and Economics. Types of Impacts, www.unep.or.jp/ietc/publications/integrative/enta/aeet/6.asp. Accessed 20 August 2011.
3 For more examples about bridging the gap between scientific research, the private sector and users, see the Centre for Research on Innovation and Science Policy, www.crispindia.org/Publications.asp. Accessed 20 August 2011.
4 Food and Africultural Organisation of the United Nations, *Climate Change, Biofuels and Land.* Infosheet. ftp://ftp.fao.org/nr/HLCinfo/Land-Infosheet-En.pdf. Accessed 4 August 2011.
5 Lansing and Singer 1988.
6 Alan Emery, 2000, *Guidelines. Integrating Indigenous Knowledge into Project Planning and Implementation*, www.worldbank.org/afr/ik/guidelines/prelims2.pdf. Accessed 21 May 2012.
7 UNESCO, Register of best practices on indigenous knowledge, www.unesco.org/most/bpikreg.htm. Accessed 20 August 2011.
8 For example, see United Nations University/Institute of Advanced Studies, 2003, *The International Regime for Bioprospecting. Emerging policies and Emerging Issues for the Antartic.* www.ias.unu.edu/binaries/UNUIAS_AntarcticaReport.pdf. Accessed 6 August 2011.

7   The moralities of production and exchange

1 This compares with an aid flow from DAC donor countries of US$129 billion in 2010 according to OECD Aid statistics website. DAC stands for the Development Cooperation Directorate. For details see www.oecd.org/document/49/0,3746,en_2649_34447_4658264 1_1_1_1,00.html. Accessed 9 September 2011.
2 http://econ.worldbank.org/external/default/main?pagePK=64165259&theSitePK=469 372&piPK=64165421&menuPK=64166322&entityID=000178830_98101911111181. Accessed 6 November 2011.
3 www-wds.worldbank.org/external/default/WDSContentServer/IW3P/IB/2000/12/13/0001 78830_98101903342884/Rendered/PDF/multi_page.pdf. Accessed 6 November 2011.
4 www.guardian.co.uk/business/2012/jan/29/business-economics-journalists-reporting-celebrities?INTCMP=SRCH. Accessed 15 February 2012.
5 Trade Justice Movement, www.tjm.org.uk/trade-issues.html. Accessed 9 September 2011.
6 'Fragments of an Anarchist Anthropology', available at http://ramshackleglory.com/para-digm14.pdf. Accessed 17 February 2012.

8   The politics of policy and practice

1   Tony Blair, Blaming moral decline for the riots makes good headlines but bad policy. In the *Observer*, 21 August 2011, p. 29, and available on the *Guardian* website, www.guardian.co.uk/commentisfree/2011/aug/20/tony-blair-riots-crime-family. Accessed 22 August 2011.

2   These observations are based on Emma Crewe's employment and research in various development agencies – grant-makers (Comic Relief, Department for International Development, Oak Foundation, Vitol Foundation, Big Lottery Fund, Baring Foundation, and the Health Foundation), international NGOs (Practical Action, International Forum for Rural Transport and Development, Womankind and ChildHope) and NGOs in Bangladesh, Ghana, India, Indonesia, Kenya, Ethiopia, Peru, Brazil, India, Sri Lanka, Tanzania and Uganda – between 1987 and 2011.

3   For more on the most popular buzzwords and fuzzwords and what they mean, see Andrea Cornwall and Eade 2010.

4   Interview with Emma Crewe, April 2006.

5   Benny Morris, Interview with Ha'aretz, www.webcitation.org/5pvy2Rvfw. Accessed 3 February 2012.

6   USAID, Where does USAID's money go?, www.usaid.gov/policy/budget/money/. Accessed 9 September 2011.

7   CRS report for Congress, *US Foreign Aid to Israel*, Jeremy M. Sharp, Congressional Research Service, January 2008, http://fpc.state.gov/documents/organisation/100102.pdf. Accessed 9 September 2011.

8   For an explanation of the wall, and its effects, see Bowman 2007.

9   *Guardian*, 'Academic claims Israeli textbooks contain bias', 7 August 2011, www.guardian.co.uk/world/2011/aug/07/israeli-school-racism-claim?INTCMP=SRCH. Accessed 9 August 2011.

10 Chicago Chapter of Jewish Women for Peace, www.nimn.org/Perspectives/international/000132.php?section=. Accessed 8 August 2011.

9   Imagining the future

1   Corporate Vision Statements, www.samples-help.org.uk/mission-statements/corporate-vision-statements.htm. Accessed 10 August 2011.

2   www.gatesfoundation.org/about/Documents/foundation-fact-sheet.pdf accessed 30 August 2011.

3   www.comicrelief.com/. Accessed 30 August 2011.

4   www.usaid.gov/about_usaid/. Accessed 23 August 2011.

5   www.fairtrade.org.uk/. Accessed 23 August 2011.

6   Emma Crewe would like to credit Chris Mowles with much more than the ideas in his articles. As Chair of ChildHope from 2010, he and his predecessor, Richard Livesey-Haworth, another management specialist, played an important role in developing management practices in ChildHope that challenged convention and focused more on the present than the past and the future.

References

Adams, A. 1979. 'An open letter to a young researcher', *African Affairs* **78** (313): 451–79.

Adams, P. 2009. *Accounting for Aid: Regimes and Practices of Spending in Development*. MA dissertation, School of Oriental and African Studies (University of London).

Agrawal, A. 1995. 'Dismantling the divide between indigenous and scientific knowledge', *Development & Change* **26**: 413–39.

Amarasuriya, H. 2010. Guardians of childhood: state, class and morality in a Sri Lankan bureaucracy. PhD thesis, The University of Edinburgh and Queen Margaret University.

Apffel-Marglin, F. 1990. 'Smallpox in two systems of knowledge', in F. Apffel-Marglin and S. Marglin (eds.), pp. 120–44.

Apffel-Marglin, F. and S. Marglin (eds.) 1990. *Dominating Knowledge, Development, Culture and Resistance*. Oxford University Press.

Appadurai, A. 2004. 'The capacity to aspire: culture and the terms of recognition', in V. Rao and M. Walton (eds.), pp. 59–84.

1986. 'Commodities and the politics of value', in A. Appadurai (ed.), pp. 34–43.

Appadurai, A. (ed.) 1986. *The Social Life of Things*. Cambridge University Press.

(ed.) 1985. *Do It Herself: Women and Technical Innovation*. London: Intermediate Technology Publications.

Apthorpe, R. 1970. *People, Planning and Development Studies: Some Reflections on Development Planning*. Brighton: Frank Cass.

1997. 'Writing development policy and policy analysis plain or clear: on language, genre and power', in C. Shore and S. Wright (eds.), pp. 43–58.

2011. 'With Alice in Aidland: a seriously satirical allegory', in Mosse (ed.), pp. 199–220.

Arce, A., and N. Long (eds.) 2000. *Anthropology, Development and Modernities*. London: Routledge.

Ariès, P. 1962. *Centuries of Childhood: a Social History of Family Life*. New York: Vintage Books.

Aronoff, M. J. 1989. *Israeli Visions and Divisions: Cultural Change and Political Conflict*. New Brunswick, NJ: Transaction.

Asad, T. (ed.) 1973. *Anthropology & the Colonial Encounter*. London: Ithaca Press.

Axelby, R. 2007. 'It takes two hands to clap': how Gaddi shepherds in the Indian Himalayas negotiate access to grazing', *Journal of Agrarian Change* **7** (1): 35–75.

Barder, O. 2007. 'Reforming development assistance: lessons from the UK experience', in L. Brainard (ed.), *Security by Other Means: Foreign Assistance, Global
Poverty, and American Leadership*. Washington, DC: Brookings Institute Press.

Barlett, S. 2001. 'Children and development assistance: the need to re-orient priorities and programmes', *Development in Practice* **11** (1): 62–72.

Barnard, A. 2000. *History and Theory in Anthropology*. Cambridge University
Press.

Barnard, A., and J. Spencer (eds.) 1996. *Encyclopaedia of social and cultural anthropology*. London: Routledge.

Barrett, C., and M. Carter, 2010. 'The power and pitfalls of experiments in development economics: some non-random reflections', *Applied Economic Perspectives
and Policy* **32** (4): 515–48.

Batliwala, S. 2007. 'Taking the power out of empowerment', *Development in Practice*
17 (4–5): 557–65.

Beall, J., T. Goodfellow and J. Putzel 2006. 'Introductory article: on the discourse
of terrorism, security and development', *Journal of International Development*
18 (1): 51–67.

Bebbington, A., S. Guggenheim, E. Olson and M. Woolcock 2004. 'Exploring social
capital debated at the World Bank', *The Journal of Development Studies* **40** (5):
33–64.

Bebbington, A., S. Guggenheim, E. Olson and M. Woolcock (eds.) 2006. *The Search
for Empowerment: Social Capital as Theory and Practice at the World Bank*.
West Hartford, CT: Kumarian Press.

Beck, T. 1994. *The Experience of Poverty: Fighting for Respect and Resources in
Village India*. London: Intermediate Technology Publications.

Bell, D. A. and J.-M. Coicaud (eds.) 2007. *Ethics in Action: the Ethical Challenges
of International Human Rights Nongovernmental Organisations*. Cambridge
University Press.

Benedict, R. 1989 [1946]. *The Chrysanthemum and the Sword: Patterns of Japanese
Culture*. Boston, MA: Houghton Mifflin.

Bentley, K. A. 2005. 'Can there be any universal children's rights', *International
Journal of Human Rights* **9** (1): 107–23.

Berthoud, G. 2010. 'Market', in W. Sachs (ed.), pp. 1–23.

Bloch, M. 1991. 'Language, anthropology and cognitive science'. *Journal of the
Royal Anthropological Institute* **26** (2): 183–98.

Bloch, M., and J. Parry 1989. *Money and the Morality of Exchange*. Cambridge
University Press.

Boserup, E. 1970. *Women's Role in Economic Development*. London: St. Martin's
Press.

Bourdieu, P. 1977. *Outline of a theory of practice* [tr. Richard Nice]. Cambridge
University Press.

Bowman, G. 2007. 'Israel's wall and the logic of encystation: sovereign exception or
wild sovereignty?', *Focaal – European Journal of Anthropology* **50**: 127–36.

Boyden, J. 1997. 'Childhood and the policy-makers: a comparative perspective on
the globalisation of childhood,' in A. James and A. Prout (eds.), pp. 190–215.

Brautigam, D. 2009. *The Dragon's Gift: the Real Story of China in Africa*. New York:
Oxford University Press.

Bremen, J. van, and A. Shimizu 1999. 'Anthropology in colonial contexts: a tale of two countries' in Van Bremen and A. Shimizu (eds.), pp. 1–10.

Bremen, J. van, and A. Shimizu (eds.) 1999. *Anthropology and Colonialism in Asia and Oceania*. Richmond, Surrey: Curzon Press.

Bush, C. G. 1983. 'Women and the assessment of technology: to think, to be, to unthink', in J. Rothschild (ed.), pp. 151–70.

Byron, G., and C. Ornemark 2010. 'Gender equality in Swedish development cooperation', *Sida Evaluation* 2010: 1.

Carrier, J. G. (ed.) 1997. *Meanings of the Market: The Free Market in Western Culture*. Oxford: Berg.

Chambers, R. 1983. *Rural Development: Putting the Last First*. New York: John Wiley.
   1994. 'The origins and practice of participatory rural appraisal', *World Development* **22** (7): 953–69.

Chant, S., and M. Guttman 2005. '"Men-streaming" gender? Questions for gender and development policy in the twenty-first century', in M. Elderman and A. Haugerud (eds.), pp. 240–9.

Chincilla, N. S. 1991. 'Marxism, feminism, and the struggle for democracy in Latin America', *Gender and Society* **5** (3): 291–310.

Chodorow, N. 1999. *The Reproduction of Mothering*. Berkeley: University of California Press.

Christiansen, C., M. Utas and H. E. Vish (eds.) 2006. *Navigating Youth and Generating Adulthood: Social Becoming in an African Context*. Uppsala: Nordiska Afrikainstitutet.

Clark, J. 2003. *Worlds Apart: Civil Society and the Battle for Ethical Globalisation*. London: Earthscan.

Clifford, J., and G. Marcus, G. (eds.) 1986. *Writing Culture: the Poetics and Politics of Ethnography*. Berkeley: University of California Press.

Cline-Cole, R. A., H. A. C. Main and J. E. Nichol 1990. 'On fuelwood consumption, population dynamics, and deforestation in Africa', *World Development* **18** (4): 513–27.

Conticini, A., and D. Hulme 2007. 'Escaping violence, seeking freedom: why children in Bangladesh migrate to the street', *Development and Change* **38** (2): 201–27.

Cooke, B., and U. Kothari (eds.) 2001. *Participation: the New Tyranny*. London: Zed Books.

Corbridge, S., G. Williams, M. Srivastava and R. Veron 2003. 'Making social science matter – I: How the local state works in rural Bihar, Jharkhand and West Bengal', *Economic and Political Weekly*, June **14**: 2377–89.

Cornwall, A. 2010. 'Introductory overview – buzzwords and fuzzwords: deconstructing development discourse', in A. Cornwall and D. Eade (eds.), pp. 1–18.

Cornwall, A., and C. Nyamu-Musembi 2004. 'What is the "rights-based approach" all about? Perspectives from international development agencies.' Institute for Development Studies Working Paper 234. www.gsdrc.org/go/display/document/legacyid/1317, accessed 21 May 2012.

Cornwall, A., and D. Eade (eds) 2010. *Deconstructing Development Discourse: Buzzwords and Fuzzwords*. Rugby: Practical Action Publishing.

Cornwall, A., E. Harrison and A. Whitehead. (eds.) 2008. *Gender Myths and Feminist Fables: the Struggle for Interpretive Power in Gender and Development*. Oxford: Blackwell.

Cowen, M. P., and R. W. Shenton 1996. *Doctrines of Development*. London and New York: Routledge.

Craig, D., and. D. Porter. 2006. *Development Beyond Neoliberalism: Governance, Poverty Reduction and Political Economy*. London and New York: Routledge.

Crate, S. A., and M. Nuttall (eds.) 2009. *Anthropology and Climate Change: From Encounters to Actions*. Walnut Creek, CA: Left Coast Press.

Crewe, E. 1997. 'The silent traditions of developing cooks', in R. Grillo and R. L. Stirrat (eds.), pp. 59–80.

2007. 'Towards better outcomes for children: Alternative Perspectives on International Development', *Journal of Children's Services*, **2** (4): 59–70.

Crewe, E., and E. A. Harrison. 1998. *Whose Development? An Ethnography of Aid*. London: Zed.

Crewe, E., and P. Fernando 2006. 'The elephant in the room: racism in representations, relationships and rituals', *Progress in Development Studies* **6** (1): 1–15.

Crewe, E., and U. Kothari 1997. Migration, work and identity. Gujaratis in Wellingborough. ESRC-funded Institute for Development Policy and Management research report. Unpublished.

Crewe, E., and A. Sarkar 2006. 'Strategic communication and institutional links in technology research and development', *Journal of Technology Management and Sustainable Development* **5** (1): 21–40.

Crisp, L. 2011. "The Danger of a Single Story": How Fundraising Images Used by INGOs Continue to Perpetuate Racism in Development. MA dissertation, School of Oriental and African Studies (University of London).

Dalton, G. (ed.) 1980. *Research in Economic Anthropology*, Vol. III. Greenwich, CT: JAI Press.

David, R., A. Mancini and I. Guijt. 2006. 'Bringing systems in line with values: the practice of ALPS (ActionAid's Accountability, Learning and Planning system)', in R. Eyben (ed.).

Davison, O., and S. Karekezi 1993. 'A new environmentally sound energy strategy for the development of sub-Saharan Africa', in S. Karekezi and G. A. Mackenzie (eds.), pp. 8–22.

De Neve, G. (ed.) 2008. *Hidden Hands in the Market: Ethnographies of Fair Trade, Ethical Consumption, and Corporate Social Responsibility*. Bingley: JAI Press.

Devereux, S. 2001. 'Sen's entitlement approach: critiques and counter-critiques', *Oxford Development Studies* **29** (3): 244–83.

Devereux, S. (ed.) 2007. *The New Famines: Why Famines Persist in an Era of Globalization*. London: Routledge.

Devereux, S. and Z. Tiba 2007. 'Malawi's first famine, 2001–2002', in S. Devereux (ed.), pp. 143–77.

Devlin, C. and Elgie, R. 2008. 'The effect of increased women's representation in parliament: the case of Rwanda', *Parliamentary Affairs* **61** (2): 237–54.

DFID 2000. *Realising Human Rights for Poor People: Strategies for Achieving the International Development Targets*. London: Department for International Development.

2010. *The Politics of Poverty: Elites, Citizens and States. Findings from ten years of DFID-funded research on Governance and Fragile States 2001–2010. A synthesis paper*. London: Department for International Development.

Doolittle, A. 2006. 'Resources, ideologies and nationalism: the politics of development in Malaysia', in D. Lewis and D. Mosse (eds.), pp. 51–74.

Douglas, M. 1987. *How Institutions Think*. London: Routledge & Kegan Paul.

Duffield, M. 2001: *Global Governance and the New Wars: the Merging of Development and Security*. London: Zed Books.

Eldelman, M., and A. Haugerud 2005. 'Introduction: the anthropology of development and globalizationisation', in Elderman and Haugerud (eds.), pp. 1–74.

Eldelman, M., and A. Haugerud (eds.) 2005. *The Anthropology of Development and Globalisation: from Classical Political Economy to Contemporary Neoliberalism*. Oxford: Blackwell.

Einarsdottir, J. 2006. 'Relocation of children: fosterage and child death in Biombo, Guinea-Bissau', in C. Christiansen, M. Utas and H. E. Vish (eds.), pp. 183–200.

Elwin, V. 1954. *Tribal Myths of Orissa*. India: Oxford University Press.

Escobar, A. 1987. Power and Visibility: the Invention and Management of Development in the Third World. PhD dissertation, University of California, Berkeley.

1991. 'Anthropology and the development encounter: the making and marketing of development anthropology', *American Ethnologist* **18** (4): 16–40.

1992. 'Reflections on "development": grassroots approaches and alternative politics in the Third World', *Futures*, **24**: 411–436.

1995. *Encountering Development: the Making and Unmaking of the Third World*. Princeton University Press.

Esteva, G. 1992. ' "Development." ' In Wolfgang Sachs (ed.), pp. 6–25.

Eyben, R. (ed.) 2006. *Relationships for Aid*. Zed Books: London.

Ferguson, J. 1990. *The Anti-politics Machine: Development, De-politicisation and Bureaucratic Power in Lesotho*. Cambridge University Press.

Ferguson, J. 1996. *'Development'*, in A. Barnard and J. Spencer (eds.), pp. 240–42.

Finnstrom, A. 2006. 'Meaningful rebels? Young adult perceptions on the Lord's Resistance Movement/Army in Uganda', in C. Christiansen, M. Utas and H. E. Vish (eds.), pp. 203–27.

Firth, R. 1981. 'Engagement and detachment: reflections on applying social anthropology to social affairs', *Human Organization* **40** (3): 193–201.

Fisher, W. F. 1997. 'Doing good? The politics and antipolitics of NGO practices', *Annual Review of Anthropology* **26**: 439–64.

Francis, P. 2001. 'Participatory development at the World Bank: the primary of process', in B. Cooke and U. Kothari (eds.), pp. 72–87.

Fukuyama, F. 1993. *The End of History and the Last Man*. Harmondsworth: Penguin.

Fuller, C. J., and J. Harriss 2001. 'For an anthropology of the modern Indian state', in Fuller and Benei (eds.), pp. 1–30.

Fuller, C. J., and V. Benei (eds.) (2001). *The Everyday State and Society in Modern India*. London: Hurst.

Gardner, K. and D. Lewis 1996. *Anthropology, Development and the Post-modern Challenge*. London: Pluto Press.

Gasper, D. 2000. 'Evaluating the "logical framework approach" – towards learning-oriented development evaluation', *Public Administration and Development* **20** (1): 17–28.

Gedalof, I. 1999. *Against Purity: Rethinking Identity with Indian and western Feminisms*. New York and London: Routledge.

Geertz, C. 1973. *The Interpretation of Cultures: Selected Essays*. New York: Basic.

Gellner, D. (ed.) 2010. *Varieties of Activist Experience: Civil Society in South Asia*. Los Angeles, CA: SAGE Publications.

Gill, K., K. Brooks, J. McDougall, P. Patel and A. Kes 2010. *Bridging the Gender Divide: How Technology Can Advance Women Technologically*. Washington, DC: International Centre for Research on Women.

Gledhill, J. 1994. *Power and Its Disguises: Anthropological Perspectives on Politics*. London: Pluto Press.

— 2008. 'Introduction: anthropological perspectives on indigenous resurgence in Chaipas', *Identities: Global Studies in Culture and Power* **15**: 483–505.

Goetz, A. M., and R. Sen Gupta 1996. 'Who takes the credit? Gender, power, and control over loan use in rural credit programs in Bangladesh', *World Development* **24** (1): 45–63.

Goldman, M. 2005. *Imperial Nature: the World Bank and Struggles for Social Justice in the Age of Globalisation*. New Haven, CT, and London: Yale University Press.

Gonzalez, R. J. 2008. 'Human terrain: past, present and future applications', *Anthropology Today* **24** (1): 21–6.

Gould, J. 2007. Maintaining good partnerships: the challenge of long distance relationships. Unpublished report, Christian World Services, Christchurch.

Graeber, D. 2009. *Direct Action: an Ethnography*. Oakland, CA: AK Press.

Gray, P. A. 2011. 'Looking "The Gift" in the mouth: Russia as donor', *Anthropology Today* **27** (2): 5–8.

Green, M. 2000. 'Participatory development and the appropriation of agency in southern Tanzania', *Critique of Anthropology* **20** (1): 67–89.

— 2006. 'Representing poverty and attacking representations: perspectives on poverty from social anthropology', *Journal of Development Studies* **42** (7): 1108–29.

Green, M. and D. Hulme, 2005. 'From correlates and characteristics to causes: thinking about poverty from a chronic poverty perspective', *World Development* **33** (6): 867–79.

Greenfield, S. 2010. 'A faith-based mental health and development project for slum dwellers in Brazil', *National Association for the Practice of Anthropology Bulletin* **33** (1): 91–104, American Anthropological Association.

Grillo, R., and R. L. Stirrat (eds.) 1997. *Discourses of Development*. London: Berg.

Grugel, J., and N. Piper 2009. 'Do rights promote development?', *Global Social Policy* **9** (1): 79–98.

Guggenheim, S. 2006. 'Crises and contradictions: understanding the origins of a community development project in Indonesia', in A. Bebbington, S. Guggenheim, E. Olson and M. Woolcock (eds.), pp. 111–44.

Gunder Frank, A. 1966. 'The development of underdevelopment', *Monthly Review*, **18** (4): 7–31.

Hagberg, S. 2001. *Poverty in Burkino Faso: Representations and Realities*. Uppsala University.

Hagberg, S., and C. Widmark (eds.) 2009. *Ethnographic Practice and Public Aid*. Uppsala: Uppsala University.

Hale, C. 2006. 'Activist research vs. cultural critique: indigenous land rights and the contradictions of politically engaged anthropology'. *Cultural Anthropology* **21**: 96–120.

Hall, A., R. Raina and R. Sulaiman 2005, 'Institutional learning and change: a review of concepts and principles', *NCAP Policy Brief*, no. 21, p. 4. National Centre for Agricultural Economics and Policy Research, India: New Delhi.

Halper, J. 2008. *An Israeli in Palestine: Resisting dispossession, redeeming Israel*. London: Pluto.

   2009. *Obstacles to Peace. A Reframing of the Israeli-Palestinian Conflict*. Jerusalem: Israeli Campaign Against House Demolitions.

Hancock, G. 1989. *The Lords of Poverty: The Power, Prestige, and Corruption of the International Aid Business*. New York: The Atlantic Monthly Press.

Hann, C., and K. Hart 2011. *Economic Anthropology: History, Ethnography, Critique*. Cambridge: Polity Press.

Harper, C., and N. Jones 2009a. 'Raising the Same: Mainstreaming Children's Rights', *Overseas Development Institute Briefing Paper*, no 56, November.

   2009b. 'Child rights and aid: mutually exclusive?', *Overseas Development Institute Background Note*, November.

Harper, I. 2011. "World health and Nepal: producing internationals, healthy citizenship and the cosmopolitan", in D. Mosse (ed.), pp. 123–38.

Harper, R. 2000. 'The social organization of the IMF's mission work: an examination of international auditing', in M. Strathern (ed.), pp. 21–54.

Harrison, T. 1959. *World Within: a Borneo Story*. Oxford University Press.

Hart, K. 1973. 'Informal income opportunities and urban employment in Ghana', *Journal of Modern Africa Studies* **11** (1): 61–89.

   2005. *The Hit Man's Dilemma: or Business, Personal and Impersonal*. Chicago, IL: Prickly Paradigm Press.

Hashim, I. 2007. 'Independent child migration and education in Ghana', *Development and Change* **38** (5): 911–31.

Haugerud, A. M., P. Stone and P. D. Little 2000. *Commodities and Globalization: Anthropological Perspectives*. New York: Rowman & Littlefield.

Hecht, T. 1998. *At Home in the Street: Street Children of Northeast Brazil*. Cambridge University Press.

Hefferan, T., and T. Fogarty. 2010. 'The anthropology of faith and development: an introduction', *National Association for the Practice of Anthropology Bulletin* **33** (1): 1–11, American Anthropological Association.

Herring, R. J. 2007. 'The genomics revolution and development studies: science, poverty and politics', *Journal of Development Studies* **43** (1): 1–30.

Hertz, E. 1998. *The Trading Crowd: an Ethnography of the Shanghai Stock Market.* Cambridge University Press.

Hewitt de Alcántara, C. 1993. 'Markets in principle and practice', *European Journal of Development* **4** (2): 1–16.

Hickey, S., and G. Mohan (eds.) 2004. *Participation. From Tyranny to Transformation?* London and New York: Zed Books.

Hilhorst, D. 2003. *The real world of NGOs: Discourses, diversity and development.* London: Zed Books.

Ho, K. 2009. *Liquidated: an Ethnography of Wall Street.* Durham, NC: Duke University Press.

Hobart, M. (ed.) 1993. *An Anthropological Critique of Development: the Growth of Ignorance.* London and New York: Routledge.

Hodges, J. 2011. 'Development smart: acknowledging the power that street children bring to the development interface.' MA dissertation, School of Oriental and African Studies (University of London).

Holdt, J. 2003. *Development Aid and Racism.* www.american-pictures.com/english/racism/articles/aid.htm, accessed 24 August 2005.

Honwara A., and F. De Boeck (eds.) 2005. *Makers and Breakers. Children and Youth in Postcolonial Africa.* London: James Currey.

Hopgood, S. 2006. *Keepers of the Flame: Understanding Amnesty International.* New York: Cornell University Press.

Hulme, D., and M. Edwards 1997. *NGOs, States and Donors: Too Close for Comfort? Save the Children.* London: Macmillan.

Illich, I. 1976. *Limits to medicine: Medicine Nemesis – the Expropriation of Health.* London: Penguin.

Jackson, C. 1992. 'Gender, women and the environment: harmony or discord?' GAID Discussion Paper, no. 6, School of Development Studies, University of East Anglia.
    1998. 'Rescuing gender from the poverty trap', in C. Jackson and R. Pearson (eds.), pp. 39–64.

Jackson, C., and R. Pearson (eds.) 1998. *Feminist Visions of Development.* London: Routledge.

James, W. 1973. 'The anthropologist as reluctant imperialist', in T. Asad (ed.), pp. 41–69.

James, A., and A. Prout (eds.) 1997. *Constructing and Reconstructing Childhood.* London: Falmer Press.

Jeffrey, C., and J. Lerche 2001. 'Dimensions of dominance: class and state in Uttar Pradesh', in C. J. Fuller and V. Benei (eds.), pp. 91–114.

Jenkins, T., 1994. Fieldwork and the perception of everyday life. *Man* **29** (2): 433–55.

Johnson, V., J. Hill, S. Rana, M. Bharadwaj, P. Sapkota, R. Lamichanne, B. Basnet and S. Ghimimire 1995. *Listening to Smaller Voices: Children in an environment of change.* Kathmandu: Action Aid Nepal.

Kabeer, N. 1994. *Reversed Realities: Gender Hierarchies in Development Thought.* New York: Verso.

Karekezi, S., and G. A. Mackenzie (eds.) 1993. *Energy Options for Africa.* London: Zed Books.

Keenan, J. 2008. 'US militarisation in Africa: what anthropologists should know about AFRICOM', *Anthropology Today* **24** (5): 16–20.
    2009. 'Al-Qaeda terrorism in the Sahara? Edwin Dyer's murder and the role of intelligence agencies', *Anthropology Today* **25** (4): 14–18.

Kertzer, D. 1988, *Ritual, Politics and Power*. New Haven, CT and London: Yale University Press.

Kuhn, T. S. 1962. *The Structure of Scientific Revolutions*. University of Chicago Press.

Kuklick, H. (ed.) 2008. *A New History of Anthropology*. Oxford: Blackwell.

Lansing, J. S. 1991. *Priests and Programmers. Technologies of Power in the Engineered Landscape of Bali*. Princeton University Press.

Lansing, J. S., and A. Singer 1988. *The Goddess & the Computer*. Watertown, MA: Documentary Education Resources.

Latour, B. 1987. *Science in Action: How to Follow Scientists and Engineers Through Society*. Cambridge, MA: Harvard University Press.

   1996, *Aramis, or the love of technology*. Cambridge, MA: Harvard University Press.

   2010. *The Making of Law: an Ethnography of the Conseil D'État*. Cambridge and Malden, MA: Polity.

Leach, E. R. 1967. *Political systems of Highland Burma* (2nd rev. edn). London: Athlone Press.

Leach, M., and R. Mearns (eds.) 1988. *Beyond the Woodfuel Crisis: People, Land and Trees in Africa*. London: Earthscan.

Lewis, D. 2001. 'Civil society in non-western contexts: reflections on the "usefulness" of a concept.' *Civil Society Working Paper series, 13*. Centre for Civil Society, London School of Economics and Political Science, London.

   2007. *The Management of Non-Governmental Development Organisations*. London: Routledge. (1st edn 2001).

   2009. 'International development and the "perpetual present": anthropological approaches to the rehistoricisation of policy.' *European Journal of Development Research* **21** (1): 32–46.

Lewis, D., and D. Mosse (eds.) 2006. *Development Brokers and Translators: the Ethnography of Aid and Agencies*. Bloomfield, CT: Kumarian Press.

Li, T. M. 2005. Neoliberal Strategies of Government through Community: The Social Development Program of the World Bank in Indonesia. IILJ Working Paper 2006/2 (Global Administrative Law Series). Available at www.iilj.org/publications/documents/2006–2-GAL-Li-final-web.pdf, accessed 28 June 2010.

   2007. *The Will to Improve: Governmentality, Development, and the Practice of Politics*. Durham, NC: Duke University Press.

Lind, A. 2003. 'Feminist post-development thought: 'women and development' and the gendered paradoxes of survival in Bolivia', *Women's Studies Quarterly* **31** (3/4): 227–46.

Linkenback, A. 2007. *Forest Futures: Global Representations and Ground Realities in the Himalayas*. Oxford: Seagull Books.

Lipton, M. 1977. *Why Poor People Stay Poor: Urban Bias in World Development*. Cambridge, MA: Harvard University Press.

Lockhart, C. 2008. 'The life and death of a street boy in East Africa', *Medical Anthropology Quarterly* **22** (1): 94–115.

Loftsdóttir, K. 2009. 'Invisible colour: landscapes of whiteness and racial identity in international development', *Anthropology Today* **25** (5): 4–7.

Lopez-Claros, A., and **S.** Zahidi 2005. *Women's Empowerment: Measuring the Global Gender Gap*. Geneva: World Economic Forum.

Luetchford, P. 2006. 'Brokering Fair Trade: relations between coffee cooperatives and alternative trade organizations – a view from Costa Rica', in D. Lewis and D. Mosse (eds.), pp. 127–48.

2008. *Fair Trade and a Global Commodity: Coffee in Costa Rica.* London: Pluto Press.

Lutz, C. 2008. 'Selling ourselves? The periods of Pentagon funding for anthropology', *Anthropology Today* **24** (5): 1–3.

Malinowski, B. 1929. 'Practical anthropology', *Africa* **2** (1): 22–38.

1945. *The Dynamics of Culture Change: an Inquiry into Race Relations in Africa.* New Haven, CT: Yale University Press.

Mamdani. M. 1972. *The Myth of Population Control: Family, Caste, and Class in an Indian Village.* New York: Monthly Review Press.

Mansuri, G. and V. Rao 2004. 'Community-based and -driven development: a critical review', *The World Bank Research Observer* **19** (1).

Marsden, D. 2010. 'W(h)ither anthropology? Opening up or closing down', *Anthropology Today* **26** (6): 1–3.

Matar, D. 2011. *What It Means to be Palestinian: Stories of Palestinian Peoplehood.* London and New York: I.B. Tauris.

Mauss, M. 1990 [1923]. *The Gift.* London: Routledge.

McCormack, C. P., and Strathern, M. (eds) 1980. *Nature, Culture and Gender.* Cambridge, London and New York: Cambridge University Press.

Meadows, D. H., D. L. Meadows, J. Randers and W. W. Behrens III (eds.) 1972. *The Limits to Growth.* New York: Universe Books.

Miller, F. 1977. 'Knowledge and power: anthropology policy research and the Green revolution', *American Ethnologist* **4**: 190–8.

Mitchell, T. 2002. *Rule of Experts: Egypt, Techno-politics, Modernity.* Berkeley: University of California Press.

Mohan, G. and K. Stokke 2000. 'Participatory Development and Empowerment: the Dangers of Localism', *Third World Quarterly* **21** (2): 247–68.

Mohanty, C. T. 1988. 'Under western eyes: feminist scholarship and colonial discourses', *Feminist Review* **30**: 61–88.

Montgomery, H. 2005. 'Gendered childhoods: a cross disciplinary overview', *Gender and Education* **17** (5): 471–82.

Moore, D. S. 2000. 'The crucible of cultural politics: reworking "development" in Zimbabwe's eastern highlands', *American Ethnologist* **26** (3): 654–89.

Moran, E. (ed.) 1996. *Transforming Societies: Transforming Anthropology.* Ann Arbor: University of Michigan Press.

Mosse, D. 2005. *Cultivating Development: an Ethnography of Aid Policy and Practice.* London: Pluto Press.

2006. 'Anti-social anthropology? Objectivity, objection and the ethnography of public policy and professional communities', *Journal Royal Anthropological Institute* **12** (4): 935–56.

2007. 'Power and the durability of poverty: a critical exploration of the links between culture, marginality and chronic poverty.' *CPRC Working Paper No. 107*, Chronic Poverty Research Centre, University of Manchester. [ISBN 978-1-906433-06-2].

2010. 'A relational approach to durable poverty, inequality and power', *Journal of Development Studies* **46** (7): 1–23.

Mosse, D. (ed.) 2011. *Adventures in Aidland: the Anthropology of Professionals in International Development*. New York: Berghahn Books.

Mosse, D., and D. Lewis (eds.) 2005. *The Aid Effect: Giving and Governing in International Development*. London: Pluto Press.

Mowles, C. 2007 'Promises of transformation: just how different are international NGOs?', *Journal of International Development* **19**: 401–11.

2008. 'Values in international development organisations: negotiating non-negotiables', *Development in Practice* **18** (1): 5–16.

2009. 'Beyond the dotted line: capacity development, power and ways of knowing. Capacity. A gateway for capacity development', www.capacity.org, issue 37, September, 12–13.

Moyo, D. 2009. *Dead aid: why aid is not working and how there is a better way for Africa*. New York: Farrar, Straus & Giroux.

Msukwa, C A P S., and D. Taylor 2011. 'Why can't development be managed more like a funeral? Challenging participatory practices', *Development in Practice*, **21** (1): 59–72.

Nandy, A., and S. Visvanathan 1990. 'Modern medicine and its non-modern critics: A Study in discourse', in F. A. Apffel-Marglin and S. A. Marglin (eds.), pp. 145–84.

Nieuwenhuys, O. 1996. 'The paradox of child labour and anthropology', *Annual Review of Anthropology* **25**: 237–51.

Nuijten, M. 2003. *Power, Community and the State: The Political Anthropology of Organisation in Mexico*. London: Pluto.

O'Neill, T. 2003. 'Anti-child labour rhetoric, child protection and young carpet weavers in Kathmandu, Nepal', *Journal of Youth Studies* **6** (4): 413–14.

Olivier de Sardan, J.-P. 2005. *Anthropology and Development: Understanding Social Change*. London: Zed Press.

2009. 'Development, governance and reforms: studying practical norms in the delivery of public goods and services', in S. Hagberg and C. Widmark (eds.), pp. 101–24.

Ortner, S. 1974. 'Is female to male as nature is to culture' in M. Rosaldo and L. Lamphere (eds.), pp. 67–88.

Ovesen, J. 2009. 'The loneliness of the short-term consultant: anthropology and hydropower development in Laos', in S. Hagberg and C. Widmark (eds.), pp. 263–86.

Panter-Brick, C. 2002. 'Street children, human rights, and public health: a critique and future directions', *Annual Review of Anthropology* **31**: 147–71.

Pels, P. 1999. 'Professions of duplexity: a prehistory of ethical codes in anthropology', *Current Anthropology* **40** (2): 101–36.

Pfaffenberger, B. 1992. 'Social anthropology of technology', *Annual Review of Anthropology* **21**: 491–516.

Pickard, M. 2007. 'Reflections on relationships: the nature of partnership according to five NGOs in southern Mexico', *Development in Practice* **17** (4): 575 – 81.

Pieterse, J. N. 2000. 'After post-development', *Third World Quarterly* **21** (2): 175–91.

Pigg, S. L. 1992. 'Inventing social categories through place: social representations and development in Nepal', *Comparative Studies in Society and History* **34**: 491–513.

Plewes, B., and Stuart, R. 2007. 'The pornography of poverty: a cautionary fundraising tale', in D. A. Bell, and J.-M. Coicaud (eds.), pp. 23–37.

Polanyi, K., C. Arensberg and H. Pearson (eds.) 1957. *Trade and Market in the Early Empires: Economies in History and Theory*. Glencoe, IL: Free Press.

Pottier, J. 1999. *Anthropology of Food: the Social Dynamics of Food Security*. Cambridge: Polity Press.

Power, M. 1994. *The Audit Explosion*. London: Demos.

Preibisch, K. and G. R. Herrejón and S. L. Wiggins 2002. 'Defending food security in a free-market economy: the gendered dimensions of restructuring in rural Mexico', *Human Organization* **61** (1): 68–79.

Price, D. H. 1998. 'Gregory Bateson and the OSS: World War II and Bateson's assessment of applied anthropology', *Human Organization* **57** (4): 379–84.

Price, D. 2002. 'Lessons from Second World War anthropology: peripheral, persuasive and ignored contributions', *Anthropology Today* **18** (3): 14–20.

Quarles van Ufford, P. 1993. 'Knowledge and ignorance in the practices of development policy', in M. Hobart (ed.), pp. 135–160.

Radcliffe-Brown, A. R. 1980 [1930]. 'Applied anthropology', in G. Dalton (ed.), pp. 123–34.

Rahman, M., R. Khanam and N. Uddin Absar 1999. 'Child labor in Bangladesh: a critical appraisal of Harkin's Bill and the MOU-type schooling program', *Journal of Economic Issues* **33** (4): 985–1003.

Rahnema, M. 1997. *The Post-Develoment Reader*. London: Zed Books.

Rajak, D. 2011. *In Good Company: An Anatomy of Corporate Social Responsibility*. Stanford University Press.

Rao, V. and M.Walton (eds.) 2004. *Culture and Public Action*. Stanford University Press.

Raynolds, L. 2002. 'Producer consumer links in fair trade coffee networks', *Sociologia Ruralis* **42** (4): 404–24.

Riedmann, A. 1993. *Science that Colonises: a Critique of Fertility Studies*. Philadelphia, PA: Temple University Press.

Robbins, P. 2003. 'Policing and erasing the global/local border: Rajasthani foresters and the narrative ecology of modernization', in K. Sivaramakrishnan and A. Agrawal (eds.), pp. 377–403.

Robins, S. 2003. 'Whose modernity? Indigenous modernities and land claims after apartheid', *Development and Change* **34** (2): 265–86.

Rosaldo, M., and L. Lamphere (eds.) 1974. *Women, Culture and Society*. Stanford University Press.

Rosen, D. M. 2007. 'Child soldiers, international humanitarian law and the globalisation of childhood', *American Anthropologist* **109** (2): 296–306.

Rostow, W. W. 1960. *The Stages of Economic Growth: a Non-Communist Manifesto*. Cambridge University Press.

Rothschild, J. (ed.) 1983. *Machina ex Dea*. Pergamon: New York.

Rudiak-Gould, P. 2011. 'Climate change and anthropology: the importance of reception studies', *Anthropology Today* **27** (2): 9–12.

Rutherford, B. and R. Nyamuda. 2000. 'Learning about power: development and marginality in an adult literacy center for farm workers in Zimbabwe', *American Ethnologist* **27** (4): 839–54.

Rydstrom, H. 2001. 'Like a white piece of paper'. Embodiment and the moral upbringing of Vietnamese children', *Ethnos* **66** (3): 394–413.

Saberwal, V. K. 1999. *Pastoral Politics: Shepherds, Bureaucrats and Conservation in the Western Himalaya*. Delhi: Oxford University Press.

Sachs, W. (ed.) 1992. *The Development Dictionary: a Guide to Knowledge as Power.* London: Zed books.

Sahlins, M. 1972. *Stone Age Economics*. New York: Aldine De Gruyter.

 1976. *Cultural and Practical Reason*. Chicago University Press.

Schech, S., and J. Haggis 2000. *Culture and Development: a Critical Introduction.* Oxford: Blackwell.

Scheper-Hughes, N. 1995. 'The primacy of the ethical: propositions for a militant anthropology'. *Current Anthropology* **36** (3): 409–40.

Schuurman, F. J. 2001. *Globalization and Development Studies. Challenges for the 21st Century*. London, Thousand Oaks, CA, and New Delhi: Sage.

Schwegler, T. 2011. 'Intimate knowledge and the politics of policy convergence: the World Bank and social security reform in Mexico', in C. Shore, S. Wright and D. Pero (eds.), pp. 130–50.

Scoones, I. 1998. 'Sustainable rural livelihoods. a framework for analysis', *Institute for Development Studies Working Paper 72*, Sustainable Livelihood Rural Programme. Institute of Development Studies: Falmer, Sussex.

Scott, J. 1985. *Weapons of the Weak: Everyday Forms of Peasant Resistance*. New Haven, CT, and London: Yale University Press.

 1998. *Seeing like a state: How certain schemes to improve the human condition have failed.* New Haven, CT, and London: Yale University Press.

Sen, Amartya 1982. *Poverty and Famines: an Essay on Entitlements and Deprivation.* Oxford: Clarendon Press.

 1999. *Development as Freedom*. Oxford University Press.

Severs, D. 2001. *18 Folgate Street. The Tale of a House in Spitalfields*. London: Chatto & Windus.

Shiva, V.1997. *Biopiracy: the Plunder of Nature and Knowledge*. Boston, MA: South End Press.

 1988. *Staying Alive: Women, Ecology and Survival in India*. London: Zed Books.

 2001. *Patents, Myths and Reality*. India: Penguin.

 2000. *Seeds of Suicide: the Ecological and Human Costs of Globalization of Agriculture*. Delhi, India: RFSTE.

Shore, C., and S. Wright 2000. 'Coercive accountability: the rise of audit culture in higher education', in Marilyn Strathern (ed.), *Audit Cultures: Anthropological Studies in Accountability, Ethics and the Academy*. London and New York: Routledge.

Shore, C., and S. Wright (eds.) 1994. *Anthropology of Policy: Critical Perspectives on Governance and Power.* London and New York: Routledge.

Shore, C., S. Wright and D. Pero (eds.) 2011. *Policy World: Anthropology and the Analysis of Contemporary Power*. New York and Oxford: Berghahn.

SIDA 2001. *A Democracy and Human Rights Based Approach to Development Cooperation*. Stockholm: SIDA.

Sillitoe, P. 1998. 'The development of indigenous knowledge', *Current Anthropology* **39** (2): 223–52.

2002. 'Participant observation to participatory development: Making anthropology work', in P. Sillitoe, A. Bicker and J. Pottier (eds.), pp.1–23.

Sillitoe, P., A. Bicker and J. Pottier (eds.) 2002. *Participating in Development: Approaches to Indigenous Knowledge.* London: Routledge.

Singer, M. 2008. 'Applied anthropology', in H. Kuklick (ed), pp. 326–38.

Sinha, S., S. Gururani and B. Greenberg, 1997. 'The 'new traditionalist' discourse of Indian environmentalism', *Journal of Peasant Studies* **24** (3): 65–99.

Sivaramakrishnan, K., and Arun Agrawal (eds.) 2003. *Regional Modernities: the Cultural Politics of Development in India.* Oxford University Press.

Skarstein, R.. 2005. 'Economic liberalization and smallholder productivity in Tanzania: from promised success to real failure, 1985–1998', *Journal of Agrarian Change* **5** (3): 334–62.

Spencer, J. 2007. *Anthropology, Politics and the State: Democracy and Violence in South Asia.* Cambridge and New York: Cambridge University Press.

Spoor, M. (ed.) 2004. *Globalisation, Poverty and Conflict: a Critical Development Reader.* Dordrecht (Netherlands) and Boston, MA: Kluwer Academic.

Stewart, F., and M. Wang 2003. 'Do PRSPs empower poor countries and disempower the World Bank, or is it the other way around?' *QEH Working Paper Series* – QEHWPS108.

Stirrat, R. L. 2008. 'Mercenaries, missionaries and misfits: representations of development personnel', *Critique of Anthropology*, **28** (4): 406–25.

Stirrat, R. L., and H. Henkel. 1997. 'The development gift: the problem of reciprocity in the NGO world.' *The Annals of the American Academy of Political and Social Science*, **554**: 66–80.

Strathern, M. 2000. 'Afterword: Accountability and ethnography', in M. Strathern (ed.).

Strathern, M. (ed.) 2000. *Audit Cultures: Anthropological Studies in Accountability, Ethics and the Academy.* London and New York: Routledge.

Streicker, J. 1995. 'Policing boundaries: race, class, and gender in Cartagena, Colombia', *American Ethnologist* **22** (1): 54–74.

Taylor, L. R. 2005. 'Dangerous trade-offs: the behavioural ecology of child labour and prostitution in rural Northern Thailand', *Current Anthropology* **46** (3): 411–31.

Tett, G. 2010. *Fool's Gold: How Unrestrained Greed Corrupted a Dream, Shattered Global Markets and Unleashed a Catastrophe.* London: Little, Brown.

Thorsen, D. 2006. 'Child migrants in transit: strategies to assert new identities in rural Burkino Faso', in C. Christiansen, M. Utas and H. E. Vish (eds.), pp. 88–114.

Turton, C. 2001. 'Sustainable livelihood and project design in India.' *Working Paper 127*. London: Overseas Development Institute.

Tsing, A. L. 2004. *Friction: an Ethnography of Global Connection.* Princeton University Press.

UN Women 2011. *Progress of the World's Women: in Pursuit of Justice.* http://progress.unwomen.org/, accessed 21 May 2012.

UNDP 1998. *Integrating Human Rights with Sustainable Human Development.* A UNDP Policy Document, www.pogar.org/publications/other/undp/hr/hr-pub-policy5-98e.pdf, accessed 21 May 2012.

UNICEF 2009. *State of the World's Childhood, Special Edition, Celebrating 20 Years of the Convention on the Rights of the Child*. New York: UNICEF, www.unicef. org/rightsite/sowc/, accessed 24 November 2009.

USAID 2006. *Policy Framework for Bilateral Foreign Aid. Implementing Tranformational Diplomacy through Development*. PD-ACG-244. US Agency for International Development.

Vasan, S. 2002. 'Ethnography of the forest guard: contrasting discourses, conflicting roles and policy implementation', *Economic and Political Weekly*, **5** (October): 4125–34.

Vermeulen, H. F, 1999. 'Anthropology in colonial contexts', in Bremen and Shimizu (eds.).

Visweswaran, K. 1998. 'Race the culture of anthropology', *American Anthropologist* **100** (1): 70–83.

Wallace, T., L. Bornstein, and J. Chapman, 2006. *The Aid Chain: Coercion and Commitment in Development NGOs*. Rugby: Practical Action Publishing.

Wallerstein, I. 1974. 'The rise and future demise of the world capitalist system', *Comparative Studies in Society and History* **16** (4): 387–415.

Wedel, J. 2004. 'Blurring the state-private divide: flex organisations and the decline of accountability', in Max Spoor (ed.), pp. 217–35.

Welker, M. 2009. '"Corporate security begins in the community": mining, the corporate social responsibility industry, and environmental advocacy in Indonesia', *Cultural Anthropology* **24** (1): 142–79.

Wessells, M. 2006. *Child Soldiers: from Violence to Protection*. Cambridge, MA, and London: Harvard University Press.

Whaites, A. 2000. *Development, NGOs, and Civil Society: A Development Practice Reader*. Oxford: Oxfam.

White, S. 1996. 'Depoliticising development: the uses and abuses of participation' *Development in Practice* **6** (1): 6–15.

1999. 'NGOs, civil society, and the state in Bangladesh: The politics of representing the poor', *Development and Change* **30**: 307–26.

2002. 'Thinking race, thinking development', *Third World Quarterly* **23** (3): 407–19.

2006. 'The "gender lens": a racial blinder?', *Progress in Development Studies* **6** (1): 55–67.

2010. 'Analysing wellbeing: a framework for development practice', *Development in Practice* **20** (2): 158–72.

Widmark, C. 2009. 'Shortcuts to anthropological fieldwork in Sida-commissioned assessments: experiences from Bolivia and Peru', in S. Hagberg and C. Widmark (eds.), pp. 287–303.

Williams, G. 2004. 'Towards a repoliticization of participatory development: political capabilities and spaces of empowerment', in S. Hickey and G. Mohan (eds.), pp. 92–109.

Wilson, R. (ed.) 1996. *Human Rights, Culture and Context: Anthropological Perspectives*. London: Pluto.

Wordsworth, A. 2007. *A Matter of Interests. Gender and the Politics of Presence in Afghanistan's Wolesi Jirga*. Afghanistan Research and Evaluation Unit, Issues Paper Series, Afghanistan.

World Trade Organization, 2010. *World Trade Statistics 2010*. Geneva: World Trade Organization.

Young, S. 2010. 'The "moral hazards" of microfinance: restructuring rural credit in India', *Antipode* **42** (1): 201–23.

Yuen, P. 2008. '"Things that break the heart of God": child sponsorship programme and World Vision International', *Totem: The University of Western Ontario Journal of Anthropology* **16** (1): 40–51.

Index